TEAM LEADERSHIP

ENDORSEMENTS

If you have a vested interest in the performance of your team, then look no further than this book for all the tools and techniques you will need to elevate team performance. *Team Leadership: Theories, Tools and Techniques* is practical – it provides theoretical context, before it swiftly moves on to explore and unpack the intricacies of team dynamics faced by team leaders. It does not stop there, but moves on to present and discuss a multitude of tools that I believe have to be in the arsenal of every single team leader. Whilst I recommend you read the book in totality, the specific chapters employ a standardised format, enabling you to move directly to a topic of interest or need. I have no doubt that I will revisit the invaluable content of this book on many occasions – I encourage you to do the same.

Janko Kotzé, Industrial Psychologist, Managing Director, Human Interest Consulting

This book offers practical guidelines for leaders in business, as well as the tools and techniques they need to apply to lead teams. The book further more provides managers, leaders and academics with sound theories, tools and techniques to use in teambuilding. The tips provided for team leaders after each chapter, is an easy reference guide to follow to improve team behaviour.

Prof Nico Martins, Department of Industrial and Organisational Psychology, Unisa,
Author of Employee Assistance Programmes: Theory and Practical Applications

Team Leadership is a valuable addition to the team leadership literature and bridges the gap between current academic (theory/research-based) and popular self-help team leadership literature through its "Integrated learning" approach.

Team development is made helpful and practical for team leaders by demonstrating the utility of a number of selected classical theories and assessment instruments in daily organisational life.

Prof Melinde Coetzee, Department of Industrial and Organisational Psychology, Unisa,
Author of Developing Student Graduateness and Employability:
Issues, provocations, theory and practical guidelines

This book is well written and structured, drawing on appropriate literature, yet written in an easy to understand language. I regularly stopped to reflect and hope that every reader will do so – particularly on identity – the authentic self and the organisational imposed, the latter of which can be "paralysing".

Prof Hester Nienaber, Research Professor (School of Public Administration and Operations
Management), Department of Operations Management, Unisa, Author of Employee Engagement in a
South African context: A scientific approach to context-specific measurement

This book is an insightful view of team dynamics that reminds the reader that team effectiveness is not as the common pervasive myth suggests, result of a team building event. Different levels of depth in human engagements exist that should be incorporated to enable meaningful change. This book takes the reader on an exploratory journey of various leadership team theories and frameworks and invites the reader to choose an approach that best resonates with him or her.

Ashnie Muthusamy, Group Manager: Talent Management, Sun International,
Author of *Succession Management: The Definite "Do's" and the Detrimental "Don'ts"*

First published in 2019.

ISBN: 978-1-86922-772-2 (Printed)
ISBN: 978-1-86922-773-9 (ePDF)

Published by KR Publishing

P O Box 3954
Randburg
2125

Republic of South Africa

Tel: (011) 706-6009
Fax: (011) 706-1127
E-mail: orders@knowres.co.za
Website: www.kr.co.za

Printed and bound: HartWood Digital Printing, 243 Alexandra Avenue, Halfway House, Midrand
Typesetting, layout and design: Cia Joubert, cia@knowres.co.za
Cover design: Marlene de Villiers, marlene@knowres.co.za
Editing: Mary Hazelton, maryhazelton@gmail.com
Proofreading: Jennifer Renton, jenniferrenton@live.co.za
Project management: Cia Joubert, cia@knowres.co.za

TEAM LEADERSHIP

THEORIES, TOOLS AND TECHNIQUES

Drikus Kriek

publishing

2019

"Coming together is a beginning.
Keeping together is progress.
Working together is success."

—*Henry Ford*

To my mother

TABLE OF CONTENTS

ABOUT THE AUTHOR

Prof Hendrik Sebastiaan (Drikus) Kriek is Deputy Dean for Pedagogy and Director of the Executive PhD at the IEDC-Bled School of Management in Bled, Slovenia. He acted as Interim Director of the Central and Eastern European Management Association in 2018 and is Associate-Professor of Leadership at the IEDC where he was instrumental in establishing the recently launched Team Development Institute. Previously he was Director of the Leadership Development Centre at Wits Business School of the University of the Witwatersrand and holds an Associate-Professorship in Human Resource Management and Leadership at WBS. He teaches Leadership, Leading High Performance teams and Organisation Development courses on various PhD, MBA and Coaching programmes. He also lectures on executive education programmes to various organisations, enterprises and clients, both locally and internationally.

Drikus consults in the field of Organisation Development and has been involved in team development, management education projects, lecturing and leadership development programmes to a variety of local and international organisations with projects in Slovenia, Russia, Croatia, Bosnia-Herzegovina, Serbia, Namibia, Botswana, Ghana, Latvia, The Netherlands and Australia. He is also director of the Team and Leadership Development Centre, which specialises in a variety of team solutions including unstructured groups, teambuilding initiatives and psychometric assessments. He was instrumental in the introduction and advancement of the Adventure Therapy industry in South Africa and has reported on his work in this industry at international academic conferences, while simultaneously applying the benefits of this approach to a variety of industries and enterprises.

Previously Drikus was an Associate-Professor in Organisational Behaviour and Leadership at the Graduate School of Business Leadership (SBL) of the University of South Africa, and is a former Head of the Strategy and Leadership Area of the school. He studied Clinical Psychology and received his MA (Clin Psych) and MBA degrees, both cum laude, from the Rand Afrikaans University and the University of Stellenbosch respectively. Drikus received his Doctorate from the University of Pretoria and is a graduate of Yale University in the United States. He spent his Sabbatical leave at the Integral Leadership Centre of the Graduate School of Management of The University of Western Australia, and has presented his research to local and international forums as well as in popular and academic outlets. His article on African Change leaders (with Prof Stella Nkomo) was awarded the Best Paper of 2011 by the Journal of Occupational and Organizational Psychology (one of the top five in the field). He completed commissioned research on Sizwe Nxasana on his change leadership during his tenure as CEO of Telkom, and completed a National Research Foundation-funded research project on African Change Leadership (linking life histories of leaders with change processes (internal and external)) with Prof Stella Nkomo of the University of Pretoria.

Drikus was named Researcher of the Year for 2006/7 at the SBL and was runner-up Lecturer of the Year (Executive Education) at WBS in 2015. He is a regular member of international accreditation panels for IQA accreditation for business schools in Europe and Asia, as well as a speaker at various conferences. Prior to his appointment at the SBL, Drikus practiced as a clinical psychologist and was CEO of Janus Data, the then largest independent storage media company in South Africa. Drikus is married to Caroline and they have two boys, Estiaan and Hanno.

INTRODUCTION

One can hardly deny the critical role that teams play in twenty-first century business; the use of teams can rightly be regarded as one of the most significant characteristics of modern organisational life. New dynamics such as virtual teams, increased diversity and specialisation, agile teams and self-managing teams are forcing us to rethink our view of teams and how to optimise them. This makes it even more crucial for managers to deepen their knowledge of teams in their organisations to maximise team performance, enhance individual and team growth, and ensure organisational alignment and benefit. It is particularly necessary for team leaders to manage their teams effectively.

The aim of this book is to help team leaders and team members to be more effective by helping them to understand teams better. The book brings together theories and research on team design, team functioning, managing teams, team growth and team development. It also describes some tools and techniques that can be used to raise the performance levels of teams and help them to be optimal. Thus, it offers a spectrum of mechanisms to apply in understanding teams, leading teams and working in teams.

It is not easy to distinguish between the terms 'theory', 'tool' and 'technique', in this context, particularly when they are presented as practical aids for team leaders and members. For example, one can argue that a theoretical framework, such as Tuckman's well-known team development theory that states that a team progresses through phases of development, is clearly a theory. So too are the self-determination and equity theories of motivation. However, when such theories are used in a team they become tools. To make matters worse, some scholars refer to their work as models, frameworks, approaches or perspectives.

For current purposes, a theory is regarded as some aspect of team operations that is conceptual, proven in research and offers general and overarching explanations of a particular phenomenon. On the other hand, teams need to know how to apply certain techniques to function optimally, thus a technique is a practical set of behaviours or actions a team can take to lead to a particular outcome. Tools are conceptualised as somewhere between theory and technique. A good example is psychological assessment instruments. While they are all based on theoretical foundations, they are not techniques but rather tools that can be applied to facilitate team functioning.

What makes this book different from others?

Since there are many books offering tools for teams, one can rightly ask what makes this one different or even why another one on teams at all. A few reasons can be offered:

- This is not a teambuilding book. Often books describing similar tools or techniques include activities, games and experiences that can be used in teambuilding sessions. These are obviously helpful and many a team will attest to the benefits that teambuilding interventions can offer, yet the focus of this book is more on how to help the team with its current operations, rather than on techniques that can be used and then need to be transferred back into the workplace.

- This book falls in the overlap between research, practice and development. It gives insight into team behaviour from an academic point of view, particularly what current science tells us on what works well to improve teams. It also links to practice in that it aims to be practical and helpful in daily organisational life. In addition, it gives leaders an opportunity to learn and grow, and therefore also has a developmental focus. The book can therefore be helpful:

  ◦ in academic class rooms (e.g. MBA classes teaching leadership or team performance) or management education and leadership development programmes;

  ◦ in the management and leadership of teams, where team leaders and their teams can use the theories, tools and techniques to improve their own team performance; and

  ◦ for personal development and growth, where managers, leaders and team members can use the theories, tools and techniques to improve their own personal functioning and effectiveness.

- The book offers a smorgasbord of carefully selected theories, tools and techniques to be applied in many contexts and at various stages of a team's development, therefore it is clear that not all of them will, or even should, apply to every context and/or leadership challenge. Leaders should draw from this book whatever they find most helpful and add it to their arsenal of techniques, tools and frameworks, as it is applied already. It is written to accompany a process of improving team performance. Once leaders have defined their preferred method of leading a team, they can select from the text which tools and techniques to apply.

- The focus in this book is on breadth of theories, tools and techniques. Thus, while a process of team development forms the backbone of the text, the book does not purport to give quintessential quick steps to solve all problems and to lead teams effectively. Leaders are exposed to a variety of tools, theories and techniques to choose from.

The structure of the book

Comment is merited on how it was decided which theories, tools and techniques to include in this book. The first point of departure was to provide the theoretical background from the world of science and academia about the optimal functioning of teams, therefore the bulk of the material included in the book has a firm theoretical foundation. In some cases, techniques are included where specific implementation demands necessitate a focus beyond theory and tools. Naturally it is impossible to provide a comprehensive compilation of all available tools, therefore the selection offered here comprises key theories and tools that have stood the test of time and which are embedded in research and practice. In addition, focus is placed on practical application to assist teams to improve their operations. The material is structured in twenty sections, which are briefly described in what follows.

A further criterion was that any item included had to fit the structure of the book. It will be obvious to anyone interested in teams that the material offered by theory and practice to include in a book of this nature is nearly endless, thus a set of topics or themes was selected to act as a framework for the book. Twenty themes were identified; within each of these themes, in order to limit the possible material, five theories, tools or techniques are presented. Which particular five was ultimately a subjective choice based on the author's judgement of the usefulness of a theory, his personal experience or proven practice. Readers will be aware that in some cases many more examples could have been included, while on other topics there is far less material. No doubt some leaders, theorists and practitioners would have chosen differently. In the end, it is hoped that the selection is found to be practical, while at the same time offering some alternative views or at least some incentive to invest in more research.

The twenty themes of the book are as described below.

Developmental frameworks
The first section describes how teams develop over time. This is to help team leaders understand the different stages, cycles and rhythms a team goes through. A variety of frameworks have been offered over the years with the all-too-familiar forming-storming-norming-performing of Bruce Tuckman heading the pack. However, beyond such linear frameworks, a variety of other frameworks show how time is important to teams and how teams show different characteristics as they develop in time. Among these are recursive, punctuated equilibrium and integrated frameworks.

Constituent frameworks
In this section, different frameworks of team composition are presented. They include hierarchical, component-based frameworks and the often-used input-process-output models. The role of external and internal components that moderate and/or mediate team behaviour are discussed next. The section is concluded with the presentation of an integrated model.

Organisational context
Any team functions in a particular context. In particular, a team's functioning is influenced by the organisational context it operates in. Thus, not only is a team embedded in a particular context, but alignment with such a context is a key team deliverable. Factors influencing the external and internal contexts of a team, its culture and the value chain wherein it operates are all discussed.

Team assessments
A key part in improving the performance of a team lies in ascertaining the current levels of composition and/ or performance of the team. This section offers objective assessment instruments that teams can use to evaluate where they stand. Instruments to assess team composition, climate, effectiveness and conditions for success are discussed. The section is concluded by describing some techniques a team can use to analyse their performance from their own point of view.

Team design

This section deals with how to set up a team, and presents important foundational elements that need to be put in place to ensure success. The initial focus is on types of teams, and then the mandate of the team. Team composition, diversity and a normative team design model complete the section.

Individual assessment instruments

One part of the composition of the team is obviously the make-up of the team in terms of members. As individual needs, skills, knowledge, preference and personality are but a few elements that distinguish between individuals, a set of instruments are offered as tools for teams to consider and to help them optimise the design of the team. Psychometric instruments that assist the team to measure personality, emotional intelligence, strengths and style are described.

Team roles

One element of team functioning that has attracted research and has been found to be practical and helpful is the manner in which team members prefer different roles. A variety of different assessment instruments designed to help teams with this part of team functioning are presented: Belbin's team roles, Team Management Profile, Kets de Vries Archetypes, Team role knowledge assessment, and Lessem's integrators.

Team tasks

Tasks a team has to execute are discussed in this section, as is the classification of tasks, how to formulate tasks, and generic tasks. The section also includes a presentation of behavioural processes that determine tasks, as well as the job characteristics model, which helps a team to design its tasks.

Teamwork

Teamwork refers to the interaction between team members as they orchestrate tasks through interdependent team activities in pursuit of goals. Teamwork is characterised by a set of flexible and adaptive behaviours, cognitions and attitudes. Teamwork is in essence the interrelated behaviours of members to co-ordinate and synchronise collective action; the specific set of competencies will differ according to the type of team.

Diverging techniques

This refers to the tools that teams can use to find new alternatives, innovative ideas and creative "outside the box" thinking. The section provides tools to help the teams with this diverging process.

Converging techniques

These tools offer ways to "funnel" the wide variety of ideas into a limited number of options and ultimately to make decisions on which alternative is preferred.

Conflict management

Conflict is a natural part of life and therefore also manifests in teams. The process that a team uses to manage conflict is the focus of this section. Types of conflict are described and one potential source of conflict, difficult people on the team, is considered. This is followed by a description of two conflict management theories: the Thomas-Killman model and a sequential-contingent view of conflict. Lastly, a process is given whereby teams can manage conflicts through what are called crucial conversations.

Communication

Whether it is verbal or non-verbal, teams function to complete tasks and to deal with interpersonal relations through communication. Some communication tools are presented starting with how communication can be used to help teams deal with conflict and crucial conversations. Communication patterns, types of interactions used in team meetings, and the theory of structural dynamics are described next. Lastly, recent types of teams, namely, agile and virtual teams, are discussed in relation to communication.

Emergent states

As teams start to function, the inevitable interaction of human beings leads various cognitive and emotional states to emerge. These play a critical part in getting the team aligned and "on the same page", but they also refer to affective attachment and connections. Frameworks of, and tools for, these critical elements of team functioning are described in this section. The emergent states discussed are cognition, learning, affect, flow, and a description of unconscious forces that influence the development of emergent states, namely (A)CIBART.

Motivational states

A few emergent states have been found to play a particularly important role in motivating team members. They are the focus of this section, as they play a large part in creating the conditions required for teams to be motivated. The five motivational states chosen here are confidence, trust, safety, cohesion and interdependence.

Motivation theory

Various tools taken from theories of motivation are offered here. These include needs-based motivational theories, expectancy theory, self-determination theory and equity theory. The section is concluded with a discussion on how nudging can be used to design the context of the team to motivate desired behaviour.

Team leadership

This section focuses on leadership and how the role of the team leader plays a part in the operations and functioning of the team. It describes different leadership theories and styles, and how the personality of the leader influences the team's journey.

Tasks of team leaders

Specific tasks of team leaders are discussed in this section. First, functional leadership tasks are described, followed by tasks related to managing change, including personal change. The role leaders can play in implementing action plans forms the last part of this section.

Coaching

In their journey to deliver on tasks, to interface with other members and to remain motivated, many team members find it valuable to enter into coaching processes whereby they are supported on their development journeys. Various coaching theories and tools can be used to help teams, thus some individual and team coaching models are presented here.

Teambuilding

Related to coaching but specifically applied to teams, some frameworks of teambuilding are presented. In this case they are tools to guide the choice of intervention, and no particular teambuilding activity or experience is presented. Rather, such activities are regarded as one "tool" (among others) that leaders can use to improve team functioning.

1

DEVELOPMENTAL FRAMEWORKS

This section deals with the development of teams over time, and the sequence of stages or phases that a team passes through. However, different views have been offered on exactly how such development takes place. Some theorists regard the progress as linear, while others hold that teams sometimes revisit previous stages. Another perspective indicates that teams find equilibrium at some point in their development, and other scholars try to integrate these different views. Thus, when looking at developmental frameworks, these various perspectives need to be taken into account.

1 | Linear development framework

Introduction

Linear development frameworks of a team's development in time posit that the process is analogous to the stages of birth, growth and death, or like organisations which are start-ups, grow in size, mature and then decline. Probably one of the most famous management, let alone team, tools of all time is the enduring linear development framework offered by Bruce Tuckman, and the subsequent adjustment thereof by Tuckman and Jenson. Derived from a meta-analysis of team research, this "conceptual statement" identifies two realms (people and task) and five (originally four) stages in the life of a team. However, the original linear development framework needs to be augmented to account for the ability teams have to re-invent themselves and, if they so desire, to continue and refresh the cycle of development. The stages in the life of a team are therefore presented in a life-cycle pattern; to utilise this ability, teams have to re-invent or re-invigorate themselves. Towards the end of a team's life-cycle, e.g. at the end of a particular project, the team has to decide whether it "adjourns" or whether it can or should be re-invigorated. A team can thus, use this tool to find key moments in its development to determine its readiness for re-invention. Edison provided an example of this type of framework which retains the initial four stages of Tuckman, but expands it with the four additions to complete a life-cycle.

In a nutshell

Development stages that a team goes through: forming, storming, norming, performing, informing, conforming, deforming and transforming.

Purpose

To help teams in their development journey from start to being fully operational.

To align team tasks with appropriate stages.

To focus attention on the realms of task and team.

To have a line of sight of a complete team life-cycle.

Description

Two linear development frameworks are presented, namely the famous Tuckman framework as well as the extension thereof by Edison.

Tuckman

Tuckman identified two "realms" and originally four stages, and showed how a team develops in each of the realms. In a subsequent study with Jenson, he added a final stage to make five stages in the development process. The realms identified are "group structure", referring to the interpersonal configuration or the way members interact with one another, and "task activity", referring to the "task at hand" for the team. In each of the five stages the team completes development tasks associated with the realms; all the stages of development can thus, be described by referring to the stages and the realms. The well-known stages that the team goes through are described below, before the additional stages are presented.

Forming

This stage refers to the group's initial testing of boundaries of interpersonal and task behaviours, as well as the establishment of dependency relationships with leaders, members and pre-existing standards. 'Testing and dependence' refers to attempts by group members to discover acceptable interpersonal behaviours, which is done by evaluating the reactions of the leader and/or members and their relation to norms and structures. During the Forming stage, the group also orientates itself to the task at hand by establishing ground rules and obtaining relevant information. Members are focused on their own objectives and a level of dependency on the leader and other members develops. Members are not clear on what they should do and since they are unfamiliar with one another, there is little trust and they spent a lot of time checking each other out.

Storming

The Storming stage is characterised by intra-group conflict, as well as hostility between members and towards the leader. This stage is also characterised by emotional responses to task demands as a form of resistance and the emergence of discrepancies in both task and interpersonal realms. Teams often exhibit polarisation around interpersonal issues, the goals of the team and the values of the team, with emotional outbursts and challenges to the leadership manifesting themselves. Splinter groups may emerge as individuals articulate agendas around power, position and responsibilities.

Norming

The third stage, Norming, brings with it a sense of cohesion with new norms, roles and standards, while intimate and personal opinions are expressed in the task realm. This third stage is identified through the emergence of group cohesion and acceptance of the members of the group. The group develops norms to perpetuate the group and avoids conflict in search of harmonious relationships. "Open exchange of relevant interpretations" takes place in the task realm of this stage; this refers to efforts to exchange information and opinions that facilitate alternative interpretations of available information. Team norms evolve that aim to perpetuate the processes and behaviours that minimise conflict and contribute to harmonious relationships. Resistance is replaced by an in-group feeling, a sense of cohesion and a growing identity. Members settle into new roles and responsibilities and relationships between team members get stronger. The leader reinforces norms and behaviours and team members themselves take responsibility to drive performance and meet demands and expectations according to (tacitly and explicitly) agreed norms.

Performing

During the Performing stage, the interpersonal structure supports the group's focus on the tasks at hand, roles become flexible and energy is channelled to the completion of the task of the group. In this stage "functional role-relatedness" refers to the group's problem-solving efforts where members feel comfortable with different roles, while the "emergence of solutions" refers to constructive efforts to complete the tasks of the team successfully. The group is very motivated, displays effective operations and has a sense of pride in their achievements. Members care about each other and work collaboratively, and all are prepared to take risks and find solutions to any problems the team faces.

Adjourning

This final stage was added later and refers to the "death of the group", where the tasks of the team are wrapped up and emotionally the members distance themselves from the team. Tuckman and Jensen did not offer specific labels for the two realms of this stage.

Edison

Edison then added four more stages to provide a complete life-cycle of team development.

Informing

This framework uses the pinnacle of the team´s performance as its midpoint, but calls it the Informing stage. This is because the team is informed by its performance to date as well as on how it should proceed; it is a tipping point that could lead to decline. There is a danger of impending dysfunction if the required corrective action is not taken. This stage provides an opportunity for the team to re-group, re-tool and re-focus, and to transform into a fully operational team. A key focus should be to evaluate how the team can provide impetus through new ideas, information or members. If this is not done, the team can relapse into a stage of decay, complacency and ultimately failure.

Conforming

This stage of team development is characterised by members' desire to conform. Where in previous stages the work ethic required collaboration, risk-taking and the infusing of new ideas, these have all stalled in the life cycle of the team. Instead, a culture evolves that subverts creativity, originality and innovation. Members display elements of "groupthink" in that they begin to think alike so that questioning and criticism of ideas and of the operation of the team are withheld. The dangers of this stage are that teams start to bask in their own success and end up reinforcing each other's ideas without critical scrutiny or openness to new initiatives and ideas.

Deforming

The team starts to decay as a functional unit and members lose interest in the team's operations; during this stage there is no energy or gratification at being part of the team. Lack of motivation manifests itself in missed deadlines, ineffectiveness and even despondency.

Transforming

This stage refers to a team taking the Informing stage, that is, the midpoint transition, seriously and learning from the lessons gained from evaluation and scrutiny of the first phase. The team progresses to being fully functional and invigorating. It allows for new ideas and members are committed to the success of the team. Thus, it allows for the team to restart a cycle of development. These transformational efforts can link to demands that individuals and the team should gain from team experience, and therefore learning is built into the new cycle of development. The team elicits contributions from members to map out how lessons from their experience to date can be utilised and taken into the next cycle of development.

Conclusion

This type of framework emphasises the ability teams have to form again and for development to be perpetuated. In this regard, it differs from the additive frameworks in that it proposes that teams evolve over time, reach a peak and begin to decline … only to start again.

The extension of the original Tuckman model by Edison therefore goes beyond the adjourning stage and emphasises that teams can rejuvenate, transform and initiate a new journey. However, it does not ignore the fact that in some cases teams do not have the ability to rejuvenate and therefore stop operating - either because the project has been completed or because the team does not have the internal ability to sustain its life cycle.

Tips for team leaders

Countless studies and practical experience over many years have contributed to the staying power of this framework and its value lies in its simplicity and focus. Although the original study was based on a theoretical meta-analysis, it has been used on actual teams and has been shown to be a very useful tool with new teams. The tool helps team leaders to "map" a way through a team's development and gives them clear guidance on what to do during the various stages of team development. However, the framework is not without its detractors and it is helpful to consider that teams do not only develop linearly and often have to "revisit" stages at different times. It is also worth mentioning that the stages do not always follow sequentially as stated here, and that teams do not spend an equal amount of time in each stage.

It has also been found that in some cases teams can "skip" a stage. What is important to know is that these stages are not discrete and exclusive but, should rather be seen as the development processes the team is going through at any given stage that is regards as critical for that particular stage of its development. For example, while a team is in the storming stage it may already be performing, but the issues and challenges related to storming will be highlighted during that stage. Lastly, it must be stated that the additions offered by Edison make for a more complete representation, and in particular, the focus on the team's ability to transform and re-ignite its performance is a valuable addition and extension of the original work.

Representation

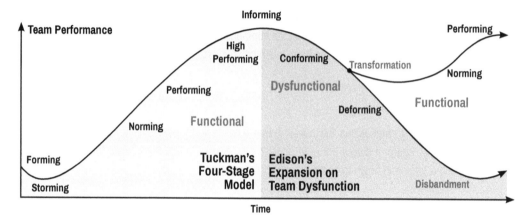

Figure 1.1: Life-cycle of a team's development

References

Edison, T. (2008). The Team Development Life Cycle: A New Look. *Defence* AT& L, 37(3), 14–17.

Tuckman, B. (1965). Developmental Sequence in Small Groups. *Psychological Bulletin*, 63(6), 384–399.

Tuckman, B. & Jensen, M. (1977). Stages of Small-group Development Revisited. *Group & Organization Management*, 2(4), 419–427.

Alternative five-stage linear frameworks

Introduction

Many researchers have offered their views on adjusting the often-used five-stage model described above or have built on it. Two variants are described here to illustrate the development of theoretical points of view within this type of framework: the classic perspectives of Katzenbach and Smith and the equally enduring version of Susan Wheelan and her colleagues.

In a nutshell

Alternative frameworks to those described above.

Purpose

To expand the understanding of the linear development of teams.

To help leaders guide teams through the development stages.

Description

Two representative theories are presented here, namely those of Katzenbach and Smith, and of Susan Wheelan and her colleagues.

Katzenbach and Smith

The alternative linear development framework offered by Katzenbach and Smith is prefaced by a comprehensive section about team components, but the most enduring legacy of their seminal work lies in the developmental path they proposed. They identified five stages on a "team performance curve".

Working group

This type of group consists of members that share information, best practices and perspectives only to enable the members to perform better individually. There is no need for cooperation towards a common goal, joint work products or mutual accountability. No incremental performance is needed, members perform better individually without a sense of common purpose, and the outcomes of the team are not dependent on collective efforts.

Pseudo-team

This team could have a significant, incremental performance needs or opportunities, but the team members have not focused on collective achievement and their efforts remain largely individual. Although members and the organisation may call this collection of people a team, there is no effort to craft a common goal or purpose. The authors regard these teams as destructive because "their interactions detract from each member's individual performance without delivering any joint benefit". The net effect of this team is worse than individual effort.

Potential team

This team tries to improve its performance collectively, but is hampered as its purpose and collective goals are unclear. Members need each other's efforts and incremental performance is required, but teams in this phase have not yet established collective accountability. The team should thus, invest in developing shared goals and purpose and should create a sense of interdependence.

Real team

A real team is defined by the authors as "a small number of people with complementary skills who are committed to a common purpose, performance goals, and approach for which they hold themselves mutually accountable". They regard it as critical that teams focus on performance as well as displaying individual characteristics. Performance refers to results, collective work outputs and personal growth. Real teams display the following basic characteristics:

- a small number of members, so that individual effort is required for collective output;

- complementary skills, including problem-solving, technical or functional, and interpersonal skills; and

- commitment.

Commitment comprises:

- A meaningful purpose: this sets the tone, direction and momentum and helps to foster commitment and aspiration. It is shaped by the team in response to a demand or opportunity from the external environment and it shapes the performance requirements of the team. The team engages in "purposing" as a constant activity as it creates, explores and agrees on goals that are meaningful to the team and the individuals in the team alike.

- Specific performance goals: these stem from the purpose of the team and from concretising and individualising this purpose to meaningful individual goals. To do this, teams define a team work-product (that is, something specific to the team that requires collective effort) that assists in shaping clear communication while facilitating constructive conflict in the team. This directs the focus of the team to attaining performance goals, which in turn enables utilising the knowledge, skills and abilities of everyone on the team. It also allows for the team to celebrate small wins, and as performance goals and the purpose of the team are aligned, it gives an opportunity for the team to mobilise effort.

- A common approach based on agreement as to how they work best to accomplish their purpose. It involves economic, administrative and interpersonal dimensions and all are equally important.

- Mutual accountability, including understanding that mutual effort is needed and should be focused towards team goals.

High-performance team

The difference between a high-performance team and a real team is that in a high-performance team, the members have also committed to one another's personal growth and success. Members help each other to achieve personal and professional goals and this commitment goes beyond organisational requirements. Katzenbach and Smith stated that such commitment fuels team processes to become nobler, team performance goals to become urgent, and team approaches to be more powerful. They proposed that high-performance teams are built by accepting the performance challenge, creating performance results, and shaping the purpose and performance goals, all of which ensures personal commitment and generates extended team effort.

Wheelan

Wheelan proposed five stages of a team's development, namely dependency and inclusion; counter dependency and fight; trust and structure; work; and impending termination.

Dependency and inclusion

The first stage is characterised by members' dependency on the designated leader, while issues around safety and inclusion in the team are also addressed. As there is still a lack of vision and trust, the leader of the team is expected to provide direction. During this stage team members engage in "pseudo-work", such as activities and discussion about topics not relevant to team goals, and may be concerned about being accepted by other members of the team, especially since they may fear rejection and feel insecure. There may be high levels of compliance and the leader is rarely challenged.

Counter-dependency and fight

During this stage there is disagreement among members about goals, procedures and tasks, and competing behaviours between members start to emerge. The outcome expected of this stage is to find a unified set of goals, values and procedures. The conflict serves the function of establishing sufficient levels of trust and security. Some teams may not be able to deal with the demands of this stage and are stuck in fighting mode or remain dependent on the leader. Conflicts around values emerge, subgroups and coalitions may form, and members challenge the leader. Both role and goal clarification start and there is a marked increase in member participation.

Trust and structure

During this stage the focus is on the roles expected from members, alignment with the organisational context and establishment of procedures. Interpersonally, members strengthen relationships between one another and communication becomes open and task-related. Trust, commitment and willingness to cooperate increase, as does member satisfaction. Cooperation between members is at higher levels, pressure to conform is heightened, and the leader becomes less directive and more consultative.

Work

This stage is characterised by the team's focus on work, increased productivity and effectiveness, and the attainment of goals. As a high performance team, it establishes clear norms and acts according to them, the team is highly cohesive, and conformity is voluntary and high. Roles are clear, there is feedback from various members, and the leader shares and delegates responsibilities according to skills, roles and abilities.

Impending termination

This stage was proposed by Wheelan, Davidson and Tilin as a final stage during which teams may experience disruption and conflict. This applies to teams that know their termination time (e.g. a project team). The framework acknowledges that the termination time or date may have a disruptive (e.g. enhanced levels of stress and conflict) or an appreciative (e.g. acknowledgement) element to it.

Conclusion

This framework expands the "traditional" development framework(s) in that it suggests that teams do not necessarily spend equal amounts of time in the various stages. It suggests that teams might regress to earlier stages or stall development at a particular stage if external changes or a disruption in membership occur. It also suggests that awareness of impending termination may disrupt the team, although it may also lead to celebration or to team members expressing appreciation of each other.

Tips for team leaders

As is clear from the illustrations of these frameworks, there are subtle differences between them (e.g. nomenclature, sequence and number of stages), but some overlap and agreement can be detected. In particular, the following stages are common to all the versions:

- Forming. An initial stage common to all theories with a focus on boundary testing, defining the task of the team and working on identity within the team.

- Conflict. Unrest, disagreement and conflict characterise this stage, with sub-groups, factions and cliques forming. Challenges to the leadership are found and disagreement can arise between members who are task-oriented and those who are more people-focussed.

- Identity. The group displays cohesion and group identity during this stage.

- Production. This phase follows after cohesion has been established and the team actively starts performing. Focus is on delivery of outcomes.

- Termination. A final phase where the team completes its tasks or disbands.

While the various alternatives point to additional elements in the development of teams and can be very helpful to guide a team's journey, they also highlight some elements leaders may need to take into account, such as:

- teams might not spend equal amounts of time in the various stages;

- teams may regress to earlier stages or stall their development within a particular stage; and

- teams may take a different journey owing to the demands of the context.

In addition, it could be asked whether these stages correctly represent the complex nature of team development and if the whole approach is not too simplistic. Further, teams certainly only start performing at the end of their life cycle and definitely react to the demands of the context more adaptively than being predestined in a singular development path.

Representation

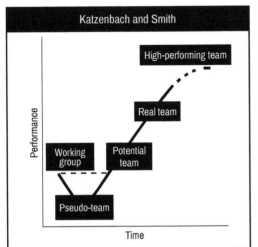
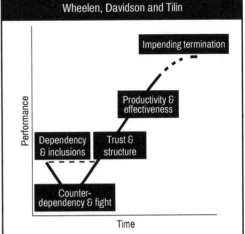

Figure 1.2: Team performance curve

References

Katzenbach, J., Smith, D. & Bookspan, M. (1993). *The wisdom of teams*: Boston: Harvard Business School Press.

Wheelan, S. (2016). *Creating effective teams: A guide for members and leaders* (5th ed.). Los Angeles: Sage.

Wheelan, S., Davidson, B. & Tilin, F. (2003). Group Development Across Time: Reality or illusion? *Small Group Research*, 34(2), 223–245.

Recursive processes

Introduction

The recursive perspective of how teams develop is the view that teams can revisit stages of development. If a team has not completed the development tasks associated with a particular stage it can "repeat" or "revisit" any previous stage or elements of a stage that have not been completed. The linear progression of a team does not always happen without obstacles, either task-related or interpersonal, and there are often disruptions in the development of a team. Conflict might develop between team members, contextual demands might change, stakeholder expectations might become different and the composition of the team might change. Although this is similar to the linear progressive views described above, it goes further by proposing that if a team does not complete the requirements of each stage satisfactorily, it will revisit the previous stage. This is described as a recursive process. One must thus make provision for the fact that a team may need to revisit some of its development tasks as time goes on.

In a nutshell

Seven stages (developmental tasks) that teams can revisit are identified, namely orientation, trust, goal orientation, commitment, implementation, high performance and renewal.

Purpose

To guide the team through its developmental tasks.

To help teams with key developmental tasks in each stage.

To allow teams to revisit previous stages to ensure appropriate completion of stages.

Description

Exponents of this perspective are Drexler, Sibbit and Forrester, who identified seven stages of team development, each characterised by key questions asked by members of the team.

Orientation

An initial stage where the team orientates itself to its task and the reason for its existence; members of the team ask "Why am I here?". If this stage is completed successfully the team finds its purpose, team harmony develops and the membership of the team is clarified. However, if not, members are disoriented and they feel fear and uncertainty about being in the team, the direction thereof or their place in the team.

Trust

The second stage is focused on building trust. Members spend time familiarising themselves with other members and want answers to "Who are you?" If this stage is successful, mutual regard develops and the team feel they can rely on one another. If it is unsuccessful, the team members mistrust one another and the team only progresses tentatively and cautiously with its tasks.

Goal orientation

The next stage answers the question "What are we doing?"; time and effort is spent orientating team members to the goals of the team. When the team resolves this stage successfully, members agree on clear and integrated goals and have a shared vision. Otherwise the team can become apathetic and sceptical.

Commitment

During this stage the team focuses its attention on "How will we do it?" and gets buy-in and commitment from its members. When this stage is positively negotiated the team members feel an increased focus on the purpose and outputs of the team, as well as how they are aligned. The team agrees on assigned roles, how resources are allocated and how decisions are made. If these issues are unresolved the team is characterised by resistance, members become despondent, the performance of the team is compromised, and interpersonal relationships deteriorate.

Implementation

The team is fully committed to delivering its tasks during this stage and therefore the questions raised are: "Who does what, when, where?" Clearly defined and effective processes are developed, the team is disciplined in their execution, and the interactions of the members are aligned. When the team does not succeed in its implementation efforts the effect is increased conflict and confusion, with the resultant missing of deadlines.

High performance

High performance is characterised by spontaneous interaction and synergy. The team performs to the best of its ability and surpasses expectations; a "Wow" feeling dominates. If this stage is not completed successfully, the team regresses into disharmony and overload.

Renewal

As the team completes its efforts the members ask "Why continue?" They perceive their task to have been completed successfully and celebrate their accomplishment. The members are empowered and bolstered by their ability to master changes and they celebrate the staying power and resolve they displayed. However, if the team does not feel its efforts were worthwhile and meaningful, members suffer from burnout and boredom and their willingness to continue is compromised.

Tips for team leaders

The main advantage of this perspective is that it allows teams to focus on the key elements that need to be addressed at each stage, but is "more realistic" in that it allows for challenges and obstacles to the team's development to be considered at any time. It also highlights a key transition period in the life of the team with a change of focus from creating the team to maintaining the team.

Representation

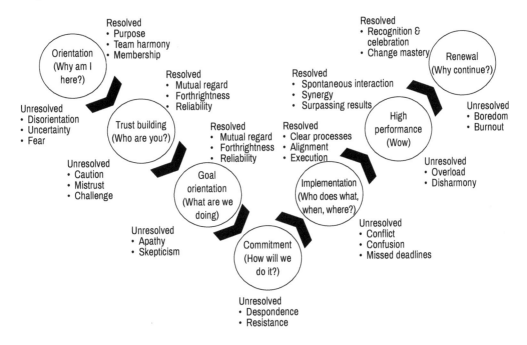

Figure 1.3: Recursive team processes

References

Drexler, A.B., Sibbet, D. & Forrester, R.H. (1988). The team performance model. In W. B. Reddy & K. Jamison (eds.). *Team building: Blueprints for productivity and satisfaction.* Alexandria, VA: National Institute for Applied Behavioral Science & Pfeiffer.

4 | Punctuated equilibrium model

Introduction

The punctuated equilibrium framework disputes the idea that teams all move linearly and contends that there is no necessarily "forward" movement in the development of a team. Proposed by Connie Gersick, this framework contends that a team is able to adjust its operations, structure and cooperation. The main contribution is the view that teams do not move through temporal stages, but rather develop two "bounded eras" that are temporal periods ("phases") that structure the utilisation of time by teams. The team's operations are punctuated with a period of transition and two phases of equal length before and afterwards. Bushe and Coetzer offered further views on how a team can utilise these two phases in its development.

In a nutshell

The development of teams in time is characterised by two phases, with a key transition stage at approximately the middle of the team's operations.

Purpose

To understand how teams progress in time.

To utilise the key moments in a team's development when it is most susceptible for intervention.

Description

Two versions of the Punctuated Equilibrium Model are offered, namely that of Gersick and the adaption by Bushe and Coetzer. The original model was proposed by Gersick after a review of laboratory teams, but it has since been extended and supported with work teams as well. The analysis of Bushe and Coetzer is included here as it links team member focus with the time periods in a team's development.

Gersick

The punctuated equilibrium model describes how teams go through two stages of relative stability "punctuated" (interrupted) by sudden, rapid change. Gersick contended that certain behavioural patterns and assumptions emerge the first time the team gets together, resulting in "bounded eras" (temporal periods or phases) that structure the utilisation of time by teams. She did not refer to hierarchical and/or progressive stages with identical sets of activities in each, but rather provided a different metaphor, namely that of a football match with two halves and a major half-time break.

Initial operational stage

The team enjoys an initial state of equilibrium throughout the first half of its life. Most often this framework evolves implicitly through what is said and done repeatedly by the team. The norms and processes that develop are robust and the team settles into a rhythm of operation. This lasts until approximately the calendar midpoint of the team.

Midpoint

At this "midpoint" a transition or paradigmatic shift occurs as the team takes stock of the learning that has taken place during the first phase and adjusts its operations for the remaining time. Members find old perspectives no longer viable and develop new ideas to use during completion of the team's work. At this point the team realises its time is limited, but this offers an opportunity to the team to calibrate its actions and to move forward. The team opens up to external influences and resources and benchmarks are set to re-chart its progress. This transition period is marked by three key conditions, namely members know their work well enough, they know that time is running out, and they understand that there is still enough time to make changes.

Second operational stage

A second phase of relative inertia follows where the team is informed by the events of the first phase and influenced by the members' expectations regarding the requirements of the last phase. Shortly before completion of its tasks, the team "launches into a final burst of activity" in an effort to satisfy outside expectation where the team experiences the positive and negative consequences of decisions it took during its operational life cycle.

Bushe and Coetzer

Bushe and Coetzer, in their attempt to reconcile disparate strands in research on group development, proposed a two-stage process consisting of membership and competence. Membership refers to individuals' efforts to "psychologically join" and identify with the team, while competence consists of the team's efforts to find ways to work together. This includes attempts to establish a "governance structure" that incorporates "issues of power and influence, task allocation, coordination of thought and action, utilization of diversity, clarification of external expectations, and management of group boundaries". This approach is "plotted onto" the punctuated equilibrium framework, in that the first phase should be completed before progress can be expected to the next phase. The authors regarded the first half of the team's operations as an attempt to move from the "actual" to the "ideal" team. In their view, the turbulence at the midpoint is due to a change of focus where the team moves from what it currently accomplishes to what it "ought" to accomplish. Unless a team progresses satisfactorily through the forming and storming stages, dysfunctional norms will be prevalent during the first phase of Gersick's framework. Where these stages are not completed effectively, relational (i.e. emotional or affective) conflict and task (i.e. cognitive) conflict will persist and teams will need a transition point earlier and more urgently. If this does not take place, the team will be dysfunctional and interpersonal relations will be problematic.

To alleviate the impact of these two possible impediments, more time will be needed for analysis of the team's framework and routines; this process should be brought forward to enable a higher quality of reflection and analysis as dysfunctional relationships make it progressively more difficult to do effective analysis and reflection. The success of the transition phase's reflection and analysis is dependent on the quality and sophistication of the facilitation thereof.

Finally, the last phase of the punctuated equilibrium framework (what the authors called "competence") consists of efforts of the team to find convergence between their (collective) perception of what it has accomplished and expectations of what it "ought" to accomplish. Although they alluded to a last phase where the team's operations are maintained or the team disperses, this part of their integration is not well-developed.

Tips for team leaders

This framework of a transition midpoint that connects two periods of stability and balance gives three natural opportunities to teams and their leaders to optimise members' willingness to learn and change.

Representation

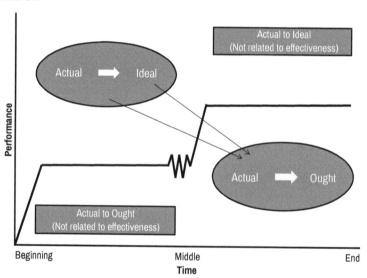

Figure 1.4: Punctuated equilibrium model

References

Bushe, G.R. & Coetzer, G.H. (2007). Group Development and Team Effectiveness: Using Cognitive Representations to Measure Group Development and Predict Task Performance and Group Viability. *The Journal of Applied Behavioural Science*, June, 184–211.

Gersick, C.J. (1988). Time and Transition in Work Teams: Toward a New Model of Group Development. *Academy of Management Journal*, 31, 9–41.

Gersick, C.J. (1989). Marking Time: Predictable Transitions in Task Groups. *Academy of Management Journal*, 32, 274–309.

Introduction

Morgan, Salas and Glickman provided an early example of integrating linear-progressive and equilibrium perspectives. Although they also identified nine "relatively informal, indistinct, and overlapping" stages, the key contribution of their view is that the team has the ability to revisit and/or repeat a stage (i.e. oscillate like a pendulum).

In a nutshell

Nine team development stages and two realms, the realm of tasks and the realm of interpersonal relations.

Purpose

To integrate development theories.

To guide teams to understand their development over time.

Description

This integrated perspective is largely based on a linear development view, but also accommodates the midpoint transition proposed by equilibrium frameworks. The authors identified nine stages, i.e. seven central or core stages, with a stage preceding and a stage following the central stages. They preferred to refer to stages rather than phases, as they regarded them as relatively informal, indistinct and overlapping time periods. They considered that in the daily operations of teams, sharp demarcations are impossible to determine. They also acknowledged that teams will spent different amounts of time (according to their individual needs and characteristics such as past experience and the nature of the team's tasks) in any of the stages, so team development is not only a linear process. The stages they identified are described in what follows.

Pre-forming

This non-core stage relates to the environmental forces (demands and constraints) that contribute or lead to the establishment of the team. The team focuses on the development of task assignments and explores or investigates the group.

Forming

In this stage the focus is on orientation to the task, testing of dependencies on the leader and other members in the team, and commitment to the goal. In this regard, the authors' views align with other views about the key development tasks that happen during the initial or forming stage of the team's development (e.g. Tuckman).

Storming

This stage is characterised by emotional responses to the task demands (on the taskwork level) and intra-group conflict on the teamwork level. It is at this stage that the team's goals are formed and committed to. While acknowledging the potentially turbulent nature of this stage, the authors pointed out that it is sometimes unstable due to the impact of the environment.

Norming

During this stage the team members make initial efforts toward accommodation of one another and start to understand what to expect from one another operationally and interpersonally. It is during this stage that the formation of roles starts to take place and members start to accept these roles. During this stage the team exhibits an open exchange of relevant interpretations, while on the interpersonal level cohesion starts to develop.

Performing – I

This stage is characterised by an initial rhythm of performance, but also by inefficient patterns. During the first operations phase solutions start to emerge and the team eagerly sets off to implement these initial solutions. While the team examines and develops role relatedness, i.e. the effectiveness of how different members occupy certain roles, it embarks on an initial operational stage. As was pointed out by Gersick, this is a relatively extended period and is only disturbed during the midterm transition of the team.

Reforming

The re-evaluation and transition stage provides an opportunity to reflect on performance to date and to scope the work ahead. During this midpoint the team adjusts its perspective and redefines its roles. This is consistent with the view that during its calendar midpoint a team has sufficient material to evaluate its performance while realisation of the limited time available spurs the team on to renewed effort. This period of turbulence focuses on keeping what has been successful, but allows for adjustment of those behaviours and practices that could hamper successful completion of its tasks.

Performing – II

This refers to the second period of stable functioning as a result of the evaluation and renewal described above. The team refocuses its efforts and performance; during this stage it optimises the use of roles and the drive to completion energises its members.

Conforming

Conforming in the sense used by these authors refers to what is required of the team to complete its tasks and deliver on its mandate. Thus, the completion of tasks and the accomplishment of goals and objectives are the key drivers on the taskwork level, while adjustment to environmental demands can be seen on the teamwork level.

De-forming

The model allows for a final stage where the team is disbanded. Withdrawal from task and a review of accomplishments are the two key elements on the taskwork level, while exiting the group and remembering the group happens on the relational level.

Tips for team leaders

This model gives a more comprehensive view of team development by integrating two prominent theories. Leaders can use this to track team development and make appropriate interventions according to the stage or level of development of their team.

Reference

Gersick, C.J. (1988). Time and Transition in Work Teams: Toward a New Model of Group Development. *Academy of Management Journal*, 31, 9–41.

Morgan, B. B., Salas, E. & Glickman, A. S. (1993). An Analysis of Team Evolution and Maturation. *Journal of General Psychology*, 120(3), 277–291.

Representation

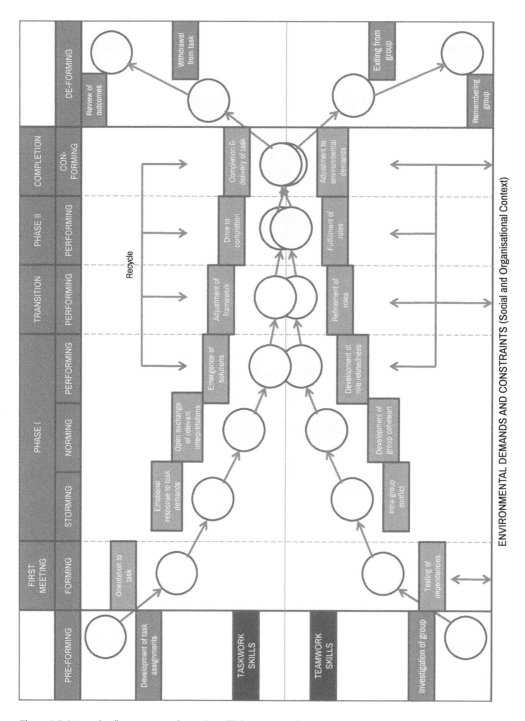

Figure 1.5: Integrating linear-progressive and equilibrium perspectives

2 CONSTITUENT FRAMEWORKS

Constituent frameworks are helpful as they provide the basic building blocks or elements that constitute a team and describe the minimum elements that need to be in place. Such frameworks can also be used to evaluate the extent to which these components are present in a team. The presence or absence of one or more of the components could indicate potential reasons for less than optimal functioning in the team. Many different frameworks or models of teams have been identified through research projects, practical experience and academic endeavour that use different components or constituent parts as a point of departure. The first to be described here are hierarchical component frameworks. These are followed by the Input-Process-Output perspective which is influenced by systems thinking. A variant of this perspective is the Input-Mediating-Output-Input framework. A further constituent framework looks at the external moderating components. Lastly, an integrated and comprehensive framework of constituent elements key to team operation is presented.

Introduction

It makes sense to think about teams as consisting of specific elements or "parts", and countless frameworks or models of this nature exist. Hierarchical models regard these constituent components to be in a hierarchical relationship with one another. Two such frameworks are presented here and although they illustrate this approach well, they differ in nature. Larson and LaFasto surveyed more than 6000 so-called "excellent" teams and described a hierarchical relationship (i.e. resembling a holarchy) between the components they found that drive performance. Lencioni, meanwhile, provided a narrative that serves as an allegory of how teams operate. He identified five stages that are premised on five "dysfunctions" and are structured in pyramidal form to indicate importance.

In a nutshell

Hierarchical relationships between components of teams, namely holarchical (team members, relationships, problem solving, leader, and organisational environment) and pyramidal (dysfunctions, i.e. absence of trust, fear of conflict, lack of commitment, avoidance of accountability and inattention to results).

Purpose

To grow the team according to the required components.

To give a template to evaluate the team.

To direct teams to what dysfunctions may prevent them from optimal functioning.

Description

Larson and LaFasto's holarchical view

The authors offered a hierarchical view where the different elements build on one another and where the one level incorporates and contains the previous (and all previous components), i.e. a holarchical relationship. They identified team members, team relationships, team problem-solving, team leadership and organisational context as key constituent parts.

Team members

In discussing what is required of team members, Larson and LaFasto made the classic distinction between task skills and team skills. They contended that working knowledge (their term for the operational, task-based skills required for success) consists of experience and problem-solving ability. The first includes the practical knowledge relevant to the team's objective as well as sufficient experience to deliver on what is required. In terms of the team skills required of members, four team skills are identified, namely openness (ability to identify, investigate and solve problems), supportiveness (willingness and desire to help), action orientation (deliberate effort to make things happen) and style (level of positivity and ability to put colleagues at ease).

Team relationships

Productive team relationships are characterised as constructive for both parties, are productive, are perceived as fostering mutual understanding and are self-corrective. Two key elements in creating such relationships in teams are openness (willingness to communicate, frequency of interaction and ability to raise an issue) and supportiveness (acceptance and affection towards others, confirmation of the worth and value of team members, and positive treatment of team members to bring out the best in them). In order to facilitate good team relationships members need to agree to constructive conversations, shape conversations towards making a difference, allow for mutual understanding of perspectives, and commit to improvements.

Team problem-solving

From their survey of teams, Larson and LaFasto showed that three key factors differentiate effective from ineffective teams. The first is the degree to which team members are focused in their efforts and are clear about what they are doing at each moment of their work. Secondly, the climate, that is, the team's mental, physical and spiritual energies, are directed at solving the goal and members feel accepted, valued and competent. Thirdly, the team makes systematic problem-solving a priority through a meticulous process.

The team leader

The following six dimensions are identified as critical for an effective team leader. To be effective, a team leader:

- focuses on the goal – the leader must articulate a clear goal in a manner that is inspiring to the point that members can repeat in "syncopated rhythm where the team is heading", believe in the direction it takes the team and inspire members to work hard to achieve it. The latter is done by demonstrating how each member contributes towards the goal;

- ensures a collaborative climate – the leader must make it safe to discuss issues, demand a collaborative approach and reward collective behaviour. Furthermore the leader must guide the team's problem-solving efforts and limit focus on his/her own needs;

- builds confidence – leaders build confidence by ensuring that results are attained, by enabling members to be smart about issues and facts, and by exhibiting trust by assigning responsibility. However, this needs to be supported by being fair and impartial, accentuating the positive, and expressing gratitude for the effort of team members;

- demonstrates sufficient technical know-how – leaders should understand the body of knowledge necessary for the achievement of the goal and be comfortable to find help if they "don't know their stuff";

- sets priorities – team leaders should focus on the crucial initiatives by clarifying what must happen and what must not, and by being prepared to adjust when priorities change; and

- manages performance – team leaders accomplish this dimension by making performance expectations clear, giving constructive feedback and resolving performance issues by both dealing with sub-optimal performance and recognising superior effort.

The organisational environment

Lastly Larson and LaFasto maintained that a supporting organisational environment drives clarity, which in turn fosters confidence, which in turn creates commitment. The three elements of the environment that influence effective teams are:

- management practices: leaders must set clear direction (clear goals and priorities), ensure resources are used in a balanced manner, and establish clear operating principles to ensure aligned effort and delivery of results;

- structure and processes: this refers to the contextual conditions that help for the best decisions to be made as quickly as possible by the right people (best equipped in terms of knowledge and managerial responsibility), at the right time, dealing with the right issue. Effective communication processes keep team members "in sync" with the task and connected with one another so that information, understanding and effort are aligned; and

- systems: the organisation must provide reliable and useful information and should focus team behaviour towards the desired results. This can take place when personal financial and psychological rewards are linked to the group goal so that team victory is more important than personal victory.

Lencioni's pyramidal framework

Lencioni provided a narrative that serves as an allegory of how teams operate. He identified five stages that are premised on five "dysfunctions" that stop teams from achieving optimal performance. To correct these dysfunctions, teams need to sort out that each preceding level is in place and operating as it should, in order to progress to the next level. Lencioni provides a hierarchical model illustrating these five potential dysfunctions.

Absence of trust

Trust allows team members to feel vulnerable in the team and to be open about mistakes and weaknesses. If there is no trust, no sufficient foundation is created whereon the team can be built. According to Lencioni, trust in a team is different from the generally understood meaning of the term; in a team it means members have confidence that the intentions of others in the team are good. There is thus no reason to be protective and careful, and members are allowed to be vulnerable. Even more, it means that members understand that any vulnerability will not be used against them. Vulnerabilities include "soft" personal and interpersonal aspects, and trust is built over time as members share their experiences. They also need the validation of follow-through and the credibility that comes from multiple occurrences; this is assisted by an in-depth understanding of the strengths, weaknesses, idiosyncrasies and unique attributes of each member. The absence of trust leads to the next dysfunction where conflict is avoided and open discussion limited.

Fear of conflict

This failure refers to the team's inability to engage in passionate debate, where it skirts issues through superficial discussions and guarded comments. In effective teams, productive ideological conflict is tolerated while destructive interpersonal conflict is minimised. The former allows for the best possible solution to emerge, for issues to be discussed in greater depth, and for members to be energised in their efforts to find alternatives rather than be left with residual feelings. By optimising conflict and making it more common and productive, teams save time and become more effective. As the team solves problems the members become fully committed to the team.

Lack of commitment

If team members can not participate openly and air their opinions, they do not become committed to the team, and may be reluctant to buy into the team's decisions and operations. This lack of commitment can be overcome by clear and timely decisions. Contrary to common wisdom, it is not always necessary for teams to achieve consensus; consensus can even lead to sub-optimal decision-making, as "groupthink" may limit a team's effectiveness. But once a clear decision is made, teams should be able to commit to the resolution and give their allegiance, even if they have a different personal opinion. In the absence of such clarity and commitment, even members fail to call each other on their actions.

Avoidance of accountability

If the team members do not feel committed it stops them from questioning their peers' actions and behaviours that are counterproductive to the good of the team. The effect is that members avoid the interpersonal discomfort of calling each other on their actions, and rather live with the consequences of not having difficult conversations. This flies in the face of accountability and effective teams will resist falling into this trap. In great teams, members indicate their respect for one another by keeping to commitments, holding each other accountable and setting high expectations of each other's performance.

Inattention to results

Avoiding accountability leads to an environment where members put individual needs and the needs of subgroups above those of the whole team. The team should focus unrelentingly on collective goals and specific outcomes. These include, but are not limited to, financial and business-driven outcomes. They should also include the growth and development goals the team members have set for themselves.

Tips for team leaders

The frameworks presented here are described as integrated, as the status of each element influences the other elements. Leaders can use these approaches to highlight the interrelation between the various elements of teams. The greatest strength of this approach is its simplicity and "check-list" nature. Leaders and members alike can evaluate their operations and interactions and determine where the team may be improved. It furthermore helps teams to find a point of entry into the team's constitution and thereby helps to determine where interventions to improve the team's success need to be implemented. When Lencioni's framework is put in a positive mode it shows that the members of a successful team trust one another; engage in unfiltered conflict around ideas; commit to decisions and actions; hold each other accountable for delivering against action plans; and focus on the achievement of collective results.

Representation

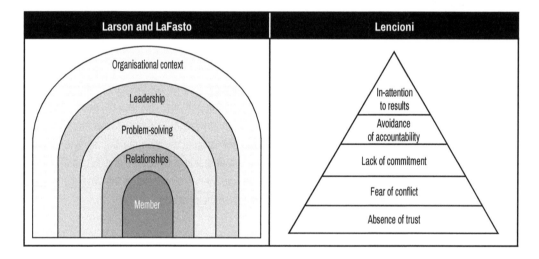

Figure 2.1: Hierarchical components

References

LaFasto, F.M.J. & Larson, C.E. (2001). *When teams work best: 6,000 team members and leaders tell what it takes to succeed*. Newbury Park, CA: Sage.

Larson, C.E. & LaFasto, F.M.J. (1989). *Teamwork: What must go right/ What can go wrong*. Newbury Park, CA: Brooks.

Lencioni, P. (2002). *The five dysfunctions of a team*. San Francisco, CA: Jossey-Bass.

Input-process-output process

Introduction

Bang and Midelfart offered a variant of the basic Input-Process-Output (IPO) perspective by preferring to use the term "throughputs" to refer to the process part. They identified a set of eight inputs, eleven throughputs and three outputs for the work of a team as constituents thereof.

In a nutshell

An IPO framework with eight inputs, eleven processes and three outputs.

Purpose

To help teams understand input, throughput and output elements in a team.

To give a checklist of each element to help gauge the performance of each.

Description

The authors identified eight inputs, eleven throughput elements and eight outputs, which resulted in 27 dimensions.

Inputs

Inputs refer to the IPO elements or conditions required to enable the team to exist and to deliver on its goals. In this version the following are included:

- Clear purpose: a clear sense of the team's role in the organisation and what value it creates. It clarifies what should and should not be addressed by the team.

- Appropriate tasks: appropriate allocation of tasks that involve the whole team.

- Appropriate size: optimal for the purpose and tasks that need to be accomplished.

- Appropriate competencies: the required professional, intellectual and interpersonal knowledge, skills and abilities to complete the tasks and achieve results.

- Balanced diversity: sufficient levels of diversity in the team to supplement and stimulate each other, while at the same time sufficiently similar to facilitate understanding, working together and harmony.

- Team-reinforcing reward systems: incentive systems that are structured to reward high quality performance as well as collaboration.

- Adequate information systems: the organisation provides sufficient high quality information to the team to enable it to execute its tasks and subsequently its mission; and

- Adequate educational systems: a system to offer development, training and education to equip members to deliver on the mission of the team.

Throughputs

Throughputs (activities and tasks that help the team to transform input into output) include:

- pre-meeting preparation: members are adequately prepared and supporting documents required in meetings are of a high quality;

- clear meeting goals: clarity on why an issue is raised and discussed, as well as clarity on what is expected of the team once deliberation is completed;

- focused communication: members focus on the issue at hand, and are not long-winded and do not drift off the topic;

- task conflict: open and healthy conflict takes place, including debating differences of opinion, entertaining diverse views and allowing different points of view;

- absence of relationship conflict: the team works well on an interpersonal level and there is no friction, tension or conflict;

- absence of politics: limited attempts by members to use covert action to raise their level of power and influence over members, the team and processes. The team functions with limited power struggles, the members provide the required information and there are no counter-productive alliances or coalitions;

- dialogue: the team allows and encourages the open exchange of ideas, willingness to explore various ideas and build on each other's ideas;

- behavioural integration: through teamwork the team exhibits a high degree of cooperation, integration and coordination, which allows for shared information and resources. Members work collaboratively and are involved with each other as they feel mutually responsible for actions and decisions in the team;

- active external relationships: constructive relationships with internal and external stakeholders are maintained;

- continuous team learning: the team constantly evaluates its own performance and work methods, and adjusts its processes according to these reflections; and

- effective team leadership: the leader ensures that the ideal conditions and processes are maintained to ensure task and team performance.

Outputs

Outputs include performance (as judged by external others), meeting the needs of team members, and viability (demonstrated by the willingness of team members to stay in the team). In the framework offered by Bang and Midelfart, team performance comprises three elements, namely task performance, team viability and individual well-being. These outputs have to meet the requirements of the stakeholders of the team, in other words they have to satisfy organisational or personal goals and meet pre-determined criteria.

Task performance is measured according to set criteria such as profit, quality or quantity. Three types of task performance outcomes are identified in this framework, namely:

* general task performance: in order to provide value to the organisation, the tasks the team has to fulfil are accomplished successfully and achieve the required results;

* decision quality: the decisions made by the team are to the benefit of the organisation and those affected thereby are generally satisfied; and

* decision implementation: the team collectively commits to its decisions and ensures their implementation.

Team viability looks at whether the team is sustainable and able to reach its targets. A team should act to ensure longer-term viability and sustainability and create a sense of belonging and cohesion for its members. This allows for members to enjoy working together and to build an environment to which they are prepared to commit and contribute. Elements of team viability include:

* psychological team safety: the team is sufficiently safe for risk taking and allows members to express their views openly, to be vulnerable and to explore without fear of negative reactions from other members;

* team spirit: a sense of cohesion that is built on members liking each other, being committed to each other and the team's goals, and generally perceiving themselves as tightly knit;

* functional team culture: the team functions with agreed values and norms (stated or understood) that foster cooperation, support effectiveness and facilitate cooperation and support for one another; and

* team efficacy: the team believes in its own ability to be successful, productive and to create high quality work.

Individual well-being comprises individual member growth and satisfaction. The consequences a group has for its members and the benefits each member finds in being part of the group should form part of the target of the team. Members participate in teams and will remain in a team for an extended period of time only when it realises sufficient benefit for the individual. Thus, a team must also provide learning and development opportunities for members to develop new skills, to fulfil their own ambitions and to grow.

Tips for team leaders

This is a very helpful tool to assist leaders to identify strengths and weaknesses in the IPO process of a team and provide an opportunity to identify where effective intervention will have the biggest impact. Based on this model, the authors designed an evaluation instrument, called "Effect", which measures the various elements of their management team effectiveness model.

Representation

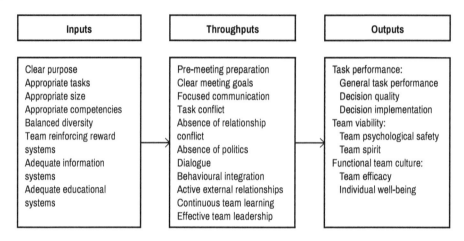

Figure 2.2: Inputs-Process-Output (IPO)

References

Bang, H. (2017). *Technical manual on effect – an inventory for measuring management team effectiveness.* Oslo: University of Oslo.

Bang, H. & Midelfart, T.N. (2017). What Characterizes Effective Management Teams? A Research-Based Approach. *Consulting Psychology Journal: Practice and Research,* 69(4), 334–359.

Hansen, L.B. (2017). The dimensionality of management team effectiveness: A psychometric analysis of the team inventory "effect". Unpublished Master's Thesis, University of Oslo.

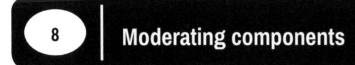

Introduction

It has long been realised that a team's performance is moderated by various factors, both external and internal. The notion that teams are embedded in layered contexts is aptly illustrated by the perspective of Sundstrom, De Meuse and Futrell, who described the components of such environmental factors. A more recent and influential attempt at demonstrating the importance of context was given by Kozlowski and Ilgen, who demonstrated the demands that context puts on a team's performance. As this context is dynamic, shifting, and complex, the team's performance is moderated from external sources. Thompson held that the context enables conditions to be in place that in turn drive performance.

In a nutshell

External contextual moderators influence team performance.

Purpose

To highlight the interrelation between processes and output.

To demonstrate that the outcomes of processes influence other team processes.

To highlight the fact that the Input-Process-Output process is not only linear.

To point to emergent states that evolve as teams develop.

Description

Three perspectives on how components moderate team development are discussed, namely "Embedded context-", "Dynamic development" and "Integrated".

Embedded context

Sundstrom and colleagues distinguished between organisational context, boundaries, team development and team effectiveness as key structural components of teams. They contended that these components are embedded in one another, and defined them as follows:

Organisational context

This comprises features of the environment external to the team, including organisation culture; task design and technology; mission clarity; autonomy; performance feedback; reward and recognition; training and consultation; and the team's physical environment.

Boundaries

The function of team boundaries is to differentiate the work unit from others; to pose real or symbolic barriers to entry and/or flow from the team; and to serve as points of external exchange with other stakeholders and teams. It mediates between organisational context and team development, and assists in defining effectiveness. Boundaries serve to integrate and at the same time differentiate:

- Integration: the team's boundaries are used to align and integrate the group into the larger system. Of specific importance is the impact that external integration has on the use of work cycles (i.e. high levels of external integration lead to shorter work cycles, while lower levels of integration may lead to single cycles or longer-term cycles).

- Differentiation: this refers to the degree of specialisation, independence and autonomy of the team in relation to other teams and stakeholders. Differentiation is determined by features including membership (i.e. composition, turnover and size); temporal scope (i.e. time spent together); and territories (i.e. the need of teams to have their own physical space).

Team development

Over time, teams develop ways of dealing with their environment, including both "group-structure" and "interpersonal processes", and norms, cohesion and roles.

Contextual influences

The authors also highlighted two related contextual influences, namely team effectiveness, comprising viability (team members' satisfaction around working together) and performance (the acceptability of the output - production and/or service). Also critical to their view is that interrelationships between the various elements and contexts are key to team performance and that they are all linked through reciprocal interdependence. The emphasis on the embedded nature of all these elements and the interrelations between them is key, according to this view.

Dynamic development

Kozlowski and Ilgen indicated that context creates the environment in which cognitive, behavioural and affective processes develop. They noted that these contextual moderators create commensurate team task demands that members have to resolve, and that team members typically combine their cognitive, motivational/affective, and behavioural resources (i.e. processes) to meet such demands. When the processes employed by the team align with the "environmentally driven task demands", the team is effective. The effectiveness of the team is determined by the manner in which the team can use processes to respond to the contextual demands, thus the team is perceived as:

- embedded in a multilevel system that has individual, team and organisational aspects. This entails that the reciprocal processes between the team and its environment are acknowledged. In particular, it is key to bear in mind that the interaction between these systems is reciprocal in that team outputs (i.e. performance) influence or resolve task demands, which in turn change the team context;

- focused on task-relevant processes as the task sets minimum requirements for the resource pool and also determines the primary focus of the team's activities. The task determines work flow structures and coordination demands. These team processes are regarded as emergent phenomena;

- incorporating temporal dynamics, which include episodic tasks (i.e. task cycles) and developmental progression (e.g. linear, phasic development); and

- influenced by factors that shape, lever or align these processes according to the performance of the team, the contextual demands and the emergent processes.

Components that influence team processes

The authors identify the following influences on team processes:

Cognitive processes and structures

Four cognitive processes and structures are identified as key, namely:

- a collective climate: a climate captures the strategic imperatives reflective of the core mission and objectives of the team. Leverage points to shape climate include strategic imperatives, leadership and social interaction;

- shared mental models: these should be accurate and correct to facilitate shared understanding relating to tasks and relationships among the members of the team, its tasks and role system, and its environment(s). Leverage points to shape development of a shared mental model include leadership, training and common experience;

- transactive memory systems: this is knowledge of member specialisation and knowledge on how to access such knowledge to enable teams to be effective; and

- team learning: collective learning efforts enhance team effectiveness.

Interpersonal, motivational and affective processes

Here the authors identified four processes that allow teams to be more effective:

- Team cohesion: teams with a greater sense of the collective task and of interpersonal cooperation will be more effective.

- Team level efficacy and group potency: as influenced by leadership and training.

- Affect, mood and emotion: these impact on team effectiveness, but research-based and conceptual work is needed to determine to what levels.

- Conflict management: skills to maximise trust and to facilitate the management of any conflict in the team.

Action and behavioural processes

Two components are identified here that assist team effectiveness:

- Coordination, cooperation and communication: these are key behavioural processes.

- Team-member competencies: the knowledge, skills and abilities of the team members required to perform and execute tasks.

Integrated

Thompson provided a perspective of teams that divided the components of team functioning into contextual and conditional components. Context comprises organisational context, team design and team culture, while the conditions that drive performance are ability, motivation and strategy. In her view, team performance includes productivity, cohesion, learning and integration.

Context

The three factors Thompson identifies as components of context are:

- organisational context: strategy, culture and processes influence optimum team performance;

- team design: the size and composition of the team are determinants of conditions required; and

- team culture: the prevailing culture in the team in terms of interpersonal relationships and mood influence conditions.

Conditions

Thompson's thesis is that three essential conditions are required for a team to produce the required performance, namely:

- ability: the members' knowledge, skills and education level, as well as the quality of information available to the team to complete its work;

- motivation: the intrinsic and extrinsic motivation required by team members to perform; and

- strategy: the communication and coordination the team employs. This last condition (i.e. strategy) seems similar to what other perspectives call a process, but in this case it is considered to be a condition.

Tips for team leaders

It is helpful to understand the critical role that context plays in determining the scope and vision of a team, as well as the fact that it provides the team with its members. As the modern-day context of organisations becomes increasingly complex, uncertain and volatile, teams will have to adjust their processes to adapt to this changing context. Thus, the moderating role of the external environment has to be taken into account when in determining the design and processes of the team.

Reference

Kozlowski, S.W.J. & Ilgen, D.R. (2006). Enhancing the Effectiveness of Work Groups and Teams. *Psychological Science in the Public Interest*, 7(3), 77–124.

Sundstrom, E., McIntyre, M., Halfhill, T. & Richards, H. (2000). Work Groups: From the Hawthorne Studies to Work Teams of the 1990s and Beyond. *Group Dynamics: Theory, Research, and Practice*, 4(1), 44–67.

Thompson, L. (2007). *Making the Team: A guide for Managers* (3rd ed.). Upper Saddle River, NJ: Pearson Prentice Hall.

Representation

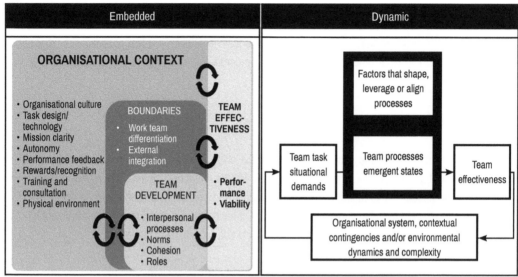

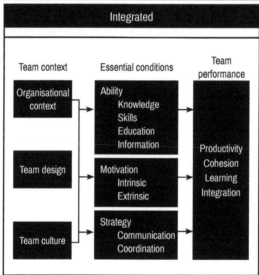

Figure 2.3: Three perspectives on how components moderate team development

Internal mediating components (IMOI)

Introduction

In a departure from the traditional Input-Process-Output perspective, Ilgen, Hollenbeck, Johnson and Jundt focused on the manner in which internal processes develop and in turn influence team performance. They offered an alternative framework to assist in their review of research, namely IMOI (input-mediator-output-input).

In a nutshell

Internal moderating factors influence team performance.

Purpose

To highlight the interrelation between processes and output.

To highlight the fact that the IPO process is not only linear.

To point to emergent states that evolve as teams develop.

Description

Ilgen, Hollenbeck, Johnson and Jundt pointed out some of the limitations of the Input-Process-Output framework, indicating that:

- many of the mediational factors included as "process" are not really processes at all, but "emergent cognitive or affective states";

- an IPO framework implies a single-cycle linear path from inputs to outcomes. This does not take into account that some emergent states influence processes which in turn potentially impact on performance; and

- the IPO framework focuses on categories (i.e. I, P or O) that follows sequentially, but it seems that other relations (e.g. between various inputs and processes (I x P) between various processes (P x P) and between inputs or processes and emergent states (ES) are also possible.

The authors thus offered an alternative framework to assist in their review of research, namely IMOI (i.e. input-mediator-output-input). They contended that substituting "M" for "P" reflects the broader range of variables that are important mediational influences, which can explain variability in team performance and viability. Adding the extra "I" at the end of the framework explicitly invokes the notion of cyclical causal feedback. Elimination of the hyphen between letters also signifies that the causal linkages may not be linear or additive, but rather nonlinear or conditional. They presented their review of studies around the three phases, each of which contains a cognitive, an affective and a behavioural component. These phases are as follows:

Forming phase (i.e. the IM-phase)

The initial phase where the team starts its operation. Three factors influence the forming phase, namely trusting, planning and structuring.

Trusting

This factor relates to the trust that exists between members and includes potency and safety. The former refers to the sense that the team has the requisite levels of competence to deliver, while safety expands this from the behavioural scope to include members' views on the intentions of their colleagues. Teams require unconditional trust and a willingness to take interpersonal risk to feel safe. The extent of this sense of trust (confidence and safety) acts as an emergent state that influences a team's processes from within.

Planning

This factor is broad enough to include planning, gathering information and developing strategy. This behavioural process impacts on team development and on the belief that the team can be successful through the way it acquires the information it needs and what is valuable to its constituencies. The second key factor that impacts on the planning of the team is how it uses this information to form a strategy to deliver on its mission. This requires focused planning, and as the team delivers on its milestones this is an internal process that influences its performance.

Structuring

Structuring includes shared mental frameworks and transactive memory. This refers to the team's development and maintenance of norms, roles, and interaction patterns. As a team interacts through delivering on its strategy, the various interactions and interpersonal relationships require that the team develop shared mental models. It is necessary for the members of the team to be on the proverbial "same hymn sheet" to know what is expected from each of them, to have a shared sense of the goals of the team and to share views on quality and norms. Furthermore, the transactive memory of the team determines knowledge of where information is "stored" in the team and how it can be accessed.

Thus, as the team completes the forming stage, its levels of trust, planning activities and structuring processes influence the manner in which the next phase, the functioning phase, is executed.

Functioning phase (i.e. the MO-phase)

During this phase the team experiences working together. Factors influencing this process include bonding, adapting and learning.

Bonding

Bonding refers to the affective feelings that team members develop toward each other, leading to a strong sense of rapport and a willingness to work together and stay together. It includes the manner in which the team manages diversity and conflict. As these two factors potentially influence the levels of bonding, they highlight the mechanisms required to facilitate bonding.

Adapting

This refers to behavioural processes related to the manner in which the team performs in routine versus novel conditions, which impact how a team adapts. This in turn helps the team to put the required actions and processes in place to help the team perform on its tasks. Crucial to this is the manner in which members of the team help one another and are willing to share the workload. As this happens it increases the team's sense of accomplishment, which in turn acts as an emergent state motivating the team.

Learning

Learning as a process refers to whether team members are willing to learn from minority views and how dissenting voices are accommodated. Again, these have a critical impact on the internal processes of the team, as these behaviours foster the affective and cognitive emergent states. These in turn act as internal moderators on team processes.

Finishing phase (i.e. the OI-phase)

This is where the team completes one episode in the developmental cycle and starts a new cycle. The authors only list this phase and don't discuss elements thereof.

Tips for team leaders

The tool is helpful as it guides leaders to think beyond a linear view of team operation, and to be attuned to the many facets of team dynamics and how team dynamics can change over time.

It is helpful to leaders to keep in mind that the successes or failures of a team's processes have an impact on the performance of the team, not only in terms of the outcomes they produce, but also in the manner in which they influence the processes the team subsequently employs.

Representation

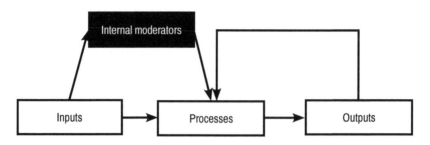

Figure 2.4: IMOI model

Reference

Ilgen, D.R., Hollenbeck, J.R., Johnson, M. & Jundt, D. (2005). Teams in Organizations: From Input-Process-Output Models to IMOI Models. *Annual Review of Psychology,* 56(1), 517–543.

Introduction

It will be obvious that all the different constituent elements of team functioning are interrelated, for instance the moderating elements and their influence should not be perceived in isolation, but as impacting on the whole life of the team. The theory of interrelations has attracted scholarly attention as it highlights the dynamics between components. A good example of such an integrated view is the Team Leadership Model (TLM) offered by Ginnet, who focused on what leaders have to do to lead teams effectively and introduced a framework that is used to guide the leader on where to intervene and lead.

In a nutshell

A team is viewed from a direction, design and development perspective.

Purpose

To demonstrate the interrelation of various constituent elements.

To highlight the dynamic interplay of components within an Input-Process-Output systems approach to teams.

Description

The Team Leadership Model focuses on what leaders have to do to lead teams effectively. The Input-Process-Output framework is used, but the multiple contexts in which teams functions are also stressed. The team aims to achieve its outcomes (stakeholder expectations, future capability and individual satisfaction) through processes (effort, knowledge and skills, strategy and group dynamics) and with inputs from an organisational level (control systems), a team level (authority domains) and an individual level (interpersonal behaviour).

Determine the outputs of the team

The point of departure in this perspective is the deliverables the team have to produce. Thus, the outputs of the team must be determined and performance levels set with regard to:

*   productive output (goods, services, decisions);

*   ability to work as a team (processes are inductive to help members work as team members in current or future teams); and

*   enhanced growth and personal well-being of members.

Evaluate the processes of the team

The processes employed provide measures of effectiveness by which the team can evaluate the ways they operate. Four process measures for the team to evaluate were identified:

- Effort - do we work hard enough?

- Knowledge and skills – do we have sufficient knowledge and skills?

- Strategy - do we have an appropriate strategy or approach to the task at hand?

- Group dynamics - how do we interact (communicate, express emotions, deal with conflict)?

Determine input factors

In order to influence the processes of a team, various input factors have to be addressed. These are the factors available to the team to do its work. Organisational systems, team factors and individual characteristics all influence team processes and each of these has a commensurate leverage point. Ginnett identified three "foundation-level variables" that impact on each of the three levels of input, namely interpersonal behaviour (on the individual level), authority dynamics (on the team level) and control systems (on the organisational level). Each of these foundation-level variables has three leverage points, namely:

- for interpersonal behaviour, the leverage points are motivations and interests, skills and abilities, and values and attitudes;

- for authority dynamics, the leverage points are team task, team composition and team norms; and

- for control systems, the leverage points are reward systems, education systems, and information systems.

Furthermore, each of these leverage points impacts on each of the process criteria. The TLM also indicates the role that the leader has to play by offering prescriptions (suggestions on how to set up a team) and diagnosis and leverage points (suggestions on where to intervene).

Prescriptions

- Dream: the leader has the responsibility to communicate a clear and engaging vision. The goal must be challenging, demanding and such that the team is involved in designing, enacting and buying into the vision.

- Design: at this point leaders have the opportunity to detect flaws in the design and make corrections to influence the processes of the team.

- Development: this is the ongoing work done by the team at the process level on how the team can improve.

Diagnosis and leverage points

The true value of the TLM is that it can be used diagnostically to determine where intervention will potentially have the biggest impact. For example, if a leader detects a problem with effort (i.e. a process problem), it could be connected with the control systems (the organisational level) or it could be that the team's lack of effort is due to issues with the reward system. However, if the process problem lies with the level of knowledge or skills, a different route is suggested.

Tips for team leaders

The contribution of Ginnet is unique in describing the link between specific control systems and authority domains, which in turn impacts on interpersonal behaviour. It offers a very clear description of how organisational context can affect a team's behaviour and how the team should deal with feedback from the environment.

Representation

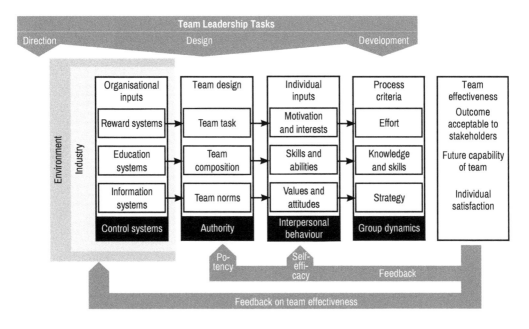

Figure 2.5: Ginnett's Team Leadership Model

References

Hughes, R.L., Ginnett, R.C. & Curphey, G.J. (2009). *Leadership: Enhancing the lessons of experience* (6th ed.). New York: McGraw-Hill.

3 ORGANISATIONAL CONTEXT

The importance of the context in which a team operates can never be under-estimated, as a team is always embedded in a larger environment. This context provides the team with its commission (i.e. its reason for existence), its purpose, and indeed the people that form the team. Thus, it shapes the goal and vision of the team and determines the make-up and composition of the team.

Context can be considered as composed of external and internal elements. The external environment is the broader societal context in which the team operates and includes political, social, economic, technological, legal and environmental factors. The internal context of the team also has an impact, as does the organisational context. The organisational context can support or limit the functioning of a team. Culture refers to the shared beliefs, values and attitudes, or what has been called the "underlying assumptions" that influence how members in an organisation (and therefore a team as well) think and behave and which emerge through the development history of the team. As the influence of culture as part of a team's internal context is particularly critical to the manner in which the team operates interpersonally and operationally, two parts are devoted to culture. Lastly, the team may also be influenced by the value chain in the organisation, and it may be helpful for the team to define where its unique position is along the value chain in relation to other teams and stakeholders.

Introduction

In the ever-changing environment in which organisations operate, keeping track of context is critical. Not only is it a key determinant for the sustainability of a team, but the team also gets its purpose from the external context, either directly if given a goal to achieve within a larger system, or indirectly when a team needs to design plans on how it will offer value to the external environment. For teams to understand the context they operate in it is helpful to use a process such as a PESTLE analysis or a Stakeholder analysis. While the latter may also include stakeholders that could be external to the team, some of them could be critical internal stakeholders. It is presented here to give a broad perspective on a team's external environment.

In a nutshell

Analysis of elements influencing the external organisational context.

Purpose

To help analysis of the organisation's external environment.

To facilitate alignment and fit with organisational context.

To map the stakeholders of the team.

To identify those with influence and those have to be influenced.

To identify those supportive of the team and those adversarial to the team.

To map allies, blockers, hostiles or supporters.

Description

Two techniques are described, the PESTLE analysis and the Stakeholder analysis.

PESTLE analysis

The elements of the so-called PESTLE model (and the terms from which the acronym is devised) are political, economic, sociological, technological, legal and environmental issues. These mega-trends impact on everyone in one way or another and therefore teams are also influenced by them. The importance in terms of teams is understanding how each one affects the specific team.

Political influences

The fact that remote trends can be of a national or global nature is probably best illustrated by the impact that the political context can have on team behaviour. Political decisions may influence aspects such as the composition of teams, or emotions could be influenced by global political events.

Economic issues

Various economic issues can influence a team and the behaviour of members within the team. Even events on a global scale, such as a recession or a downturn in markets far removed from their own, can impact on the team. Such impact may influence the perspectives members have of each other and of the aims and goals of the team.

Sociological influences

The importance of race or gender issues and the cultural valence attached to specific behaviours are examples of sociological influences that have a potential impact on a team's interpersonal relationships.

Technological influences

The effect of technology can best be illustrated by how the notion of virtual teams brings new challenges. The demands of technology through the so-called fourth revolution and the changes it has brought to lifestyles has an enormous impact on teams, as they operate today in a society with more information facilitated by technology.

Legal influences

Teams operate within larger organisational and societal environments and are therefore not exempt from the legal framework of those environments.

Environmental influences

These days organisations have become increasingly aware of the critical responsibility they have regarding sustainability, which goes beyond contact with the environment to include corporate social responsibility. Many team decisions and outputs could be influenced by stricter environmental awareness and international control measures.

Stakeholder Analysis

While in the past stakeholders have been viewed rather narrowly, there is now much clearer consensus that the stakeholders of teams are varied and multiple and all stakeholders impact on a team's performance in a variety of ways. For this analysis, the team compiles a list of the stakeholders of the team. Most teams will know intuitively who their critical stakeholders are, but care should be taken to ensure that all are included. Once the list is complete, each of the stakeholders is entered onto a matrix to indicate their perceived influence on, and support of, the team. The matrix is drawn by indicating on a graph's vertical axis "People with influence" at the top and "People that are influenced" at the bottom. The horizontal axis is used to indicate those "In favour" and those "Against" the team. The various stakeholders are then plotted on the graph according to their perceived level of influence and degree of support.

Once plotted, stakeholders can be categorised as:

- allies (supporters of the solution that have influence);

- hostiles (stakeholders against the solution that have influence);

- supporters (stakeholders influenced by and in favour of the solution); and

- blockers (stakeholders influenced by the solution but against it).

This method allows the team to identify critical stakeholders and devise appropriate action where necessary.

Tips for team leaders

This is helpful to understand the drivers and dynamics of the organisational context the team operates in and to help the team understand its own position in the broader system. It is a key function of leadership to align the team with the demands of the external environment, therefore changes in its context should be noticed timeously to enable the team to adapt its operations to meet such demands.

Representation

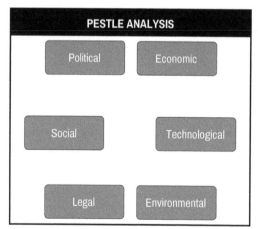
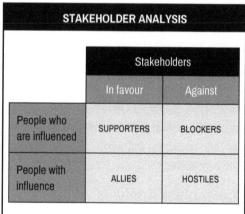

Figure 3.1: PESTLE and Stakeholder analysis

References

Kriek, H.S. (2007). *Creative problem solving: Techniques for South African teams.* Pretoria: Mindmuzik.

Introduction

For current purposes the Burke and Litwin model and the McKinsey 7S model are presented to help teams analyse the internal organisational context and get a perspective of the key elements that affect them. Considering the various components of the organisation and the interaction between them can help the team to evaluate its organisational context and understand how elements external to the team, but within the organisation, could influence dynamics within the team.

In a nutshell

The internal organisational context of a team, comprising elements such as leadership, strategy, culture, policies and procedures of the organisation.

Purpose

To help the team analyse the organisation, i.e. its internal context.

To understand drivers of organisational behaviour.

To align and fit with the internal organisational context.

Description

Burke and Litwin

Burke and Litwin identified the following elements that could impact on a team from an organisational development point of view:

- External environment: As any business operates in a larger context, this environment guides the strategies, operations and ultimately the manner in which the teams in the organisation operate, not only because the organisation offers services and products to meet the needs of the environment, but also because the environment provides the context from which talent for the organisation (and teams) are sourced. In a broader sense, the organisational context can be said to consist of various stakeholders (see the Stakeholder analysis above) and the demands they put on the organisation may influence the organisational response.

- Leadership: The role of leadership is primarily to enable the organisation to meet the demands of the context. Therefore leadership takes responsibility to identify these demands, and then to devise and implement strategy and to foster and strengthen culture.

- Strategy: Leadership is responsible for the strategic direction of the company and should ensure that the vision, mission and objectives of the organisation are aligned.

- Culture: The second key responsibility of leadership is to ensure that the culture of the organisation (especially values) is supportive of the strategy and enables the staff to deliver on the strategy.

- Structure: Structure should be supportive of strategy and the organisational design should enable the strategy to be implemented. Organisational structure can take many forms, such as hierarchical, project-based, geographically designed or divisionally designed, but the chosen structure should be the one that best supports the strategy.

- Policies and procedures: Underscoring and supporting the organisational culture are the formal (e.g. regulatory framework) and informal (e.g. rituals) policies and procedures that the organisation employs.

- Processes: These last four elements (strategy, culture, structure and policies/procedures) interact in organisational processes. These processes require financial, human and physical resources.

- Climate: The interaction of all the above elements impacts on the team climate. This is regarded as the outcome of the interaction, but teams should remember that it also acts as an input to the team as it influences the mood and operations of the team and acts as motivation to the individuals.

- Motivation: The organisational climate provides the context or conditions that interact with and provide impetus to the motivation levels of individuals. This is influenced by the tasks and skills of the members on the one hand and individuals' own needs and values on the other.

- Task requirements: The tasks that individuals have to complete have certain requirements and need certain skills to be completed. At the same time, the tasks feed into the structure and strategy of the organisation to enable the organisation to deliver.

- Individual values and needs: Individuals have different needs and different values. This influences the manner in which they approach their jobs and also influences the processes and culture of the organisation. This in turn affects the motivation levels of the individual.

- Individual and organisational performance: Ultimately the individual and the organisation perform according to how they are influenced by all these components, which reinforces the circular nature of the model.

McKinsey 7S Model

Waterman, Peters and Phillips devised this model to analyse performance in a company, but it is also a valuable tool for teams to use to find their fit in the larger organisational context. Each of the factors identified influences the other and they are regarded as equally important. The model divides the organisational context in terms of seven factors, each with the initial letter S.

*   Strategy: the direction, vision and goals of the organisation; teams can find it valuable to link their own actions with the strategy of the larger organisation, which often helps them to find meaning in their own actions.

*   Structure: the manner in which the various parts of the organisation are organised and how the different parts interact and relate with one another. This can take various forms, from strictly hierarchical, matrix, or project structures to ad hoc structures, and the demands of this structure may play a significant role in how the team needs to connect to other parts of the organisation.

*   System: this refers to the business processes, systems and procedures that the organisation employs, for example operational, informational, educational and developmental systems. It goes without saying that these will impact on the team in ways such as the availability of resources and so on.

*   Shared values: refers to the beliefs, values and overarching vision or purpose the organisation wants to achieve. This impacts on employees' behaviour, thinking processes and actions, and influences interactions and interpersonal relations in the team as well.

*   Skills: the competencies, capabilities and skills of the organisation and the employees. Naturally this should be aligned with the organisation's vision and strategy, and therefore what is required from an organisational perspective will also influence what is required by the team.

*   Staff: this is the factor that focuses on the people in the organisation and their nature, type and general abilities.

*   Style: the last factor refers to the organisational culture and leadership style, which has a direct impact on the internal context of the organisation (and teams), but also influences how the organisation is viewed from the outside.

Tips for team leaders

These analyses are helpful to understand the drivers of the organisational context the team operates in and help the team comprehends its own position in the broader system. The context of the organisation provides the strategy, culture, staff and resources that the team requires to be successful, and an understanding of this internal context can help the team with its positioning in the system.

Representation

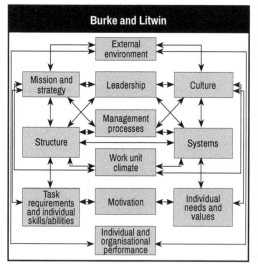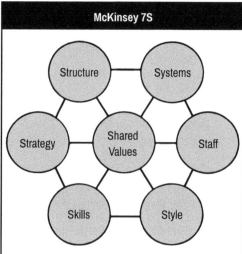

Figure 3.2: Internal organisational context

References

Burke, W.W. & Litwin, G.H. (1992). A Causal Model of Organisational Performance and Change. *Journal of Management,* 8(3), 523–546.

Peters, T. & Waterman, R. (1982). *In search of excellence.* New York: Harper & Row.

Waterman, R.H., Peters, T.J. & Phillips, J.R. (1980). *Structure is not organization.* Bridgeport, Conn.: M. Wiener.

Introduction

Any team that works within a bigger organisational system is exposed to larger social dynamics of which the organisational culture is a key part. This culture forms part of the team's context and can assist team performance, but can also inhibit optimum output. Two different tools to help leaders think about the impact of organisational culture on the team are presented, namely Johnson and Scholes' Cultural Paradigm and Baghai and Quigley's Cultural Archetypes.

In a nutshell

Organisational cultural paradigm and archetypes as contextual influences on the team.

Purpose

To highlight views on organisational culture.

To facilitate thinking on organisational cultural influences.

To help teams to position themselves within organisational cultural spheres.

Description

Cultural paradigm

Johnson and Scholes claimed that although each organisation develops its own unique culture, similar dimensions underly them all. The manner in which each organisation chooses to highlight or activate some of these dimensions allows a unique culture to develop. They identified the following different dimensions.

Stories

This refers to the prevailing stories in a company that are told in the passages. A story that still goes the rounds illustrates this well. A famous business leader called into his office some of his staff whose cars were dirty and unkempt. He said: "If you don't look after your own things well, how can I expect you to look after my company well?" Told year in and year out in the organisation, the message was created that you should take good care of the company - in fact look after the company as if it were your own.

Structure

Organisations can be very structured and formalistic and in many cases this overlaps with the manner in which the organisation is structured in terms of hierarchy. A variety of different structures can be identified, which can also influence team behaviour. Amongst these:

- line organisation: the familiar hierarchical bureaucracy with team members reporting in a "line" of authority;

- matrix organisation: where members report into a line, but also have to report to managers responsible for support across the organisation, such as where a representative of HR reports to the management as well as to an HR director;

- profit centres: where organisations are structured across lines and divisions related to cost or profit;

- strategic alliances: where teams are formed across companies for strategic alignment purposes; and

- process organisation: the team is structured by using a value chain or specific processes in the team.

Rituals and routines

The manner in which companies structure routines and how rituals evolve tell us something about the culture of the company or can influence the culture. Think for example how major achievements are celebrated or how procedures are made into routines.

Symbols

This goes beyond logos and brands (although these also impact on culture) to include the manner in which symbols are displayed in a company. In this regard the symbolic valence of separate tea rooms, parking spots or allocation of resources such as offices, equipment or cars are examples of symbols that influence and build culture.

Power

This refers to the formal or informal differences that exist between different members of the organisation, which can be based on, for example, agency, reference, knowledge, and/or position. It gives teams guidelines for formulating and observing the core set of assumptions and beliefs that drive the organisation; the "perceived wisdom" of how to operate successfully.

Control system

This element of the cultural web is about what things are monitored, controlled and regulated in the organisation. This gives an indication of how a culture is enforced and maintained and it allows team leaders the opportunity to understand what to focus attention and activity upon.

Cultural archetypes

Baghai and Quigley looked at how some archetypal organisational cultures can be distinguished. They used a two-axis model to identify organisational culture, where the y-axis reflects how power is exercised while the horizontal axis indicates the nature of individuals' tasks and how work is organised. The vertical axis shows how culture is influenced by whether leadership is top-down and authoritative, or whether there is opportunity for employees to be involved in co-constructing an emerging culture. It thus distinguishes between the influence of a leader with clear direction, active involvement, a strong focus and an authoritarian and domineering manner at the extreme end of the spectrum, and a limited leader authority with a focus on followers to determine their own way and direction on the other. The horizontal axis shows the degree to which employees are allowed freedom to be creative or whether their actions and behaviours are scripted. These authors were also at pains to point out that culture is a "two-way" street, with the manner in which the leader is involved with the employees creating a symbiosis that brings forth a culture. This leads to different archetypes, which are described below.

Landlord and tenants (e.g. Apple)

This archetype represents a clear control and power base where the leader gives direction and enforces the rules of the game. Best performing "tenants" are rewarded by the "landlord", who solves any conflict. There are clear rules of the game and a definite game plan, and the leader has the power to ensure everything is implemented exactly according to plan. A clear sense of authority with near absolute decision-making power is vested in the leader.

Architect and builder (e.g. Tata Nano)

"Freedom within a frame" best describes this archetype, which allows for a somewhat less direct impact of the leader than the previous type. In this case the leader offers the dream (e.g. revolutionary dream) and allows freedom for the organisation to find the best way to fulfil that dream. Success is determined by the delivery of tasks on time, according to the aspirations and demands of the leader. Members are connected as through a chain and all are committed to delivery.

Producer and creative team (e.g. Cirque du Soleil)

Here the level of authority of the leader is nearly completely dissipated and members are given complete freedom to deliver what they would like. Success is defined through the levels of creativity and the innovative ways in which the organisation's elements can work together. Close co-operation is essential for the team to deliver on the direction that is given.

Senator and citizens (e.g. WL Gore)

This archetype can be seen as a "Constitution", where values determine the direction and action of the workforce. There are clear principles and values and strict adherence to collective action and working together. Individual autonomy is non-negotiable and active participation is expected.

Community organiser and volunteers (e.g. Linux)

At the opposite end of the scale to the authoritarian leader, this cultural archetype transfers the energy, drive and direction of the organisation to the people. Here, as illustrated by the classic Linux example, the culture emerges from volunteers who are independent or perceived to be independent, working of their own volition on objectives they determine. They are looking for the same opportunities and expect to be treated the same, with equal rights. The power of the "people" increases as the number of volunteers grows.

Captain and sports team (e.g. Dabbawallas)

Dabbawalas is the famed Indian system whereby home-cooked meals are delivered across various cities by thousands of delivery people. In a culture that demonstrates such an archetypical form there is a limited hierarchy, yet tasks and processes are clearly defined. Members are committed to a shared identity yet pursue personal goals. The culture is based on extensive internal communication, but a large degree of freedom exists for members to excel according to their own personal development goals.

Conductor and orchestra (e.g. Medco)

In this archetype, clearly defined tasks and roles are scripted and no deviation is allowed from these processes and roles. There is uniformity across the organisation (even across geographical areas) and the same experience is expected at all locations. This is only possible if each member works to an incredibly tightly scheduled mode of operation. No room for error or diversion is allowed. The team functions virtually without the clear presence of the leader during the time of operation, but detailed and carefully scripted processes determine their actions and responses. As each member has clearly defined tasks, success depends on how each member completes his or her own responsibilities.

General and soldiers (e.g. Marriot)

The last archetype manifests where an organisation operates like a general and soldiers. Here there are clear authority lines and directives and the organisation has an established hierarchy and ranks. The tasks, roles and responsibilities expected are highly specialised and are often displayed through uniforms and rituals.

Tips for team leaders

To understand the driving culture in an organisation helps team leaders to interact with team members about "how we do things here" and to shape interventions if necessary.

Representation

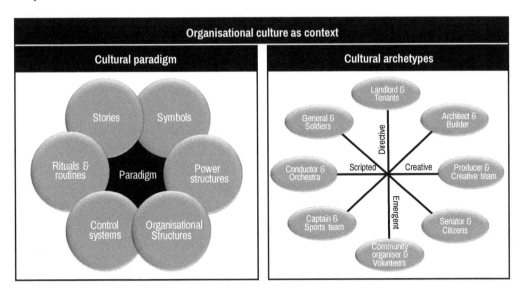

Figure 3.3: Organisational culture as context

References

Baghai, M. & Quigley, J. (2011). *As one*. New York, NY: Portfolio Hardcover.

Johnson, G. & Scholes, K. (1997). *Exploring corporate strategy*. Verlag: Prentice-Hall.

Culture: Reinventing organisations

14

Introduction

Frederic Laloux looked at organisations with a development lens and in particular how the development of human consciousness impacts on the manner in which organisational culture manifests.

In a nutshell

Development of organisational culture through distinctive stages.

Purpose

To help the team understand the organisational context.

To align and fit the team with cultural demands.

To evaluate organisational culture for cues to shape team culture.

Description

Laloux's development theories presuppose the following principles:

- Development is accelerating.

- There is no preferred or better level of consciousness. This fundamental principle is key for this perspective to be helpful. Often it is explained by pointing out a toddler can't be "better" than an adolescent, yet it is clear that we can expect different behaviour, development or reflective ability because the adolescent can think in more sophisticated ways. This moves the question away from whether one person or route is better than another to which is more appropriate given the demands from the environment at a particular moment. Similarly, organisational culture also displays different levels of development and this can impact on team behaviour.

- It is easier to see the level 'below" than to look at higher levels of development.

- Development levels are holarchical, meaning that higher levels include those below (very much like Matryoshka (Russian) dolls).

- Different paradigms can live alongside each other and individuals, teams and even divisions in an organisation can display different prevailing and preferred levels of consciousness. However, organisations reflect societal changes (in particular consciousness) and the dominant element in each era is likely to be dominant in organisational culture as well.

- Organisations develop incrementally and during each change everything changes (systems, mental models, views of success and power structures), which impacts on teams as well.

Laloux used earlier development theories as a point of departure, but in contrast to them, his focus was on organisations. This allows inclusion here as it impacts on culture and could also influence team behaviour. He identified the following stages of development of organisations:

Red

The first organisational level is labelled red, and the example used to explain this is a pack of wolves. In such an organisation there is clear and definite exercise of power by a single figure of authority. The power associated with this positon is used to keep troops in line and fear is used to keep the organisation together. The leader displays predatory and command authority focused on reactive, short-term gain. Examples include street gangs, war lords and egocentric leaders. The lasting result of this approach is the division of labour, which was demanded by overlords, but which is still a feature of many modern businesses.

Amber

The amber stage is dominated by the power in the system; where changes occur, they still have to fit with existing organisational systems. Here the military or army is an example; highly formal roles within a hierarchical pyramid are characteristic of such a culture. Top-down command and control is displayed and clearly defined rules, regulations and system-based requirements exist for what to do and how to do it. Rigorous processes ensure stability and balance, and limited change or turbulence is the prevailing expectation. A paternalistic and authoritative leadership style is displayed and the organisation is structured as a social hierarchy where conduct is scripted according to strict codes of conduct. Organisations such as the church and government agencies display amber characteristics.

Orange

In this organisation, competition and productivity are the main drivers. As in a machine (the preferred metaphor for this stage), focus is on effectiveness and efficiency; most multinational companies display such characteristics. The goal is to beat competition, achieve profit and growth, and stay ahead. Driven by societal demands like globalisation, capitalism and performance, this stage dictates adversity and achievement. The notion that science and technology allow for the better use of resources in order to maximise profit and to reach objectives underpins this stage. It has introduced performance-based meritocracy and has led to innovation and technological breakthroughs. The leadership style required by this stage is decisive, often backed up by scientific support (e.g. computer-based decision-making), and is goal- and task-oriented.

Green

This stage is characterised by the colour green, but this should not be equated with modern parlance where it relates (is almost limited) to a conservation and environmental focus. Here the emphasis is broader and is more like the example of a family. It allows a pyramid structure, but participative and collective behaviour is expected. In such organisations, the focus on relationships, culture and empowerment leads to employee motivation where consensus and engagement are valued. Members are treated as stakeholders, and breakthroughs of this type of stage are the increased importance of empowerment and an extended view of stakeholders beyond shareholders. Many culture- and value-driven organisations where the leadership style is focused on consensus are examples of green organisations.

Teal

Teal organisations are fewer in number, but Laloux indicated that some organisations that display these characteristics have been around for a long time, e.g. W.L.Gore. Here the metaphor is a living organism, and the drive, energy and leadership is dispersed throughout the system. In this type of organisation self-management replaces the traditional, hierarchical pyramid and the organisation is rather seen as a living entity, with its own creative potential and evolutionary purpose. The role of the leader becomes blurred and the organisation displays distributed leadership, with inner rightness and purpose as the primary motivator and guideline. Breakthroughs brought by teal organisations are a focus on self-management, wholeness and evolutionary purpose.

Tips for team leaders

The graphic way of depicting organisational culture and its development makes it easy for teams to detect what type of context they operates in. Although Laloux did not focus on teams' drivers and needs, his analysis is also applicable at the team level.

Representation

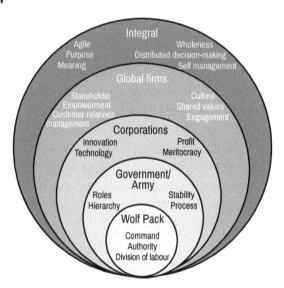

Figure 3.4: Development of organisational culture through distinctive stages

Reference

Laloux, F. (2014). *Reinventing organizations: A guide to creating organizations inspired by the next stage in human consciousness.* Brussels, Belgium: Nelson Parker.

15 | Value chain

Introduction

It can be helpful for teams to evaluate the context they operate in by analysing the company's value chain. This allows a team to track a product or service throughout the "value chain" and teams can see where they fit into the larger organisational context. For example, a manufacturing team or a sales team can use the tool to understand key stakeholders, as well as to find the meaningful contribution they make to the organisation as a team. The Business Model Canvas developed by Osterwalder and Pigneur can help the team to evaluate where it stands within the organisational context. While (as the name suggests) this is actually a tool to help an organisation evaluate its business model, it can be helpful for executive and management teams evaluating the organisation (especially when it is a fairly young company), as well as for teams to evaluate their own operations from a business model perspective. Thus, it provides an evaluation opportunity that gives an overview of the team's operations and may open fresh perspectives of what the team does. Another helpful approach to assist teams with where they fit into an organisation's value chain or to determine their own value chain is the original work of Michael Porter, whose contribution is considered first in what follows.

In a nutshell

To assess the position of the team in the value chain of the organisation.

Purpose

To present an overview of the team's operations.

To understand the flow of activity throughout the organisation.

To find the "fit" of the team in the value chain.

To direct the team's focus.

Description
Porter

Originally designed by Michael Porter, the value chain analysis allows organisations to understand where their competitive advantage is. The team uses the template and populates each of the elements of the organisation's value chain. They may not have all the information, but it helps to understand where each element fits and how the team connects with other parts of the organisation. The nine elements are split into two parts, namely primary activities and support activities.

Primary activities

- Inbound logistics. The input part of the process refers to the relationship with suppliers and what is required to receive and store raw material. If any preliminary work needs to be done to the raw material, that is also dealt with here.

- Operations. The manufacture, production or creation of a product or service are seen as the operations of a team.

- Outbound logistics. The focus here is on the transportation, storage and distribution of the final product to the customer.

- Marketing and sales. The function whereby customers are made aware of the product and where it is supplied to them.

- Service. Any after-sales services or additional contact that is required falls into this part of the value chain. Examples like training, maintenance or repairs are included.

Support activities

- Infrastructure. The organisational hierarchy, strategic planning processes and implementation, and various control systems (including financial and quality) are part of the infrastructure support activities.

- Human resource management. The recruitment and training of potential and existing staff as well as performance management systems are included as part of this activity.

- Technology development. All operational processes require some technological assistance and resources and these are dealt with here. In particular, hardware, software, procedures and technical knowledge are distinguished.

Osterwalder and Pigneur

Osterwalder and Pigneur designed the business model canvas in such a manner that it gives nine clear elements to consider. When this is applied to a team (or an organisation) the key areas where the team should put its focus are revealed. In fact, the business model is helpful in more than one way. When the model is applied to the organisation the team understands what its role is in the bigger organisational context, but it can also be used to evaluate its own processes. The following elements are presented:

- Key partners. For a team this would refer to other stakeholders (internally in the organisation and external to the organisation) that impact on the team, namely those members and other teams that assist with input and whose support or physical inputs are critical for the team to deliver on its mandate.

- Key activities. Key tasks and operations the team needs to complete.

- Key resources. Physical, financial and human resources the team needs to operate effectively.

- Value proposition. In start-ups or teams where the business consists of the team, this is particularly critical as the value proposition of the team is what sets it apart from the rest of the organisation and why the contribution it makes to the organisation is critical. However, in traditional teams it is as critical to understand the value proposition of the team.

- Customer relationships. The manner in which the team relates to its customers, both internal and external, is evaluated in this element.

- Channels. Options about delivery and how the team gets its products or services to the key customers.

- Customer segments. If the team has to deliver to more than one stakeholder or customer segment, this is considered part of this element.

- Cost structure. How the team's cost structure is set up and the flows of money in the team's operations.

- Revenue streams. How the team is responsible for income.

Tips for team leaders

The value chain of the organisation drives its activities and where the team fits into the larger context determines its stakeholders, in particular other parts of the organisation that provide inputs into the team and who are "customers" of the team. On the other hand the model can be applied at team level to determine the nine elements the canvas identifies and to apply them to the team itself.

Representation

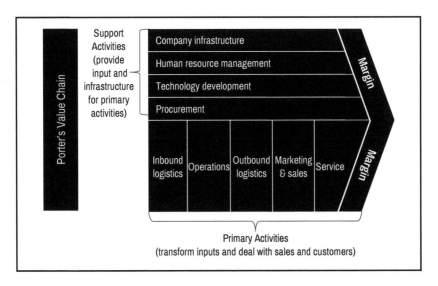

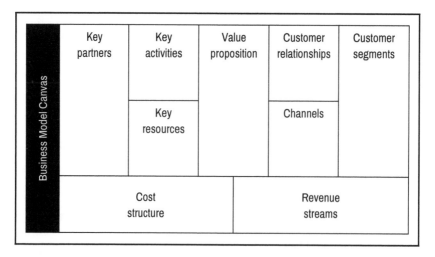

Figure 3.5: Value chain analysis

References

Osterwalder, A. & Pigneur, Y. (2010). *Business model generation: A handbook for visionaries, game changers, and challengers.* Hoboken, NJ: Wiley.

Porter, M. (1985). Competitive advantage: Creating and sustaining superior performance. New York, NY: The Free Press.

4 TEAM ASSESSMENTS

A variety of team assessment instruments are available and just about every aspect of team functioning can be assessed. The tools presented here between them provide a good overall picture of the assessment of team functioning and give teams a proverbial bird's eye view.

Firstly, three instruments to assess the composition of the team are described: the Team Excellence Questionnaire, the Klein Group Instrument and the Team Architect. Another key element of team functioning is climate, so the next part presents the Team Climate Inventory developed by Anderson and West. This gives teams an idea of how they shape up according to participative safety, support for innovation, vision, performance and social desirability.

The next set of instruments focus on effectiveness. Here the Team Effectiveness Assessment and Team Effectiveness Profile are presented for teams to use as tools. The former measures a team against the standards and practices of high-performing teams, while the latter aims in particular to help a team remove blockages in its operations and increase its level of performance. These are followed by The Team Diagnostic Survey (TDS), which measures the effectiveness of a team according to its productive output and how well members work together.

The last assessment tools offered in this chapter use subjective assessment. It is sometimes helpful for a team to evaluate its own performance from an internal perspective and to evaluate what it does through introspection and gauging members' views. Examples are questioning (stock questions, repeated questions and question words); the familiar SWOT analysis; and representational techniques including "fishbone", "cause-effect tree" and "force-field".

Introduction

There are numerous frameworks, conceptualisations and assessment instruments based on a list of team characteristics or components, which are all helpful for teams and can be employed to great benefit. Three are presented as examples of what is available, namely the Team Excellence Survey (developed by Larson and LaFasto), the Klein Group Instrument and the Team Architect (based on the 7T model of team effectiveness by Lombardo and Eichinger).

In a nutshell

Psychometric instruments for assessing the components of teams.

Purpose

To assist teams in optimising the requisite components to become high performing.

To identify strengths and weaknesses in the team's current performance.

To identify development opportunities.

To aid teams in discovering ways to enhance teamwork and increase productivity.

To provide action steps to boost performance.

Description

While each of the three instruments highlights different, yet complementary, components, it is helpful to have an overview of the theory behind each in order to pick the most suitable.

Team excellence survey

Eight components were identified by Larson and LaFasto for this questionniare. Distinctive of this approach is the fact that the eight different components are perceived to be equally important and no hierarchy or connection between elements is assumed. The eight components are as follows:

- A clear, elevating goal which gives the team a clear understanding of what is to be achieved and which the team regards as compelling.

- Results-driven structure to facilitate problem solving, creative effort and tactical outcomes. A team's structure should have clear roles and accountabilities, an effective communication system, monitoring of individual performance followed by feedback, and facts-based judgements.

- Competent members that have the required technical skills as well as the personal characteristics to provide excellence.

- Unified commitment generated by a clear articulation of the goal (often by the leader) and active participation in strategising and planning to achieve this.

- Collaborative climate characterised by trust. Trust is generated through openness, respect, honesty and consistency.

- Standards for excellence enforced by factors including personal pressure, team pressure, task demands, the team leader, and external factors.

- External support and recognition by a conducive organisational environment that is serious about tangible and psychological rewards.

- Principled leadership demonstrated through commitment, consistent behaviours and collaborative interaction.

The Team Excellence Questionnaire gives a team an indication of how well it performs on each of the components.

Klein Group Instrument

The Klein Group Instrument (KGI) uses four major scales that are broken down into nine subscales. It provides detailed personalised feedback through graphs that indicate preferences on each of the scales and subscales, and gives information on what the team enjoys, what challenges exist, and what behaviours will help in the growth and development of the team. The major scales with the corresponding subscales are as follows:

Leadership

This scale measures the ability of a team member to guide the group towards meaningful collaboration and successful task completion. The subscales are:

- assertiveness: the opportunity each member in the team has to contribute and to have his or her views heard;

- group facilitation: the extent to which members share facilitation duties of a task and interpersonal nature. It includes constructive feedback and how the human consequences of decisions and actions impact on the team; and

- initiative: the extent to which members are prepared to take centre stage, attempting to influence other members and efforts to energise colleagues in the team.

Negotiation orientation

The next scale measures the ability of members to listen closely to one another and to construct mutually acceptable agreements. It measures:

- perspective taking: the ability to step into the shoes of others and expand your own perspective by looking at the world through the eyes of others; and

- constructive negotiation approach: this is the extent to which the team sets a positive tone for negotiation and discussion, how members' interests and concerns are addressed, and how new solutions are proposed. It is focused on finding alternatives and whether the team is able to accommodate various views which still lead to agreement.

Task focus

Directing attention to the operations of a team, this scale measures the ability of members to devise a sound strategy for the task and to carry out the plan fruitfully. It consists of the following subscales:

- task analysis: the extent to which the team analyses its tasks and particularly how it considers a range of solutions and then structures its activities to facilitate achievement of the solution; and

- task implementation: the necessary steps to follow through on a decided path or action, tracking progress towards achieving the goal, and making adjustments when necessary. The members must maintain clear communication, stay focused on their own responsibilities and collaborate efficiently.

Interpersonal focus

The interpersonal scale measures the ability of members to develop a team spirit and to attend to "feeling issues" in the group. The subscales are:

- positive group affiliation: the extent to which members know and trust one another and how it manifests in cohesion, identity and spirit; and

- feeling orientation: the extent to which the team members feel comfortable expressing their feelings (even in periods of conflict) and how in tune the team is with any emotional undercurrents. The receptivity of the team to verbal and non-verbal emotional communication and sensitivity to potential emotional consequences of their actions are also considered.

It is a strength of the KGI that for each subscale it provides detailed, actionable suggestions for improving performance. The KGI helps improve team communication, morale and engagement, and helps members to appreciate complementary skills. It is practical and focused on each of the subscales. It identifies training, development and coaching opportunities, and the instrument can be taken from either a specific or general team perspective.

Team Architect

Originally developed by Lombardo and Eichinger, the T7 Model of Team Effectiveness identified seven components that all starts with the letter T, hence the name. In the original theory the developers identify two clusters of components which they regarded as influential to team functioning, an internal cluster of five components and an external cluster consisting of the two remaining components.

Internal components

The five internal components are:

- thrust: a common purpose about what needs to be accomplished, divided into identify clarity, commitment and management of thrust;

- trust: in each other as teammates through truthful communication, trust in actions, and trust inside the team;

- talent: the collective skills of the team members to get the job done through talent acquisition and enhancement as well as talent allocation and deployment;

- teaming skills: the fourth component assesses whether the team is operating effectively and efficiently as a team; resource management and team learning are identified as parts of this component. Team learning refers to a team's ability to make decisions, deal with conflict, manage its processes and manage the atmosphere of the team; and

- task skills: refer to whether the team is executing its tasks successfully or whether it is getting the job done. In particular it refers to focusing, assignment flexibility, measurement and how the team is executing its tasks.

External components

The two external components are:

- team-leader fit: the degree to which the team leader satisfies the needs of the team members; and

- team support from the organisation: the extent to which the leadership of the organisation as a whole enables the team to perform.

Tips for team leaders

These instruments provide helpful methods of assessing a team so that the leaders can determine where there are potential areas for improvement. They also help the leader to understand the key components of a team, and to what extent each of these components is present in the team to be evaluated. This evaluation allows leaders to adjust their team operations, use the information to inform the team of any proposed adjustments, and make improvements. Leaders should, however, be aware that these three instruments are presented here as examples and other assessment instruments are also available.

Representation

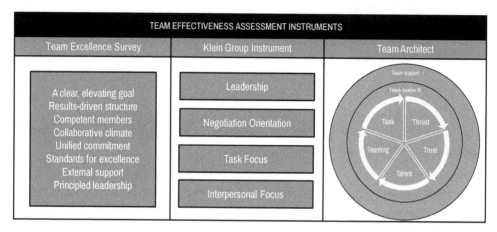

Figure 4.1: Composition assessment instruments

References

De Meuse, K. (2009). *Driving Team Effectiveness. A Comparative Analysis of the Korn/Ferry T7 Model with Other Popular Team Models.* Available from: https://www.kornferry.com/media/lominger_pdf/teamswhitepaper080409.pdf.

Klein, R. (2008). *The Klein Group Instrument manual.* Gainesville, FL: The Centre for Applications of Psychological Type.

Larson, C.E. & LaFasto, F.M.J. (1989). *Teamwork: What must go right/ What can go wrong.* Newbury Park, CA: Brooks.

LaFasto, F.M.J. & Larson, C.E. (2001). *When teams work best: 6,000 team members and leaders tell what it takes to succeed.* Newbury Park, CA: Sage.

Lombardo, M.M. & Eichinger, R.W. (1995). *The team architect® user's manual.* Minneapolis, MN: Lominger Limited.

17 | Climate assessment

Introduction

A good team climate is an environment where members experience sufficient levels of affiliation and togetherness for them to feel free to participate. It also requires trust in team members' competence, integrity and benevolence, which is built through communication and the belief that the team can be successful. A further element of team climate is a willingness to be innovative, to change things, to learn, and to feel empowered to share new and creative ideas. Anderson and West developed the Team Climate Inventory to add assessment of the climate in teams to the many individual instruments available. It is used as a performance improvement tool in many industries and with a variety of types of teams (including management teams).

In a nutshell

The team assesses its climate through measuring participative safety, support for innovation, vision, performance and task orientation.

Purpose

To assess the team climate.

To improve performance.

To highlight areas where improvement may be expected.

To link safety, innovation, vision and performance.

Description

The basic inventory consists of four scales, namely participative safety, support for innovation, vision and task orientation. The original has been adapted to a 14 item instrument as follows.

Participative safety

This scale indicates the level of collaboration and support, as well as how psychologically safe members feel to provide input and new ideas. Subscales for this construct are:

*   information sharing: the level of real attempts at sharing information as well as the frequency of such attempts. It measures how team members keep each other involved with work-related information and how different members obtain the necessary information;

- safety: the comfort members of the team feel to contribute their ideas and information. This is based on the notion that members are more likely to contribute in a climate of support;

- influence: the ability to influence each other; and

- interaction: the frequency of contact with one another, the levels of integration, and the manner in which members keep in touch.

Support for innovation

The second scale measures the degree of practical support through the following subscales:

- Articulated support: members' openness to new ideas as well as their support for developing new ideas and finding solutions.

- Enacted support: cooperation and sharing of resources through active behaviour.

Vision

The next scale relates to how clearly the vision of the team is defined. The following aspects of vision are measured:

- Clarity: how clearly the vision and objectives of the team are articulated.

- Perceived value is thus how meaningful the goals of the team are for individuals and how useful and appropriate members regard the goals to be. Thus, perceived value is assessed with an individual and a collective view.

- Sharedness: the extent to which members share the same vision and are in agreement as to its meaning.

- Attainability: the level to which members think the goals can actually be achieved. This involves members' views about the appropriateness of the vision, whether they are willing to pursue this vision, and their views on the capability of the team to attain these goals and vision.

Task orientation

This relates to how the team performs. It measures the team's commitment to excellence and what measures they have put in place to ensure that goals are attained and achieved. The following subscales are used for measurement:

- Excellence: the level of concern in the team that the highest standards must be achieved and their collective views of such standards. It also assesses the efforts the team puts in place to achieve such standards and the degree to which they are willing to dedicate themselves to such excellence.

- Appraisal: this refers to the appraisal and evaluation of the operations of the team. It also assesses the team's commitment to the standards that the team has set (based on internal or external norms) and appraises the level of outputs.

- Ideation: how team members contribute ideas, how these ideas can energise the team, and to what degree colleagues are prepared to build on these ideas.

A fifth scale, namely social desirability, has been added as a measure to limit faking and detect the impressions of participants that complete the questionnaire. This scale tests social and task aspects of social desirability.

Tips for team leaders

This is a comprehensive instrument that helps leaders to identify the climate in the team, and to determine the role of affect. The four scales give a clear indication of where the team may improve or where intervention is needed. It has been used to good effect to assist teams in evaluating the climate with regard to innovation and teams' readiness and willingness to be open to new ideas. Using the assessment results, leaders can help teams to agree upon realistic objectives, facilitate participation in decision-making, build commitment to high performing standards and support innovative ideas as a means to develop team climate and thereby develop new ideas and working methods.

Representation

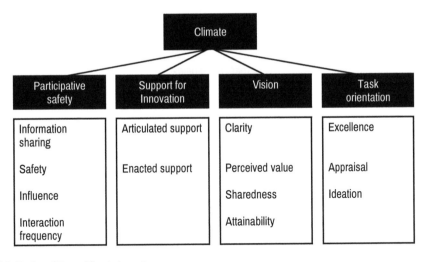

Figure 4.2: Scales of Team Climate Inventory

Reference

Anderson, N. & West, M.A. (1996). The Team Climate Inventory: Development of the TCI and its Applications in Teambuilding for Innovativeness. *European Journal of Work and Organizational Psychology*, 5(1), 53–66.

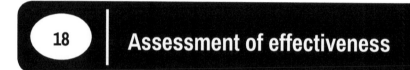

Introduction

Effectiveness refers to how successfully a team utilises its resources to meet its outcomes. It can be said that effectiveness is a measure of the actual outputs of the team in relation to the desired outputs. Obviously this will be related to what the team regards as outcomes and its target will influence the unique outcomes of each team. Scholars have proposed various instruments to measure team effectiveness, two of which are the Team Effectiveness Assessment (TEA) and the Team Effectiveness Profile (TEP), which are offered here as widely used tools.

In a nutshell

Instruments to measure team effectiveness.

Purpose

To evaluate team performance.

To provide information about a broad array of team functioning aspects.

To suggest improvements in team effectiveness.

Description

Each of the factors assessed by the TEA and TEP are described in order to understand the evaluation scope of each of the instruments.

Team Effectiveness Assessment (TEA)

This tool is designed to help a team set an improvement agenda based on the standards and practices demonstrated by high performing teams. It identifies the critical drivers of team effectiveness and gives insights into what a team can do to improve team performance. It further offers an assessment of five factors that all influence team effectiveness.

Capabilities and infrastructure

This indicates the extent to which the team has sufficient support processes, decision authority, knowledge, understanding, skills and leadership to be successful. It considers:

- organisational support: The extent to which the organisation provides resources, decision authority, and infrastructure to support the team;

- working knowledge: the extent to which team members have the necessary understanding, information and concepts to execute the team's mission;

- virtual infrastructure: the extent to which the team is supported to collaborate; and

- aligned leadership: the extent to which the team has adequate guidance, facilitation, direction and coordination.

Goals and purpose

This factor addresses the question: "Are we focused?" It indicates the team's sense of shared purpose and priorities, whether it has a mission that demands interdependence, and a clear understanding of each member's accountabilities. Subscales of this factor are:

- meaningful mission: the extent to which the team has a clear and challenging purpose and an indication of how this energises the team;

- clear priorities: the extent to which the team is clear about specific goals and work outputs;

- team commitment: the extent to which team members are committed to the team, its success, and the success of each other; and

- strong accountability: the extent to which the team assigns and accepts responsibility for results.

Roles and individual expectations

The third factor deals with the rules of engagement employed by the team on how to use power, how they relate to one another and how much experimentation is allowed. It therefore represents a "guide" to individual behaviour and performance. This factor comprises:

- collaborative partnerships: the extent to which team members are oriented to cooperate with others to achieve shared results;

- inclusion and engagement: the extent to which members feel included and motivated to do their best;

- leveraged diversity: the extent to which the team values and learns from others' ideas, opinions and points of view; and

- innovative experimentation: the extent to which team members allow each other to innovate, take risks and explore intuitions.

Interactions and team processes

The next factor gives an indication of work and team interactions; how these are coordinated in effective processes, conversations and decision-making; and how the team deals with conflict. Thus, it reveals how work gets done in the team. It is subdivided as follows:

- powerful conversations: the extent to which team members speak openly, listen carefully, and encourage others to do the same;

- productive conflicts: the extent to which team members confront and resolve conflicts through sharing information and appreciating opposing views;

- efficient team processes: the extent to which the team has productive work processes and methods of running effective meetings; and

- effective decisions: the extent to which team members use a systematic and participative process to make decisions and solve problems.

Learning and results

This factor relates to how the team thrives and whether it gets better at what it does. It looks at the feedback the team receives and how it adapts to the environment, gets results, and is rewarded. It is subdivided as follows:

- metric based feedback: the extent to which the team has ways to measure and understand customer satisfaction, output quality, team competency and overall effectiveness;

- evolution and adaptation: the extent to which the team can generate an understanding of its own dynamics and results, and can self-design and self-manage change;

- great results: the extent to which the team produces quality outputs and exceptional results; and

- rewards and recognition: the extent to which the team is appropriately recognised and compensated for both individual and team performance.

The TEA provides a comprehensive report to participants that includes an explanation of the model, as well as an interpretative guide, team profile, verbatim comments and a team development plan.

Team Effectiveness Profile (TEP)

This instrument helps teams to improve their output and work satisfaction. In particular it aims to help a team remove blockages in its operations and increase its level of performance. It is a test that measures members' perceptions on team activity and the 50 items are rated on a 5-point scale. The following constructs are evaluated.

Mission, vision, and goals

This evaluates the team's vision and how well-defined and communicated it is. It gives an indication of the levels of collaboration in the planning process and whether work is managed against goals or objectives. When teams have blockages in this area they do not spend sufficient time in articulating a vision, they are not sure about the team's purpose, and planning may be haphazard or top down.

Team roles

Teams that experience blockages in this area have ill-defined roles, relationships and accountabilities. This scale of the TEP indicates the extent to which members of the team experience this type of blockage. It assesses the use and understanding of standard job descriptions, identification with tasks and responsibilities, and clarity of roles.

Operating processes

This scale assesses whether policies and procedures employed by the team support both task and maintenance needs. Task needs refer to activities required to accomplish work objectives, while maintenance needs refer to human or interpersonal needs. Evaluating this team component gives an opportunity to the team to see whether they meet regularly enough, how decisions are made and how their communication processes lead to effective operations, solving of problems and handling of conflict.

Interpersonal relationships

Effective teams need good interpersonal relations and the relationship realm has been highlighted both theoretically and practically as key to effectiveness. In particular, effective teams need trust, interaction with colleagues and solutions to interpersonal problems. This scale provides a measurement of the perceptions of team members regarding interpersonal relationships in the team. Ineffective teams may display caution in their disclosures and willingness to take personal risks and constructive feedback may not be the norm. This scale provides the team with information for understanding and improving interpersonal dynamics.

Inter-team relationships

Where unhealthy competition exists in a team it may lead to sub-optimal performance. In this scale the instrument goes beyond the boundaries of the current team and measures the relations the team has with external stakeholders. As the team is embedded in larger systems the manner in which it aligns with the bigger context gives an indication of how effective it could be; in other words, this scale gives valuable insight into the team's operations. It evaluates issues of time, goals, interpersonal relations and internal structure orientation.

The instrument rates the team on each of these scales as either immature, fragmented, cohesive, effective or synergistic. The report gives scores on each of the subscales and provides a team profile score, which is a broad overview of the team's effectiveness. It further highlights how the team operates on a five-point scale ranging from very ineffective to very effective. It also gives mean scores on each of the five team constructs. Finally, the report gives guideline questions on how to discuss some of the potential blockages with the team.

Tips for team leaders

These tools offer steps that can be used in team development, and leaders of teams can use them fruitfully in devising improvement steps for their teams. They help teams to identify current patterns, point the way to address some of the issues, and show where to intervene. The tools provide generic explanations of each of the factors (in terms of how they manifest) and offer "actions to consider" to team leaders. Both instruments focus specifically on effectiveness; they give a clear indication of where intervention could be needed to facilitate improvement. Sharing this information with the team also allows for shared mental models to be expanded and for collaboration to be improved.

Representation

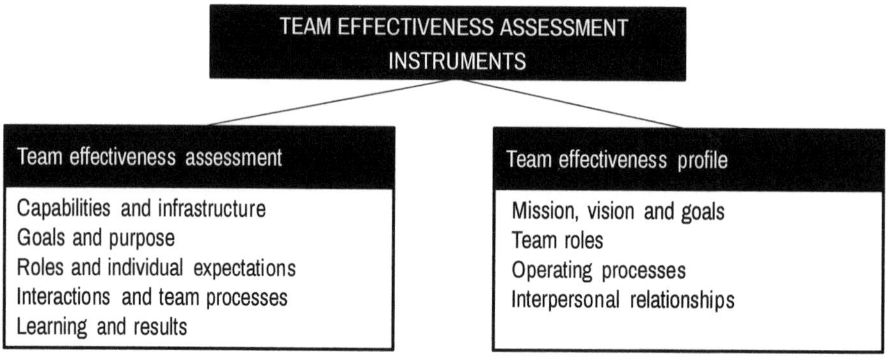

TEAM EFFECTIVENESS ASSESSMENT INSTRUMENTS

Team effectiveness assessment

Capabilities and infrastructure
Goals and purpose
Roles and individual expectations
Interactions and team processes
Learning and results

Team effectiveness profile

Mission, vision and goals
Team roles
Operating processes
Interpersonal relationships

Figure 4.3: Team Effectiveness Assessment Instruments

References

Linkage Incorporated. (n.d.) *Team Effectiveness Assessment*. Available from: www.linkageinc.com.
Glaser, R.O. & Glaser, C. (1992). *Team Effectiveness Profile: How is your team working?* King of Prussia, PA: Organization Design and Development.

Team diagnostic survey

Introduction

The Team Diagnostic Survey (TDS) assesses team effectiveness by building predominantly on the theoretical work of Richard Hackman. This view measures the effectiveness of a team according to its productive output (products, services, or decisions taken) and whether it meets or exceeds required standards as set by team stakeholders. It also looks at how well members work as a team (i.e. with increased levels of interdependence and being more capable at the end than when they started) and whether the team fosters positive contributions to individual members' learning and well-being. To accomplish this, teams must be a "real" team, defined as one with a compelling direction, an enabling structure, supporting context and expert coaching. The instrument assesses the state of the team on each of these constructs and advises on strengths and weaknesses.

In a nutshell

The instrument assesses a team's direction, structure, context, and level of coaching to decide whether it is a "real" team.

Purpose

To indicate the effectiveness of a team (not perception of performance as experienced by customers).

To highlight strengths and weaknesses.

To assess the five key antecedents of team effectiveness.

Description

Real team

A "real team" displays clear boundaries that distinguish members from non-members; interdependence towards a common, (potentially) measurable outcome for which members are collectively responsible; and stability of membership. This last condition includes identifying team tasks – the tasks that in fact require a team. Although this may sound unnecessarily specific, in many instances tasks are assigned to teams that would be better completed by individuals, as no sense of interdependence is needed or felt by either the team or the individual.

- Boundaries: teams need to have the right level of boundedness as this is a key element to create identity. Sometimes a team is over-bounded and becomes an island drifting on its own, and could even be so tightly knit through groupthink and commitment to each other that they do not connect well with the greater organisational environment. On the other hand, teams can also be under-bounded, with lack of clarity of who is on the team and who is not. In some cases, focusing on the core members of the team and building boundedness around them could be helpful as it gives opportunity to then involve some of the peripheral members.

- Interdependence - this relates to the team's ability to execute, monitor and manage, design and set direction.

- Stability - members that stay together in a team develop a sense of familiarity that enable them to grow a shared mental model that includes who knows what in the team and who is best equipped to complete specific tasks.

Compelling direction

A compelling direction is one that is challenging (which energises members), clear (which orients them to their main purposes), and consequential (which engages the full range of their talents). It describes a situation where clear and specific ends are given to the team, but the team is left to its own means to accomplish the tasks.

Enabling structure

An enabling structure in terms of task design, team composition and core norms of conduct is the next construct that is measured. The structure should be aligned with the team's purpose, but tasks should be designed to contain "motivating potential", including that the "team task (a) is a whole and meaningful piece of work, (b) for which members have autonomy to exercise judgment about work procedures, and that (c) provides members regular and trustworthy knowledge of results". Team composition relates to size (as few members as possible to ensure the task is accomplished), ample presence of task and interpersonal skills, and sufficient diversity i.e. "neither so similar to one another that they duplicate one another's resources nor so different that they are unable to communicate or coordinate well with one another". Clear norms of conduct (imported, evolving or explicit) that are focused on good performance processes help the team to scan its performance situation and plan performance strategies.

Supporting context

Hackman's approach highlights the requirement that leaders of teams should focus on providing the conditions for effective team performance. In particular, it highlights the different roles played by a supporting context and expert coaching. These act as moderating factors that influence all the other components. A supporting context includes the reward system, the information system, the educational system, and material resources. The reward system should provide an opportunity for reward and recognition that reinforces excellent performance yet encourages members to operate in a manner supportive of team goals. The information system of the team should provide it with the required information to be effective, while the education system should provide growth and development to ensure there are sufficient skills for the team to deliver on its mandate.

Expert coaching

Expert coaching should address the three main elements of team effectiveness, namely member effort, performance strategies, and skills and knowledge levels. Coaching can be used to minimise coordination and motivation problems that are affecting commitment; improve performance by, for example, limiting inappropriate habitual routines; and increase skills and knowledge levels by encouraging team members to share their expertise with each other. The TDS offers scales for evaluating team coaching (assessed through coaching availability, coaching helpfulness, leader coaching, interpersonal coaching and the presence of unhelpful directives) and peer coaching (assessed through task-focused coaching, interpersonal coaching, and the existence of unhelpful interventions).

Tips for team leaders

This is a well-researched theory with a clear conceptual foundation that is helpful for leaders to determine what they should do to ensure the conditions required for performance are in place.

Representation

Process criteria	Real team	Compelling direction	Enabling structure	Supporting context	Expert coaching
Effort Performance strategy Team social processes Quality of interaction Relationship satisfaction Individual well-being Internal work motivation Growth satisfaction General satisfaction	Bounded Interdependent Stable	Clarity Challenge Consequentiality	Team composition Size Diversity Skills Task design Whole task Autonomy/judgement Knowledge of results Group norms	Rewards/recognition Information Education/consultation Material resources	Team coaching Coaching availability Coaching helpfulness Coaching (Leader; Task focused; Operant; or Interpersonal) Unhelpful directives Peer coaching Unhelpful interventions

Figure 4.4: Team Diagnostic Survey (TDS)

Reference

Hackman, J.R. (2002). *Leading teams: Setting the stage for great performances*. Boston: Harvard Business School Press.

Introduction

The assessment instruments discussed thus far are all based on the objective assessment of teams, and while generic in nature, they can give teams an indication of where there are opportunities for improvement and where intervention can be directed. This part of the section offers a more subjective approach that teams can use to evaluate their own performance and effectiveness. Three techniques that are often used for other purposes as well are presented here. Through applying these techniques a more subjective appraisal of the team's performance emerges.

In a nutshell

A team can assess its own performance through questioning, SWOT-analysis and visual representation techniques.

Purpose

To help teams evaluate their own performance

To give a subjective analysis of performance

To indicate potential direct intervention

To find opportunities for, and eliminate threats to, the optimal performance of the team

Description

Questioning techniques, SWOT-analysis and visual representation are discussed.

Questioning

When analysing a team or an aspect of team functioning or behaviour, it is often helpful if the team has the skills to question the problem to enable a drill-down investigation. By using a set of stock questions or repeatedly asking a particular question, the team gains insight into the nature and extent of the problem.

Stock questions

The team decides on a question word or sentence that they think would best suit their needs. This choice depends on the type of problem addressed. A list of question words with examples of how they can be applied can assist the team in deciding what to use. Possible questions are: Why? What for? What happened then? And then? What happened before or after…? What was the effect thereof? What is the reason for …? Cause of…? Six question words (who, when, what, why, where and how) are often referred to as 5Ws & H. The team uses the 5Ws & H question words and formulates questions that can be applied to the problem. Each type of question is posed to the problem and the team examines the answers they provide to better understand the team. Results are used to facilitate an understanding of the team.

Repeated questions

Once the team has decided on a question word to use they apply the question to the initial formulation of the problem. After an initial answer is obtained the same question is repeated and the team keeps on providing answers. The team continues with this process until they agree that the issue has been explored to their satisfaction and in sufficient depth, breadth or detail. The answers are analysed and evaluated in terms of the new insights they provide and are used to reformulate the problem.

SWOT analysis

While SWOT analyses are more usually applied during strategic planning at an organisational level, it can be a helpful tool for teams to use in evaluating their own operations. The team identifies the most critical strengths, weaknesses, opportunities and threats facing them in relation to its operations.

- Strengths include specific skills and expertise, but also the team's (or organisational) competitive capability.

- Weaknesses are things the team lacks, for example it does not perform to its full capability or there is a condition that puts it at a disadvantage.

- Opportunities are situations that could benefit the team and might be attractive for the team to invest resources in.

- Threats come from the external environment and could affect the team's plan, position or standing.

The team clusters and collates the results of the analysis. It then prioritises the various SWOT-elements identified and evaluates their impact on team performance and effectiveness.

Visual representation techniques

Three such techniques are presented, namely Fishbone, Cause-and-effect analysis and Force-field analysis.

Fishbone

This technique was first described by Kaoru Ishikawa of Japan, and is one of the Japanese tools that has spread beyond its shores to influence management practice around the world. The fishbone diagram (alternatively called the Ishikawa diagram) provides a clear, visible presentation of a problem and is helpful for exploration and in-depth analysis. It gives a presentation of antecedents or causes of a problem and allows for clustering, prioritising and indicating inter-relationships between elements of the problem. Once discussion is exhausted, the outcomes of the discussion are presented graphically by using a depiction of a fishbone. This is done by drawing a straight line (representing the backbone of a fish) across a blackboard or flip-chart. The team draws a fish's head and tail at the respective ends of the line as well as "bones" of the fish at approximately forty-five degree angles on both sides of the horizontal line. Each "bone" is then labelled with one of the identified constituent elements.

Cause-effect tree

Similar to the fishbone technique, the cause-effect tree also identifies antecedents to problems. However, the technique uses the metaphor of a tree instead of a fish and moreover focuses on causes as well as effects. The team uses any process to generate the main causes and effects of the problem. The team draws a horizontal line in the middle of a flip-chart page or a white/blackboard. This represents the ground. A perpendicular line is then drawn to be the "stem" of the tree and the various causes of the problem are indicated as branches attached to the stem of the tree. Each of the respective influences can then also be indicated as having supporting influences or substrata of influences working to ever-smaller branches of the tree. Evaluate to ascertain what new insights have been generated regarding the problem of the team.

Force-field analysis

The originator of this technique is the American Gestalt psychologist Kurt Lewin. He regarded problems as presenting fields of pressure or fields of influence. Thus, in any given situation, there are various forces exerting influence on the field wherein the problem exists. The basic philosophy underscoring the tool is that in any system there are forces supporting its performance while simultaneously there are forces constraining its success. The team's current position is visually presented as somewhere between an ideal "to be" state where the team experiences optimal performance and a "zero" position where the restricting factors prevents the team from functioning at all. The team's position can thus be assessed as being somewhere between the helping and the restricting factors. These helping and restricting forces are then prioritised in terms of the extent of each one's impact (positive or negative) on the performance of the team.

Representation

Questioning	SWOT-analysis	Visual representation
Stock questions Repeated questions Question words	SWOT-analysis	Fishbone Cause-effect Force-field

Figure 4.5: Subjective assessment techniques

References

Kriek, H.S. (2007). *Creative problem solving: Techniques for South African teams*. Pretoria: Mindmuzik.

Ishikawa K. & Loftus, J.H. (1990). *Introduction to quality control*. Tokyo, Japan: 3A Corporation.

5

TEAM DESIGN

It is important for leaders to know the key elements to be considered when designing a team. Firstly, a theory on types of teams is presented, which distinguishes between three key elements, namely skills, authority, and stability over time. This is followed by a section on team mandate. The mandate of a team includes its vision, mission, values, targets and objectives. A charter concretises the mandate of the team and helps members to understand their roles and responsibilities. The next part describes a model that identifies six team design elements to be considered, namely traditional (personnel-position) fit; traditional fit plus teamwork skills; relative contribution; team profile; time; and fluidity of membership. This is followed by a normative team design model which looks at team design under the topics of job design, interdependence, composition, context and process. The last element of team design to be discussed is diversity. Diversity is understood in different ways and can be analysed in relation to a team in different ways.

Introduction

Many different types of teams exist and various dimensions are used to depict differences. This leads to teams being described as, for example, project teams, traditional work teams, action teams, parallel teams, (top) management teams, decision-making teams, self-managed teams, ad hoc teams, or crews, depending on the dimensions applied. A more extensive typology can also be used and will be provided here.

In a nutshell

A typology of team types using skill differentiation, authority differentiation and temporal stability.

Purpose

To depict, compare and contrast different types of teams.

To evaluate whether some dimensions could or should be adjusted.

To determine the impact of the type of team on its performance.

Description

Here models that differentiate between types of teams according to particular dimensions are illustrated, which are followed by a comprehensive typology of teams.

Dimensional models

It is almost impossible to provide a comprehensive scheme that covers all types of teams. Researchers often use a single dimension to differentiate between teams and here levels of authority, different team functions and differences in duration in time are used to illustrate different types of teams.

Authority

Hackman classified teams according to the type and extent of authority. Teams differ in the level of responsibility assigned to the team or to the management of the team. The following types of teams can be distinguished:

- Manager-led teams: the team has limited authority and managers take responsibility for the team's direction, execution of work and direction.

- Self-managing teams: team members execute the tasks of the team, but in addition take responsibility for measuring and managing the team's performance.

- Self-designing teams: this type of team has authority over the design thereof and some aspects of its context.

- Self-governing teams: members of the team have authority over all four functions of the team and decide what must be done, structure its context and manage its own performance (including execution of tasks).

Functions

To classify teams according to their function, i.e. what the team actually does, a number of different approaches have been offered. For example, Sundstrom distinguished between six types of teams according to function, namely:

- production teams: this type of team repeatedly produces a specific outcome, for example a factory team;

- service teams: transactions that are conducted between team members and clients/customers identify this type of team;

- management teams: this type of team consists of managers or executives who plan, develop policies or strategies, and coordinate the activities of the organisation;

- project teams: experts that come together to perform a specific task within a defined period of time;

- action or performing teams: groups such as sports teams or entertainment groups that engage in brief activities or performances that are repeated in different settings, but which require specialised skills and extensive training and/or preparation;

- parallel teams: these teams exist outside the normal work, and are temporary teams that provide suggestions or recommendations to change an organisation.

Type/duration

Devine used product type and duration as dimensions to classify teams. Furthermore, they distinguished between two "product types", namely tasks that revolve around processing information (e.g. planning, creating, choosing) and tasks that require hands-on physical activity. They also distinguished two temporal dimensions, namely short-term, ad hoc teams for one task cycle, and long-term, ongoing teams that may continually be assigned new tasks or who complete tasks in a cyclical fashion. The resulting four types of teams can be described as follows:

- Ad hoc project teams. These exist for a finite period of time to complete specific tasks, which could be solving problems, creating solutions, making decisions, or interacting with clients.

- Ongoing project teams have no specific known end date and have relatively stable membership.

- Ad hoc production teams are temporary and established on a case-by-case basis to perform tasks such as building, assembling, performing or rendering a service.

- Ongoing production teams are standing teams that perform the same tasks as ad hoc teams, but do so on an ongoing, regular basis.

The purpose of classifying teams is to draw attention to the particular context. It does not really matter which type of team it is, whether it is a production team (function) operating as an ad hoc project team (time) with self-management (authority), or it is an ongoing service team, but virtual in nature. What the leader needs to consider is how this particular context may impact the team, in other words, how does the context frame the operations of the team?

Typology of teams

Hollenbeck, Beersma and Schouten provided a spectrum or continuum along which teams can be assessed according to three different dimensions, namely skill differentiation, authority differentiation and temporal stability.

Skill differentiation

This dimension refers to the specific functional responsibility of the individual or the degree to which members have differentiated skills levels. Any skill that impacts on the ability of the team member to perform his or her work can be regarded as a specific skill, e.g. experience, education, culture or profession. Depending on the skill levels required it may be more or less difficult to substitute members. Teams on the higher end of the continuum are typically more stable; it takes a longer time to develop requisite skills and members are not easily interchangeable. On the other hand, when a team is characterised by low skill differentiation members are are not bound to one unique role and their roles and tasks can be shared easily. Typical examples of teams on the continuum are:

- x-teams, on the high end of the continuum. This type of team is defined by their members' unique relations with outside groups and very specific skills that transcend the boundaries of the current team;

- cross-functional teams are constituted by members of various different functional backgrounds where each takes responsibility related to a specific discipline, function or expertise;

- extreme action teams where team members have unique skills, but also need a specific set of shared or common core skills to function in the team;

- crews are further along the continuum, and are characterised by high levels of role differentiation and role standardisation. When considering the two sets of skills, task-related skills and interpersonal skills, it could be that crews have high levels of specialisation, but in some cases members might be new to the current crew and are thus substitutable in this sense;

- fully cross-trained teams – where a larger degree of skill is required which could be dependent on specific training, but since all members have same levels of skills it would be easy to substitute a team member; and

- behavioural teams are at the lowest end of the of the continuum. In these teams one team member can quite easily fulfill different roles. Typically teams of this nature do not require specific skills and therefore members of such teams can be replaced with ease.

Authority differentiation

The vertical dimension of the proposed chart provides a continuum relating to who has responsibility for making decisions: individual members, subgroups, or the team as a whole. It relates in particular to where authority resides when there is disagreement. At one end of the spectrum teams have a formal leader with full authority to make decisions, while at the other end the team has full leader control and complete self-management. The following typical teams occupy the various levels:

- Judge-adviser systems where the judge and the advisers do not share in the outcome of the decision, and where there is disagreement in the team a single point of authority with assigned leadership makes a unilateral decision.

- Hierarchical decision-making teams where there is some input from the team, but the final decision is rendered by the authority figure.

- Traditional work teams managed, directed and led by supervisors who make most of the decisions.

- Situation-specific emergent leadership or rotated leadership teams. Such teams are mostly stable over time, but depending on the demands of the situation different leaders may emerge to assist in decision-making, mostly because of the specific requirements of the situation.

- Democratic teams where team members are involved through public debate and decisions are made by voting between various options. Here the team members have to "live with" the consequences of the decision taken by the team and majority rules apply.

- Consensus teams are similar to democratic teams, but they require consensus to solve disagreement and they rely on the input and contribution of all members.

- Self-managing teams, where the decision authority lies in the hands of the team members themselves and they decide for themselves how they want to manage any disagreement.

Temporal stability

Temporal stability is determined by the influence of time, both past and future. It refers to the degree to which team members have a history of working together and whether it is expected that the team will continue working together in the future. Whether the team is short-term or long-lasting could impact on the interpersonal connection of team members, and therefore the degree of temporal stability could impact performance. The following types of teams illustrate the differences on this continuum:

- Real teams are stable and have a history and future together; in this type of team membership is stable and could be intact for as long as ten years.

- Ongoing teams are intact teams that work together continuously over a long period of time.

- Long-term teams work together on specific projects, but stay together for up to a year.

- Student project teams and ad hoc teams are short-term teams that may work together for 10 to 15 weeks.

- Short-term advice groups may meet three to five times over the course of two to eight weeks.

- One-shot laboratory teams get together for a specific reason and may only work together for a few hours.

Using these three dimensions the team can plot itself onto a three-axis matrix, which can assist in understanding how the dynamics of the specific type of team may influence design requirements. The authors claim that not all teams should be treated equally, but that teams should be designed appropriately according to their characteristics. Each of these dimensions can also be used to evaluate the team's current performance and to assist in adjusting actions and behaviour to align better with the organisation.

Tips for team leaders

It is necessary for team leaders to have a clear understanding of the type of team they lead as this impacts directly on some of the design decisions they have to make. It also impacts on views of efficiency, effectiveness and how performance should be regarded. The tool can help leaders to understand where their specific team resides in this conceptual space and could assist them to predict the opportunities and threats to the team depending on the relative position. It could then also help the leader to consider which direction the team could move on the continuum and the potential consequences of such a move. For example, a team could make a decision on whether it is beneficial to move "up" or "down" the authority dimension. If the team operates in a very hierarchical organisational culture it may be difficult for them to adjust and to use a more self-managed authority style.

Representation

The graphical representation used by Hollenbeck, Beersma and Schouten (2012) is presented here to facilitate understanding of their typology.

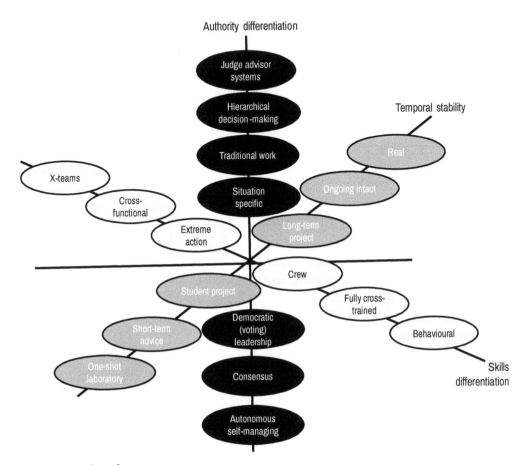

Figure 5.1: Typology of teams

References

Devine, D., Clayton, L., Philips, J., Dunford, B. & Melner, S. (1999). Teams in Organizations: Prevalence, Characteristics, and Effectiveness. *Small Group Research*, 30(6), 678.

Hackman, J.R. (2002). *Leading teams: Setting the stage for great performances*. Boston: Harvard Business School Press.

Hollenbeck, J.R., Beersma, B. & Schouten, M.E. (2012). Beyond Team Types and Taxonomies: A Dimensional Scaling Conceptualization for Team Description. *Academy of Management Review*, 37(1), 82–106. http://dx.doi.org/10.5465/amr.2010.0181.

Sundstrom, E., McIntyre, M., Halfhill, T. & Richards, H. (2000). Work Groups: From the Hawthorne Studies to Work Teams of the 1990s and Beyond. *Group Dynamics: Theory, Research, and Practice*, 4(1), 44–67.

22 | Mandate

Introduction

The mandate of a team can be discussed in terms of vision, mission, values, targets and objectives. Two theories around team mandate that have received research attention are described here, namely the use of a charter and goal-setting theory. The former method concretises the mandate of a team and helps members to understand their roles and responsibilities, while goal-setting theory has been proven to be helpful in guiding teams towards realising their mandate.

In a nutshell

A key element of a team is its vision or goal, which summarises the raison d'etre of the team.

Purpose

To help the team focus and find direction.

To energise the team.

To provide measurements for achievement.

To use as ground rules.

To shape behaviour and ownership.

Description

Elements of a mandate

The mandate of a team is a concretisation of its overall assignment; its raison d'etre. It makes clear what is expected of the group and who it is responsible to deliver to. It defines the alignment of the team with the organisation as it defines its scope and determines the measurements used to evaluate its performance. The following elements constitute the mandate of a team: vision, mission, goals and objectives, core values, and team targets.

Vision

Hackman claimed that a team's vision provides a compelling direction and serves to energise, direct and engage the team members.

- Energise: the vision should be sufficiently challenging to members of the team to facilitate motivated engagement.

- Direct: the clarity of the vision aligns the strategy of the team with the team's purpose.

- Engage: the vision should help individuals in the team to regard their actions as meaningful and consequential and foster the utilisation of each member's knowledge and skills.

Mission/purpose

A mission reflects the primary purpose or reason why the team exists. It is a concise version of what the team regards as important, who the team serves and what it wants to accomplish.

Values

The values of a team reflect the core principles that the team will stand and abide by. It is based on core beliefs and includes how the team expects its environment to function. Values are aspirational, but also constrain behaviour in that they guide and direct behaviour. They provide the foundation on which strategic, operational and interpersonal decisions are based, and also demonstrate integrity to the team's stakeholders.

Targets

The next element of the team's mandate is its targets. Every team must have the following four components of performance covered to ensure its targets are reached:

- Production output: Every team delivers on a particular outcome; one can hardly deny that this is probably the most important element of the target. The manner in which the team delivers on task demands and the processes it employs should be focused on delivering an outcome. How and what is measured to describe this output is unique to each team. The production output of the team is also determined by the stakeholders or customers of the team. These can be internal (e.g. the next department in a value chain) or external (e.g. the end user of a product). The output can also be evaluated according to quality (e.g. levels of customer satisfaction) or quantity (e.g. the number of a particular product that is produced).

- Individual member growth and satisfaction: The consequences a group has for its members and the benefits each member finds in being part of the group should form part of the target of the team. For example, the benefits for the individual of belonging to and contributing to the team could be career advancement, personal satisfaction, or fulfilling other personal needs and motives. Members participate in teams and will remain in a team for an extended period of time only when this realises sufficient benefit for the individual. Thus, a team must also provide learning and development opportunity for members to develop new skills, to fulfil their own ambitions and to provide the opportunities to grow. Successful teams understand that they have to create a context in which individuals can be empowered, and therefore have to have a keen interest in the members as individuals.

- Team development: this refers to the viability of the team. A team must ensure that it is sustainable and able to reach its targets. A team should act to ensure its longer term viability and sustainability and create a sense of belonging and cohesion for its members. This allows for members to enjoy working together and to build an environment where they are prepared to commit and contribute.

- Organisational alignment and benefit: a team can only be successful once it meets the key demands of individuals, the team and the organisation. With regard to the latter, a team should have as part of its target an evaluation mechanism to determine whether it benefits the organisation and whether what it does is aligned with the organisational strategy. This requires that the team is sufficiently networked with the rest of the organisation.

Objectives/Goals

Once the team is clear on its vision or goal, it has to produce the action steps required to accomplish its vision. This is done by deciding on appropriate plans of action and articulating the action steps required to ensure their implementation. This is done by clearly formulating the actions in terms of concrete outcomes. This is where goal-setting theory as outlined by Locke and Latham is useful. According to this theory, goals motivate individuals to increase performance, therefore goals should be future-orientated and guide behaviour to facilitate satisfaction as reward. The following characteristics must be present:

- Challenging: a challenging goal has clarity, provides an appropriate level of difficulty (challenging, but not impossible to achieve), and feeds the participants' sense of self-efficacy (the belief that the goal can be accomplished).

- Mediators: successful performance is mediated by direction, persistence, effort and task strategy.

- Moderators: the performance is always moderated by ability, goal commitment, feedback and task complexity.

A team is always under pressure to find the proverbial "sweet spot" where the goals are not too narrow, but at the same time not too broad, so that team members feel energised and engaged.

Charter

The use of a charter or contract in a team is based on the assumption that agreeing formally on intended behavioural and process norms early on in a team's development has long-lasting effects. A charter is designed to establish a common frame of reference and to establish a common set of expectations regarding goals, responsibilities and processes, and make it clear to the team what its overall assignment is. As has been widely recognised, teams are influenced by both task and interpersonal relations components, and it is helpful to structure a charter to reflect these elements as well as the processes the team needs to agree on to ensure implementation of its mandate. According to Whichard and Kees, a team's charter should include:

- a purpose: to define why it exists, how it aligns with the organisation's strategy and who its key stakeholders are. it states who in the organisation it reports to or who its customers are, as well as how the team benefits the organisation;

- goals: this includes what the teams want to deliver, who is responsible for various parts of the delivery and when it will accomplish its mission;

- roles: each member's role(s) and subsequent expectations thereof, commensurate with members' skills, expertise, competencies and experience, should be included. in addition, the persons responsible for each of the actions and goals should be indicated; and

- ground rules: the rules ("how we do things here") should be agreed and included in the charter.

The charter can include personal information that it could benefit the rest of the team to know, such as contact details, work history, strengths and weaknesses including knowledge, skills and ability, experience related to the team's mandate, personality preferences e.g. an MBTI type preference or a DISC profile, and other related issues that may influence teamwork, such as religious practices that entail not working on particular days.

Lastly, the charter must also define its operational processes, in other words how teams plan to work together and how interpersonal relations will be handled. This includes (but is not limited to) information and agreement on:

- policies, procedures (including technical procedures) and regulations;

- decision-making: how do we make decisions?;

- guidelines for communication in terms of how to reach one another;

- agreement on procedures for meetings, regarding attendance, interruptions, lateness;

- participation: what are the expectations regarding participation?; and

- conflict: how will healthy and unhealthy conflict be dealt with and how will differences of opinion be handled?

The following questions help a team to define its mandate: What are we expected to deliver? What will it look like when delivered successfully? How does our charge align with the organisation? The focus is not only on the statement of the mandate, but on the process of defining the mandate. This process often assists the team in defining, delimiting and construing what it actually is that they have to deliver.

Representation

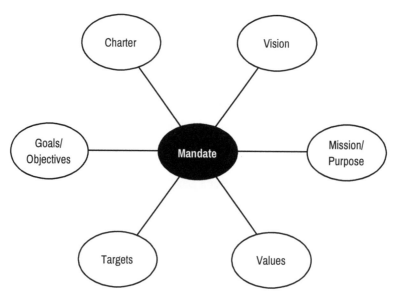

Figure 5.2: Mandate

References

Hackman, J.R. (2002). *Leading teams: Setting the stage for great performances.* Boston: Harvard Business School Press.

Locke, E.A. & Latham, G.P. (1990). *A theory of goal setting and task performance.* Englewood Cliffs, NJ: Prentice-Hall.

Whichard, J. & Kees, N.L. (2006). *Manager as facilitator.* Hartford, CT: Praeger.

23 | # Team composition

Introduction

Six determinants of what should be taken into account when making decisions regarding the composition of a team are presented by Mathieu, Tannenbaum, Donsbach and Alliger. This approach provides a broader and more comprehensive view on how to manage the composition of a team.

In a nutshell

Things to consider in composing a team: traditional (personnel-position) fit; traditional fit plus teamwork skills; relative contribution; team profile; time; and fluidity of membership.

Purpose

To help with the composition of the team.

To facilitate understanding of what is needed to improve performance.

Description

Six factors to keep in mind when constituting the composition of a team are presented:

Traditional (personnel-position) fit

The first way of composing teams is identified as the traditional personnel-position fit model. This is what can be called the "all-star model" where individuals who are experts in a specific task or discipline are picked because of the specific knowledge, skills and abilities they have to fulfil a particular position. It assumes that if you get the best set of persons the performance of the team "rolls-up" to lead to superior performance. However, in essence this treats each position in a team as though it is an individual job in an organisation, without considering contextual demands or issues of group dynamics. Implicit in this is the assumption that exact and ideal job profiles would be required to enable each to be filled with specialists who can occupy the position and perform optimally to the demands of the position - hence the notion of personnel-position fit. Furthermore it suggests that team performance will be dependent on how well each incumbent performs the demands of the specific position, and that the aggregation of performance will influence performance levels.

Traditional fit plus teamwork skills

This approach to staffing a team remains focused on the individual, but in addition to position-fit competencies, team-relevant competencies are also considered. Here the level of interdependence as well as the position requirements are indexed and the skills required to work across situations in a team setting are added to the consideration. Thus, it is not only position-specific skills that are considered, but also how individual members contribute to the team as a collective. The skills set is therefore expanded to include team-generic competencies that are valuable across the team's operations and time together. Examples are adaptability, shared situational awareness, performance monitoring and feedback, leadership/team management, interpersonal relations, coordination, communication, and decision-making. The inclusion of members that possess these competencies will enhance team performance.

Team profile

This factor views the team as a collective and looks at various combinations of team compositional properties; it looks at the distributional features of member composition, i.e. how the team collectively display a particular construct. For example, how is the composition of the team in terms of diversity, balance of roles or personality, or even when someone in the team needs to contribute something that is to the benefit of the whole team? Thus, the complete team is taken into account and the leader determines what is needed from the perspective of the team. As is explained here, while external demands may influence decisions about the team profile, team performance measures also impact decisions on composition. In this regard the profile of the team should be evaluated for the potential impact on performance. For example, role or personality balance could impact team performance. A further aspect of how the team profile and the needs of the team could determine its composition is where the team may be in need of a specific skill. In this regard it is important to know that the need for this skill should be one that the team in general requires to be successful, and the need of the team is just that someone and not necessarily a particular person or position needs the skill. Examples include knowledge of a local language, knowledge of customer needs, or a high level of understanding of information technology.

Relative contribution

This is about the fact that in teams not all contributions are necessarily equally important for team success. It requires a perspective of a team as a network where the interconnections need to be in place to the benefit of the team as a whole. It thus acknowledges that members' contributions need not be viewed or weighted equally. The competencies and contributions of the weakest and strongest members in the team obviously have a different impact on the success of the team, especially in situations where there is a high incidence of task interdependencies. In such cases the stronger and weaker members can either carry or undermine the entire team effort. Thus, in considering the composition of a team, a leader should consider the potential negative impact of disproportionate influence on overall team functioning.

Time

As is common knowledge, teams develop and different tasks and actions are required at different times. It is therefore also important to evaluate the composition of a team from the perspective of how the team will develop. At the start a different skill set may be required to set up the team, to plan and to give direction. Later on, more focus should be on action while the mid-term transition may need a special skill set. How to balance the team over its lifetime is highlighted by this determinant.

Fluidity of membership

Very few teams are stable over their complete life cycle and membership is therefore fluid and dynamic. Many organisations make exclusive use of temporary teams (e.g. consulting teams, film production teams or project teams). This determines the composition of a team as members leaving or joining a team impact on its performance. Thus, whenever a change to the composition occurs, the dynamics of the team are affected which can have a positive or negative impact on the team. For example the addition of members may allow the team to adjust better to environmental or customer demands. It may also offer new ideas, transfer of knowledge, improvement of best practices and improve the team's adaptability and flexibility to demands. However, on the negative side it may diminish stability or drag the team down because time needs to be spent to bring the new member "on board". New members may also take time to find their feet and feel comfortable and safe, therefore their contributions may take time to take effect. The addition of a member may also destabilise patterns, sub-groups and power relations, which could impact on performance. In this way the composition of the team is influenced by leavers and arrivers, and the knowledge, skills and ability sets brought in or lost should be considered in terms of task, interpersonal skills and interdependence levels.

Tips for team leaders

These factors influence the composition of every team. However, leaders need to discern the importance of each of these according to the demands of their team at a particular time, and should use these factors selectively to compose their teams given current imperatives, challenges or demands.

Representation

		Focus	
		Individual	Team
Static	Individual member	Traditional Personnel position fit	Personnel model with team considerations
	Team members	Relative contribution model	Team profile model
Dynamic		Time	Stability of membership

Figure 5.3: Determinants of composing a team

Reference

Mathieu, J.E., Tannenbaum, S.I., Donsbach, J.S. & Alliger, G.M. (2014). A Review and Integration of Team Composition Models: Moving Toward a Dynamic and Temporal Framework. *Journal of Management,* 40(1), 130–160.

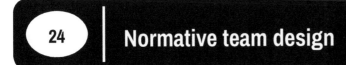

Normative team design

Introduction

Normative views of team design contend that there is a "correct", i.e. normative way to design a team. The work of Campion, Medsker and Higgs provided a comprehensive analysis and their components of a normative team are described here as an example of this approach. They identified five design themes related to team effectiveness, and in addition highlighted a total of 19 characteristics within these themes that can be used to guide team design.

In a nutshell

Five team design themes, namely job design, interdependence, composition, context and process.

Purpose

To describe five broad design themes and their components to help teams set up effective teams.

To help teams design themselves to ensure effectiveness.

To provide a checklist for design and evaluation.

Description

The authors provided five design themes and the various components of each theme.

Job design

Self-management, participation, task variety, task significance and task identity are regarded as the elements impacting on job design.

Self-management

This characteristic relates to autonomy: whether a team has to manage its own actions and the authority to make its own decisions. The larger the degree of self-management, the larger the levels of responsibility and sense of ownership can be expected. In particular, decisions regarding scheduling, methods to be used and procedures employed are made at a team level and are not only the responsibility of the leader.

Participation

This relates to the degree to which all members are free to participate in the decisions. This means placing the location of decision-making as near as possible to operational problems and uncertainties, and increases responsibility and ownership in the team.

Task variety

This characteristic allows members to use different skills. With this approach either boring or interesting tasks can be shared among members. Members get a chance to learn new skills and task assignments can change on a daily basis to meet the workload needs of the team.

Task significance

If members of a team feel that their actions and tasks have significance to the various stakeholders and meaningful consequences for its customers, they will be more committed and ownership will increase.

Task identity

This characteristic can also be regarded as task differentiation; it refers to whether a team takes responsibility for a whole or separate piece of work.

Interdependence

The authors identified task and goal interdependence and interdependent feedback and rewards as elements of this design factor.

Task interdependence

This relates to how members of a team interact and depend on one another to complete the work. It builds a sense of responsibility for others' work and enhances the reward value of the team's achievements and accomplishments.

Goal interdependence

This type of interdependence relates to how individuals and the team as a whole are dependent on one another to reach the team's goals. The team's goals must be linked with the goals of individuals and the fact that they need each other to accomplish both team goals and individual goals must be stressed.

Interdependent feedback and rewards

This is also called outcome interdependence and is linked to how collective rewards and feedback can be used to motivate members in the team.

Composition

Compositional factors identified are heterogeneity, flexibility, relative size and preference for group work among members.

Heterogeneity

The influence of heterogeneity on team effectiveness is based on the assumption that a variety of skills and experience will improve effectiveness. This is especially so because it provides opportunities for team members to learn from one another and to utilise the knowledge, skills and expertise that each member brings to the team.

Flexibility

When members are flexible the effectiveness of a team is enhanced. This flexibility refers to whether members of the team can stand in for each other and whether the team is flexible enough to accept new members.

Relative size

Obviously some teams have a pre-determined number of members prescribed by external factors such as regulatory demands, but in most cases the number of members on a team is more discretionary. Since the optimal size of a team is the smallest number needed to do the work, team size is a relative number and should be controlled to ensure effectiveness.

Preference for group work

Individuals differ in their preferences, with some embracing the opportunity to work in a team, while others could be more reluctant. In terms of team design, the authors contended that a team's effectiveness will increase if the majority of members prefer to work in teams compared to on their own.

Context

The importance of context was acknowledged by the authors as a key design factor, in that training, managerial support and communication/cooperation between groups all impact on team performance.

Training

Training in group decision-making, interpersonal skills and technical knowledge increases team effectiveness; the team needs to ensure that the opportunity for such training forms part of the plans for the team.

Managerial support

As management controls the allocation of resources it is clear that a team needs their support. Furthermore, management plays an important role in setting and enhancing organisation culture, which may impact on the team's performance. Also considered here is the level of support that management has for the notion and use of teams in general.

Communication/cooperation between groups

This refers to the connection the team has with other stakeholders and how well communication and cooperation between the team and external stakeholders take place. This requires the team to evaluate the level of competition with other teams and individuals and how well teams in the organisation cooperate to get work done.

Process

Process consists of potency, social support, workload sharing and communication/cooperation within groups.

Potency

Potency is the sense or self-belief a team has that it can be successful in delivering on its mandate and be effective. It is similar to the more colloquial concept of team spirit and is related to the individual sense of self-efficacy.

Social support

This refers to teams whose members have positive social interpersonal relations and are prepared to help each other or to perform back-up behaviours to ensure the team's tasks are completed.

Workload sharing

This concept distinguishes between individualised measured outputs and team output. It is also concerned with whether individual outputs are perceived to be significant to the tasks and outcomes the team as a whole needs to deliver. It deals with whether everyone does their fair share of the team's work in that no member of the team depends on or expects another to do their work for them. Furthermore there must be a perception that work is distributed equally.

Communication/cooperation within groups

This relates to the teamwork behaviour that manifests in teams. It refers to how likely members are to share information with each other and whether there are clear patterns of communication and optimised levels of cooperation.

Tips for team leaders

This model provides a clear list of normative design features that leaders can use to set up their teams and to optimise the design of the team to ensure effectiveness.

Representation

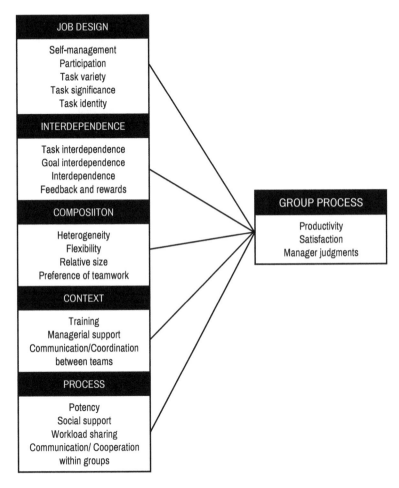

Figure 5.4: Normative design themes

Reference

Campion, M.A., Medsker, G.J. & Higgs, A.C. (1993). Relations Between Work Group Characteristics and Effectiveness: Implications for Designing Effective Work Groups. *Personnel Psychology*, 46(4), 823–850.

Introduction

When considering diversity it is first necessary to consider why organisations use diverse teams. On the one hand, it is done to improve performance and profit and therefore organisations espousing this view try to optimise profits using a diverse workforce. This is the so-called business perspective on diversity. However, a counter view (the equality perspective) holds that whether it makes business sense or not, teams need to include diversity considerations in their composition and operations since it is the "right thing to do". This perspective advocates doing the morally correct thing by addressing issues relating to the past in terms of diversity and not viewing organisational endeavours to address diversity only from a "value-in-diversity" perspective. The model described here, the Categorisation Elaboration Model, contends that how you categorise people moderates the impact diversity has on a team, and therefore diversity can lead to the elaboration of task-relevant information and perspectives, which in turn leads to increased performance. However, first a description of different types of diversity is presented.

In a nutshell

Teams elaborate on different categories (i.e. diversity) to enhance performance.

Purpose

To give an integrated view of diversity.

To show the benefits of diversity.

Description

Types of diversity

Harrison and Klein used diversity "to describe the distribution of differences among the members of a unit with respect to a common attribute, X". In other words, they regarded it as attribute-specific, in the sense that a team cannot be diverse per se, but can only be regarded as diverse in relation to the specific elements, attributes or features of its members. They contended that diversity should be considered in relation to the extent of separation, variety, or disparity of a particular attribute.

Separation

This refers to key differences in position or opinion among unit members. The authors viewed such diversity as the manner in which members differ from one another on a single continuum with regard to a single value, belief or attitude (e.g. positive affect, perceptions of leader charisma, or experience of organisational commitment). This type of diversity also manifests where there is difference of opinion, disagreement or opposition. Separation can also refer to physical location, that is, how close or far apart members are situated. Obviously these differences in separation may have consequences such as higher or lower cohesion. Where separation is high one can expect more interpersonal conflict, distrust and decreased task performance.

Variety

This refers to how members differ from one another qualitatively in terms of a categorical attribute, e.g. functional background or source of external information. Thus, variety reflects the differences in composition in kind, source or category of relevant knowledge or experience in terms of how it holds unique or distinctive information. A team can also differ in the extent to which its members are evenly spread across all the categories of variety or whether there are broader levels of difference. The authors held that the distribution of variety indicates the number and spread of "batches" of information, content, experience, or unique network ties available. A higher level of variety in a team broadens the cognitive and behavioural repertoire of the team and generally has positive effects (such as in the quality of problem-solving or group decision-making). Teams with a high level of variety will be more creative, with increased flexibility and higher levels of innovation. However, one can also expect increased levels of task conflict and disagreement.

Disparity

This refers to the differences in concentration of valued social assets or resources. According to the authors, members in a team can differ in the extent to which they hold or receive a share, amount, or proportion of an attribute. In some respects the distribution could be equal, while in other teams the same attribute could be held in disproportion. Some consequences of this type of disparity are an increase in within-unit competition, reduced input, less interaction between members of the team and deviance from the norms.

Categorisation Elaboration Model

Researchers have tried to understand the manifestation of diversity through two main theoretical lenses, namely:

- social identification theory: this contends that individuals have a more favourable evaluation of in-group members, i.e. people similar to them. The effect of such identification is that inter-group bias can occur. This similarity attraction paradigm states that when an individual experiences similarity in values and beliefs it is perceived as pleasurable and therefore more likely to lead to group formation;

- the information/decision-making approach: conversely, this view contends that there is value in diversity and the more diverse a team is, the more it will benefit from diverse task-related knowledge and perspectives.

The Categorisation Elaboration Model (CEM) tries to integrate these two perspectives of diversity by asking how, since diversity exists in any event, it can be "elaborated" to the benefit of the team. At first the model states that all dimensions of diversity can be used for social categorisation and for elaborating information and task-relevant information, yet how a team goes about doing this (and therefore whether it uses diversity to its benefit or detriment) depends on how it utilises categorisation. To answer this the CEM explains how categorisation (the potential strengthening and institutionalisation of different elements of diversity) moderates the elaboration of diversity, i.e. how it is used to increase task-relevant information and perspectives and in turn increase performance. This happens through three processes, as the manner in which this categorisation occurs depends on the:

- normative fit, i.e. the importance attached to salient features by the individual, e.g. how "visible" it is made or how important it is evaluated. Normative fit relates to how a team regards a particular feature of difference, i.e. the diversity of a team exists and some attributes thereof indicate difference when these attributes are compared to one another (comparative fit). The team then decides (not necessarily consciously, but through social identification) to regard this attribute as important (normative fit);

- accessibility, i.e. how willing the individual is to access the cognitive representation of the attribute and how easy it is to ascertain and access such attribute; and

- comparative fit, i.e. the extent to which the particular attribute can be used to determine difference. In a team the extent of social categorisation is influenced by how easy or difficult it is for a team to use cognitive representation (as moderated by normative fit and accessibility) of a particular attribute, in other words, the extent to which an element of (perceived) difference is regarded as important.

Thus, the importance attached to, the accessibility of and the comparative fit of an attribute is used in the social categorisation processes by a team to determine whether it is beneficial to be diverse or not. These attributes that are then used as comparative fit, i.e. used to differentiate each other. This is particularly salient when they relate to so-called fault lines. Fault lines can be perceived as the existence of multiple attributes shared by particular subgroups in a team. This leads to the formation of subgroups that are relatively homogenous on a number of shared attributes. For example, if in a particular group two subgroups exist that each share the same nationality, language and profession, such a team has a clear fault line and the impact of diversity could be exacerbated. The CEM furthermore contends that the team's elaboration efforts are moderated through social categorisation efforts, which lead to affective and evaluative reactions. These could be relational conflict, cohesion, identification or commitment. The theory contends that all of these have the potential to serve as enhancements to the elaboration processes of the team and can be helped to grow the team's output. However, the CEM states that these affective and evaluative reactions are negatively influenced when it is perceived that:

- the social identity of the team or subgroup as established through social categorisation is threatened. Once this happens the social identity group retreats and guards its actions, and the elaboration efforts of the team are limited as it impacts the team through increased relational conflict; lack of cohesion; problems identifying with the team, and lack of commitment; and

- task specific influences, including task informational and decision requirements, task motivation, and task ability.

Lastly, it is also important to understand the importance put to perceptions of diversity. In this regard, diversity is not only something that manifests objectively, but that the subjective perceptions regarding the importance a particular member may put on a particular attribute may also influence the experience and manifestation of the effects of diversity.

Tips for team leaders

The CEM enables leaders of teams to use diversity to their benefit for both the business and moral argument thereof, and makes it clear where to intervene in a team to benefit from diversity, while understanding different types of diversity helps leaders to design teams to be more effective.

Representation

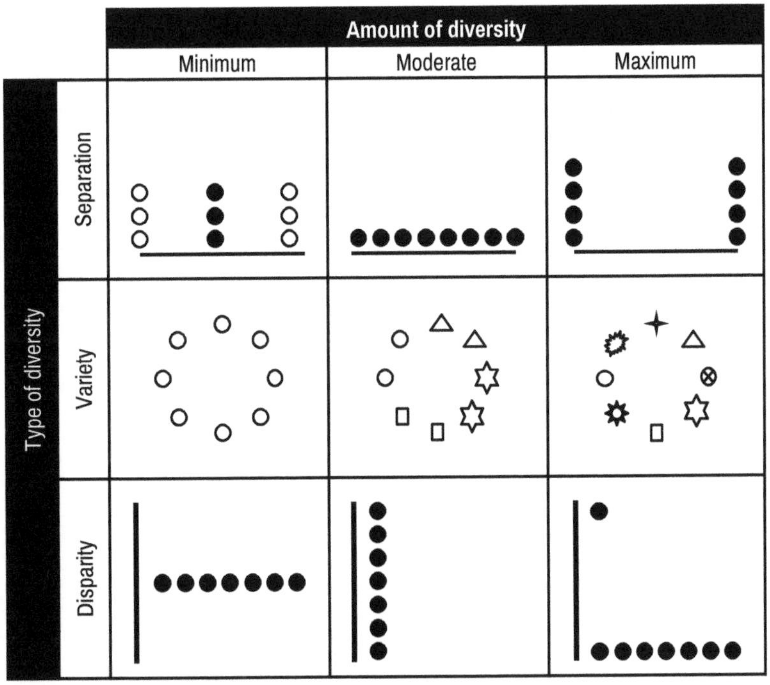

Figure 5.5: Different categories of diversity

Reference

Harrison, D. A. & Klein, K. J. (2007). What's the Difference? Diversity Constructs as Separation, Variety, or Disparity in Organizations. *Academy of Management Review*, 32(4), 1199–1228.

Van Knippenberg, D., De Dreu, C.K.W. & Homan, A.C. (2004). Work Group Diversity and Group Performance: An Integrative Model and Research Agenda. *Journal of Applied Psychology*, 89(6), 1008–1022.

INDIVIDUAL ASSESSMENT INSTRUMENTS

The use of psychometric instruments has had a long and enduring relationship with organisational life and leaders of teams have used them extensively to assist in developing their teams and improving performance. In this section, instruments to measure personality type, personality traits, individual emotional intelligence, competencies or strengths, and individual style are described, as they can be particularly helpful for teams to understand how differences between members can be discerned and optimised. All these instruments assess "individual traits", which plays a critical part in how members interact in teams. While it has many detractors, the classic Myers-Briggs Type Indicator remains a popular and useful tool to assist leaders and team members alike. A more recent and also more robust assessment of personality is the Big Five personality trait assessment. The next set of instruments relates to the increasingly influential focus on emotions and the ability to recognise and manage emotions, i.e. Emotional Intelligence. Three different assessment instruments (each with a different focus) are presented here, namely the Mayer-Salovey-Caruso Emotional Intelligence Test (emotions as a cognitive intelligence element), Bar-On's EQ-I (emotional intelligence elements that include behaviour, traits, social interrelations and awareness) and the Multifactor Emotional Intelligence Scale (assessing the ability to perceive, identify and understand emotions). A different perspective of what individuals bring to the team is to assess their competencies. The Clifton Strengths Finder (CSF) measures personal talent through highlighting what strengths people utilise and display. The last tool described here relates to individual leadership style and identifies six different styles, namely commanding, authoritative, pace-setting, visionary, coaching and affiliative.

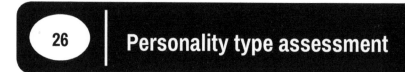

26 | Personality type assessment

Introduction

Personality is the relatively stable set of characteristics that influence a person's behaviour. As it determines to a large extent who we are, it goes without saying that it will also form part of the building blocks of a team. One of the most popular methods of measuring personality as part of team development is the Myers-Briggs Type Indicator (MBTI). The MBTI is based on the work of Carl Jung and was developed by Isabel Myers and Katherine Cook Briggs.

In a nutshell

Identifying personality type according to extraversion/introversion, sensing/intuition, thinking/feeling, and judging/perceiving.

Purpose

To help members identify their own personality preferences.

To facilitate understanding amongst team members.

To determine optimal engagement styles.

To limit conflict

Description

The MBTI distinguishes four sets of opposites that influence personality, namely:

	How we are energised?	
(E)	Extraversion ———————————————— Introversion	(I)
	Where do we get our information from?	
(S)	Sensing —————————————————Intuition	(N)
	How do we make decisions?	
(T)	Thinking————————————————Feeling	(F)
	How do we organise our world?	
(J)	Judging———————————————— Perceiving	(P)

Letter 1 – Extraversion (E) or Introversion (I) (the attitude type)
Letter 2 – Intuition (N) or Sensing (S) (the information-gathering function)
Letter 3 – Thinking (T) or Feeling (F) (the decision-making function)
Letter 4 – Perception (P) or Judgement (J) (the lifestyle type)

Every person tends to display one of each pair of opposites more than the other, i.e. a team member may be an extrovert as opposed to an introvert. The same applies for the other three sets of opposites. Thus, by combining the four different scales, 16 different personality types are distinguished, each displaying its own characteristics. For example, someone with an ESTP type would probably be adaptable and pragmatic, like things mechanical and to work with his or her hands, and like to sort out problems or issues on the spot. While the developers provided an extensive description of each type, they also offered a short summary of each as part of the questionnaire which are reproduced here as an illustration of each type.

Table 6.1: The 16 personality types

ISTJ	Quiet, serious with a logical decision-making style. Value traditions, are loyal, and take pleasure in an orderly and organised environment.
ISFJ	Steady, friendly and conscientious with concern for how others feel. Can be thorough and painstaking, and strive to create an orderly and harmonious environment.
ISTP	Quiet and observant yet reacting quickly with logical analysis of data sets to determine the core of practical problems; value efficiency, logical principles and focused effort.
ISFP	Friendly, sensitive and present in the moment. Like individuality and independence, and are committed to their values and to people they regard as important. Dislike conflict and do not force their opinions or values on others.
ESTP	Focus on immediate results, display flexibility and tolerance, and want action. Focus on the here and now and enjoy each moment they can be active with others.
ESFP	Flexible, spontaneous and adaptable to new settings with an outgoing, friendly, and accepting nature. They are exuberant lovers of life and of people, and enjoy working with others to make things happen. They are realistic and fun and bring commonsense to work.
ESTJ	Practical, realistic and matter-of-fact. They focus on results, action and getting things done. They like routine and have a clear set of logical standards that they systematically follow and require others to follow.
ESFJ	Looking for harmony, this generally cooperative type prefers to work with others to complete tasks accurately and on time. Want to be appreciated for who they are and for what they contribute.
INFJ	Committed to firm values and serving the common good, they seek meaning and connection in ideas, relationships, and material possessions. Want to understand what motivates people, are contemplative and insightful.

INTJ	Original minds with a great drive for implementing their ideas and achieving their goals, however they tend to be sceptical and independent, and place high value on standards of competence and performance.
INFP	Values and people who are important to them are key drivers. They want to understand, help and lead others to fulfil their potential. They tend to be adaptable, flexible and accepting unless a value is threatened.
INTP	Theories are more important to them than social interaction. They have a propensity to delve deep into solving problems and to find logical explanations to things they find interesting. They can be sceptical, sometimes critical, yet always analytical.
ENFP	With life seen as full of possibilities, this type displays warm, enthusiastic and imaginative behaviour and disposition. They seek affirmation from others, and readily give appreciation and support. Spontaneous and flexible, they often rely on their ability to improvise and their verbal fluency.
ENTP	Adept at reading other people, but also at generating conceptual possibilities, they analyse others strategically and solve challenges resourcefully. This type does not like routine and can be seen to turn from one new interest to another.
ENFJ	Warm, empathetic, and focused on the emotions, needs, and motivations of others. They find potential in everyone, and want to help others to fulfil their potential.
ENTJ	Decisive and forceful in presenting their ideas. They often assume leadership. Good analytical ability sees them offering long-term plans, solutions to challenges and efficient procedures and policies. Tend to be well-informed and willing to pass knowledge onto others.

Tips for team leaders

The MBTI is a widely used instrument and while not without its distractors, it does provide leaders with helpful insights into personality and how to adjust behaviour to align team members best with their type. For example, leaders can:

- allow members of the team (each with his or her own type preference) to explain to others in the team which interaction styles they prefer to optimise their contributions;

- give an opportunity to members to experiment with behaviour that is not their natural preference; and

- adapt their leadership style to connect optimally with members from different style preferences.

Representation

ENFJ Teacher	INFJ Counsellor	INTJ Mastermind	ENTJ Field marshall
ENFP Champion	INFP Healer	INTP Architect	ENTP Inventor
ESFP Performer	ISFP Composer	ISTP Operator	ESTP Promoter
ESFJ Provider	ISFJ Protector	ISTJ Inspector	ESTJ Supervisor

Figure 6.1: Myers-Briggs Type Indicator (MBTI) personality preference types

References

Mayer, J.D., Salovey, P., Caruso, D.R. & Sitarenios, G. (2003). Measuring Emotional Intelligence with the MSCEIT V2.0. *Emotion*, 3(1), 97–105.

27 | Personality trait assessment

Introduction

Probably the most commonly used tool to assess personality is the so-called Big Five or Five Factor instrument. These five factors are generally regarded as the main constituents of personality and the instrument can be applied fruitfully by leaders to help them understand their team members.

In a nutshell

An assessment of a team member's personality in terms of five factors: openness, conscientiousness, extraversion, agreeableness and neuroticism.

purpose

To assess individual members' personality traits.

To help members understand colleagues better.

To align individual preference to team tasks.

Description

The Five Factor Model is a valuable framework for understanding and describing personality. It provides a taxonomy for understanding its parts, its organisation and its definition, even though it does not comment on how personality develops within an individual. The following five factors are differentiated:

Openness

This relates to a person's willingness and preparedness to seek new experiences. It points to the individual's curiosity, creativity and need to seek novelty. In teams it reflects through openness to new ideas, willingness to experiment and attitude to experiment. People who are open are willing to work in more complex environments where change occurs often, and do not require strict structure, routine or order. The scale measures levels of curiosity or preference for consistency and caution. A person's level of openness indicates to what degree they embrace, appreciate and seek new experiences, while the opposite (rigidity) indicates narrow interests, dogmatic thinking and being set in one's ways.

Conscientiousness

This factor refers to efficiency and propensity to organise on the one hand and a tendency to be relaxed, careless and easy-going on the other. The measure indicates how members in a team prefer challenges to achieve, how meticulous, organised and dutiful they are, as well as how self-disciplined they are. It is associated with long-term planning, striving towards goals, and achievement. Conscientiousness refers to a person's level of reliability and propensity to work hard and be organised, while being self-directed, dependable and persevering.

Extraversion

This factor describes how energetic, outgoing and spontaneous people are compared to being reserved, content to be on their own and individualistic. This measure indicates drive, energy and surgency, and can be helpful to teams as it gives an indication of levels of assertiveness, sociability and social interaction as well as of the need for social stimulation. Extraverted people are more assertive and gregarious while introverted people tend to be reserved, aloof and quiet. Also linked to extraversion is ambition or dominance, which corresponds to the need for power.

Agreeableness

The next factor describes how compassionate, involved and empathetic people are with other members on a team. Its counterpart on the scale relates to the level of detachment, indifference and distance that members could feel towards colleagues. Agreeableness refers to a person's level of compassion and disposition to be cooperative, helpful and trusting.

Neuroticism

The last factor gives an indication of a person's propensity to feel insecure, anxious or less confident. The tendency to experience unwelcome, uncomfortable and unpleasant emotions and have difficulty in dealing with them is indicated by a high score on this scale. At the other end of the scale are those who are comfortable with a broad repertoire of emotions, display emotional stability and do not easily submit to feeling stressed, depressed or anxious. Neurotic people often feel insecure or hostile as opposed to being calm, self-confident and cool-headed.

DeYoung's recent conceptualisation of the Big Five views these factors as indicative of either stability (neuroticism, agreeableness and conscientiousness) or plasticity (extraversion and openness/intellect). He also added two sets of traits to each of the Big Five categories to indicate a spectrum, as follows:

- neuroticism: withdrawal and volatility;

- agreeableness: compassion and politeness;

- conscientiousness: industriousness and orderliness;

- extraversion: enthusiasm and assertiveness; and

- openness/intellect: intellect and openness.

Tips for team leaders

The Five Factor Model is the most widely accepted view of personality structure and has been found to be relatively stable over its life span. Although the Big Five Factors are not described in terms of a spectrum, it is sometimes helpful for leaders to consider the concepts in terms of opposites, such as extroversion/surgency versus introversion/timidity, or agreeableness versus coldness and independence. This allows leaders to view subtleties in behaviour and to understand the full range of personality traits.

Representation

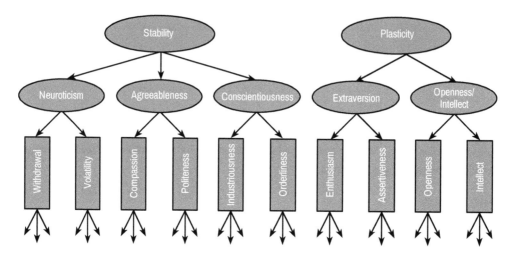

Figure 6.2: The Five Factor Model

References

DeYoung, C.G. (2010). Personality Neuroscience and the Biology of Traits. *Social and Personality Psychology Compass*, 4(12), 1165–1180.

DeYoung, C.G., Hirsh, J.B., Shane, M., Jones, C.S. & Hartley, N.T. (2013). Comparing Correlations between Four-Quadrant and Five-Factor Personality Assessments. *American Journal of Business Education*, 6(4), 459–470.

Hogan, R. & Hogan, J. (1995). *Hogan personality inventory manual*. Tulsa, OK: Hogan Assessment Systems.

Judge, T.A., Piccolo, R.F. & Kosalka, T. (2009). The Bright and Dark Sides of Leader Traits: A Review and Theoretical Extension of the Leader Trait Paradigm. *The Leadership Quarterly*, 20(6), 855–875.

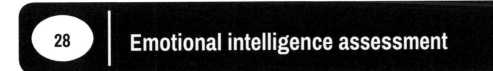

28 | Emotional intelligence assessment

Introduction

Ever since the concept of Emotional Intelligence (EI) was popularised through the work of Daniel Goleman, the notion of EI has entered into mainstream organisational life and its influence in teams has also not been insignificant. Three different assessment instruments, which each highlight a different aspect of emotional intelligence, will be presented. The score obtained on this test is known as an Emotional Quotient (EQ), but the terms EI and EQ are often used interchangeably. The Multifactor Emotional Intelligence Scale measures how tasks are performed based on the ability to perceive, identify and understand emotions. Bar-On's EQ-I is based on an expanded view of emotional intelligence to include behaviour, traits, social interrelations and awareness, and gives a broad overview of how an individual displays EI, while the Emotional Competence Inventory gives an opportunity for evaluation of a person's emotional intelligence as perceived by others.

In a nutshell

Assessing Emotional Intelligence through the Multifactor Emotional Intelligence Scale, Bar-On's EQ-I and the Emotional Competence Inventory

Purpose

To assess Emotional Intelligence

To give views on different aspects of Emotional Intelligence

To develop teams' Emotional Intelligence competencies

Description

Three different assessment instruments that highlight a different aspect of emotional intelligence are described here. Original interest in the concept of EQ started with the work of Salovey and Mayer, who highlighted the "mental ability" component of EI and regarded it as a cognitive function. Goleman and his colleagues built on these views and not only popularised EQ, but also included the ability of a person to experience and manage emotions by extending it to include an eclectic mix of traits including dispositional traits such as happiness, self-esteem, optimism, and self-management. Bar-On used a broadly defined interpretation of EI that included the emotional, personal and social dimensions of one's general intelligence. This can be regarded as a "mixed model" because it includes non-cognitive capabilities, competencies, and skills that influence a person to cope with environmental (and consequently emotional reactions) demands.

This leads to different approaches to EI (traits-based and mixed) as well as three sets of assessment instruments. Each of the three assessment instruments allows for a different perspective and each could be useful to a team.

Mayer-Salovey-Caruso Emotional Intelligence Test (MSCEIT)

The developers of this test describe the concept of Emotional Intelligence as follows: emotions refer to feelings and intelligence refers to the ability to reason about something. They therefore viewed EQ as "the capacity to reason with emotions and emotional signals, and the capacity of emotion to enhance thought". Consistent with their view of Emotional Intelligence as the ability someone has to recognise and engage in sophisticated processing of their own and others' emotions and behaviours, their focus on the ability part and therefore EQ is reflected in what one can accomplish once emotions are recognised. This ability enables a person to pay attention to, use, understand and ultimately manage emotions. These four levels of Emotional Intelligence are arranged hierarchically (indicated here from the lowest to the highest), and are tested as follows:

Perceiving emotions

In the MSCEIT, the ability to perceive emotions is measured through subscales called faces and paintings. The testee looks at a picture of a face and indicates to what degree each of five specific emotions is displayed. In the pictures subscale, pictures of landscapes and abstract designs based on cartoon faces are evaluated.

Facilitate thinking

The ability to think about emotions is assessed by participants imagining certain emotions and indicating how they match certain situations. The second manner of assessment of the use of emotions is called facilitations; here the extent to which certain emotions can assist in cognitive tasks or behaviours is determined.

Understanding emotions

This level is evaluated by the subscales called blends and changes. The former requires participants to identify basic emotions and combine them into more complex feelings, while the latter refers to intensification of emotions, i.e. how a certain emotion increases or decreases.

Managing emotions

In this case two subscales are also used, namely emotional management and emotional relationships. For emotional management, participants indicate how effective certain actions might be in regulating certain moods, while in the emotional relationships subscale participants are asked to indicate how effective certain actions of a person might be in regulating or managing the emotions of another.

EQ-I of Bar-On

The Bar-On EQ-I is a self-scoring test that measures five main elements deemed to constitute an individual's Emotional Intelligence. The original instrument contained 133 items, but Bar-On has since developed a short version (EQ-i: S) containing 51 questions to measure the same five main components.

Intrapersonal scale

This component refers to an individual's self-understanding, self-awareness, and ability to express feelings and ideas. This is measured with the following subscales:

*   Self-regard i.e. to accurately perceive, understand and accept oneself.

*   Emotional self-awareness i.e. to be aware of and understand one's emotions.

*   Assertiveness i.e. to effectively and constructively express one's emotions and oneself.

*   Independence i.e. to be self-reliant and free of emotional dependency on others.

*   Self-actualisation i.e. to strive to achieve personal goals and actualise one's potential.

Interpersonal scale

The next component is the ability to be aware of, appreciate, and understand the feelings of others, as well as the ability to establish and maintain mutually satisfying relationships with others and relate well with others. The three subscales measure:

*   empathy, i.e. to be aware of and understand how others feel;

*   social responsibility, i.e. to identify with one's social group and cooperate with others; and

*   interpersonal relationship, i.e. be able to establish mutually satisfying relationships.

Stress Management

Emotional management and regulation refers to how one copes with stressful situations and the level and extent of control of one's emotions.

*   Stress tolerance: to effectively and constructively manage emotions.

*   Impulse control: to effectively and constructively control emotions.

Adaptability

Adaptability includes accurately assessing one's feelings in the context of objective external cues and accurately assessing the situation one finds oneself in. It also refers to the propensity to be emotionally flexible and adapt one's thoughts in changing environments, and how to apply this in problem-solving situations.

- Reality-testing: to objectively validate one's feelings and thinking with external reality.

- Flexibility: the ability to adapt and adjust one's feelings and thinking to new situations.

- Problem-solving: to effectively solve problems of a personal and interpersonal nature.

General mood self-motivation

This is the final component, which covers general moods such as optimism, positivity and enjoying oneself and others. It is divided into:

- optimism: to be positive and look at the brighter side of life; and

- happiness: to feel content with oneself, others and life in general.

The Emotional and Social Competence Inventory (ESCI)

The ESCI is a multi-rater (360-degree) tool that assesses the emotional competencies of individuals, teams and organisations. It gives detailed feedback about an individual's strengths and development opportunities, indicates to the participant which of the competencies will improve his or her EI, and indicates where potential gaps may be. The Emotional and Social Competence Inventory 2.0 (ECI) measures 12 competencies, which are organised into four clusters as follows:

Self-awareness

This involves knowing one's internal states, preferences, resources, and intuitions, and comprises emotional awareness, that is, recognising one's emotions and their effects, and having an accurate assessment of oneself in terms of strengths and weaknesses.

Self-management

The next scale refers to how internal states, impulses, and resources are managed. The following subscales are distinguished:

- Emotional self-control: keeping disruptive emotions and impulses in check.

- Adaptability: flexibility in handling change.

- Achievement: striving to improve or meet a standard of excellence.

- Optimism: persistence in pursuing goals despite obstacles and setbacks.

Social awareness

This scale refers to how people handle relationships and their awareness of others' feelings, needs and concerns. The following two competencies make up the cluster:

- Empathy: sensing others' feelings and perspectives, and taking an active interest in their concerns.

- Organisational awareness: reading a group's emotional currents and power relationships.

Relationship management

The last scale concerns the skill or adeptness at inducing desirable responses in others. This cluster consists of six competencies, namely:

- conflict management: negotiating and resolving disagreements;

- coach and mentor: developing others by sensing others' development needs and bolstering their abilities;

- influence: wielding effective tactics for persuasion;

- inspirational leadership: inspiring and guiding individuals and groups; and

- teamwork and collaboration: working with others toward shared goals and creating synergy in pursuing collective goals.

Tips for team leaders

The value of Emotional Intelligence as a leadership quality is regarded as increasing in importance and leaders can find great benefit in understanding their own levels thereof and that of the members in the team. The assessment instruments offered here are all valuable and the unique intricacies they add to an assessment of EI make them valuable to use for purposes unique to the needs of each team.

Representation

Emotional Intelligence Assessment		
MSCEIT	Bar-On's EQ-I	Emotional & Social Competence Inventory
Perceiving emotions Facilitate thinking Understanding emotions Managing emotions	Intrapersonal Interpersonal Stress management Adaptability	Self-awareness Self-management Social awareness Relationship management

Figure 6.3: Emotional Intelligence Assessment instruments

References

Bar-On, R. (1997). *Bar-On emotional quotient inventory: A measure of emotional intelligence.* Toronto: Multi-Health Systems Inc.

Goleman, D. (1995). *Emotional intelligence: Why it can matter more than IQ.* New York: Bantam.

Mayer, J.D., Salovey, P. & Caruso, D.R. (2004). Emotional intelligence: Theory, Findings, and Implications. *Psychological Inquiry,* 15(3), 197–215.

Mayer, J.D., Salovey, P., Caruso, D.R. & Sitarenios, G. (2003). Measuring Emotional Intelligence with the MSCEIT V2.0. *Emotion,* 3(1), 97–105.

29 | **Strengths Finder**

Introduction

The basic premise of this type of assessment is embedded in the notion that people perform best when working in their areas of strength, and teams perform best when the team itself has a balanced, complementary set of strengths. The Clifton Strengths Finder (CSF) (which is now called Clifton Strengths) is an online measure of personal talent that identifies areas where an individual's greatest strengths exist.

In a nutshell

Assessment of an individual's strengths in four clusters, namely strategic thinking, influence, relationship building, and execution.

Purpose

To focus on individual members' strengths.

To help team members engage with their strengths.

To build balanced teams in terms of strength distribution.

To understand follower needs through trust, compassion, stability and hope.

Description

This measure developed by Tom Rath was tested through a large survey done by Gallup and distinguishes four domains of leadership strength (i.e. executing, influencing, relationship building and strategic thinking) that are critical to the effectiveness of a team.

Strategic thinking

This is about focusing on the big picture and towards the future with the potential of the team in mind. Leaders who display strategic thinking provide challenges and stretch the team. Sub-categories include:

- context: focused on history, they try to make sense out of the present through the lens of the past;

- futuristic: inspired by the future they energise others with their views of the future;

- ideation: inspired by ideas, thoughts and seemingly disparate phenomena, such people can find interactions and interrelations;

- input: people exceptionally talented in this area have a craving to know more; and often they like to collect and archive all kinds of information;

- analytical: always questioning and probing, they search for reasons, causes and answers;

- intellection: intellectual discussion and debate drive these people;

- learner: the process of learning, the knowledge learned and the need to continuously improve enthuses these individuals; and

- strategic: it is easy for them to find alternatives and they can quickly spot relevant patterns and issues.

Influence

Promoting the team's ideas internally and externally to the organisation, leaders displaying this strength inspire others to adopt their ideas and move the team forward. They are natural persuaders (although they may differ in how they do the persuasion) and can be motivating to energise the team.

- Activator: excels in turning thoughts into action.

- Command: they can take control and make decisions.

- Communication: good presenters, communicators and easy for them to put their thoughts into words.

- Competition: they like to compete, to strive to be the best and to measure themselves against others.

- Maximiser: they tend to focus on strengths as a way to stimulate personal and group excellence and seek to transform something strong into something exceptional.

- Self-assurance: they are confident in their ability to manage their own lives and rely on an inner compass to guide them.

- Significance: they are independent; they want to be recognised and well regarded by others.

- Woo: they are natural networkers who love to meet new people and win them over; to break the ice to connect with someone else.

Relationship building

The third domain of strength focuses on how people create and maintain relationships. With emphasis on the whole being bigger than its parts, such people highlight connections, interpersonal relations and cooperation between members, and act as the glue that keeps the system together. Strengths include:

- adaptability: they are happy to flow along with the processes of the team and to take things as they come

- developer: they are focused on development, and on progress and potential in others

- connectedness: they find meaning in links they discover between people and things

- empathy: they are able to step into the shoes of others, and understand the emotions, perspectives and feelings of others;

- harmony: they try to build consensus by minimising conflict and increasing areas of agreement;

- includer: they are sensitised to those on the outside, and are able to include and bring others into the fold;

- individualisation: they are intrigued with the unique qualities of each person and allow each team member to excel in their own way;

- positivity: their upbeat enthusiasm acts as an inspiration to others; and

- relator: they see colleagues as friends and prefer to work hard with them to achieve a goal.

Execution

People with strengths in this domain know how to get things done. This domain is characterised by the following types or strengths:

- Achiever: a hard-worker that enjoys being active, busy and productive.

- Arranger: as natural organisers they want maximum productivity by linking and organising systems.

- Belief: core values determine purpose for their lives.

- Consistency: equality and equitability in the manner they treat people help them to set rules "to live by".

- Deliberative: they are careful about how they make decisions or choices.

- Discipline: order, stability, routine and structure are important to them.

- Focus: they set priorities to drive their action, can steer a path forward, and excel in adapting to new demands while following through on their set path.

- Responsibility: they value honesty and loyalty and take psychological ownership of what they say they will do.

- Restorative: they are good at figuring out what is wrong, how to resolve it and how to deal with problems.

Tips for team leaders

This assessment forms part of a larger study, which gives information on what competencies team members require; from their leaders to follow effectively. These are:

- trust: employees who trust (inclusive of respect, integrity and honesty) their leaders are much more likely to be stable and produce better outcomes, in terms of both production and personal satisfaction;

- compassion: people want leaders who care about them. In a team where compassion – caring and friendship – is displayed, members are more engaged and productive and there is a higher retention rate;

- stability: team members need security, strength, support and peace, and a sense that there is a steady hand at the helm of the team. People want stability and confidence and this is a key prerequisite for change to happen; and

- hope: while people want stability on a daily basis, they also want hope for the future. Direction, faith and guidance are required from their leaders. This hope and optimism inspires employees, gives them something them to live and strive for.

Representation

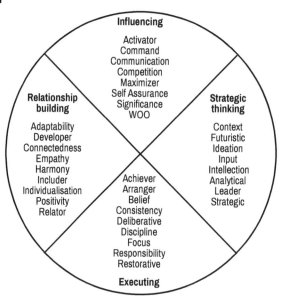

Figure 6.4: Strengths Finder clusters of strengths

References

Rath, T. (2008). *Strengths-based leadership: Great leaders, teams and why people follow*. New York: Gallup Press.

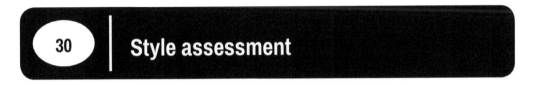

Introduction

Although theories of different leadership styles and behaviours have been around for decades and come from a number of different sources (e.g. the Situational Leadership theory), here a more recent theory of style is presented, namely the work of Daniel Goleman. Building on his work on Emotional Intelligence, Goleman together with Boyatzis and McKee described six different leadership styles which can apply to team leaders and team members alike.

In a nutshell

Commanding, authoritative, pace-setting, visionary, coaching and affiliative styles are explained.

Purpose

To help teams understand the style preferences of the leader and team members.

To assist in expanding the role repertoire of leaders and members.

To allow members to evaluate styles and their usefulness.

To raise awareness of the danger of using a particular style when not appropriate.

Description

Goleman and his colleagues identified six leadership styles that are built on views of EI. Each style reflects the leader's underlying capabilities, and their recognition and management of their own and others' emotions.

Commanding

This type of leader gives direction, focuses on achievement and drives for their success. They know how to deliver when problems arise or calm things down in a crisis. They demand compliance, believing that they know best, regardless of the situation. Using this style soothes fears and builds security in the team as the powerful stance of the leader commands respect. The focus of this style is based on the assumption that team members must comply immediately with the leader's views. This style is best employed in times of crisis when unquestioned rapid action is needed. On the other hand, this style can be associated with tension and lack of contribution from the team because of the forceful stance of the leader. The key phrase to summarise this style is "Do what I tell you".

Visionary

The visionary leader moves people towards shared dreams, is able to articulate a vision and creates a sense of direction. Such leaders encourage change, are self-confident and empathetic, and mobilise the team towards its vision. The visionary leader tells the team where to go, but not how to get there. The thrust of this style is based on providing long-term direction and creating a context wherein the team functions. The style is best used when new direction is needed. It may not always be suitable when trying to motivate experts or peers. The key phrase to summarise this style is "Come with me".

Affiliative

This classic "people-focused" style builds relationships and teams. Such leaders create harmony through building emotional bonds, believe in interpersonal relations and affiliation, and focus on team members' need to belong, in order to help the team to be successful. This style is best suited when conflict needs to be addressed, to mend relationship damage, or where harmony is needed in the team or organisation. It is collaborative and inclusive, and focuses on emotional needs over work-related issues. This stye is positive as it creates a harmonious climate and is often used alongside visionary leadership, but it can be perceived as soft, indecisive and too focused on relationships. The key phrase to summarise this style is "People come first".

Democratic

This style of leadership creates buy-in or consensus by involving people and valuing their input. Such leaders value collaboration, teamwork and cooperation and try to involve the team in decision-making. A democratic leader values inputs and commitment via participation, and listens to both the bad and the good news. Building commitment and generating new ideas whereby members are included in processes of the team are key factors of this style. It is best for situations where buy-in is needed or when simple inputs are required (for example, when the leader is uncertain). The key phrase to summarise this style is "What do you think?"

Pacesetting

In the pacesetting style the focus is on setting challenges that high performers can achieve and expecting high standards of performance. Achievement, drive and initiative are valued and encouraged. The leader who uses this style builds challenges and exciting goals for people. Their drive means that they expect excellence from others and often go to great lengths to exemplify it themselves. They identify poor performers and demand more of them by showing the way and pushing them for improvement. They are not afraid to step up and deliver themselves and therefore the slogan "Do as I do, now" is often associated with this style. They demand a lot from their staff and expect the team to know what to do.

Coaching

The coaching style manifests where leaders are focused on the needs of their followers. They concentrate on the development of team members and help them improve their performance. They align employee goals with those of the organisation and create a variety of development opportunities to enable members to reach levels that they regard as within their reach. This type of leader is prepared to go beyond what is required by the workplace and reaches out to help team members understand their strengths and weaknesses and help them to address their weaknesses. They are good at delegating challenging assignments and their actions are built on the belief that the staff is capable of doing what is required and committed to doing it. This style is focused on the long-term development of others and it demands high levels of loyalty. The key phrase to summarise this style is "Try this".

Tips for team leaders

It is necessary for leaders to be flexible and to employ more than one leadership style, and in particular to discern when to use a particular style. As most people tend to favour a particular leadership style leaders must take care not to over-use their preferred style as a go-to behaviour and run the risk of using it inappropriately. While these styles originated in leadership studies they also apply to leaders or members of teams. Thus, not only does it happen that these styles are displayed and used in a team, but it could also be that the team allows specific styles to manifest and to be accepted, even though this may not be the style best suited for the demands of the particular moment. The authors of this theory linked each style to associated outcomes, which will help leaders to evaluate their usefulness.

Representation

Style	Phase	Description of style
Commanding	Do what I tell you	Achievement drive, initiative taking and self-control
Visionary	Come with me	Catalysing change, forward focus and vision
Affiliative	People come first	Relationship building and empathy
Democratic	What do you think	Collaboration, communication and cooperation
Pacesetting	Do as I do, now	Conscientiousness, initiative and drive
Coaching	Try this	Empathy, developing others and self-awareness

Figure 6.5: Leadership styles

Reference

Goleman, D., Boyatzis, R.E. & McKee, A. (2002). *Primal leadership: Realizing the power of emotional intelligence.* Boston: Harvard Business School Press.

7

TEAM ROLES

A role in a team can be seen as the manifestation of thoughts, feelings and behaviours by individuals on behalf of and to the benefit of the team's psychological life. Roles develop in a dynamic fashion and their developmental processes are dependent on a team member's propensity for a particular role, but also on the broader team context, particular situation and deliberate or unconscious allocation of roles among team members. Various authors have proposed theories (and associated assessment instruments) to help explain team roles. While the famous and widely-used model of Meredith Belbin is most popular, alternative views proposed by Margerison and McCann, Kets de Vries, Mumford and colleagues and Ronnie Lessem provide a broad array of views on how roles play a part in team performance.

While there are overlaps between some of these sets of roles, it appears that scholars do not agree on a universal set of roles. However, it seems clear that different team members prefer, and therefore enact, different roles, and teams can utilise this understanding to improve overall performance.

Introduction

Belbin originally studied team management in a computerised, laboratory simulation, but his theory has been applied and tested beyond those original settings and has become one of the standard-bearing perspectives on team roles. The nine roles that he distinguished help team members to understand their preferences and enable teams to allocate their resources in a balanced manner. This balance of roles leads to improved performance.

In a nutshell

Nine team roles are identified, namely implementer, co-ordinator, shaper, plant, resource-investigator, monitor-evaluator, team worker, completer-finisher and specialist.

Purpose

To assist teams in identifying team roles.

To help teams balance themselves in terms of role resources.

To assist members of the team to be allocated functional roles aligned with team role preferences.

To help teams identify areas where they do not have role representation and to adjust accordingly.

Description

Belbin originally proposed eight roles, but later added a ninth role, while also making some changes in the names applied to each role. His theory rests on the following principles:

- Each team member displays a preferred team role determined by personal qualities and preferences (e.g. the professional and/or technical knowledge required to participate in the team's work).

- Each of these roles is characterised by unique patterns of interaction.

- Successful teams acquire optimal balance between functional roles and roles that are aligned with the team's objectives and goals.

- A team's effectiveness is enhanced when members recognise their own roles, and adjust them according to the balance displayed by the team, the role needs of the team and the objectives of the team.

Belbin furthermore clustered the various roles according to whether they are more focussed on thinking (monitor-evaluator, plant and specialist), action (implementer, shaper and completer-finisher), or people (co-ordinator, teamworker and resource-investigator).

Thinking

The three roles that make up the thinking or cognitive cluster are monitor-evaluator, plant and specialist.

Monitor-Evaluator

This role is characterised by the incumbent's ability to analyse problems and complexities with sober and unemotional assessment. Such people like to assess problems and ideas to ascertain their feasibility, practicality and value to the team's endeavours. Their contribution to the team is to interpret challenges, evaluate innovations and give balanced views on their viability and utility. They are able to step back and view team problems objectively and are often considered to be cold and dispassionate. They excel in analytical ability and can be perceived as shrewd, calculating and serious-minded. The critical ability of this person is often helpful to a team to prevent them from embarking on misguided projects and tasks, and their application of sound judgement is the most valued contribution to the team.

Plant

This describes an unorthodox and individualistic intellectual who advances new ideas and charts new courses of action. Such people bring creativity and innovation to the team's operations. They are assertive and socially venturesome and are prepared to take on challenges, especially those that involve ideas and imaginative effort. Their ideas often serve as seeds for other ideas to flourish and enhance the team's collective innovative efforts. They are constantly searching for new ideas, original approaches and ways to improve the performance of a team. Sometimes they can be overly fixed on their own ideas with a habit of retracting (often with feelings of hurt) if their ideas are not adopted or are challenged. They are "big picture" people and do not like to be bogged down with detail, specifics or minutiae. To them it is important that the "grand scheme of things", overall vision and broad issues are used to guide the performance of the team.

Specialist

This is a single-minded, self-driven individual who possesses unique knowledge, skills or abilities critical to the team. Such people like to be known for the contribution of their unique skill set. Specialists prefer to contribute on a technical, narrow level and can lose sight of the bigger picture. They sometimes lose interest when their services are no longer required and prefer to move on to more challenging environments rather than remain in a team where they feel their contribution is no longer of importance.

Action

In the category focusing on action or execution, again three roles are distinguished, namely implementer/ company worker, shaper and completer-finisher.

Implementer/Company worker

This describes a conscientious team member who transforms talk and ideas into practical activities. A company worker excels in clarifying goals and objectives and sorting out details of implementation. This team member prefers stability and does not always deal well with change or adjustments to predetermined plans. Such people have a natural ability to create order and structure and prefer to work systematically, methodologically and conservatively. They are practically oriented, with a realistic view of the goals and operations of the team. They are sometimes regarded as conservative given their preference for systems and authority. They tend to be stable and dependable, and are known for their perseverance.

Shaper

A dynamic, high-achiever occupies the shaper role. Such a person seeks patterns in group discussions and pushes for decision-making. He/she "shapes" the behaviour of the team, coordinates its tasks and intervenes when the team veers off course. The shaper is inspiring, enthusiastic and instils energy into the team. This role is often associated with someone who is perceived as anxious, self-assured and dominant. While this role is good for the momentum of the team, it comes with the risk of damaging interpersonal relations. A shaper can be seen as the "director of operations" who can direct the energy of the team into successful performance.

Completer-Finisher

This role can be likened to that of an inspector or controller. The objective of someone occupying the Completer-Finisher role is to ensure perfection in execution and meticulous adherence to controls, standards and system requirements. When tasks require close attention, detailed scrutiny and thorough controls, the outputs of this role are most beneficial to the team. People acting as Completer-Finishers struggle with delegation and are often preoccupied with order, detail and schedules. Their focus on detail sometime leads them to forget the overall objectives. They can become tense and anxious as they are preoccupied with thoughts of what could go wrong and how the team could be jeopardised. The team benefits from people in this role because they are key in the completion stages, and like to bring tasks to conclusion on time and ensure that projects are completed as well as possible.

People

The final cluster consists of roles that focus on interpersonal relationships (i.e. people); the three roles in this category are coordinator/chairperson, resource-investigator and teamworker.

Coordinator/Chairperson

This team member is someone who clarifies goals and objectives, allocates responsibilities and duties, and displays self-confidence and positive thinking. The objective of a coordinator/chairperson is to control and organise, and they are helpful to teams in the manner in which they allocate and direct resources.

As natural organisers and coordinators they fill the role of clarifying objectives and setting the agenda. It is easy for them to keep fellow members following the team's deadlines and milestones, controlling the achievement and performance of the team. They stand out in the way they coordinate colleagues' actions and how they take responsibility to identify weaknesses and build on strengths. People who enact the role of coordinator present as emotionally stable, calm and assertive, and tend to be good supervisors and delegators. As good communicators these people do not dominate, but rather assist members to fulfil their potential and help them to do what they can do best. They are able to balance interpersonal demands with the challenges of the workplace.

Resource investigator

This team member has perfectionist tendencies, focuses on detail and introduces external information including negotiation with outsiders. Their main aim is to explore alternatives, find new ways of doing things and evaluate resources. They excel as networkers and often provide the team with contacts in the external environment. They are inquisitive, positive and relaxed, and are often prepared to help individuals and other teams. Resource investigators are able to find and utilise human resources, innovative ideas, and material to the benefit of the team. However, resource investigators are known to leave some tasks and initiatives incomplete and to "jump" from one area of focus to the next without "closing the deal".

Team worker

This describes a sensitive and team-oriented individual who gives personal support and help to others. Such people are easy to work with and are the natural "helpers" in a team; the ones you can depend on and whose doors always stand open to other colleagues. Their biggest contribution is to support members, to build on others' ideas and to foster team spirit. They are admired for their humility, assistance and encouragement, and they are popular members of the team. They are sometimes perceived as too soft and too accommodating. They are conscientious and the well-being of the team and its members is their foremost priority. They are loyal, easy to get along with and stable. They are "peacemakers" whose benefit comes to the fore when "times are tough" and teams are facing challenges. In such scenarios they rally the troops, get morale up and focus on the tasks at hand.

Tips for team leaders

Some team roles are more helpful at certain stages of the team's development and the leader may utilise such roles at the appropriate stage of development. For example "plants" are best utilised early on in a team's life while a "completer-finisher" may be best deployed towards the end of a project. It is helpful to assist members in understanding their preferences and to adjust functional work to be aligned with team roles. Team roles may have to be adjusted according to the needs of the team, and willingness of members to understand each other's preferences may help the team in allocating resources optimally. A major weakness of the theory is that balance is not clearly defined and it is not clear what type of balance is needed for different types of teams and situations. It is not clear if all team roles contribute equally to team performance and success.

Representation

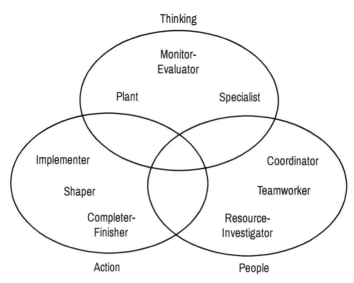

Figure 7.1: Belbin's team roles

References

Belbin, R.M. (2004). *Management teams: Why they succeed or fail* (2nd ed.). Oxford, UK: Butterworth-Heinemann.

32 | Margerison and McCann's team management profile

Introduction

Margerison and McCann identified "key work functions" that they argued are needed in a well-balanced and effective team. These are discussed as generic tasks (see Section 39 Team Tasks). The researchers then looked for the relationship between individuals' preferences for certain types of work and the various tasks, from which they identified eight team roles.

In a nutshell

Eight team roles are identified, namely reporter-advisor, creator-innovator, explorer-promoter, assessor-developer, thruster-organisor, concluder-producer, controller-inspector, and upholder-maintainer.

Purpose

To emphasise that team members prefer different roles.

To indicate how teams can maximise these preferences.

To balance teams according to team roles.

To link individual preferences to team tasks.

Description

Margerison and McCann identified "key work functions" that they believe are needed in a well-balanced and effective team. The researchers then found a correlation between individuals' preference for certain types of work and the various tasks. By adapting the work of Jung to the environment of work they determined four dimensions of personality that different individuals prefer:

- Relationships: how do you prefer to relate to others? The authors here made use of the differences between extraversion and introversion, as they believed that relationships are influenced and maintained by this use of energy.

- Information: how do you prefer to gather and use information at work? People differ in the manner they prefer to gather and use data. Some people are practical and like concrete information while, others prefer to generate information, find out new ways of doing things and be innovative.

- Decisions: how do you prefer to make decisions at work? People are driven by differences in their preference for analytical, logical decision-making or more belief- and value-based decision-making.

- Organisation: how do you prefer to organise yourself and others at work? This refers to whether people prefer structured or flexible work environments, and how they organise their worlds accordingly.

They went on to identify eight roles that team members fulfil whilst operating in a team.

Reporter-Advisor

The preference of persons who play this role is to gather and share information, and they tend to be supporters and helpers. They are knowledgeable and want to ensure that the information available to the team is correct and valuable, and that everyone is as informed as possible. They like it when the decisions of the team are based on solid information and their forte is therefore to produce and accumulate data and to synthesise it so that it is useful to the team.

Creator-Innovator

The person in this role is often the source of innovation and creativity. They are not scared to think out of the box, challenge convention and bring new ideas to the team. They may interrupt the traditional way things are done and excel when they feel their ideas are valued and that they have freedom to express them. They are imaginative, future-oriented and comfortable with complexity and challenge. They are independent thinkers who like to push the issue and enjoy developing their own ideas.

Explorer-Promoter

They are the persuaders and like fast-paced, stimulating work environments. They are often energisers with an influential and outgoing focus. They are "broad picture", "grand scheme" people whose benefit to teams is their ability to explore contacts, potential and challenges external to the team. As motivators and persuaders they are able to inspire colleagues to see the way forward as the team pursues its vision. They are classically the ones who are able to see beyond the horizon and will challenge members in the team to look for opportunities beyond the current and everyday slog of the task at hand. Members preferring this role tend to be persuasive, influential and outgoing, and like tasks involving the investigation and presentation of new opportunities.

Assessor-Developer

This role is characterised by an analytical and reasoned approach to work; these people tend to be practical. They can see possibilities, but like to make them workable and realistic. They want to go beyond the idea and the grand scheme to see how the ideas can come to fruition. They prefer work that involves planning to ensure the feasibility of ideas, and they tend to be analytical, objective and experimenting.

Thruster-Organiser

These are people who are spurred on by action, performance and getting results. They want to go beyond discussion, ideas and experiments and be actively involved in the production and completion of the work. They like to organise and implement, are quick in their decision-making processes and want things to be completed. They excel in setting up systems where the value of the process can be tracked. They can take ideas of others in the team and make them work more efficiently and effectively through planning, organising and scheduling. They are energised when they see their actions materialise into something concrete.

Concluder-Producer

These people like to work to a set standard, according to schedules and procedures, and also like to produce things. They tend to be more traditional in the way they set up work and like to see that their contribution and skills are utilised optimally. They are comfortable working according to rigorous and tried and tested procedures to ensure results. As concluders, they are helpful in the final stages of a project to ensure the final touches are complete.

Controller-Inspector

The key characteristic of people in this role is their emphasis on control. They like to control, inspect and audit work processes to ensure that the team operates at optimal levels of efficiency and effectiveness. They are detail-oriented and like to work to strict standards and procedures. They display a limited need for people and are often quite happy to remain on their own and complete tasks involving small detail and facts. They are meticulous and conscientious and will ensure that facts and figures are correct. They can devote long periods of work to in-depth work.

Upholder-Maintainer

This person enjoys taking care of both human and technical systems. They are often adept at keeping the balance between the human and physical needs of the team and hold definite views on the key demands on the team to ensure its effectiveness. They are often a source of strength and support to the team. Such peope tend to be conservative, loyal, supportive and ethical.

Linker

The Team Management Profile also describes a linking role of being at the hub of the 'wheel' and claim that ideally this is the role of all team members because they are all expected to help link, through communication, their own personal roles with the personal roles of other team members. Linking often becomes the responsibility of a leader in a team, although the theory holds that leaders also act according to their own role preferences.

The authors identified six people skills, five task skills and two further general skills that are required for linkers to be effective. The people skills are:

- communication: effective communication is regarded as a key team component and clear channels of communication are particularly relevant to build trust;

- active listening: clearly indicating a willingness to listen and to understand the viewpoint of other team members;

- good team relationships: built on mutual trust and respect;

- problem-solving and counselling: this relates to the availability of members of the team to help and to find solutions when problems arise;

- participative decision-making: this is about involving all stakeholders in the decision-making process to ensure optimal outcomes and to promote ownership of solutions; and

- interface management: by this term the authors mean the role leaders play in linking the team with its external environment.

The task skills of the linker role are:

- work allocation: assignment and alignment of specific members of the team to specific tasks according to the skills set of the particular member;

- team development: developing the competencies and preferences of members that facilitate good team performance;

- delegation: the process of coaching and mentoring individuals on the team to allow them to develop new skills and competencies and to facilitate their journey to excellence;

- setting of objectives: to read helps the team to build confidence and a sense of achievement as they reach the outcomes required by each goal; and

- quality standards: the linker helps to define standards that meet the requirements of the client.

The two general skills are of a different type from the rest. The authors maintained that the manner in which they are used determines the effectiveness of the team. These two skills are:

- motivation: this concept is slightly different from the more general view of motivation. It refers specifically to the sense of confidence and subsequent motivation that members find when they consider that their leader is fighting for them and is prepared to take a stand in their interests when controversial issues arise; and

- strategic thinking: the ability to analyse situations clearly and correctly and to guide the team towards appropriate strategic (re-)positioning in the face of challenges.

Tips for team leaders

The instrument is very helpful in assisting teams to ascertain their composition and balance. It also helps teams to determine which of the different tasks required for teams to be effective are addressed. It is particularly successful as a leadership development tool and gives people valuable insight into their behaviour and preferences. The tool is often used as a teambuilding intervention as it allows members to learn from one another and gives insight into how balance in the team could be used to improve performance. According to the theory it is important to remember that the team needs to be balanced in the distribution of roles according to the task and purpose of the team. Thus, the goals and outputs required of the team should guide decisions on how to balance the team according to team roles. Furthermore, it is not necessary that all the roles are present in the team, but the preferences associated with each role must be performed by someone. The authors added that team members have a predominant role preference, but also display characteristics of up to two supportive roles. This requires a balance of roles in that the team members need to take responsibility and ensure that all the tasks required (see generic tasks) are covered. It is not imperative that all the roles be represented by particular individuals; if some roles are not present then the team has to make an extra effort to ensure that the tasks associated with the 'missing' roles are covered by members jointly.

Representation

Figure 7.2: Team management profile

References

Gordon, J. (2002). A Perspective on Team Building. *Journal of American Academy of Business,* 2(1), 185–188.

Margerison, C. & McCann, D. (1996). *Team management: Practical new approaches.* Chalford: Management Books.

33 | # Kets de Vries' archetypes

Introduction

Another approach to roles is that defined by Kets de Vries, which identifies what he termed "leadership archetypes". He described the purpose of these archetypes as helping leaders to define their style in order to balance a team, to determine the best roles for each team member, and to create teams best suited to meet specific challenges. The approach is based on personal preferences and requires the team to be balanced and informed on how to deal with team members with different preferences.

In a nutshell

Eight archetypes, namely strategist, change-catalyst, transactor, builder, innovator, processor, coach and communicator.

Purpose

To help members understand the archetype they prefer.

To balance the team.

To find the best role for a team member to play in a team.

Description

The Leadership Archetype Questionnaire was designed to assess which of the following archetypes best describe a leader or team member.

Strategist

Strategists focus on external environments to the team (and organisation) and help to set its vision and strategic direction. As a metaphor they can be seen as viewing leadership as a game of chess. Being skilled in observation, "connecting the dots" and seeing patterns, they are good at dealing with developments in the organisation's environment. They provide vision, strategic direction and out-of-the-box thinking to create new organisational forms and generate future growth. They are good at abstract, imaginative thinking and presenting different options. They can simplify complex situations and excel in finding new ways through unconventional thinking.

Change-catalyst

This archetype is characterised by the ability to find order in messy and fuzzy situations and excels in creating new blueprints and templates. These people thrive in complex and volatile environments and excel at "re-engineering and creating new organizational 'blueprints'". They are skilled at recognising opportunities or selling the need for change. They can make abstract concepts practical and are good at implementation. They are prepared to take on risky assignments and challenges and their sense of urgency allows them to make difficult decisions. They possess the ability to align vision, strategy and behaviour, and are comfortable setting standards and monitoring performance.

Transactor

Transactors are good at finding new opportunities, negotiating, and tackling new challenges. They are good deal-makers and excel in identifying opportunities. They do particularly well in complex environments where their negotiation skills are optimised. They have a natural preference for novelty, adventure and exploration. They embrace change and the demands of day-to-day management are onerous to them. They display great tolerance for risk and their enthusiasm and dynamism make them proactive. They often display a need to accumulate wealth and have great adaptive capacity.

Builder

This archetype describes people who are focused and determined and have the ability to make their dreams come true through their development efforts and determined work. They view leadership as an entrepreneurial endeavour. They like to build new opportunities and have the drive to make them come true. They display a need to be in control, to act independently and to make their own way. They show great drive and energy, and display single-mindedness and perseverance. They are decisive and able to endure in insecure and ambiguous circumstances, where their capacity to thrive under pressure suits them well. They have a long-term focus in what they do, display high achievement orientation and high, but calculated risk-taking propensity. They are able to convince others to buy into their dreams and are motivated to create something. They sometimes lack the required social skills and may display difficulties in dealing with authority.

Innovator

These natural innovators excel in finding new ideas, ventures and opportunities, and like to find solutions to problems. They are energetic and driven to pursue their ideas and display creativity and imagination in looking for future possibilities. They enjoy challenges, excel in trying to solve complex problems and strive for "stretch goals" at whatever needs to be accomplished. They are at times eccentric, are not driven by financial gain and can be ineffective in communication. They have a long-term view of personal success and show perseverance and endurance to succeed in what they set themselves to do.

Processor

The processor archetype puts systems, structures and order in place to ensure the smooth functioning of the team. They are determined to establish efficiency and view the team or organisation as a well-oiled machine. They are adept in finding practical action in complex situations and can simplify difficult situations. They provide structural or process boundaries and since they do not operate well in unstructured contexts, they set forth to create rules, procedures and systems to facilitate order and structure. They adhere to rules and procedures and keep to what is required from them. They are good team members and show loyalty and commitment to team members and the organisation. They are good networkers and have a natural ability to be persuasive and to get people to see different perspectives.

Coaches

They are focused on team members and their well-being, and contribute towards getting the best out of people on the team. They are key to creating a high performing culture. They display empathetic behaviour, are good listeners and inspire trust. They enjoy it when people cooperate and excel at handling interpersonal relationships. They are great motivators, can give feedback and since they have good communication skills, they help the team to create a collaborative and high-performance culture. They are good delegators, have a positive outlook and are adept at facilitating and driving change initiatives.

Communicators

Communicators are good influencers, impact their environment, can spur followers on and view leadership as a stage. They are excellent at communicating broad themes and presenting the big picture. They have a natural way with language and through story, metaphor and theatrical skills can be persuasive and motivating. They are focused on the broader parts of plans and through their networking ability they can influence others. They are able to use experts well and are very good at managing the stakeholders of the team.

Tips for team leaders

Each person has a preference for a particular archetype, but may display characteristics of more than one. The task of the leader is to find a balance of roles. Leaders can use the Leadership Archetype Questionnaire (LAQ) to assess which archetype best describes a person.

Representation

Archetype	Description of archetype
The Strategist	Leadership as a game of chess
The Change-Catalyst	Leadership as a turnaround activity
The Transactor	Leadership as deal-making
The Builder	Leadership as an entrepreneurial activity
The Innovator	Leadership as creative idea generation
The Processor	Leadership as an exercise in efficiency
The Coach	Leadership as a form of people development
The Communicator	Leadership as stage management

Figure 7.3: Kets de Vries' archetypes

References

Kets de Vries, M.F.R. (2007). Decoding the Team Conundrum: The Eight Roles Executives Play. *Organizational Dynamics*, 36(1), 28–44.

Kets de Vries, M.F.R. (2011). *The hedgehog effect: The secrets of building high performance teams.* London: Wiley.

34 Team role knowledge

Introduction

Roles are used in teams to facilitate the execution of internal tasks, to manage a team's relationship with its external context, and to meet the interpersonal and socio-emotional needs of its members. Where other perspectives on team roles are based on the personalities of the members, Mumford, Van Iddekinge, Morgeson and Campion had a different perspective. They proposed that what they called "team role knowledge" be used to align roles with team contexts and situations. By "team role knowledge" they meant the knowledge a member of a team possesses about the palette of roles and the situational contingencies that determine their use. They extended role theory by indicating the specific contexts in which each of the roles contributes optimally.

In a nutshell

Ten different roles, namely contractor, creator, contributor, completer, critic, co-operator, communicator, calibrator, consul and coordinator.

Purpose

To help team members occupy preferred and different roles.

To build on previous experience and the propensity of members to define roles.

To optimise talent.

To align team situations with role preferences.

Description

Ten different roles are described which are grouped into three clusters, namely task, social, and boundary-spanning roles.

Task roles

The first cluster focuses on how the team gets its work done and how it is organised to ensure it delivers on its goals. Five roles are distinguished and are described here.

Contractor

This role focuses on the task behaviours of the team. A contractor prefers to organise and coordinate the actions of the team, allocating tasks, setting deadlines and putting systems in place to sequence tasks and organise workflow. They motivate and mobilise team members to achieve team goals and keep track of progress with achieving goals. They focus on task issues, keep track of progress and assure team members that their time spent on team tasks is used efficiently and that it is worthwhile to continue.

In the team context, this role is optimal in situations where there is work ambiguity and uncertainty about the work to be done or the strategies required to perform. It is particularly relevant where tasks are technically complex, or where members are inexperienced or have not worked together very long.

Creator

These people are initiators who can structure processes and strategies at the start of a team through introducing change in the current modus operandi or by setting new directions. They can articulate new and novel ideas, are able to provide compelling visions of what the team has to do, and can use goals to energise the team. They are able to "reframe" the objectives and vision of the team as well as what is required to achieve that by looking at the bigger picture. They provide creative solutions to the problems the team is facing and their vision of the future provides motivation to the team.

In teams, creators come into their own in situations of creative or strategic stagnation, where the team needs creativity and innovation to recharge. They are best utilised where members have little task experience, where the purpose is unclear, and where current strategy is not meeting demands. They are particularly helpful at the beginning (formation) of a team and during the midpoint transition.

Contributor

People that enact this role prefer to contribute critical information or expertise to the team. They tend to be assertive in their area of expertise yet they are prepared to share this knowledge with the team. They may engage in self-promotion in an effort to establish credibility and credentials in the team. Their strength lies in their ability to articulate members' abilities, resources and responsibilities, and they are willing to train and develop other members as well as the team in general. They possess unique expertise that puts them in a comfortable position in the team, yet they are willing to share that with others.

In the team context, the contributor is most effective in situations where distributed expertise is needed and tasks are heterogeneously distributed among the team, particularly when the work requires choice and (autonomous) decision-making and team members have little experience of working together. Situations where there are high status differentials also provide an opportunity for contributors to provide the expertise aligned with this role.

Completer

This role is associated with behaviours that are individual-oriented and focused on execution and implementation. Sometimes this involves preparatory work to facilitate the effective completion of tasks, e.g. preparing for team meetings. Completers are keen to volunteer to take personal responsibility to complete tasks and help others to complete their work. They are willing to follow through on commitments made within the team.

An individual-oriented setting is best suited to completers, in particular when there are tasks to be executed by individuals working alone outside the team environment. When the allocation of tasks and roles within the team has been completed and a clear line of sight exists in terms of what everyone must do, this role becomes valuable.

Critic

The critic is prepared to go against the flow, to counter-act and to reflect critically on actions, processes and goals. Their main contribution to optimum team functioning is to contribute critical evaluation and scrutiny. They question the purpose or actions of the team or ideas. Their critical and examining inclination make them valuable to evaluate "worst case scenarios," point out flaws in current thinking and signpost assumptions the team is making. Since reflection and questioning come easily to critics, they are willing to put forward counter-arguments, deal with negative information, and challenge leadership on the functioning and expectations of the team.

The team context best suited for this role is described as unscrutinised concurrence. This describes situations where the team is approaching consensus or finalising a decision without adequate analysis of positive and negative contingencies, critical reflection or required evaluation. This occurs when a team is seeking concurrence prematurely, where there are high levels of trust and cohesion. This role is particularly useful with decision-making tasks, in situations of technical and/or social complexity, and when a team is insulated or in stressed circumstances.

Social roles

The next cluster consists of co-operator, communicator and calibrator, who between them effectively manage interpersonal processes to ensure success and maintain the social environment in which teams function.

Cooperator

This role is characterised by an ability and preparedness to conform to team goals, decisions and operations. Cooperators conform to the expectations and influence attempts of the leader and other members, and work to align the team to the goals of the organisation. It can be seen as a proactive and critical role where willingness to conform does not come without scrutiny, but once established it facilitates alignment with and support for the aims of the team. Once cooperators have made the decision to conform, cooperate and align and have provided input and buy-in, they are sources of energy to drive the team forward.

The authors defined the context that this role is best suited for as "scrutinised concurrence", that is, situations in which the team has critically evaluated a decision and determined its merits. This happens when there is adequate differentiation before seeking concurrence and where the nature of the tasks are "negotiation" oriented. When tasks require distributed expertise and where high status differentials exist the cooperator helps the team to act as supporter and collaborator.

Communicator

This role helps the team to create a social environment that is conducive to collaboration, support and interaction. Communicators are empathetic and pay attention to the feelings of others while listening to their opinions and contributions. They are good communicators and have a calming influence in conflict situations and when things get tough. They have a subtle style of influence and prefer to be on good terms with everyone on the team.

Where social sensitivities abound, the communicator facilitates interactional processes and helps the team in its collaborative efforts. Especially where the team needs to negotiate task, where tasks demands are complex and the context is emotionally demanding or stressful, it is helpful to use the communicator role. The role can also be applied effectively where diversity levels in terms of attitudes and values reveal fault lines.

Calibrator

This role focuses on team process issues instead of task issues and involves overt action to create new norms for the team to deal with such issues. Calibrators may try to intervene and initiate discussion to solve power struggles, deal with tensions or settle disputes in the team. The role also includes behaviour to obtain feedback and evaluation of effort and pass that on to the team. Calibrators summarise the state of the team in terms of relationships and gauge performance levels. They observe social processes, raise awareness thereof and suggest changes to align them with functional social norms.

This role is most needed in circumstances where there are non-functional processes and/or where functional patterns of social interaction have not been established or where they have been disrupted. When team members are new to each other or have not worked together for long periods of time, the calibrator is effective. If members do not have shared experiences or where there are changes in team composition and subsequent disturbances in norms and behaviours, teams need the skills of a calibrator. They are particularly useful if there is emotional or task-based conflict, distrust, or the context is socially demanding.

Boundary-spanning roles

Based on the understanding that teams are embedded in larger systems, two roles (consul and coordinator) are identified here.

Consul

This role is focused on external relations. The consul collects the information and resources needed by the team. As representatives of the team, they present the team, its goals, interests and performance in a good light to external stakeholders and other relevant parties. In particular they attempt to influence perceptions, views and expectations regarding team success.

The consul unlocks external resources and so works best where a team is dependent on such resources. This could be physical resources, but extends to include support, information or staff. It seems that the role is particularly beneficial to teams that are new, somewhat experimental, and where constituents need status updates.

Coordinator

Coordinators are involved in interactions that take place primarily outside the team setting. The role acts on the interdependence needs of the team and facilitates its contact with external stakeholders. They interface with constituents of the team and coordinate the team's interactions with other parties. In particular they solicit feedback from the external context regarding the team's performance levels.

Situations that emphasise and require external activity interdependence are where this boundary-spanning role is best suited. Where activities of the team must be coordinated with those of other stakeholders outside the team, and specifically when the team is interdependent with activities of other teams, this role succeeds.

Tips for team leaders

One of the biggest benefits of this approach is the link the authors make to the contexts in which the identified roles are most helpful. This view of teams allows members to expand their respective "role repertoires" and adjust and adapt to changing and complex environments.

Representation

Task roles	Social roles	Boundary
Contractor Creator Contributor Completer Critic	Co-operator Communicator Calibrator	Consul Coordinator

Figure 7.4: Team role knowledge

References

Mumford, T.V., Campion, M.A. & Morgeson, F.P. (2006). Situational judgment in work teams: A team role typology. In J.A. Weekley & R.E. Ployhart (eds.). *Situational judgment tests: Theory, measurement, and application*. Mahwah, NJ: Erlbaum.

Mumford, T.V., Van Iddekinge, C.H., Morgeson, F.P. & Campion, M.A. (2008). The Team Role Test: Development and Validation of a Team Role Knowledge Situational Judgment Test, *Journal of Applied Psychology Association*, 93(2), 250 –267.

35 | Lessem's integrators

Introduction

A further model that can be used to understand roles in teams is the integrated model offered by Lessem. The theory builds on the concept that each individual displays a particular combination of their cognitive, emotional and behavioural faculties. Different people tend to focus on one of these more than the others, and the dominance of the preferred function in relation to the other two creates a unique behavioural set associated with the preference. In teams, these can be regarded as team roles.

In a nutshell

Eight roles: innovator, developmental, analytical, enterprising, change, people, action and adopter.

Purpose

To explain various team roles.

To allow members to enact their preferred roles.

To generate balance in a team.

To optimise team members' preferences.

Description

This model presents a cast of eight personality types derived from the mix of cognitive, emotional and behavioural faculties found in each person. Each of these roles is assigned a colour.

The innovator (violet)

This team member is very creative and innovative, with the ability to seemingly create something out of nothing. They excel through employing their powerful and expressive imagination to find solutions to problems and to inspire team members. They can craft an inspirational dream, often in vivid, graphic detail, of the state of the team once its vision has been completed. However, they are often perceived to be lonely and idiosyncratic, which can lead them to be isolated and withdrawn in a team if they feel they are not valued and understood.

Developmental manager (indigo)

Developmental managers are able to see value in complexity and diversity and have the ability to balance the demands of the environment to the benefit of the team. This manager thrives on cooperation and interdependence and seeks to optimise the contribution of each member as it relates to the outcomes of the team. They are true harmonisers who enjoy developing colleagues and processes alike, and their contribution is through insight, breadth of exposure and the ability to hold equilibrium.

Analytical manager (blue)

This role enjoys bureaucracy and is the classical manager. They work well in environments that are stable, orderly and certain. They are objective, able to take distance and prone to being perceived as impersonal. They struggle with complexity and volatility in the environment and prefer to follow well-laid plans than having to deal with constant change. Regarded as a source of stability and order in the team, they prefer to be in leadership positions where authority, responsibility and rules can be enforced. They are good organisers that excel in keeping the team on their set goal paths and helping them to keep to milestones.

Enterprising manager (green)

These managers are proactive and constantly on the move, seeking new opportunities and challenges. They enjoy the rough and tumble of organisational life and thrive on risk and challenge. They tend to be "larger than life" characters who can be perceived as overbearing by some members. They love action and are energised through efforts to meet deadlines and challenging demands, though often in order to serve their own individual needs. They are attracted to influence and power and are prepared to go to great lengths to retain that in a team.

Manager of change (yellow)

This role characteristically emphasises intellectual ability rather than emotional or practical foci. To them a mentally stimulating environment is of key importance and they prefer professional development to tangible reward. They enjoy working in diverse environments and naturally involve the external environment (network and sphere of influence) to solve problems in the team. They are prone to resisting authority and become (intellectually) argumentative when they feel they are not considered or valued for their contribution.

People manager (orange)

Team members in this role are naturally sociable and warm. They enjoy working with people, are able to understand other people's emotions and are sensitive to the needs of others. To them cooperation is a key word. They consider good relationships to be essential and learn by interacting with others. Leaders who are people orientated have confidence in themselves. In team situations this role can become too focused on being nice to others, or alternatively lead to "us-them" or "clique-ish" behaviour.

Action manager (red)

Action orientated leaders are decisive, energetic and act fast. They can jump from one idea to the next without hesitation and value deeds more than words. The ways in which they process ideas are pragmatic and to the point. Action orientated leaders are indeed quick thinkers, but in the same breath, can be impatient. They thrive when being challenged and they take pleasure in moving ahead. They are productive, efficient and respond well to change. They benefit from feedback and work well when given objectives and clear expectations. These leaders value experience and are performance driven.

Adopter manager (grey)

These people immerse themselves in the team to such an extent that they take on the identity of the team completely. They become totally subordinated to the team and unselfish in the manner they strive to be available for the team. They are natural followers and will go to great ends to do what a leader requires and what is demanded by the team, both interpersonally and operationally.

Tips for team leaders

Team leaders need to look for a balance of roles and allow for each member to operate by using his or her preferred role. The framework is helpful to team leaders in the way it explains variety in preferences. Members can then be utilised according to their preferences to the benefit of the team.

Representation

Role	Colour	Description of role
Innovator	Violet	Creative and innovative and able to create something out of nothing
Developmental	Indigo	Sees value in complexity and diversity; balances contextual demands
Analytical	Blue	Classical manager that likes stability, order and certainty
Enterprising	Green	Often a "larger than life" character that loves action and challenge
Change	Yellow	Prefers intellectually stimulating environments and challenges
People	Orange	Sociable and warm and likes to work with people; empathetic
Action	Red	Decisive, energetic and fast; likes action
Adopter	Grey	Merges with team and takes on identity of the team

Figure 7.5: Lessem's integrators

Reference

Lessem, R. (2016). *The integrators: The next evolution in leadership, knowledge and value creation*. London: Routledge.

8

TEAM TASKS

In designing a team it is helpful to understand the various elements of team tasks as well. First a classification system of team tasks is presented as proposed by McGrath. She contended that tasks can be categorised to reflect four basic processes, namely generating, choosing, negotiating and executing. This classification system is positioned on a circumplex with two axes; one reflecting the extent to which a particular task requires cognitive versus behavioural performance, and the other whether the task is cooperative or conflictual. In the next part, attention is given to how teams can formulate their tasks. Tasks are differentiated according to various attributes, and in addition certain principles for formulating tasks are presented. Guidelines include systems with mnemonics such as SMART(ER) and POSERS. This is followed by a theory of behavioural processes that determine tasks. These behavioural processes are clustered in three sets, namely action, transition and interpersonal processes. In a different vein, Margerison and McCann identified generic tasks that all teams have to complete and execute to ensure optimal performance. In the last part of this section, the Job Characteristics Model of Hackman and Oldham is described. This is an organisational behaviour classic and has shown its enduring quality by being as popular now as when it was first proposed. The authors contended that core job characteristics influence critical psychological states in workers, which in turn affects personal and work outcomes. They also associated particular task characteristics with particular psychological states.

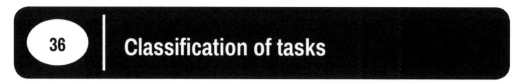

36 | # Classification of tasks

Introduction

This section presents the classic system of McGrath for differentiating between the tasks that members fulfil.

In a nutshell

To classify tasks using a circumplex.

Purpose

To design individual members' tasks to optimise performance.

To structure team tasks to maximise opportunity to deliver on what the team requires.

To use a classification system for various tasks.

To help teams design their taskwork.

Description

McGrath postulated that tasks can be categorised into four basic processes. They are described as:

- generate: tasks that require generation of ideas like brainstorming, finding new solutions, being innovative and setting agendas;

- choose: in this case the task requires some intellective or judgement components where a correct answer needs to be found and where consensus is needed among the team;

- negotiate: this type of task requires resolution of conflicting viewpoints; and

- execute: a task that requires physical movement, coordination, or dexterity is regarded as representative of this type.

Task circumplex

McGrath went further to view the classification of tasks as if positioned on a circumplex with two axes. The horizontal axis reflects the degree to which the task requires cognitive versus behavioural performance. Tasks that require a choice between two or more options are positioned at the cognitive end of the spectrum. When a task requires execution it is positioned on the behavioural end of the spectrum. The vertical axis shows the degree to which tasks are cooperative (at the top of the axis) or conflictual (at the bottom of the aixs). Co-ordinated tasks are positioned in the middle of the spectrum. The distinction between these three options is made according to the level of diversity in perspectives, interests and alternatives. Thus, tasks that require generation are seen to be more collaborative, while negotiation is required when resolution needs to be found for a conflict situation. This then allows for each of the tasks to be positioned in terms of whether it is cognitive or behavioural, and in terms of the degree of cooperation, coordination or conflict resolution it requires. Eight task descriptions are therefore possible.

Creativity tasks

Collaborative or cooperative tasks where no single solution is required, but every member can make a contribution to find alternatives or new ideas. A good example is brainstorming tasks where collaborative and cooperative efforts are needed, but no single correct option exists and members' contributions are not evaluated. There is little requirement for interdependence and each idea increases the group's collective effort.

Planning tasks

Here collaboration is required and the manner in which the planning of behaviours is carried out is highlighted. An example is setting an agenda. These are still in the creative domain, but are also more executive as on a behavioural level outcomes are expected.

Psychomotor tasks

These are tasks that require physical execution and include associated behaviours, execution and performance.

Contests or battles

Tasks that fall in this category aim to resolve conflicts of power such as contests, competition and adversarial behaviour, including resolution of challenges, debates and conflicts of opinion.

Mixed-motive tasks

These types of tasks involve resolving conflicts of motive and require a high degree of negotiation between the team and members of the team.

Cognitive conflict tasks

Where there are conflicts of viewpoint or differences of opinion, resolving these is classified as a cognitive conflict task.

Judgment tasks

These tasks require deciding on issues and then choosing a preferred answer, but here discussion needs to take place between members to reach consensus, hence it is closer to the negotiate end of the vertical axis. Judgment tasks are also potentially subject to multiple and conflicting viewpoints and perspectives and the "correct" answer may not be readily available. Coordination is thus required to persuade members (in the absence of convincing factual information) to agree to a team solution. The contributions that each member makes depend, in part, on the contributions of other members.

Intellective tasks

These tasks have demonstrably correct answers and it is easy to come to agreement on the solution (through consensus or not) as the appropriate action is recognised by one or more members of the team. In principle it means that if one member of the team finds a solution it can be applied to the whole team, therefore the level of collaboration is limited and merely coordination is required. In these cases one answer is correct and once agreement is reached there is little debate.

Tips for team leaders

It is helpful for leaders to define clearly what the task of each individual on the team is and to ensure the responsibility of the task is assigned to a team member. Once this is done the characteristics of tasks as defined here can help to optimise the manner in which members respond to what had been assigned to them.

Representation

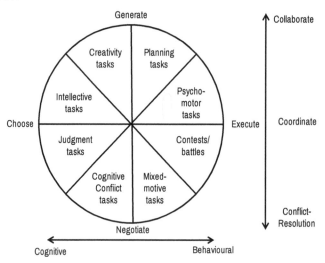

Figure 8.1: Task circumplex

References

McGrath, J.E. (1984). *Groups: Interaction and performance*. Englewood Cliffs, NJ: Prentice Hall.

Strauss, S.G. (1999). Testing a Typology of Tasks: An Empirical Validation of McGrath's (1984) Group Task Circumplex. *Small Group Research*, 30(2), 166–187.

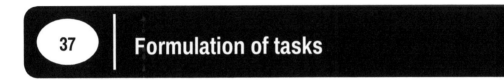

Introduction

This section focuses on the formulation of the tasks of a team. Generic task attributes are discussed first, followed by approaches to defining the particular tasks the team has to fulfil. A properly defined set of tasks helps the team to ensure that members stay committed and that their knowledge, skills and abilities are utilised to the optimum. It is important to note that these factors are driven by individual team member needs as well as what the team needs to deliver and produce.

In a nutshell

Attributes of team tasks and methods for defining team tasks.

Purpose

To design individual members' tasks to optimise performance.

To structure team tasks to maximise opportunity to deliver on what the team requires.

To help the team define its tasks.

To assist in focusing effort on key tasks.

Description

The task attributes that should be considered when designing team tasks are presented first, whereafter principles and methods of formulating tasks are described.

Attributes of tasks

Tasks can be conceptualised in terms of various attributes and understanding these attributes can help the team leader in allocating tasks to team members.

- Variety: this refers to the degree to which a particular team task requires a range of of activities, and as a consequence requires the team member to apply a range of skills and talents to complete the task. In this regard, allowing different members to do different tasks could expand the skills base of team members, reduce boredom and allow for flexibility where members can substitute for one another.

- Difficulty: some tasks are easy and do not take a lot of effort, while others are more difficult and require extreme levels of skill. The level of difficulty of the different tasks influences the allocation of resources, human and other.

- Expected occurrence: some tasks the team needs to complete are standard and can be expected, which enables the team to be prepared for what is expected of them.

- Complexity: some tasks can be complex in terms of number of outcomes, levels of abstraction, number of stakeholders and difficulty of the challenges. The levels of complexity that many managers deal with are increasingly high in executive teams.

- Tempo: this variable refers to the length of time it takes to complete tasks. It also includes contextual constraints that can influence the completion of tasks, such as when a hold-up occurs because paint has to dry, chemical processes must take hold or when safety concerns dictate time limits.

- Significance: the level of impact a particular task has on other members of the team. This relates to the level of interdependence of tasks (see Section 75). Some teams are highly dependent on the impact of each other's actions because of the integrated nature of what they are doing.

- Relevance: teams sometimes have to complete tasks that are not directly relevant to their own production outcomes, but serve purposes beyond that of the team, e.g. attend a culture workshop. These tasks are key for the team's organisational alignment, but in some cases can inhibit the performance of the team or delay outcomes.

- Identity: some tasks are in themselves a whole job, while others are only an identifiable part thereof.

- Episodic tasks versus repeatable tasks: some tasks are once-off while other tasks are repeated more than once or over and over again.

- Demonstrability: some teams need to deliver on a task that is defined and no deviation from the blueprint expected of the team is allowed. Think of a project team that has to deliver an architect's plan of a building. There is one correct way and the team has to deliver. On the other hand, some teams operate where more than one alternative exists and the team could execute one or more thereof. Examples are a problem-solving team, a consulting team or a management team searching for a solution to a problem. These teams execute a non-demonstrable task, in that it is not known in advance what they are going to do.

Principles of formulating tasks

Tasks can also be defined in terms of what is expected of them as objectives. In this regard tasks need to be:

- Individualised: the team member that is supposed to deliver the task should be clearly stated and the individual effort required to accomplish the task documented. Tasks should be allocated to specific members or where that is not possible, it must be clear that it is a collective responsibility;

- Specific: the outcome must be specific and concrete with a clear description of what constitutes the task and the successful outcome thereof. This helps members to be clear on exactly what they are responsible for, which makes it easier for them to be optimal in what they have to deliver. On the other hand, if the tasks are not specified clearly members can find it difficult to know what is required of them and in the confusion on role clarity work can be left out;

- Measurable: criteria to measure task performance include quality, quantity, cost-effectiveness and timeliness;

- Quality: the expected level of performance according to agreed standards or norms must be indicated;

- Quantity: a number that is required to be performed provides clear objectives and should be specified;

- Cost-effectiveness: the relationship between the outcomes that are expected and the costs associated with their delivery;

- Timeliness: Tasks need to be delivered at a particular time and according to plans and schedules; and

- Aligned with available resources: In addition, the physical resources, financial resources and human capital required for any task should be stated.

Task description

Action plans are described by formulating the outcome in one sentence and making it concrete and realistic. Three different sets of guidelines have been offered in the literature to help teams to describe their tasks. Each uses a different mnemonic, namely SMART(ER), the expanded version thereof (SMART PURE and CLEAN), and POSERS.

SMART(ER)

The original version of this tool, as proposed by Doran, was comprised of five attributes, captured by the mnemonic SMART. A later revision added "evaluate" and "review", which gave the version SMART(ER). Each of these two variants can be used by teams. Activities or tasks should be Specific, Measurable, Attainable and Realistic, and have a stated Time by when they must be completed. In addition, the team leader must be able to Evaluate the team's efforts, and Review them, that is, give feedback to the team members.

Whitmore's task description guidelines

Whitmore noted that any goal should be SMART, PURE and CLEAR, thus he extended the "SMART" requirements described above by adding two more acronyms that identify additional task descriptors.

PURE stands for:

- positive: actions should be stated in the positive and negative formulations should be avoided;

- understood: in terms of performance required and appropriately aligned with culture;

- relevant: related to the bigger goals and aims of the team; and

- ethical: structured according to the ethical norms and standards required and aligned with personal ethical points of view.

CLEAR stands for:

- challenging: the task must have an element of stretch in it to be motivating and energising;

- legal: the task must meet legal and regulatory requirements and people cannot be expected to contribute to illegal activities;

- environmentally sound: the task should fall within the ambit of and be aligned with responsible management and enterprise practices;

- appropriate: the appropriateness of a task is measured in terms of how it aligns with what the team needs to deliver; and

- recorded: a proper system where the task descriptions are recorded helps the team in its task design endeavours.

POSERS

This set of guidelines is derived from neuro-linguistic programming, but as applied here is somewhat narrower than the original intent. It is used to guide a team to formulate its tasks, not to describe a problem or help realise an objective as originally intended. The acronym POSERS refers to the following critical elements:

- Positive: actions should be stated in the positive and negative formulations should be avoided.

- Own part: each person's part of the action needs to be stated clearly.

- Specific: the outcome must be specific and concrete.

- Evidence: evidence of when and how it will be attained needs to be provided.

- Resources: resources needed should be stated.

- Size: the extent of the outcome needs to be stated.

Tips for team leaders

These tools help leaders to formulate exactly what team members have to deliver and to ensure clarity of task and responsibility.

Representation

Formulating tasks				
Attributes of tasks	Principles of formulating tasks	Task description		
		SMART(ER)	Whitmore's guidelines	POSERS
Variety Difficulty Expected occurrence Complexity Tempo Significance Relevance Identity Episodic tasks versus repeatable tasks Demonstrability	Individualised Specific Resources Measurable Quality Quantity Cost-effectiveness Timeliness	Specific Measurable Attainable Realistic Time Evaluate Review	SMART plus PURE Positive Understood Relevant Ethical CLEAR Challenging Legal Environmentally sound Appropriate Recorded	Positive Own part Specific Evidence Resources Size

Figure 8.2: Formulation of tasks

References

Doran, G.T. (1981). There's a S.M.A.R.T. Way to Write Management's Goals and Objectives. *Management Review* 70(11), 35–36.

Whitmore, J. (1996). *Coaching for performance: Growing people, performance and purpose.* London: Nicholas Brealey.

Introduction

Behavioural processes refer to "how" teams complete the tasks they have to execute. A process is an interdependent act that a team executes to convert inputs into outcomes. The manner in which team members interact with one another, how they utilise and employ resources, and the manner in which they operate independently can be viewed as the processes of a team. In their taxonomy, Marks, Mathieu and Zaccaro described ten such processes.

In a nutshell

Ten team processes clustered as action, transition and interpersonal processes.

Purpose

To highlight the temporal nature of team processes.

To facilitate understanding that processes happen in cycles.

Description

Marks, Mathieu and Zaccaro held that team processes operate in "recurring phases", i.e. the team oscillates as if on a pendulum of temporal cycles and identifiable periods of *action* (activities related directly to goal accomplishment) and *transition* (reflecting on past performance and planning for future action periods between actions). They also described *interpersonal* processes that occur throughout the lifespan of the team.

Action phase processes

This type of process occurs during periods where the team is conducting activities leading directly to goal attainment. The action phase processes they identified include monitoring processes towards goals, systems monitoring, team monitoring and back-up responses.

Monitoring progress towards goals

Three elements make up the monitoring processes employed by teams, namely tracking the process a team makes towards accomplishing its goals, interpreting information in terms of what is required to complete the tasks, and transmitting information on such progress to its members.

Systems monitoring

The tracking of team resources and environmental conditions to ascertain how any could influence the team accomplishing its goals. In particular it refers to monitoring of internal systems (e.g. staff, resources, information) and external environmental monitoring (e.g. conditions relevant to the team).

Team monitoring and back-up responses

This is when teams provide verbal feedback or coaching to members in the team to assist them to do their task; when they help one another and when they assume or complete a task on behalf of another member of the team.

Coordination

This process includes orchestrating, sequencing and timing of team member actions.

Transition phase processes

These are evaluative and/or planning periods where the team reflects on its accomplishment of the goals it set out to achieve. Three are identified, namely mission analysis, goal specification, and strategy formulation and planning.

Mission analysis

This is characterised by the team interpreting and evaluating its main tasks and mission, monitoring the operative contextual conditions and evaluating the tools and resources available to the team to deliver on its mandate.

Goal specification

Identification, articulation and prioritisation of goals to ensure accomplishment of the mission of the team.

Strategy formulation and planning

The devising of alternative courses of action to ensure accomplishment of the goals of the team. This process displays three separate dimensions, namely deliberate planning (i.e. formulation of the principle plan of action); contingency planning (i.e. design of alternative plans and strategy adjustments in the face of anticipated changes in the performance environment); and reactive strategy adjustment (i.e. the adjustment of existing strategy and plans in response to unanticipated changes).

Interpersonal processes

The last type of processes occur throughout the lifespan of the team and comprise managing conflict, managing affect, and motivating the team and building members' confidence.

Conflict management

Two types of conflict management are identified, namely pre-emptive and reactive processes. The former refers to establishing conditions to prevent, control or guide conflict prior to its occurring, while reactive conflict management is working through disagreements (either task, process or interpersonal) when they occur.

Motivating or confidence building

This refers to efforts the team takes to build cohesion and a sense of collective confidence that they can deliver on their goals.

Affect management

This refers to regulating the full range of emotions teams may experience in accomplishing their goals. These processes are structured according to the rhythm the team employs and can vary in length.

Tips for team leaders

The duration of time a team spends in each of these cycles stems from the manner in which it operates, their use of technology and the nature of its tasks, but this is a helpful tool for leaders to guide the actions of the team.

Representation

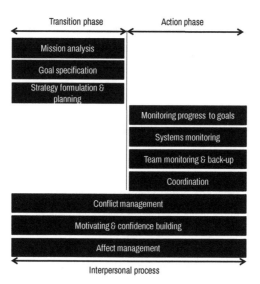

Figure 8.3: Behavioural processes

Reference

Marks, M.A., Mathieu, J.E. & Zaccaro, S.I. (2001). A Temporally Based Framework and Taxonomy of Team Processes. *Academy of Management Review*, 26(3), 356–376.

Introduction

In their analysis of what effective teams do, Australian researchers Margerison and McCann identified eight generic tasks that all teams have to complete to ensure success.

In a nutshell

Teams have to promote, develop, organise, produce, control, maintain, advise and innovate to be successful.

Purpose

To help a team evaluate how they utilise the eight generic tasks.

To help teams balance their resources.

To ensure teams address all tasks and not only those preferred by members.

To align members' inputs with generic tasks.

Description

The framework of Margerison and McCann asserts that all teams need to address eight generic tasks to be effective. These tasks underly all the direct and obvious tasks a team performs and the team needs to fulfil all of them to ensure optimum performance. The eight tasks are described here.

Advising

The term advising is somewhat confusing as it refers primarily on the task a team must fulfil to find information in its context and then to advise on this information. Thus, the team needs to gather information and data and report on these to ensure it is informed as best as it could be to react to demands, challenges and operations. This could entail scanning of the environment to ensure the team reacts to the correct stimuli from its context or to research particular topics and to be focused on particular sets of information required to inform the team. Therefore, benchmarking of other teams and what is happening in the industry environment is helpful to assist the team to be informed. The task of advising allows the team to calibrate their actions against best practice, and to be prepared for what comes from the environment and what they need to do to be prepared and to deliver on their mandate.

Innovating

This refers to the requirement that teams have to create ideas and to be innovative on what they do, how this is accomplished and how to find improvements on their performance. The team needs to find alternatives to current practices and solutions and to improve on its actions and performance. Thus, it has to experiment with new ideas and try to find ways to look beyond current practice to find alternatives. It includes the creative processes of the team and challenges the commonly perceived manner in which things are done in the team. It allows for "outside the box" thinking and aligns the team's operations to technological and other advances. It therefore requires each team to be focused on invigorating and improving its tasks.

Promoting

No team can exist without being in contact with its environment. The promoting task ensures the team explores the opportunities presented and takes advantage of them. The networking responsibilities of the team are addressed through the task of promoting. The internal and external stakeholders of the team need to be aware of what happens for them to be informed about the operations of the team. In particular this is of importance to the team as the sourcing of financial, people and physical resources could be dependent on stakeholders actually knowing what is happening in the team.

Developing

This task refers to the necessity for teams to assess and test the applicability of new ideas. It entails the activities the team employs to meet the needs of its stakeholders. The team needs to cultivate opportunities, but needs to ensure its work is planned, molded and shaped to align with what it is to produce.

Organising

The generic task "Organising" refers to the requirement a team has to establish and implement ways to get things done; i.e. to make things happen. It ensures team members know what to do, when to do it and how to perform. The team provides plans with clear objectives and milestones on how the performance of the team should be enacted and the team's resources are allocated to ensure optimal performance. In particular, the team needs to ensure members are allocated tasks that fit their knowledge, skills and abilities; and that the distribution of work is balanced and allows the outcome of the team to be accomplished.

Producing

Because any team has to deliver at least one outcome, the focus of this task is how the team delivers products and services. To enable this it is required that the team delivers on its mandate: something must emanate from the team's efforts. Furthermore, it is a requirement that the team has to be effective and efficient in its production processes. Thus, merely plodding along in a sub-optimal manner does not allow for the team to reach its targets or for members to be committed. The producing task sees to it that the team monitors what it is supposed to deliver and that implementation behaviours are in place.

Inspecting

Inspecting refers to control and audit systems through regular checks on what the team does. This task relates to the control function the team employs to ensure compliance with the various standards and norms it has to adhere to. For example, some legal requirements may be in place and the team has to adhere to regulations, laws or prescriptions. Other requirements could be regarding safety and security and measures on how the team adheres to them. This task also includes the financial control systems wherein the team needs to operate.

Maintaining

The final task ensures the team upholds and maintains standards and effective work processes of operational systems (e.g. the resources the team employs) and the social systems (e.g. interpersonal relations and customer satisfaction) wherein it operates. Thus, the team ensures that the machines, physical resources and operational requirements are maintained. Regular "service" checks are clear examples of this task. On the other hand, a team also has to maintain its interpersonal relations with all stakeholders. In this regard the satisfaction of members of the team and other stakeholders needs to be monitored and addressed. Maintaining thus refers to efforts to ensure the smooth running of the team.

Tips for team leaders

All tasks should be aligned with role preference and an assessment thereof is advisable. This view of generic tasks is good to help the team to balance its resources and can be used to determine where more or less action is required.

Representation

Figure 8.4: Margerison and McCann tasks

173

References

Margerison, C. & McCann, D. (1984) Team Mapping: A New Approach to Managerial Leadership. *Journal of European Industrial Training,* 8(1), 12–16.

Margerison, C. & McCann, D. (1996). *Team management: Practical new approaches.* Chalford: Management Books.

Introduction

The Job Characteristics Model of Hackman and Oldham is a classic and its influence is well-established. In their overview of the last hundred years of scholarship into work design, researchers Parker, Morgeson and Johns attested to its significance by claiming it is "the 2nd most highly cited JAP article of all time" (JAP refers to the Journal of Applied Psychology, which is widely believed to be one of the most influential scholarly journals in the field of organisational psychology). The key features of this model are helpful in assisting a team to design the various tasks members have to fulfil to ensure effective outcomes.

In a nutshell

Work design in terms of job characteristics, psychological states and outcomes.

Purpose

To help teams design their tasks optimally.

To ensure personal and work outcomes.

Description

The model proposes three elements leaders of teams can use in designing work, namely core dimensions, psychological states and outcomes. These elements feed into one another in the sense that the design (i.e. core dimensions) influences the psychological state of employees and this in turn impacts on the outcome of the particular individual's efforts. They identify five core dimensions (skill variety, task identity, task significance, autonomy and feedback) that impact on three psychological states (meaningfulness of work, responsibility of outcomes and knowledge of results). The outcomes of these efforts are high intrinsic motivation, high job performance, high job satisfaction, and low absenteeism and team member turnover. While all dimensions and psychological states impact on all the outcomes, they propose a more direct relationship between some of the dimensions and the psychological states, i.e. they contend that some dimensions impact directly on particular states. The psychological states are described first, followed by the core dimensions that impact directly on these states.

Psychological states

The three psychological states influencing work outcomes are:

- meaningfulness of work: employees will experience this psychological state if they regard the individual experiences of completing the job to be generally meaningful, valuable and worthwhile;

- responsibility for outcomes: this psychological state is experienced by individuals as they evaluate the degree to which they feel personally accountable and responsible for the outcomes of the work; and

- knowledge of results: this refers to the degree that individual workers are informed and understand whether they are effective in delivering what is required in performing the work assigned to them. This feedback needs to be provided on a continuous basis to influence the psychological state of knowledge of the results of one's efforts.

Core dimensions of work design

Five elements of work design influence the psychological states in the following manner. The first three influence the state of meaningfulness, while the other two influence the state of feeling responsible and the state of knowing about the results respectively:

- Skill variety, task identity and task significance influence meaningfulness at work. Skill variety refers to the degree to which a particular job requires a variety of skills and talents to be brought to bear on a variety of different activities. In particular, when the task requires an element of challenge or stretch and draws on several skills, it is perceived to be meaningful. Task identity refers to how a particular task requires completion of a "whole" and identifiable piece of work. It states that when a team member is responsible for a particular task from inception to completion and where a visible outcome is observed it leads to the task being experienced as meaningful. Task significance refers to how the task is perceived to impact on the lives or work of other people. This makes clear how the particular task has broader significance in influencing other people, leading the task to be perceived as more meaningful.

- Autonomy is the work dimension that impacts on a worker's psychological state of responsibility for the outcomes. The degree to which the individual experiences freedom, independence and discretion in scheduling the work and determining the procedures is regarded as an indication of the level of autonomy offered by the task. When the outcomes of such tasks are believed to depend on the individual's own efforts, initiatives and decisions rather than on the adequacy of instructions from the boss or on a manual of job procedures, the individual's sense of autonomy is enhanced. This in turn impacts on the experience of responsibility the worker has for the outcomes of the task.

- Feedback impacts on the need individuals have to know whether their efforts produce the required results. Thus, for workers to experience the psychological state of "knowledge of results" it is important that sufficient and continuous feedback is provided on the effectiveness of their performance.

The Job Characteristics Model also offers a mathematical indication of the motivating potential of each job and team leaders can calculate such potential. The formula they offer is based on the assumptions that when a job is high on each of the dimensions impacting on meaningfulness of work, high on autonomy and high on feedback, the motivating potential will be high. The degree to which this is present and experienced increases the opportunity for the design of the tasks to be motivating. The formula states:

$$MPS = \frac{\dfrac{Skill\ variety + Task\ identity + Task\ Significance}{3}} {} + Autonomy + Feedback$$

Lastly, the model contends that the dynamics of these interactions are moderated by the strength of the growth need of the individual, knowledge and skill of the employee and context satisfaction. The authors recognised that people are inherently different, and proposed that each individual's level and desire for personal growth will influence the motivational impact of job design on their efforts. Thus, they suggested that individuals with high growth needs will experience more intensely the psychological states influenced by task design, and will be more motivated by the experienced psychological states to deliver the outcomes expected.

Tips for team leaders

The tool is helpful to assist teams to design work according to individual preferences and to allow members of teams to be utilised according to the motivation needs important to each. Two assessment tools, the Job Diagnostic Survey and the Jobs Characteristics Inventory, are often used to assist in the design of work characteristics and to assist in establishing the motivating potential of jobs.

Representation

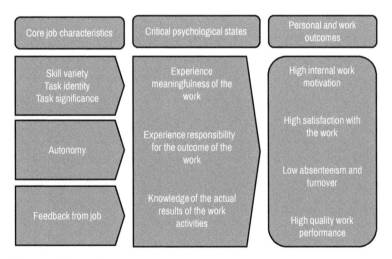

Figure 8.5: Job characteristics model

References

Hackman, J.R. & Oldham, G.R. (1975). Development of the Job Diagnostic Survey. *Journal of Applied Psychology*, 60, 159–170.

Hackman, J.R. & Oldham, G.R. (1976). Motivation Through the Design of Work: Test of a Theory. *Organizational Behaviour & Human Performance*, 16, 250–279.

Hackman, J.R. & Oldham, G.R. (1980). *Work redesign*. San Francisco, CA: Addison Wesley.

Parker, S.K., Morgeson, F.P. & Johns, G. (2017). One Hundred Years of Work Design Research: Looking Back and Looking Forward. *Journal of Applied Psychology*, 102(3), 403–420.

9

TEAMWORK

Teamwork refers to the interaction between team members as they orchestrate tasks through interdependent team activities in pursuit of team goals. Teamwork is in essence the interrelated behaviours of members to co-ordinate and synchronise collective action. It includes efforts to cooperate and coordinate the activities of the team and also refers to processes the team puts in place to facilitate effective completion. In this regard, processes to solve problems, to manage conflict and to make decisions are all dependent on the levels of teamwork in the team. For these to be accomplished successfully a team needs to consider what actions are teamwork actions, what are the dimensions thereof, and what specific techniques could help them to be effective in their teamwork efforts.

Salas, Sims and Burke proposed a model offering key dimensions of such teamwork, called the "Big Five". They also identified three coordinating/supporting mechanisms that need to be in place for successful teamwork. Another theoretical view of the teamwork tasks of a team is that of Salas, Shuffler, Thayer, Bedwell and Lazzara, who carried out a meta-analysis on teamwork and identified nine critical considerations or dimensions that facilitate effectiveness. Six of these are core processes or emergent states, while three are influencing conditions.

The next parts in this section offer information on how teams can go about facilitating teamwork. In the first, two possible intervention stances are described: Heron's six categories of intervention and Van Maurik's "Styles of Processes of Facilitation". This is followed by techniques called "Liberating Structures". A selection of liberating structures devised by Henri Lipmanowicz and Keith McCandless is presented. The last tool in this section is a fairly new methodology borrowed from the military world. It is the so-called "red teaming" and represents a structured approach to challenge assumptions about what is expected to happen in the future. It also facilitates understanding of the potential unintended consequences of plans and actions. This approach prevents complacency and enables the team to implement better plans by limiting the effects of any decision biases.

Introduction

Salas, Sims and Burke proposed five key dimensions of teamwork that affect team performance, namely team leadership, team orientation, back-up behaviour, mutual performance monitoring and adaptability. These dimensions are supported by three coordinating mechanisms that moderate the five factors.

In a nutshell

Five teamwork components (team orientation, team leadership, mutual performance monitoring, back-up behaviour and adaptability) and three supporting mechanisms (shared mental models, trust and closed-loop communication).

Purpose

To indicate key coordinating or supporting mechanisms that facilitate effective teamwork.

To help teams understand the Big Five components of teamwork.

Description

Teamwork components

The following five components are identified:

Team leadership

Leaders in teams facilitate effective teamwork by focusing on creating, maintaining and ensuring the accuracy of the team's shared mental model as it relates to team objectives, the expected roles of members, information and available resources, and monitoring the internal and external environment to facilitate team adaptability. Leaders must ensure the team is well-prepared for any changes in the environment by ensuring the team's skills levels are sufficiently developed to meet the demands of the context. Establishing and maintaining behavioural and performance expectations through available talent and facilitating interaction through an understanding of interdependence are also part of team leadership.

Mutual performance monitoring

This dimension refers to the responsibility team members take to keep each other on track and to monitor individual and collective efforts to ensure that quality and performance standards are maintained. It also involves shared responsibility that processes, procedures and responsibilities are followed according to agreed expectations. Two prerequisites for effective mutual performance monitoring have been identified, namely shared understanding of task and team responsibilities, and an open, trusting and cohesive team climate. This dimension extends the responsibility of team performance beyond that of leadership; its inclusive nature requires shared effort to ensure performance.

Back-up behaviour

This type of team behaviour happens when team members provide feedback and coaching to improve performance, assist another member to execute a task, or complete a task when another member of the team is overburdened. Thus, it is the "discretionary provision" of effort relating to tasks, resources and information to help others in the team when there is a workload distribution problem.

Adaptability

This is the ability to recognise that the team has to adjust its planned actions because of changes in the environment, internally or externally. This requires a global and strategic perspective on the team task, how roles may have to be changed and the ability to detect the need for such changes in the first place. Adaptability is required to shape the coordinating actions of members according to demands from the environment, however such adaptability must be aligned with the team's purpose, and team processes must be continually assessed to ensure that they are sufficient and optimal.

Team orientation

This refers to the attitude team members display towards the team, team members and the tasks the team has to fulfil. This refers to a preference to work in teams, and a tendency to enhance individual performance through coordinating, evaluating and utilising input from others in a team setting. It manifests in the cohesion in the team and the degree to which members value team membership through assigning high priority to team goals and participating willingly in team actions.

Coordinating/supporting mechanisms

The three coordinating mechanisms that provide the supporting context are shared mental models, trust and closed-loop communication.

Shared mental models

Mental models are the cognitive processes team members use to organise or encode information to allow them to function together. Two types are often distinguished, namely team- and task-related mental models. The former refers to how team members view working together and what expected behaviours are, while the latter refers to how information about materials and processes is shared. These models also include shared views on appropriate response patterns to demands of the environment.

Closed-loop communication

This supporting condition relates to how the communication processes in the team operate. The authors contended that this type of communication involves a sender sending a message, which is received, and then as a third and key step the recipient makes sure that the message he or she received was indeed the intended message.

Trust

In the absence of sufficient trust, members will use their time and energy to protect, check and inspect each other rather than to collaborate. Trust is described as the understanding between team members that each will perform what they are supposed to and that members can rely on one another to protect and guard the interests, rights and safety of each other. This condition is particularly important for teamwork as it directly influences the behaviour of members (e.g. back-up behaviour) and other teamwork dimensions (e.g. performance monitoring). When there is sufficient trust in a team, members feel comfortable that actions by colleagues are for the good of the team.

Tips for team leaders

This tool can guide leaders to ensure supporting mechanisms are in place and to understand key behaviours of teamwork.

Representation

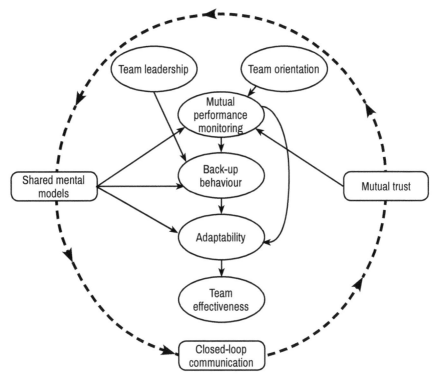

Figure 9.1: Five key dimensions of teamwork

Reference

Salas, E., Shuffler, M.L., Thayer, A.L., Bedwell, W.L. & Lazzara, E.H. (2015). Understanding and Improving Teamwork in Organizations: A Scientifically Based Practical Guide. *Human Resource Management,* 54(4), 599–622.

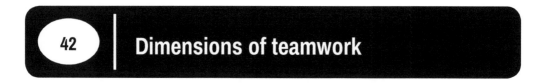

42 | # Dimensions of teamwork

Introduction

After doing a meta-analysis on teamwork, Salas, Shuffler, Thayer, Bedwell and Lazzara came up with an expanded description of the dimensions of teamwork. Nine critical considerations that facilitate effectiveness were identified, six of which are core processes or emergent states, while three are influencing conditions.

In a nutshell

Nine dimensions of teamwork, namely cooperation, conflict, coordination, communication, coaching, cognition, composition, context and culture.

Purpose

To help teams understand the dimensions of teamwork.

To highlight the conditions required for effective teamwork.

To help teams ensure all factors for effective performance are in place.

To provide a gauge to evaluate teamwork dimensions.

Description

The authors distinguished between six core processes and emergent states on the one hand, and three influencing conditions on the other.

Core processes and emergent states

These refer to the conversion of inputs to outputs through the team's cognitive, affective and behavioural processes. Once the team starts this conversion process, members interact with one another and through these interpersonal relations emergent states or resultant properties of the team develop. The factors that constitute these core processes and emergent states are cooperation, conflict, coordination, communication, coaching and cognition. These are overarching in nature and sub-elements (e.g. trust or cohesion) can be identified within these broader concepts.

Cooperation

This entails the attitudes, beliefs and feelings of the team that drive behaviour and facilitate cohesion, performance and effectiveness. Cooperation consists of the following elements:

- collective efficacy, i.e. the sense of competence or ability to control their environment that teams feel. Through early wins, momentum can be built that helps teams towards greater teamwork and cooperation;

- trust, i.e. the belief team members have that all members in the team will contribute appropriately and will be willing to protect the team when required. Trust can be fostered through building on the notion that perceived similarity (i.e. members of a team focusing on things they share) breeds predictability and comfort between people. It is particularly helpful if teams discuss past experiences prior to new projects or tasks.

- team (learning) orientation, i.e. the belief team members have that working in teams is beneficial and facilitates better performance, especially if it is geared towards learning; and

- goal commitment, i.e. the determination that team members share to attain the goals they set out to achieve.

Conflict

Conflict is regarded as "perceived incompatibilities in the interests, beliefs, or views held by one or more team members" and can relate to tasks, relationships or processes. The first relates to differences regarding the execution of tasks, relationship conflict refers to interpersonal differences, while process conflict involves the division, delegation and distribution of tasks, responsibilities and expectations of team members. Research is unclear on the exact impact of and relations between these different types of conflict, with some theorists pointing out that conflict can have benefits, for example task conflict can lead to broader views and better results, while others warn that relationship conflict limits performance, especially as the initial beneficial impact may wane over time. It furthermore seems that relationships moderate performance, with positive interpersonal relations leading to improved performance when the team experiences task conflict, while interpersonal relations lead to exacerbated task conflict and lower performance. The authors suggested that clear norms and processes on dealing with conflict must be agreed up front, and that once conflict arises it must be dealt with immediately and according to the agreed principles and processes.

Coordination

This relates to how the sequence and timing of interdependent actions can be seen as the behavioural enactment of tasks that transforms resources into outcomes. Coordination is explicit when actions are directly planned and communicated, while it manifests implicitly when members anticipate needs and adjust behaviours according to these perceptions. As coordination is based on interaction and information, successful teams have a seamless flow of information and effective coordination assists in positive performance, while the converse is true for ineffective coordination. To facilitate effective coordination, team roles must be clearly spelled out, but they must not be overly rigid in order to enable flexibility and autonomous action. Furthermore, debriefing and reflecting opportunities regarding the coordination of the team could assist in increasing performance.

Communication

This critical component of teamwork relates to the role effective communication plays in coordination, conflict and interpersonal relationships in teams. It can be explicit (direct and overt delivery of messages) or implicit (passively conveyed messages) and verbal or non-verbal. Team communication is improved through members sharing unique information and by expanding access to information. In addition, closed-loop communication patterns should be established beforehand and used during action to ensure that members send, receive, share and process relevant information appropriately.

Coaching

The authors viewed coaching as internal or external leadership behaviour enacted to establish goals and set direction to ensure team success. Leaders need to understand that the impact on task performance may be indirect in that addressing the needs of members or the team can impact on performance. Critical though is the need to diagnose and address problems as soon as they arise. Furthermore, the distribution of leadership responsibilities beyond the leader to multiple individuals helps teams to perform better and helps to disperse leadership throughout the team.

Cognition

This refers to the shared understanding between team members and includes shared mental models and transactive memory systems (see Section 66). The former refers to the baseline and common understanding members share about what is expected from each other, task requirements and performance levels to enable them to describe, predict and explain the behaviour of team members. It also refers to members' knowledge of their roles and responsibilities, objectives, norms and the team's context, and familiarity with teammates' knowledge, skills and abilities. A team's transactive memory system refers to the collective memory members have about where information is located, either internally with members or where it can be found if located externally. Establishing a clear shared understanding of team functioning, objectives, roles, responsibilities, expertise and situational variables are necessary for teams to build team cognition. Cross-training of members to foster understanding of roles and how these roles fit together also helps.

Influencing conditions

In order for the team's core processes and emergent states to be effectively utilised, three influencing conditions need to be in place. These are dimensions that determine the extent to which the other dimensions can be employed by the team and they therefore play a key role in the success of the teamwork. These conditions are the composition of the team, its context and the culture of the team and organisation.

Composition

This refers to the knowledge, skills, abilities, personality, experience and expertise of team members. Individual characteristics relate to elements like cognitive ability and personality traits. The ability a member has to work well in a team is another factor of composition that influences performance. In this regard, an individual's adaptability, problem-solving skills and acceptance of feedback may help a team to perform better. The make-up of a team also influences some team level factors such as where a team displays a strong team orientation or where members thrive in collective environments. Apart from individual and team characteristics, the specifics of the contextual demands should also influence its composition. Therefore, teams should be composed with both taskwork and teamwork in mind and the diverse mix of the team should be such that it assists the team in its performance.

Context

Context can be viewed as the characteristics or events of a particular situation that influence behaviour and refers to how a team is influenced by its environment. Broadly it can be seen as the larger organisational context, where the various systems (i.e. reward, performance, operations, training and management support) assist or hinder team performance. Of particular importance is how the organisational climate (i.e. the procedures, policies and practices) are conducive to teamwork. The physical context of a team refers to aspects of the work setting, including availability of resources. The task environment of a team refers to the manner in which tasks need to be performed and includes the performance norms and measures of excellence the team puts in place. For example, where external threat impacts on a team (e.g. a fire squad) or where a team is geographically dispersed, the task context may impact on performance. Thus, the context provides the palette on which the teamwork of the team is enacted.

Culture

Culture is defined "as the assumptions people hold about relationships with each other and the environment that are shared among an identifiable group of people (e.g., team, organization, nation) and manifest in individuals' values, beliefs, norms for social behaviour, and artefacts" and is "a driving force for member values, norms, and behaviour and can originate from any collective, including teams, the organization as a whole, a field or discipline, or at the national level" (Salas et al.). Culture influences how members view themselves in the team and their interaction, commitment and contribution to the team. The greater the cultural diversity of any organisation or team, the greater effort should be made to understand cultural preferences, e.g. differences in individualism versus collectivism. Thus, organisational culture can be seen as an enabling or supporting mechanism that facilitates teamwork.

Tips for team leaders

The model is helpful in the manner it identifies the enabling conditions for processes and emergent states to evolve. Leaders can use this framework to direct their attention to the key dimensions that facilitate teamwork, in order to guide their own teams. It is a comprehensive set of dimensions that are well researched and can be used as a guide, assessment instrument or facilitation tool, and members of the team can be asked to include their own assessment of performance regarding the levels of teamwork. It is also helpful to solicit ideas and contributions from team members on how teamwork can be improved.

Representation

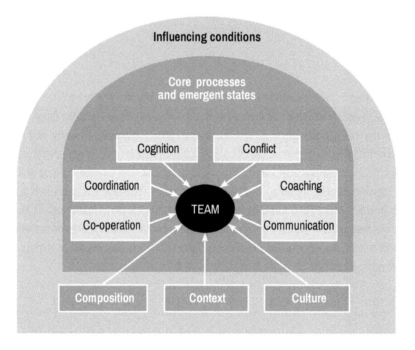

Figure 9.2: Nine dimensions of teamwork

References

Dinh, J.V. & Salas, E. (2017). Factors that influence teamwork. In E. Salas, R. Rico, & J. Passmore. (eds.). *The Wiley Blackwell handbook of the psychology of team working and collaborative processes*. Chichester, UK: John Wiley & Sons.

Salas, E., Shuffler, M.L., Thayer, A.L., Bedwell, W.L. & Lazzara, E.H. (2015). Understanding and Improving Teamwork in Organizations: A Scientifically Based Practical Guide. *Human Resource Management, 54*(4), 599–622.

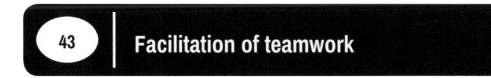

43 | **Facilitation of teamwork**

Introduction

Two different frameworks on facilitation are presented here, namely Heron's six categories of intervention and Van Maurik's "Styles and Processes of Facilitation". Both of them can be applied to facilitate teamwork, but they are also useful when helping an individual performing teamwork.

In a nutshell

Two approaches to facilitate teamwork are presented.

Purpose

To illustrate different categories and styles of facilitating teamwork.

To allow flexibility in style of facilitation.

Description

Heron's six categories of intervention

The six categories of intervention offered by Heron are helpful in situations where leaders want to support, give guidance to or provide feedback to team members. He distinguished between authoritative categories (i.e. prescriptive, informative and confrontational intervention styles) and facilitative categories (i.e. cathartic, catalytic and supportive styles).

Authoritative

This type of intervention enables the leader to maintain some degree of control in the relationship, and is used where the focus is on giving direction and/or information.

Prescriptive

The leader offers advice and directs the individual towards a preferred solution. Recommended phrases are "You need to consider ..." or "It would be useful to ...". The leader is in an expert position and directs the team in a specific direction.

Informative

The focus here is on giving useful information or instructions to help with a situation and to guide a team member to a solution. Leaders use expressions such as "This happens because …" or "The reason for that is …".

Confrontational

To use this category the leader needs to be assertive, forceful and positive. He or she challenges the team members by confronting behaviour, views or performance in order to direct them to a solution or course of action. Helpful ways to address a team could be: "You said this happened while instead …" or "Given the circumstances, why did you …?"

Facilitative

Cathartic

This is the first of the participative categories and when a leader uses this it encourages members to express their feelings and release built-up stress. This relieves tension and mitigates animosity between members. It is helpful to use empathy-driven questions like: "If that person was here, what would you like to say to them?" or "How did that make you feel?"

Catalytic

This approach promotes others to be reflective and to identify their own solutions. Focus is directed at the follower and feeds into his or her ability to reflect on the particular situation. The leader could ask: "How could that situation have been handled differently?" or "What would've made a difference?" or "In your view, what was the effect of this?"

Supportive

When leaders use this style they try to build rapport, create a sense of belonging and cohesion and indicate to members that they are on their side. They build their confidence by emphasising their achievements, competencies and capabilities. Helpful remarks include: "You must have felt …"; "it is clear you wanted to achieve…" or "this is really one of your strengths".

Facilitating excellence: styles and processes of facilitation

Van Maurik described four different modes or styles of facilitation that can be used to assist teams in their teamwork.

Intellectual Command (IC)

The first approach is characterised by a high degree of input from the leader that comes in the form of sharing data, opinions and/or information. The leader provokes, sets challenges, provides direction and gives necessary facts and knowledge to guide the team. There is limited input from the team as they depend on the input from the leader, who answers questions, sets goals and challenges and provides information from an expert stance. The leader is authoritative, objective and confident enough to state his or her views, yet should be open to view the issues at hand from various angles.

Incentives Approach (IA)

This approach demands input by the team and emphasis is put on the contribution of the members through various processes and by expecting a high level of input to the knowledge base of the team. Often teams that require this type of approach are stuck in negativity, cynicism and lack of commitment. This may lead them to question why the team exists at all, and why their actions matter. It requires the leader to demonstrate benefits and positives in the team and can be seen as a "carrot-and-stick" approach.

Creative Group Catalyst (CG)

This approach uses limited intervention, but there is also limited focus on facts and opinions of members. Typically teams that are confident in their own problem-solving abilities value this approach. For the most part, the leader in cases like this guides the team towards its goal achievement objectives, sets an agenda and ensures that the team's attention is addressed to relevant issues. The approach is characterised by thought-provoking questions, challenging prompts and emphasis to the team that they have achieved their goals independently.

Supportive Coach (SC)

This approach uses a low level of knowledge or content input, but requires a higher level of participation and intervention in team processes. It is particularly helpful where teams lack confidence in their own ability, find the tasks and objectives difficult and challenging, or do not have a clear idea where to go next. Leaders need to listen carefully to what is communicated (content and process), encourage effort, be helpful and empathise with the feelings the team conveys. The focus of this approach is on building the confidence of the individuals and the collective sense of efficacy of the team.

Tips for team leaders

Leaders can assist the teamwork of their teams by adjusting their facilitation stances or by using various styles.

Representation

AUTHORITATIVE	FACILITATIVE
Prescriptive	**Cathartic**
Direct advice Expert Lead in a direction	Encourages to express feelings Relieves stress Mitigates animosity
Informative	**Catalytic**
Giving useful information Offering instructions Explaining a situation Sharing expertise	Promotes reflection Allows identification of own solutions Builds sense of potency
Confrontational	**Supportive**
Assertive and forceful Challenges by confronting be- haviour Direction to solution	Builds rapport Creates sense of belonging Develops cohesion Emphasises achievements

LEVEL OF INTERVENTION

Intellectual command	**Creative group catalyst**
Stating and opinion Providing and answering questions Setting and receiving challenges Leading from the front	Setting the agenda Stimulating the team Leading from the middle Being the chief explorer

SCALE OF INPUT

Incentives approach	**Supportive coach**
Driving the learning Focusing the team Drawing positive and negative emotions Handling conflict Giving a reason to learn Leading from the front	Being overtly helpful Catching those in difficulty Guiding action plans Leading from the rear Listening Encouraging

Figure 9.3: Two approaches to facilitate teamwork

References

Heron, J. (1999). *The complete facilitator's handbook*. London: Kogan Page.

Van Maurik, J. (1994). Facilitating Excellence: Styles and Processes of Facilitation. *Leadership & Organization Development Journal*, 15(8), 30–34.

44 | Liberating structures

Introduction

Facilitating and leading cooperation and coordination efforts of teams are among the most challenging of a leader's tasks. A set of very helpful "liberating structures" were offered by Henri Lipmanowicz and Keith McCandless in their attempt to help groups and teams to be more energised and liberated from real and perceived confines.

In a nutshell

Twenty-seven (out of thirty-three) liberating structures are described.

Purpose

To mobilise and energise the team.

To facilitate teamwork.

Description

A selection of the liberating structures is presented that are most applicable to facilitating teamwork:

- 1-2-4-All: in response to a question each member first answers it individually, then it is discussed in pairs, then in groups of four and finally the whole team.

- Impromptu networking: ask a group engaging questions and give the team a change to answer in pairs.

- Nine why's: repeatedly ask "why?" (even repeating it nine times) in response to an answer.

- Wicked questions: the team considers key paradoxes in its operation. This is done by discussing burning issues and answering "What opposing-yet-complementary strategies do they need to accomplish simultaneously in order to be successful?"

- Appreciative interviews: members in the team interview each other where one tells a success story of something they really feel proud of. These are shared with the team to look for patterns and opportunities to build on.

- TRIZ (a Russian acronym meaning the "theory of the resolution of invention-related tasks"): this technique uses "reverse logic" to challenge sacred cows by identifying what must be stopped (as it may (unwittingly) produce unwarranted results) or by exploring what should be done to get the worst possible results.

- 15% solutions: the team explores what each can do to effect change, to complete a task or to energise the team immediately, i.e. what actions they can take with current resource levels and within their control to make a positive change.

- Troika consulting: three peers form a consulting group and give solutions to a key challenge a team member is struggling with. Once the challenge is described, the presenter of the problem turns his or her back to the other two members. The presenter listens to (and writes down) ideas, solutions or alternatives offered by the other two in the troika, but is not allowed to discuss it with the colleagues while they brainstorm.

- What, So What, Now What?: team members share their experience of an event ("What"), discuss the meaning thereof ("So what?") and then decide what actions need to follow ("Now what?").

- Discovery and action dialogue: the team asks the following progressive questions to probe deeper into a challenge: How do you know when problem X is present? How do you contribute effectively to solving problem X? What prevents you from doing this or taking these actions all the time? Do you know anybody who is able to frequently solve problem X and overcome barriers? What behaviours or practices made their success possible? Do you have any ideas? What needs to be done to make it happen? Any volunteers? Who else needs to be involved?

- Shift and share: team members split up individually or in smaller teams to find solutions to problems and put the key elements of any proposed solution on a flip-chart. After completion, all members have an opportunity to "visit" each of these work stations, listen to the proposed solutions and improve the suggested solutions.

- Wise crowds: a process of peer-to-peer coaching similar to Troika consulting (see above), but where more members in each of the groups help a volunteer to find solutions to a challenge.

- Min specs: in order to identify the minimum set of rules required for the team to meet a challenge, they identify all the rules they have to adhere to first and then limit them to the absolute minimum.

- Improve prototyping: teams act out or role play scenarios related to the problem they want to address. Through this effort to share explicit knowledge and discover tacit knowledge through observation and the emergence of latent knowledge, new ideas are generated. Some members role play while others observe what was successful and suggest ways to improve.

- Heuristic help: using groups of three (client, coach and observer), the client presents a challenge and the coach responds with one of four response patterns, namely quiet presence, guided discovery, loving provocation or process mindfulness. The client presents his or her challenge four times and the coach responds each time in a different pattern.

- Conversation café: the team gets an opportunity to speak four times on an issue or topic. During the first two and the last rounds a "talking object" is used (only the person who has the object can speak at any time), while in the third (longer) round the use of a talking object is optional. Each member is given an opportunity to share their views on the topic and by using the talking object the leader makes sure that everyone gets a chance before the next round can commence.

- Heard, seen, respected: in an effort to highlight the value of empathy, team members are asked to share an experience where they *did not* feel heard, seen or respected. Once these stories are told the team reflects on its impact and how to improve interpersonal relationships in the team.

- Drawing together: each individual in the team draws an individual or team challenge by using only the following symbols with their attached meanings: Circle = wholeness; Rectangle = support; Triangle = goal; Spiral = change; Star person (equidistant cross) = relationship. They then share with the team the journey they faced or how they dealt with the challenge.

- Design story board: the team devises ways to address a challenge by using a design story board template that comprises the agenda item, the goal, the facilitation technique used and why, the action steps or timing and the facilitator and participants.

- Social network webbing: the team explores its network by allowing each member to share who they currently work with, are in contact with, know or have access to. This is mapped to improve understanding of the team's network and stakeholder structure.

- What I Need From You (WINFY): individuals state what they need from other members and once everyone has shared what they want from each other, each one in the team responds by stating "yes", "no", "maybe" or "whatever (meaning too vague and unclear)" to indicate their commitment to action.

- Generative relationships (STAR): teams evaluate their relationships in terms of separateness (diversity in perspective, expertise and background), tuning (level of listening, reflective and collective sense-making), action (opportunities to act or innovate) and reason (the reason and benefits together).

- Integrated-Autonomy: teams evaluate how their purpose could be best served through a combination of (balancing act between) integration and autonomy, standardisation and customisation, and freedom and control.

- Critical uncertainties: the group explores anticipated critical uncertainties by plotting them on one axis of a matrix (positive and negative) and the potential impact (big or small) on the other axis, and finds ways to address these uncertainties.

- Ecocycle planning: teams plot all their current activities on a matrix using four developmental phases: birth, maturity, creative destruction, and renewal. It can also be used with metaphors to describe the major leadership style each member prefers, namely entrepreneur (birth); manager (maturity); heretic (creative destruction) and networker (renewal). A further use is to use the cycle to identify how obstacles, i.e. the rigidity trap (not letting go) and the poverty trap (not getting enough resources invested), impact on key activities.

- Panarchy: the team visualises how it is embedded in various systems that are embedded in yet more systems, i.e. a panarchy of systems. This helps them understand how these interdependencies influence the operations of a team by considering the impact or spread of change.

- Purpose-to-practice: the team finds the purpose of why they are together and determines the supporting elements, namely principles (rules we must obey), participants (contributors to reach purpose), structure (how to organise control) and practices (what we have to do to reach the purpose).

Tools focusing on larger groups (e.g. 25/10 Crowd Sourcing) are not included here, but they and detailed descriptions of how to use all the techniques can be found on the website (www.liberatingstructures.com).

Tips for team leaders

These are very helpful techniques to energise the team and can be used with more traditional facilitation techniques, including brainstorming and screening, to help the team in its teamwork processes.

Representation

Liberating structures		
1-2-4-All	Shift and Share	Design story board
Nine why's	Wise crowds	Social Network Webbing
Wicked questions	Min specs	What I Need From You (WINFY)
Appreciative interviews	Improv prototyping	Generative relationships STAR
TRIZ	Heuristic help	Integrated-Autonomy
15% Solutions	Conversation café	Critical uncertainties
Troika consulting	Heard, Seen, Respected	Ecocycle planning
What, So What, Now What?	Drawing together	Panarchy
Discovery and Action Dialogue		

Figure 9.4: Liberating structures

Reference

Lipmanowicz, H. & McCandless, K. (2013). *The surprising power of liberating structures. Simple rules to unleash a culture of innovation*. Columbia, SC: Liberating Structures Press.

45 | **Red teaming**

Introduction

Although the origins of so-called red teaming can be found in 19th century European warfare with the Prussian army using Kriegsspiel to train military officers, it has found recent revival through the American military and is making inroads into corporate life as well. Ultimately it is a way to prevent groupthink, to stimulate alternative thinking and to allow for different points of view to come to the fore by scrutinising what could go wrong. It therefore prevents a team from being overly comfortable with the status quo of how they do things and challenges assumptions on what is expected in the future by questioning assumptions and understanding and identifying the possible unintended consequences of plans and actions. It therefore enables the team to implement better plans by limiting the effects of decision biases on the team's strategies and plans.

In a nutshell

Red teaming strengthens planning processes by deliberately looking at alternatives or what could go wrong.

Purpose

To assist teams to make better decisions.

To help teams make better plans.

To prevent unforeseen mistakes.

To scrutinise team assumptions.

Description

Red teaming can be described as a mind-set or approach to dealing with issues in a team as well as a set of tools and techniques that help the team question, challenge and interrogate assumptions, plans and actions. Red teaming could be viewed as a group version of using a Devil's advocate to challenge the legitimacy of a particular view. Traditionally a red team is a separate team set up to critically and objectively analyse each aspect of a team's strategy, plan or operations, and assist organisations or teams to evaluate their decision-making, assumptions and potential routes forward. "Red teaming" refers to a mind-set that should be cultivated to achieve the same results without creating a separate, external group. The team is requested to analyse its own actions, strategies and assumptions from a red teaming perspective. In other words, the mind-set associated with red teams should be adopted. In addition, some of the specific techniques can be very helpful to challenge the status quo.

Four ways of seeing

This tool is a way of evaluating the potential impact of a plan on various stakeholders. It uses a familiar matrix with four quadrants: How X views X, How Y views Y, How X views Y, and How Y views X. The team can use this by regarding any of the stakeholders in an X-Y format and evaluating perceptions between various stakeholders. It can also include itself as either X or Y, which will yield an evaluation of how the team perceives various stakeholders and where perceptions and assumptions can be tested.

Outside-in thinking

This tool starts from outside the team and analyses its environment first, to detect potential impact on the team and what the team's issues are. It uses the following steps:

- List all major external forces that impact on a problem, i.e. political, technological, social and other potential forces.

- Determine which of these forces can impact you or you can influence.

- Consider how these forces (for example stakeholders, policy-makers, business partners or other teams) can impact on the challenge positively or negatively.

- Determine how your team can influence these forces according to the needs of the team and the challenge it is facing.

Alternative futures

This technique looks at outside forces and stakeholders to determine how the team should react to potential impact from them. It follows the following process:

- Determine key forces (stakeholders).

- Identify the two whose impact would be most critical to the team.

- Determine a spectrum of potential positive and negative impact and describe how each would look.

- Devise a matrix superimposing these two on each other.

- Speculate on the four potential "alternative futures" shown in each of the quadrants.

Pre-mortem

This analysis assumes that a plan has failed and then tries to determine what the causes of such failure could have been. The following steps can be used:

- Assume failure. Imagine complete failure or disaster of the plan and assume complete failure of the proposed plan.

- Determine causes. List all potential causes for such imagined failure and allow members to share their individual views of potential causes.

- Determine most likely causes of failure. Through a screening technique the team determines the most critical potential causes of failure.

- Adjustment. Adjust the plan and work out mitigating action plans to address potential calamity and failure.

Be your own worst enemy

This is a roleplay activity where the team acts as the opposition. It uses the availability of various levels or degrees of information to determine what course of action the "worst enemy" would follow to attack the team.

What if

This activity involves objectively analysing what the consequences of implementing a plan would be on the team or organisation. It does not focus on what could potentially cause the team to fail, but on what the consequences would be once the plan is implemented, both positive and negative. The following steps are helpful:

- Imagine an event that would have a major impact on the team.

- Determine the potential impact of this on all stakeholders of the team.

- Figure out one or more plausible ways this could occur and describe that in as much detail as possible.

- Identify triggers that would activate this event.

- Determine signposts of change that would indicate whether this foreseen event is about to unfold.

- List what the team should to do to bring about positive impact or to minimise potential negative impact.

Us-them

The team devises two different, competing courses of action and develops both in order to evaluate the potential impact of each.

Devil's advocacy

Deliberate questioning by a member or subgroup of the team around strategic assumptions by making a compelling case that the actual opposite of such assumptions is actually the case.

Tips for team leaders

Red teaming does not replace the traditional planning and operational processes of a team, but rather adds to them. It is about finding better solutions and limiting risks and mistakes by analysing what could lie in the future of the proposed plan or action.

Representation

Four ways of seeing	Pre-mortem	What if
Outside-in thinking	Risk analysis and failure analysis	Us-them
Alternative futures	Be your own worst enemy	Devil's advocacy

Figure 9.5: Red teaming

Reference

Hoffman, B.G. (2017). *Red teaming: Transform your business by thinking like the enemy*. London: Piatkus.

10

DIVERGING TECHNIQUES

Diverging techniques help teams to solve problems and expand their views by generating new ideas and alternatives. Although some of these have received research attention through a broader focus on problem solving and innovation, the application thereof in teams has been more limited in scope and allows for more practical considerations to help teams. Here the focus is therefore on how practical tools (that have been reported in literature) can be used to assist teams in their problem-solving efforts.

Five broad categories of techniques or tools are discussed and examples and variants in each of these are offered to provide teams with an array of alternatives and opportunity to experiment. The five clusters are brainstorming and its variants, attribute exploration, checklists, semantics and representational techniques.

46 | Brainstorming

Introduction

One can hardly discuss diverging elements of the creative problem-solving process without starting with brainstorming. Originally devised by Osborne, this technique rests on the assumption that team members can spur each other on to be more creative. It assumes that team members will be motivated by the efforts of others and more creative results will follow as members "build" on each other's ideas. Through this cooperation it affords individuals an opportunity to maximise synergistic effort and facilitates divergent thinking.

In a nutshell

Team members generate diverging ideas by naming anything that could potentially expand on prevailing thinking.

Purpose

To tap on the creative potential of all team members.

To allow open and unrestricted creative effort.

To energise the team.

To solicit collective effort.

To generate alternatives.

Description

Team members offer random and unrestricted ideas on what potential solutions to the problem could be, using classical brainstorming, variants thereof, and structured brainstorming.

Classical brainstorming

While it is hardly necessary to describe the process of brainstorming (where members call out any idea, solution or alternative that they think relates to the issue at hand), it is helpful to keep in mind the four following rules (Thompson), which are adaptations of the original rules by Osborne:

- Everything goes (i.e. expressiveness): an attitude of "everything goes" or "try anything" must prevail and any idea, no matter how strange, weird or fanciful, should be expressed.

- Suspend judgment and evaluation (i.e. non-evaluation): ideas and contributions should not be criticised during the process (critical evaluation is suspended until a later part of the process) and all ideas are considered valuable.

- Generate as many ideas as possible (i.e. quantity): the principle that quantity breeds quality is followed and the more ideas that are generated, the better the opportunity exists that a good one will develop.

- Build on each other's ideas (i.e. building): ideas that are generated are regarded as the collective effort of the team and expansion of each other's ideas is encouraged.

All ideas, including outrageous, funny or non-topical comments, are recorded in the contributor's own words or in a rephrased version thereof. Time is allowed to record all the ideas. After this process has been exhausted, the ideas are combined, collated and sorted to form clusters or groups of ideas.

Brainstorming variants

Scholars and practitioners have developed and added an array of variants of the original brainstorming process. Some of these are presented here.

Brainwriting

Once the team has decided on a well-defined problem they want to address, members write ideas, contributions, solutions or alternatives to solve or address the problem *individually* on a sheet of paper. Once they have listed all their contributions, they pass the sheet of paper to the person sitting next to them. Each participant uses the ideas on the paper to act as stimuli to generate more ideas and records them on the sheet of paper. These ideas are in addition to those already on the sheet and should be new ideas and not ideas recorded previously. The process is continued until every team member has had a chance to view each of the other members' contributions and is completed when members receive their original sheet back. Since the additions to their original ideas might spur them on to generate new ideas, each member then has a final opportunity to make contributions.

Brainwriting pool

Each member writes as many ideas, contributions or alternatives as possible on a sheet of paper. Once members feel satisfied that they have exhausted their own lists of ideas, they put their sheets (face down) in the middle of the table. Each member then takes any sheet (other than their own) from the pile and uses the ideas on that paper to generate new ideas.

Braindrawing gallery

Each member of the team makes a drawing, sketch or model of the problem. The contributions are passed on to the next person (like the brainwriting process) or put in the middle of the table (like the brainwriting pool). Each visual representation is amended or expanded to provide more insight into the problem. Members can also use the drawings and initiate new drawings if they find a drawing leading them to different ideas. Once completed, the various sketches are displayed in "gallery" style (e.g. posted onto a wall). Team members then put the key elements provided by the sketches into words and the content is examined for common themes, links and relationships.

Reverse brainstorming

This technique constrains the team to generate ideas that are negative or the opposite of what is required. It is, however, important to reverse this back to positives at the end of the process.

Rolestorming

Team members generate ideas through brainstorming (or any of its variants), but from the perspective of a different role than their current work-related position. Any role can be chosen; the following are given as examples of what can be used:

- Significant stakeholders such as the CEO; customers; lobbyists or professions (e.g. an auditor or engineer).

- Fantasy characters: assuming roles based on fantasy rather than real persons could assist in the process.

- Animals: different roles from the animal kingdom can be used. Examples include ants, a lioness, an eagle, a hyena or a mouse.

- Team roles: Members brainstorm from the perspective of different formal or informal roles present in the team.

- A real person from outside the work environment: members then brainstorm around the issue from the perspective of that individual.

"Wacko Jacko"

The team uses this tool to generate any idea that they find to be completely outrageous or "out of this world" to solve a problem. This technique requires the team to provide the most outrageous solution to a particular problem. The "irrational" idea allows opportunity to stretch perceptual boundaries that might limit solutions to the problem. It lets the team examine their assumptions and the perceptual boundaries influencing their problem-solving efforts, and may lead to investigation of aspects of the problem not previously explored.

Structured brainstorming

The team decides on the topic for which they would like to generate ideas. The normal brainstorming process and rules apply, but structural constraints are applied, for example theme constraints, where participants are limited with regard to the themes they can contribute, e.g. strengths, weaknesses, opportunities or threats in a SWOT-analysis.

Nominal group technique

Although strictly speaking this is not a brainstorming technique, the process is sufficiently similar to allow for its inclusion here. Each participant individually writes ideas, solutions or alternatives on a piece of paper. The leader starts by asking the first member to give their first item. Then the next member is asked to do the same, and the process is continued to allow opportunity for everyone's contributions to be collated. The facilitator (or scribe) writes down the contributions. Whenever a member's point has already been presented they are requested to provide the next one on their list. The whole team is given an opportunity to present their contributions in this manner and the facilitator allows for time to write them all down. This allows for deliberate contributions from each member and eliminates the risk that members do not contribute.

Force-fit

The team is divided in two randomly selected groups and the process is explained to the teams. One team is asked to give a word, idea or concept that is not related to the problem at all. The second team is given a few minutes to come up with a solution on how to address the problem at hand using the idea provided by the first team. While the second team is busy devising plans, the first team is tasked to provide another unrelated and outrageous idea or concept. After a number of rounds, the roles are reversed and the second team gives an idea that the first team must use to devise a solution. These seemingly unrelated and impossible ideas are scrutinised for possible use in the problem-solving process.

Dreams

There are many examples where solutions to problems and/or famous inventions resulted from information or ideas contained in dreams. For example, team members could be asked to record their dreams and reflect on what these might tell them about the conscious problem-solving process. As a variant of brainstorming, members diarise their dreams and brainstorm about the potential rich unconscious messages they could reveal. This may appear unrelated, but the brainstorming potential "meaning" of such dreams often yields surprising results and alternatives.

In-out listening

This activity records the thought processes of individuals while they are involved in activities that are not necessarily directly related to the problem being considered. For example, when listening to a speech, a lecture or a presentation, or while in a meeting, members write down ideas. Members are asked to write down issues that are "in", i.e. relating to the topic being discussed, or "out", i.e. not related to the problem, but interesting, helpful or related to other parts of the team member's work life. Team members can then brainstorm on the items listed on the "in" and "out" columns.

Idea diary

Although this was originally designed to be used in larger organisations and with larger groups, it can be applied with great benefits to a team's divergent actions as well. The leader provides each team member with a notebook with a problem statement and some suggestions on how to go about brainstorming about the idea. Team members use the notebook as a "idea diary" by recording a single idea, solution or alternative about the challenge or problem each day. This project can be protracted over an extended period of time (e.g. two weeks). At the end of the period the team leader collates the material and summarises the contributions of the team.

Representation

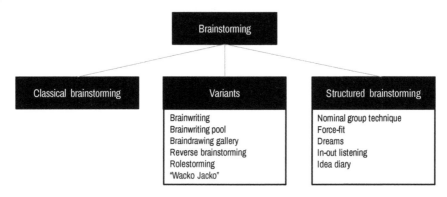

Figure 10.1: Brainstorming

References

Delbecq, A.L., Van de Ven, A.H. & Gustafson, D.H. (1975). *Group techniques for programme planning*. Glenview: Scott, Foresman.

Geschka, H., Schaude, G.R. & Schlicksupp, H. (1973). Modern Techniques for Problem Solving. *Chemical Engineering*, Aug, 91–97.

Kriek, H.S. (2007). *Creative problem solving: Techniques for South African teams*. Pretoria: Mindmuzik.

Osborne, A.F. (1963). *Applied imagination* (3rd ed.). New York: Scribner.

Thompson, L. (2007). *Making the Team: A guide for Managers* (3rd ed.). Upper Saddle River, NJ: Pearson Prentice Hall.

Van Gundy, A.B. (1988). *Techniques of structured problem solving* (2nd ed.). New York: Van Nostrand Reinhold.

Introduction

Another way to solicit divergent thinking is to explore the sub-elements or attributes of the idea, challenge, product or problem. Variants of attribute explorations are described to utilise the benefits afforded by looking at the components of what is explored.

In a nutshell

Divergent thinking through the use of attribute listing, combining and association.

Purpose

To facilitate divergent thinking.

To help get new ideas and generate new perspectives on the problem.

Description

Three different ways of exploring attributes are illustrated. The first is to list the attributes and to explore how that can lead to new ideas. In the second variant, these attributes are combined to explore new ways to view the issue at hand, while in the last variant team members make associations linked to the attributes of the problem. For example the team could consider the material of an object and explore various different materials that could replace the current material. Through exploring a variety of different materials (and/or other attributes of the material currently being used) new ideas are generated.

Attribute listing

The team lists all the attributes or sub-attributes of the problem. Members list as many analogies to the different categories or sub-attributes as they like. Once their ideas are exhausted the different analogies are used to find new ideas. The team identifies three to five different dimensions they wish to explore. These new ideas are entered into the problem-solving process. Once the team has agreed on the dimensions, they list as many different sub-divisions or elements within each of the dimensions they like. For example the dimension could be colour and a list of different colours can be made, or it could be "material" and a list of materials such as wood, plastic, metal, etc. could be provided.

Attribute combinations

Once all attributes have been explored the different results are compared and combined. Combinations of "new" attributes are then investigated for the insights they bring to the problem. These combinations can be explored through matrices, idea strips, concentric circles or cards.

Matrices

A matrix is generated where the various components of the first item are listed on one axis and the components of the other item are listed on the other axis. The different combinations are evaluated by:

- eliminating combinations of the components of the item that already exist;

- listing those cells where the combination between the two components seems immediately valuable; and

- listing those ideas that seem promising in the sense that they might allow some opportunities to emerge.

The last step consists of entering ideas and opportunities that emerge from the previous process into the problem-solving process and exploring any new ideas generated.

Idea strips

The team prepares one cardboard strip (approximately 3cm by 20cm) for each of the dimensions and writes the name/definition of each dimension as a heading on a strip, used lengthwise. Each of the attributes or components of each dimension are written on the strip one underneath the other. For example, if four dimensions have been identified you will have a list of possible attributes or components for each of the four strips. Put the four cardboard strips/columns next to each other and ensure that you can slide the cardboard columns up and down. By systematically moving the cardboard columns you will allow for each attribute or component on each strip to be seen in combination with all the attributes on all strips. The combination of four attributes (if four dimensions are chosen) allows opportunity for new perspectives on the problem to emerge.

Concentric circles

The same principle of component combination can be employed by using concentric circles and a tool can be constructed with four circles being put on top of each other. For example, on cardboard make a circle with a diameter of approximately 25 cm and cut it out. Make an additional three (or four depending on the number of dimensions) similar cardboard circles each about 10 cm in diameter larger than the other. Thus, if four dimensions are used you will have four circles each 10 cm larger than the other. It is often helpful to have them in separate colours as well. Stack the four circles on top of each other and connect them at the centre with a pin. It should now be possible to turn each of the circles independently. Subsequently write the different aspects of each dimension on each of the circles. Display this to the team and systematically turn the various circles to enable different combinations to be explored.

Cards

A further variant (that is easier and quicker) is to use index cards and write each aspect of each dimension on a separate card. Again it is helpful if different coloured cards can be used. Randomly select a card from each of the dimension stacks and display the four cards to the team by sticking them next to each other on a board. Allow time for exploration. The different permutations or combinations between different words are then generated by moving the strips, circles or cards to allow different words or concepts to be adjacent to each other.

Attribute association

Basic association

The team lists all the attributes or sub-attributes of the problem. For each of these the first word that comes to mind and that seemingly does not relate to the attribute or problem is listed. Once the list is complete this word (i.e. the association per attribute) is used in a free association process to generate ideas. Two variants of the association technique are described here, namely an association chain and a context chain.

Association chain

Members of the team are each asked to provide a word that is related to the problem or challenge and a word that is seemingly unrelated to the issue at hand, but for which a relationship can become apparent once it is explained. The team then takes these word pairs and must each suggest a word related to each of these two words. Once these words are collected the team is asked to link the two words stated initially with an association chain. This means that the different ideas and concepts provided by the rest of the team are used to create a chain of ideas to link the two initial words, which act as starting and finishing points respectively. Once a few of these rounds have been completed the team uses the different ideas to generate more ideas. It is key to the process that the links must be established through a reasoned and logical sequence. Both the association chain and any word within the chain can be used to generate more ideas. A variant of this type of association chain is to limit the association to context. Each team member is then asked to name an unrelated context and the different attributes are inked to the various contexts. The story lines or associations generated through developing the context chain are used for generating ideas.

Tips for team leaders

Ideas generated in any of these ways can be grouped into three major categories, namely:

* ideas that already exist;

* promising or provocative ideas; and

* ideas that can be used immediately.

Teams can also use computer-assisted search engines, random words or input from a thesaurus to help them generate words and ideas to explore and find associations.

Representation

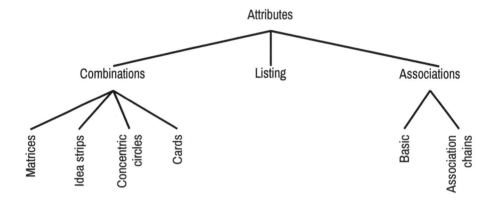

Figure 10.2: Attribute exploration

References

Kriek, H.S. (2007). *Creative problem solving: Techniques for South African teams*. Pretoria: Mindmuzik.

Van Gundy, A.B. (1988). *Techniques of structured problem solving* (2nd ed.). New York: Van Nostrand Reinhold.

Introduction

While it is often by thinking outside of conventional wisdom that new ideas appear and teams often succeed by looking beyond the ordinary to find solutions, the use of checklists offers a more structured and linear approach. This may sound counter-intuitive, but the use of checklists often provides new ways of thinking about the issues at hand that had not been considered before. By using various checklists the team interrogates the problem and tries to find new ways, alternatives or options to think about or approach the problem. It allows for diverging thinking, and new perspectives on the problem may arise.

In a nutshell

The team uses checklists to find new ways to look at a problem.

Purpose

To expand ideas.

To find new ways of looking at a problem.

To stimulate creativity.

To follow a structured way of interrogating the issues at hand.

Description

An example of a basic checklist is given here, followed by four different examples of helpful checklists offered by Osborne, Davis and Scott, Eberle, and Shore. Teams can use them independently or can apply more than one at the same time and investigate the problem from different angles.

Basic checklist

Teams can utilise a basic set of questions or they can devise their own questions to interrogate the issue at hand. As has been indicated earlier, they can also use the questions to assess their own team. Some basic questions include:

- Why is it necessary?

- Where should it be done?

- When should it be done?

- Who should do it?

- What should be done?

- How should it be done?

Osborne's checklist

Osborne, the originator of brainstorming as a technique, devised a list of questions that can be applied as a checklist to good effect.

- How can the product be modified?

- How can I add to the product to magnify it?

- How can I take away to "minify" the product?

- What can I do to substitute products or components of the product?

- How can the product's composition be altered or rearranged?

- How can the product be turned around or reversed?

- What can be combined with the product to make a new one?

Davis and Scott's checklist

The checklist offered by these two authors is particularly helpful when products are investigated for improvement or new ideas.

- What can be added or subtracted from the product?

- How can the colours be changed?

- How can materials be varied?

- How can the product's parts be rearranged?

- How can the shape be varied?

- Can the size be changed?

- Can the design or size be modified?

Eberle's checklist (SCAMPER)

Eberle created a checklist with a mnemonic that makes it easy to remember the elements of the list. Using the key word in each sentence the mnemonic SCAMMPEERR can be spelled. Bear in mind that the "m", "e" and "r" each has two words in the list, but convention dictates that "SCAMPER" is used rather than the awkward longer version:

- What can be Substituted to enhance the product?

- How can the product be Combined to form a new product?

- In what way can the product be Adapted?

- How can we Minify the product or components thereof?

- How can we Magnify the product or components thereof?

- How can the product or parts thereof be Put to other uses?

- Can elements of the product be Eliminated?

- Can elements of the product be Elaborated?

- How can the product be Rearranged?

- Can the product be Reversed?

Shore's checklist (CREATIVITY)

"Creativity" is another mnemonic, again made up of the key words in the checklist. It is particularly useful for providing new ideas on products or in challenging thinking on problems.

- How can the product be Combined to be enhanced?

- Can the product be Reversed?

- Can anything be Enlarged?

- Can anything be Adapted?

- What can be made Tinier?

- Can anything be done or used Instead of what is used currently?

- What insights does a Change of viewpoint bring?

- Are there things that can be used In other ways?

- Are there things that can be put To other uses?

- Yes?

Tips for team leaders

It is helpful to ask team members to go through the chosen checklist individually first to determine what they regard as the most critical questions. Sometimes the use of a checklist reveals a need for information and data that are not immediately available to the team. Time should be allocated to find this information. It is sometimes necessary for teams to meet specific demands within their organisations. Teams should augment and expand the checklist to ensure that it covers all their requirements. The use of checklists should be to explore and investigate, therefore this approach can be used during other problem-solving processes as well.

Representation

Checklists				
Basic	Osborne	Davis & Scott	Eberle (SCAMPER)	Shore (CREATIVITY)

Figure 10.3: Checklists

References

Davis, G.A. & Scott, S.A. (1978). *Training creative thinking*. Huntington: Krieger.

Eberle, R. (1996). *Games for imagination development*. Buffalo: D.O.K. Press.

Kriek, H.S. (2007). *Creative problem solving: Techniques for South African teams*. Pretoria: Mindmuzik.

Osborne, A.F. (1963). *Applied imagination* (3rd ed.). New York: Scribner.

Shore, S. (1972). *Creativity in action*. Sharon: Connecticut.

Semantics

Introduction

By utilising "semantics", the team combines various words or uses words in combinations to explore ideas of how the team operates or to find alternatives to solve a problem. The technique utilises the opportunities that can emerge from combining different sets of words and exploring the nature of the combination to find new combinations or explore the issue at hand.

In a nutshell

By exploring relationships between words the team gets creative input.

Purpose

To explore new ideas.

To find innovative and novel ways of exploring the problem by combining different words.

To explore relationships between elements of a problem.

To interrogate interrelations and interactions between systems.

Description

Semantics gives teams language tools to apply to various challenges and problems. These tools elicit relationships, open new opportunities and expand ideas to help the team to find new connections. Here two main types are described, namely grammatical combinations and relationship exploration.

Grammatical combinations

This application facilitates the idea-generating process by exploring combinations of particular morphological pairs. The team makes four columns on a piece of paper, flip-chart or spreadsheet and labels the columns Nouns, Verbs, Adjectives and Adverbs. The team then writes any word they can think of related to the problem in the appropriate column. Once the list has been generated, the words are combined in pairs in any grammatical combination, e.g. noun-verb or adjective-noun. The resulting combinations are used to find new ideas. The team explores new insights into the problem that these word pairs might bring. The team may also randomly select any two words from the list and explores if any combination of these words could lead to new ideas about the problem.

Van Gundy's word diamond

This technique is based on the same idea, but the four word categories are assigned to the four corners of a diamond shape. The words generated by the team in connection with the problem or issue at hand are then written in the appropriate corner of the diamond. The team then makes a variety of word combinations as before, exploring these combinations for ideas.

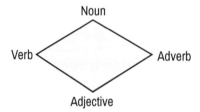

Relationship exploration

Ask the team to apply any set of words to the problem at hand to explore the relationships between elements or components of the problem. This can be done by using relationship words (see below) or unrelated words. A further way to explore relationships is to construct relationship chains by combining various words.

Unrelated words

The team lists as many words, ideas or concepts as possible related to the problem at hand. As a second step they make an additional list of unrelated words. The challenge for the team is to find analogies between a related and an unrelated word. The list can be from the environment, from magazines, from personal experience or any source that can assist the team to list words or concepts unrelated to the problem.

Relational words

Provide each team member with a sheet of relational words or display the list to the team in some way. These words, all prepositions or conjunctions, are used to link various attributes or components of objects and concepts, and thus different relationships between them are established and can be examined. Through this exploration and examination new ideas might arise that can be used in the problem-solving process. For example, two components are chosen and a different relational word is inserted between them. Nuances that transpire are included in the idea-generating process.

List of relational words

About	Above	Across	After	Against	Along
Amid	Among	Around	As	At	Because
Before	Behind	Beneath	Beside	Between	Beyond

By	Down	During	For	From	If
In	Into	Near	Of	Off	On
Opposite	Or	Out	Over	Past	Round
Since	Until	Then	Through	Until	To
Towards	Underneath	Up	Upon	While	With
Within	Without				

Relationship chain

The team chooses one word related to the topic in hand and one unrelated word. They then have to try and find a chain of thought between the two words by using relational words. The two words are written on a flip-chart with the first one at the top and the second at the bottom. The team must now provide a chain of ideas (i.e. a train of thought) to link the two concepts by using the list of relational words or another set of unrelated words. Every word chosen must thus be related to the preceding word. This reveals the analogous elements between concepts and objects. Key to the activity is that there need to be at least five steps between the two original words. Thus, the word originally chosen (and related to the problem) must be linked to five subsequent words until a relationship with the second word originally chosen (i.e. an unrelated word or concept) can be established. Once the chain has been established it is used to generate ideas regarding the problem the team is addressing.

Tips for team leaders

Exploration of grammatical combinations and other word relationships can be used by teams to find novel and innovative relations between different concepts, products or systems. It is often useful for the team to generate specific attributes or components and then apply relational words to that single idea. It can be used as a kind of checklist to expand one's ideas regarding the attribute or component and once new relationships are constructed, they can be employed usefully to find new products or different ways to address issues and challenges. The same approach can be used to evaluate current team performance.

Representation

"Semantics"	
Grammatical combinations	Relationship exploration
Van Gundy's word diamond	Unrelated words Relationship words Relationship chains

Figure 10.4: Semantics

Reference

Kriek, H.S. (2007). *Creative problem solving: Techniques for South African teams*. Pretoria: Mindmuzik.

Van Gundy, A.B. (1988). *Techniques of structured problem solving* (2nd ed.). New York: Van Nostrand Reinhold.

Representational techniques

Introduction

This technique represents ideas, information, problems or alternatives in a visual fashion. It is particularly helpful to provide a visual presentation of problems and to indicate relationships between different aspects thereof. It helps to show major components of an issue or to cluster various aspects that belong together, and when the team observes and analyses the visual representation new ideas about the problem or challenge may come to the fore. Different types of representation are offered, namely mind-mapping, projective techniques and time-related presentations.

In a nutshell

The team uses a representation of an issue, problem or challenge to generate new ideas.

Purpose

To give a visual representation of the issue at hand.

To use a projective technique to elicit the team's understanding of issues.

To understand dynamics and interrelationships between elements of the problem from different perspectives.

Description

The well-known concept of mind-mapping is presented first, after which three projective techniques, i.e. metaphors, collage and Gestalt, are described. Lastly, techniques that consider an issue in relation to time are presented.

Mind-mapping

Buzan is accepted as the father of this technique, which is used beyond the boundaries of idea-generation. Here the focus is narrower, i.e. to explore the team's divergent efforts around an issue or problem. The issue the team is addressing is written in the centre of a flip-chart sheet or blackboard. It is preferable to circle the issue or to demarcate it as the core of the issue. A new branch is then drawn from the core for each sub-topic or cluster. The branch or cluster is labelled with the concept best describing the cluster. A circle, block or "cloud" can be used to enclose the title of the sub-topic. Each of these clusters is dissected and analysed in turn and different branches of each identified and labelled. The interrelation and interaction of the various branches, clusters and sub-topics should be indicated by numbers, colours or lines. Aspects can be duplicated on different branches where required.

Projective techniques

The use of projective techniques gives an opportunity to the team to present perceptions, feelings and ideas about how the team functions through metaphors and analogies rather than having to express them directly. As a projective technique it creates a sense of safety and often brings surprisingly candid and honest views about the team. There are a number of variants, of which three are described here to illustrate their potential application: metaphor, collage and Gestalt.

Metaphor

Each team member is asked to describe a metaphor that best represents how he or she views the problem or that describes the problem best. The metaphor can also be supplemented with an adjective to expand and enrich the metaphor. Once each member has contributed, the different metaphors are compared and insights into the team are extrapolated. Thus, the team lists all the characteristics of the metaphor, the adjective as well as the context. It explores insights that the metaphor and its descriptors provide, and common themes or shared characteristics are collated. The team is then asked to use these shared ideas to form a new metaphor that incorporates as many as possible of the characteristics.

Collage

The facilitator hands out old magazines or newspapers to the team. They are asked to make an individual or team collage of the problem. They cut out any number of pictures or words and paste them onto a sheet of paper (A1 or flip-chart sheet). This collage of pictures and words can then be displayed to the team and used as a way of exploring the problem for insights it reveals. These insights can be used to redefine the problem, to ensure that the team agrees on what the real issue entails, and to explore solutions.

Gestalt

The activity consists of the team "sculpting" the team by using their own bodies to do the presentation. It is, therefore, a kind of Gestalt in that it involves the whole team. The team is then debriefed regarding the insights that were revealed through the activity (i.e. the team "being" or "playing" the team). Variants include:

Real-life presentation

The team considers a metaphor they think will depict the problem best. They then sculpt the problem as this metaphor (i.e. build the sculpture by using their bodies and/or positioning themselves). In this regard it is beneficial to ask every member to position themselves in a specific position aligned with their individual views of the team.

Acting

The team discusses the issue and provides a story or a narrative to explore and explain the problem. Often it is helpful if it is a fable or a fairy tale. The idea is that a story is told (or enacted) that allows the problem to be presented in a somewhat distant manner. Sometimes teams find it helpful for a problem to be presented as if it is not their own problem. For example, it is quite different to portray a large ogre screaming and fighting with a dwarf than to acknowledge that a boss or a superior is arrogant and brash with his or her staff. Presenting the problem in terms of a narrative also allows an opportunity to introduce a variety of characters to play about with the context of the problem.

Floating team sculpt

Hawkins provided an elaborate and powerful combination of these metaphors with what he called a "floating team sculpt". In brief this consists of a team finding a metaphor of what is at the heart of the team and putting it in the middle of the team. Each member is then requested to position him or herself around the "heart" of the team and in relation to other members in the team. Members then express how it feels to be in this particular position, i.e. in relation to the centre and to other team members. Opportunity is given to team members to adjust their position and discussion follows on what such changes entail for others. Team members are then asked to reframe the metaphor by reflecting on its nature, for example to describe it as if it was a family, or a television programme, or a country. As a final step, members are allowed to leave their positions and review the sculpture from different angles and vantage points to facilitate discussion.

Timeline

The team presents the problem as if on a timeline. A starting point is determined and a long, single line is drawn to the envisaged end. This gives the team an opportunity to view the problem from different perspectives (as if on a timeline) and allows a variety of new insights to come to the fore. Variants described include gap analysis, travel in time, act out and emotional map.

Gap analysis

This technique is a useful tool to give a graphic presentation of the team's current position as well as to indicate where it would like to be in the future. It is used extensively in organisational strategic processes, but can be simplified for teams and their problem-solving efforts. It makes use of three "states" the team has to address, namely the:

- "to be" or desired state: this refers to the position where the team wants to be once the problem has been resolved. It is future-orientated and assists the team to look beyond current constraints to an ideal position. Often it is helpful to use this stage to explore possibilities and every member's contribution and dreams for the team should be included;

- "as is" or current state: this describes the current issues of the team and is dependent on the team's assumptions and perceptions. It is critical that the team is realistic in its analysis of the current state, and it can be helpful to elicit feedback from other stakeholders or to obtain information that can assist the team in constructing the "as-is" state; and

- "implementation" or transformation state: this refers to the part of the process where change takes place from the current position to the desired state.

Travel in time

This technique is used to provide different perspectives on the problem as the team "travels in time" and reviews the problem from different temporal vantage points. It is often helpful to allow the team to physically act out this concept. In this case, a line is drawn on the floor. The team is then asked to act out the problem or to view the problem from various positions on this line. The members physically stand at different positions on the line. In this way the team can view the problem from the start or origin thereof, at a critical junction or from the end. The end-state is the desired outcome where the team addresses the issue from the point where it has been solved successfully. Another way is to "move up the timeline" to critical junctions or to certain milestones. The team can then speculate on events that might influence the progress of solving the issue.

Act out

The facilitator can give the team the opportunity to role-play critical positions on the timeline. For example there are roles that might be explored, hiccups or difficulties in the process, or even celebrations that can be acted out. This allows the team insight into some of the critical factors influencing the problem and allows the opportunity to view the impact or effect of the systems it operates in.

Emotional map

The team considers the problem on the timeline and each member indicates the emotional response it elicits from them. If possible use a metaphor to describe the effect it has on you. For example you can say it makes you feel like a dinosaur, a vice grip or a watch. Each team member's perception of the progress of the team is indicated on the line at the corresponding place and is relative to the start and finishing positions.

Tips for team leaders

Sometimes it is helpful if the metaphor is contextualised (e.g. by giving a location where the metaphor is to be found). The location adds to how the problem is perceived and could reveal boundaries or hidden assumptions the team harbours regarding the problem. For example the problem can be described as a hairy spider lurching in the night or an old train engine on a deserted station. These contexts can then be explored for how they might influence the team's perspectives.

Representation

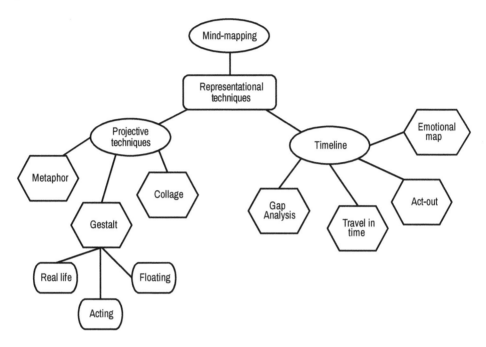

Figure 10.5: Representational techniques

References

Buzan, T. & Buzan, B. (1993). *The Mind Map book: How to use radiant thinking to maximize your brain's untapped potential*. New York: Plume.

Kriek, H.S. (2007). *Creative problem solving: Techniques for South African teams*. Pretoria: Mindmuzik.

Hawkins, P. (2017). *Leadership team coaching: Developing collective transformational leadership*. London: Kogan Page.

11

CONVERGING TECHNIQUES

For any team it is critical to use appropriate techniques to limit the various ideas and potential solutions that are generated through any of the suggestions described in the previous section, and to make appropriate decisions from a list of alternatives.

The first part of this chapter presents screening criteria to help a team find boundaries and therefore to eliminate some of the alternatives that have been produced. Snowball techniques help the team to cluster and evaluate lists of alternatives, and teams can also use matrices to limit and cluster the ideas. Next, the normative decision-making model of Vroom-Yetton-Jago is presented. This model can be applied to help leaders choose the style of decision-making best suited for any particular setting. The section continues with a description of various voting methods. The last two parts describe biases and logical fallacies that can interfere with rational argument and other common decision-making problems that may arise, such as groupthink and related scenarios.

Introduction

Once a team has generated a large number of ideas through exhaustive creative processes, all those potential ideas have to be screened in order for the most useful ones to be taken further.

In a nutshell

The team screens a large number of ideas to select the most useful.

Purpose

To limit a large number of ideas to a more useful list.

To cluster ideas produced by the team.

Description

An obvious way to screen a number of alternatives is to allow each member a limited pre-determined number of votes, which are subsequently counted. However there are various other ways of examining and prioritising the ideas, divided here into screening criteria.

Screening criteria

Ideas can be sorted according to the following criteria:

*   Implementability: all ideas are screened and sorted according to how easy or difficult it would be to implement them.

*   Potential: the potential of the ideas are screened by clustering ideas into "Yes" (can be explored more), "No" (it is not beneficial to investigate the team's resources on the issue) or "Maybe" (adapting some future use could be explored).

*   Shared characteristics: similarities are used to put various ideas into clusters, including "Use" (helpful and implementable as is), "Combine" (ideas that can form part of other combinations or systems) or "Trash" (ideas that are not immediately helpful).

*   Concerns: ideas are categorised as "Plusses" (the biggest advantages offered by the idea), "Potentials" (potentially good ideas are identified) and "Concerns" (doubts, scepticism, second thoughts and suspicions regarding the value of the idea are raised).

- Enablers and inhibiters: this evaluates solutions or ideas in terms of whether they enable or inhibit the solution-seeking process.

- "Pro's or con's": the team gets an opportunity to provide immediate responses regarding the benefits or disadvantages of a proposed idea or solution.

- Solution-specific criteria, e.g. acceptability: the alignment of the solution with the goals of the team; practicality: the extent to which the solution could be adopted within the existing financial or time constraints; and originality: an evaluation on whether the solution provides a significant contribution and/or improvement on the situation.

After classifiying the ideas or solutions into clusters through any of these methods, the team then decides on the next steps to be taken.

Snowball techniques

Another technique for dealing with a list of generated ideas is called the snowball technique. In these methods, these ideas are clustered in the same way as "a snowball becomes bigger".

Elementary snowball

The facilitator starts with the first idea and the team decides whether it is a valuable idea. If they agree that it is valuable for further use it is labelled as "number one" or "A". The next idea is considered. If it is related to the first, it is again denoted with a "one" or "A". However, if the team thinks it is a new category it is denoted with a "two" or "B" and if it is not of value it is discarded. The team evaluates all the ideas according to these classifications.

Itemised snowball

Each idea is transferred onto an index card. Only one idea is written on each card. The team then sticks or pins the cards onto a clean surface (e.g. a wall or whiteboard). Once all the ideas are all displayed, the team collectively sorts the ideas according to any organising principle of their choice, moving the cards around to present the clusters visually. This can be done by merely pinning the different idea cards that belong to the same theme close to each other or in a vertical column (resembling an organogram). Every team member is given as an opportunity to change any idea and move any of the cards between the emerging themes and/or categories. The clustering ends once the team reaches consensus on the organising principle and the classification or categorisation of the different themes.

Emotional snowball

Although the process can be completed at this stage it is sometimes helpful to stress the emotional attachment between the items and the team members. This "connection" is explored by allowing each member to examine the list in silence and to identify those ideas that appeal to them or what they find intriguing. The team discusses these emotional connections and why an idea is meaningful to the particular member. The objective is to screen out some ideas that cannot proceed to the next levels of the process, but this should not be regarded as the final evaluation. Rather, care should be taken not to discard any disagreement or alternative clustering too quickly.

Idea cards

Each of the ideas is written on a separate index card (i.e. an idea card). The cards are collected and laid out on a table. Each one is read out aloud as it is put on the table. The ideas that are related and "belong together" are grouped together. Some ideas might not seem to relate to any other ideas initially. These idea cards are not discarded, but are kept on the table. The team continues with the process until as many as possible of the idea cards are grouped together. The groups of cards are then labelled. The name or label of each of the groups are written on another card and put on top of the pile of cards. Often it is helpful to use different coloured cards for naming the groups. The process is repeated, now using the group titles and the "wild-cards" to see if logical connections, relations or associations can be found. This is obviously a higher level of abstraction, where the stacks of cards and any wild-cards found to be related are sub-sets of a "higher" level. These "higher" level sets are labelled and a different coloured idea card is again used to denote the cluster.

Sorting techniques

The team evaluates all alternatives and distributes them on a normal distribution graph (a Bell curve) according to each alternative's perceived utility. The team agrees on the 50 to 100 items that need to be sorted, and the number of categories they prefer to work with. It is often helpful to have an uneven number of categories as it assists the process of decision-making. Five, seven or nine categories usually work best. The team calculates how many items must be in each of the categories given the number of ideas that have been generated. The team then evaluates the various ideas and puts them into the specific categories according to the number of items allowed per category. For instance, if 70 items had been generated and the team decides on nine categories to consider, the most important two items will be put in the first category and the least important two will be put in the last category (and thereby will be eliminated). The next most important four and the next least important four will be put into the next categories. All the ideas are then entered into the appropriate category. Once the categorisation has been completed, the team decides on a specific cut-off point of what they want to include in their discussions for further examination.

Matrices

The use of matrices can be regarded as synonymous with management and a large variety have been proposed to help managers. In this instance we refer to matrices used to help teams to evaluate various ideas in order to decide which to keep and use. Three different matrices are described here, namely a basic matrix, a control/energy matrix and the so-called COCD box (Byttebier). The team inserts the various ideas they have generated in the appropriate quadrant and is then in a position to decide on the appropriate next steps.

Basic matrix

Any two key decision criteria (see above) can be put on a matrix with appropriate evaluating criteria such as good/bad, strong/weak or important/not important on the other axis. All the ideas can then be put in the appropriate quadrants.

Control/energy matrix

In this matrix activities or ideas are categorised according to the locus of control (i.e. within or outside the team's control) on one axis and energy expenditure (i.e. the team should or should not spend energy on the particular issue) on the other axis. Regarding the former, the team evaluates its activities according to whether it is within the team's control to carry out the idea or activity, or not. The second axis addresses the advisability of spending energy on the action. All the ideas and/or alternatives are put in the appropriate quadrant.

COCD box

A similar matrix is used to classify ideas in terms of originality versus potential for implementation:

- Originality: is the proposed direction of the team novel, yet aligned with organisational or industry constraints including product ranges and technological advances and developments?

- Potential for implementation: is there a high or low potential for implementation? Costs, technical demands, fit with strategic objectives and legal compliance are all aspects that are considered when deciding on the implementation potential of each idea.

The quadrants of the matrix are colour-coded:

- Blue ideas: left bottom quadrant, indicating the overlap between ideas with the potential to be implemented, but which are not original and novel. These ideas are handy and useful, but do not provide anything special.

- Red ideas: right bottom quadrant, indicating the overlap between ideas with the potential to be implemented and which are also original and innovative. These ideas generate a positive emotional response with members and are motivating and energising.

- Yellow ideas: right top quadrant, indicating the overlap between ideas that are not immediately possible to realise, but that are original, innovative and novel. The team must ensure that these ideas are not lost as they might be useful at another stage (e.g. with a different budget) or might be able to be transformed into something useful (e.g. through utilising some elements for something else).

- White ideas: left top quadrant, indicating ideas that are discarded as they are not original and moreover do not have the potential to be realised.

The team allocate each of the ideas to the appropriate quadrant of the matrix and each of the three coloured quadrants are then entered into further stages of the problem solving process. Care should be taken to determine the selection criteria and to ensure that members agree on the categorisation of different items.

Tips for team leaders

Screening techniques give opportunities to teams to limit the various and sometimes unnecessary long lists of ideas and alternatives. Through screening, ideas are clustered and the more helpful ones are identified. It is the responsibility of the leader to guide the process and to ensure that valuable information is not lost through a screening process that is too narrow or alternatively too broad and general.

Representation

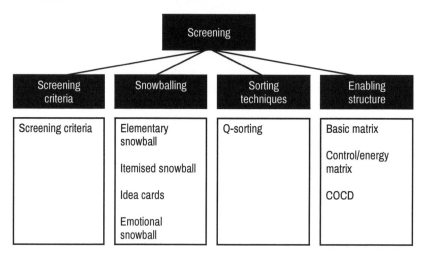

Figure 11.1: Screening techniques

References

Byttebier, I. (2002). *Creativiteit Hoe Zo?: Inzicht, inspiratie en toepassingen voor het optimal benutten van uw eigen creativiteit en die van uw organisatie*. Tielt: Lannoo.

Kriek, H.S. (2007). *Creative problem solving: Techniques for South African teams*. Pretoria: Mindmuzik.

Van Gundy, A.B. (1988). *Techniques of structured problem solving* (2nd ed.). New York: Van Nostrand Reinhold.

52 | Decision-making techniques

Introduction

Once a team has identified a limited list of potential ideas it is helpful to pick the best solution using voting variants. Sometimes it is helpful for teams to rank the various alternatives and to decide according to how each alternative is evaluated against the other alternatives. Obviously, computer systems and technology are becoming more widespread for complicated decisions and a number of scientific disciplines (e.g. Operations Research) are devoted to the improvement of decision-making. In particular, estimations that assist with scenario planning, risk analysis and decision trees can be mentioned, and teams will be well-advised to use them in complicated business decisions. Here the focus is on how to help teams in their daily functions and how basic decision-making techniques can help them to improve the performance of team-related issues.

In a nutshell

The team uses various forms of voting and ranking to make a decision.

Purpose

To decide on the preferred solution.

To ensure a fair decision-making process.

To facilitate balanced decision-making.

To determine preferred alternatives.

To organise a set of options.

Description

One of the following methods is employed when the number of alternatives has been limited and a decision on the preferred option is required.

Voting

The team votes by using any of the following types of voting modes:

Direct voting

This is a system of counting votes for and votes against a particular issue at hand. The argument or viewpoint with the most votes is the one the team prefers.

Minimum number of votes

Sometimes it is helpful for a team to decide beforehand on a certain minimum number of votes that will be regarded as a threshold. After a vote, only those options that received a pre-agreed number of votes will be entered into subsequent rounds.

Reverse voting

Sometimes it is helpful to vote first for the option that the team wants to eliminate and then continue by a process of elimination to determine the preferred choice(s).

Run-off voting

After an initial round of voting, the top two alternatives are entered into a final voting procedure. Every team member then votes again, but this time has only the two top options to choose from. This allows for team members that have preferred any other alternatives to apply their minds to the key alternatives, and this generally increases the quality of the outcome.

Voting with criteria

The team generates minimum criteria and/or standards and agrees that they will be used to evaluate alternatives. It is critical to understand that determining the criteria to be used is a key part of the process as it can influence the outcome. A matrix with the alternatives in a vertical column and criteria on a horizontal row is provided. The team evaluates each of the alternatives by assessing to what extent they satisfy each criterion. The alternative that satisfies all or the most criteria should be the preferred option.

Weighted averages

The team generates and agrees on the criteria that will be used to evaluate alternatives and determines a relative weight and/or importance for each criterion. A matrix is produced with the alternatives in a vertical column and the criteria entered in a horizontal row. Each alternative is evaluated by assessing to what extent it satisfies each criterion. The score obtained by each alternative on each criterion is therefore multiplied by the weight attached to the criterion. The alternative that attracts the highest score is chosen. The criteria must be relevant and applicable and care should be taken not to make them too broad. Therefore, care should be taken that the process does not contain hidden assumptions guiding the selection of criteria and that the process does not favour solutions that might not be the best outcome.

Ranking

Forced Ranking

Each team member ranks the alternatives individually and they are therefore "forced" to give their preferences. Scores are calculated to determine the preferred option. Three different types of ranking criteria are explained here, namely quantitative, qualitative and criterion-based ranking.

Quantitative ranking

Options can be calculated by the members indicating the most preferred option with "1", the second most preferred alternative as "2", etc. Once completed the leader tabulates the votes by:

*   adding the rank order votes (remember the one with the least number of votes is the preferred option); or

*   calculating the number of times an alternative was picked as the preferred option.

Qualitative ranking

This technique gives the opportunity to rank items through qualitative assessment, by indicating the level of like or dislike of a particular item. This can be done by assigning either one, two or three stars according to the strength of the preference and indicating that in the particular block on the matrix where the different items are compared.

Criterion-based ranking

Each alternative is ranked according to its advantages, limitations and unique qualities by applying the following process:

*   Generate as many advantages of each alternative as possible. Any idea-generating technique can be applied.

*   Then generate all the limitations that you can think of.

*   Lastly make a list of all the unique or unusual attributes and/or qualities of the alternative.

The other alternatives are examined in the same way. The results are used in a final decision-making process.

Paired comparison

Once a team has produced a list of items that need to be ranked, the process of paired comparison can commence. Write down an item on each line and each column of the matrix. In other words, each item is written on the vertical as well as the horizontal axis. Each item is compared against each of the other items and for each pair a preference is decided. In the corresponding block the preferred item is encircled. Once all the items are compared against each other, the number of circles obtained by each of the items is written down in the total section. This provides the rank of the different items.

Hierarchical ranking

The Analytic Hierarchy Process (AHP) was originally developed by Saaty to derive ratio scales from paired comparisons. A paired comparison refers to a relative scale to measure how much one option is preferred over another. The AHP technique is helpful in providing a ranking of various alternatives or items. It compares the various alternatives with one another and thereby determines the order of preference of the team. Thus, the technique establishes which the team regards as the most important, which is the next most important, and so on, and how each of the alternatives compares with the others. The method is analytical and structures the problem as a hierarchy. It is useful as it helps to determine a process to select between alternatives.

Decision tree

This technique provides a graphic display of the decision process. It is particularly helpful in situations of uncertainty and risk and helps the team to determine possible outcomes of various decisions. It is often used in situations where a sequence of decision-making options is required. A decision tree is based on the following fundamental concepts:

- Alternatives: this is an alternative course of action, strategy or implementation plan a team might choose. A decision-node is used to indicate an opportunity where a decision between a number of alternatives is required by the team. There will always be at least one set of alternatives since the team can decide to do nothing or something.

- State of nature: this represents situations in the future that would be likely to impact on the final outcome. Often it is something over which the team has no control, such as a competitor launching a new product or increases/decreases in interest rates.

- Conditional value or payoff: for any alternative and any particular state of nature there is usually a consequence or an outcome which is the conditional value. Although it is not always the case, this value is most often expressed as a monetary value. This is also called the pay-off of the decision.

- Probability: this is the team's assessment of the likelihood that a state of nature will occur.

At first it is sufficient to indicate the various states of nature that might occur. Once the tree has been constructed, probabilities can be assigned to the likelihood that particular states of nature will occur. This is based on the assessment of the team and any technique can be used to ascertain the team's decision. Estimate payoffs for all the combinations of alternatives and states of nature. This is done by working from right to left in the decision tree and calculating the expected monetary values for each state-of-nature node. Decide on the best alternative depending on the calculations.

Tips for team leaders

Consider more than one way of voting on the quality of decision-making. While using criteria may look instantly appealing, this method can lead to less than optimal decisions should the criteria not be selected with care. By using various ranking options teams can find common ground more easily and can use mathematical tools to help them in their decision-making. The use of complicated and comprehensive electronic decision-making tools enhances decision-making and leaders should utilise these to augment the techniques described here.

Representation

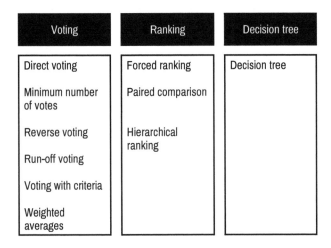

Figure 11.2: Decision-making techniques

References

Kriek, H.S. (2007). *Creative problem solving: Techniques for South African teams*. Pretoria: Mindmuzik.

Saaty, T.L. (1980). The *Analytic Hierarchy Process*. Available from: https://www.sciencedirect.com/science/article/pii/0270025587904738.

Saaty, T.L. & Vargas L.G. (2001). *Models, methods, concepts and applications of the analytic hierarchy process*. Dordrecht: Kluwer.

53 | # Normative decision-making model (Vroom-Yetton-Jago)

Introduction

The normative decision-making model aims to determine the management style best suited for a particular situation. It was developed by Victor Vroom and Phillip Yetton, and later with the help of Arthur Jago was augmented to its current form. Here the Vroom-Yetton-Jago normative decision-making model is presented from a group (i.e. team) perspective. It is necessary to keep in mind that it is a normative model and is therefore best used as prescribed.

In a nutshell

Steps to follow in a normative decision-making process.

Purpose

To guide a team to more effective decision-making.

To decide on appropriate decision-making processes.

Description

The original perspective identified five decision processes or styles that range from highly autocratic through consultative to highly participative (i.e. consensus). However, the framework is contextual and argues that the decision processes a leader employs are dependent on situational variables. The decision on which of these five styles to employ is thus determined by the situation the team faces, and in this regard the authors propose seven situational variables to consider when choosing how to proceed. The model is by definition suited for teams as it describes the leader's interaction in terms of groups, but for the sake of completeness the individual decision-making nodes are also included here.

Decision processes

The five decision processes or styles that are distinguished to move from no team member participation, to considerable participation in the decision-making process.

Autocratic style

Two different versions of this style are identified.

Autocratic style 1 (A1)

The leader makes the decision individually and independently, using only information that is available at the time. Based on the knowledge or information the leader already has, the leader solves a problem, gives advice or makes a decision.

Autocratic style 2 (A2)

The leader makes a decision without involvement from subordinates in this style as well. The difference is that the leader may require information from team members (e.g. a report or data set), but then decides on a solution to the problem alone. Members are not involved in any discussion on the problem and their views are not considered; assistance from the team is limited to providing information.

Consultative Style

Consultative 1 (C1)

The first level of consulting with the team (CI) allows individual discussion and soliciting views and ideas from individual members. This can be done through discussion, sharing reports, or asking for their ideas. However, the leader does not bring the team together and discussion is limited to individual one-on-one discussions. The leader until makes a decision individually and the decision may or may not include the suggestions and views of the team members.

Consultative 2 (C2)

In this style the leader extends the consultative effort by meeting with the team. Again, opportunity is given for the team to make suggestions and share their ideas, but this time it is collective and in a meeting or workshop setting. This allows for discussion with the leader and among the group, and the leader could share in the discussion and be influenced by it. However, the final decision remains that of the leader and again it may or may not include the views, ideas and suggestions of the team.

Group style

Group 1 (G1)

This style is characterised by a more inclusive and collective decision-making process. The leader shares the problem with the team and together they generate and evaluate alternatives. Attempts are made to reach consensus, but it is not necessary as long as the team is involved and a collective decision is made, e.g. after discussion a vote determines the selected solution. In this style the leader acts as a chairperson who coordinates the discussion, focuses on the problem and makes sure that critical issues are discussed. A key difference from the previous styles is the willingness of the leader to be open to solutions of the team and to accept the team's view as binding. The leader does not try to get his or her views adopted by the team, but rather is prepared to be persuaded and accept the preferred solution of the team. The role of the leader in this style is to ensure the team supports the solution and that there is sufficient "buy-in" for the team decision to be implemented.

Situational variables

The seven situational variables (see below as questions used in the decision tree) that influence which style should be used have been developed from the original list offered by Vroom and Yetton. The authors contended that three factors of the situation should guide the leaders to choose which decision-making style to use. These three main factors work together, namely quality, the potential for collaboration, and the amount of time available.

Quality

The quality or rationality of the decision refers to how critical it is to come up with the right decision. While it seems obvious that one should always make the right choice, reality determines that some decisions are regarded as more important than others. For instance, more resources should be allocated to decisions that are truly going to shape the future of the team or that will require a change of direction or use many resources. Quality also dictates that the future (potential) consequences of the decision should be considered.

Commitment

The next situational factor to keep in mind is whether the acceptance or commitment of the team are required to execute the decision effectively: in some cases such commitment will have a direct and strong impact while in other cases a lack of commitment may have no effect. If, 'buy-in' from the team is required, it will be beneficial to include them in the decision-making process. Thus, this situational factor evaluates the extent to which collaboration and consultation are needed from the team involved.

Time

The timeline required for effective implementation of a decision is the next situational factor to consider. Leaders have to assess the amount of time required to make the decision and the availability of time will determine whether others in the team could be included in the decision-making process. This should be weighed against the opportunities afforded by involving more members on the quality of the end product.

Decision tree

Vroom and Jago offered the following questions to guide the decision-making process:

- Is there a quality requirement such that one solution is likely to be more rational than another?
- Do I have sufficient information to make a high-quality decision?

- Is the problem structured?
- Is acceptance of the decision by subordinates critical to effective implementation?
- If I were to make of the decision by myself, is it reasonably certain that it would be accepted by my subordinates?
- Do subordinates share the organisational goals to be attained in solving this problem?
- Is conflict among subordinates likely in preferred solutions? (This question is irrelevant to individual problems.)
- Do subordinates have sufficient information to make a high-quality decision?

The authors used a decision tree to help leaders understand the various options and the representation below shows how it works. The leader uses the questions at the top and in each "column" makes a "yes" or "no" decision. Moving from left to right, the responses to each of the subsequent questions clarify the situation more, and in the end offer the leader an indication of which style is best suited for the particular situation.

Tips for team leaders

One of the main benefits of this model is its flexibility in the way it encourages leaders to expand their repertoire of styles to fit particular situations. Thus, the spectrum of styles is very helpful, including the reality that sometimes the autocratic style is most appropriate. While Vroom and his colleagues tried to include human factors, the model is rather mechanistic and leaders should make deliberate efforts to include interpersonal relations as part of using this process. The model can also provide a process for leaders to experience the decision-making process as an objective.

References

Vroom, V.H. (1974). Decision Making and the Leadership Process. *Journal of Contemporary Business*, 3(4), 47–64.

Vroom, V.H. (2000). Leadership and the Decision-making Process. *Organizational Dynamics*, 28(4), 82–94.

Vroom, V.H. & Jago, A.G. (1988). *The new leadership: Managing participation in organizations*. Englewood Cliffs, NJ: Prentice Hall.

Vroom, V.H. & Yetton, P.W. (1973). *Leadership and decision making*. Pittsburgh, PA: University of Pittsburgh Press.

Representation

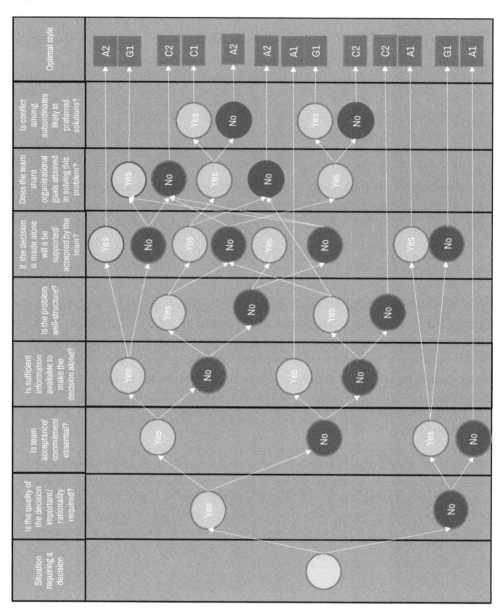

Figure 11.3: Normative decision-making model

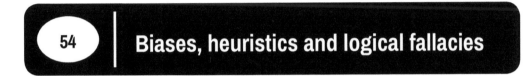

54 | **Biases, heuristics and logical fallacies**

Introduction

For their work in understanding the impact of human brain systems on decision-making, researchers Kahneman and Tversky received international acclaim (indeed the former received the Nobel prize in Economics; the prize is not awarded posthumously therefore Tversky could not be a recipient). They utilised the fact that the human brain has a faster, instinctive and associative component (System One) and a slower, rational and more sophisticated component (System Two). While we tend to think that the second system determines our decision-making they showed the role of cognitive biases and heuristics in the process. Cognitive biases refer to predictable patterns in our cognitive processes that are systematic and flawed, while heuristics are mental shortcuts we take to guide our decision-making. In addition to cognitive biases and heuristics there are some logical fallacies that teams often use; being aware of their potential impact may help teams to limit their influence on decision-making processes.

In a nutshell

Cognitive biases, heuristics and logical fallacies that can influence decision-making processes.

Purpose

To improve decision-making.

To raise awareness of cognitive biases and heuristics.

To limit the impact of cognitive biases, heuristics and logical fallacies on decision-making.

Description

Some cognitive biases and heuristics that could impact team decision-making processes are given first, followed by a description of some logical fallacies.

Cognitive biases and heuristics

Heuristics can be seen as the mental shortcuts or rules of thumb our minds make in the presence of endless data, complex environments and multiple stimuli to simplify decisions. When these heuristics are applied incorrectly or inadvertently it opens a team up to poor decision-making. Biases can be seen as inherent and systematic errors that humans (and therefore teams) make according to predictable patterns. These biases can skew reasoning and a team should keep them in mind when they make decisions.

Hoffman provided an eloquent discussion of such biases and heuristics, of which a selection applicable to teams is presented here:

- Affect heuristic. The old adage "keep the emotions out of it" may ring true as sometimes teams are more likely to make decisions on emotional responses than using objective data. Both negative and positive emotions can skew teams in their decision-making efforts.

- Anchoring. The first piece of information (often numbers) we receive is given inordinate prominence and guides our decision-making. In other words, our thought processes are anchored by what we receive first.

- Availability heuristic. People give more prominence and attention to information already available to them. Thus, teams react to what they are already aware of, even if this information is subconscious. The effect is aggravated if the information is emotional or dramatic.

- Bandwagon effect. We are more likely to believe something is true if the rest of the team believe it to be true. Since we have a bias to conform we are more likely to go with the opinions of the rest of the team than to resist and express opposing opinions.

- Base rate fallacy. The innate tendency to ignore general information and prefer data that are more specific, less meaningful and confirm our existing point of view.

- Clustering bias. In an effort to "make sense" we cluster information together into patterns and groups, but often these are based on limited or inadequate data sets. It is thus helpful for teams to ensure that an alternative interpretation of data is also considered.

- Confirmation bias. This refers to the tendency we have to give more credence to information that confirms what we already believe or validates decisions we already made. It is also true that we are more aware of such information and that we are more likely to ignore information that is in contradiction to these views.

- Existence bias. The belief something is good because it already exists and the team is familiar with it.

- Framing effect. The manner in which data, facts and narratives are presented to us influences the way they are perceived. Thus, if something is provided in a positive light we are more likely to view the data positively, while conversely if it is presented as negative we may find it less attractive.

- Hindsight bias. We erroneously believe after the fact that we should have been able to predict the outcome of events before they occurred.

- Illusions of control. The overestimation of our ability to control the external environment and of the impact our actions could have in averting danger. Teams also fall into the trap where they think that they have more control over events or circumstances than is really the case. This leads them to overlook real causes and teams are therefore well-advised to explore all potential causes of a particular circumstance.

- Loss aversion. People are more likely to avoid losing something than considering what potential benefits could accrue to them.

- Longevity bias. The belief that something is to be preferred because it has been in existence for a long period of time with preference to those having been impacting on the team for longer.

- Normalcy effect. The belief that things will stay as they are, with the result that we fail to plan for disaster, negative effects or worst case scenarios.

- Negativity bias. Our inclination to recall negative events and impacts on the team more vividly than positive effects. This may help the team to take distance and evaluate events from an objective and dispassionate vantage point to limit the effects of this bias.

- Overconfidence. The phenomenon that we place too much confidence in our own efforts and abilities and sometimes make decisions by ignoring hard data in favour of our own (inflated) opinion of our own abilities.

- Ostrich effect. The effect of ignoring information that is bad or not aligned with the team's position or beliefs and not taking into account views that challenge our assumptions.

- Status quo bias. Preference to things that exist already instead of those that need to be created and require change. This is particularly pronounced where the options increase and decision-making becomes more complicated.

- Sunk cost fallacy. The reluctance to "let go" or cut one's losses even in the face of obvious evidence that the current state or plan of action will lead to even greater losses.

- Temporal discounting. We focus on instant gratification and are more likely to make decisions with immediate positive effects than to focus on potential longer term negative effects.

Logical fallacies

Hoffman differentiated between biases and heuristics that are hardwired into the human brain and logical fallacies teams sometimes fall into, which are caused by sloppy thinking or a lack of critical thinking. He also put forward a more sinister view that proposed that sometimes these fallacies are deliberately and dishonestly applied by members who want to make a stronger case for their own point of view. A list of logical fallacies that often influence teams in their decision-making follows:

- *Ad hominem* attack: the saying "playing the man rather than the ball" describes this fallacy, where the person making the argument is criticised rather than the argument itself.

- Appeal to age or tradition: the assumption that previous generations or the team in earlier time periods were better equipped, wiser or knew more than the current team.

- Appeal to emotion or fear: using emotions like playing on people's heartstrings or anxieties instead of the argument at hand.

- Appeal to novelty: preferring an option merely because of its perceived novelty or because it is new. This leads to current products or prevailing views to be discarded for the sake of novel ideas.

- Appeal to questionable authority: when little scrutiny or critical evaluation of sources are used to base an argument on and decisions are made without a proper critique of facts, assumptions and perceptions.

- Appeal to ridicule: rejecting an idea because of the potential it may have to open the team to mockery.

- Begging the question (in the original meaning of the expression): circular reasoning where the result of the argument is predicated on its premise (e.g. "It would be good to team up with Team X for this, because Team X has proven in the past that this is their strength.)"

- Biased sample: weak statistical evidence or unsubstantiated verification are used to support an argument; arguments are made on the basis of inadequate samples.

- Confusion of cause and effect: teams are often prone to the effects of this fallacy, which is based on the mistaken belief that correlation implies causation.

- Explaining by naming: to imply that you have resolved an issue simply because you have identified it or understand it better.

- False dichotomy: oversimplifying the argument by reducing it to black-and-white choices and ignoring that there could be nuances and various alternative positions.

- Faulty analogy: using a comparison that does not support the conclusion that is being drawn from it.

- Glittering generality: using a generalisation, an appealing phrase or an uncontested statement to hide the core of the argument and allow it to go untested.

- Hasty generalisation: to base an argument, a potential solution or make assumptions based on insufficient or limited evidence.

- Loaded question: posing a query that cannot be answered without appearing as if a particular point of view is preferred.

- Middle ground: settling for a middle-ground compromise between two extreme points of view on the assumption that it will satisfy everyone.

- Oversimplification: when a complex issue that has different, interrelated causes is viewed from a narrow perspective where a single cause is assumed to be the problem. This leads the team to think that the solutions should be focused on the easier, more basic cause rather than spend time understanding real causes.

- *Post hoc, ergo propter hoc*: this Latin phrase (i.e. "after this, therefore because of this") refers to the fallacy that it is assumed something caused something else merely because the first occurred before the second. Thus, causality is ascribed because of the occurrence in time of two events that may not be related.

- Red herring: when an irrelevant topic is used and introduced in the discussion to avert attention from the original issue. This may be a deliberate attempt to move the discussion away from uncomfortable or opposing points of view.

- Slippery slope: assuming or claiming that a proposed action will set off a series of undesirable events in the face of evidence that this may not be the case and for which preventing mechanisms exist.

- Straw man: distorting or exaggerating an argument in order to make it easier to attack. Since the distortion or exaggeration allows negative perceptions to enter the fray, it becomes easier to make a substantial argument since the impact of straw man thinking has skewed the decision-making process.

- Wishful thinking: assuming a premise or argument is true or preferable merely because it is in your interest or to your benefit that it is to be true.

Tips for team leaders

By being aware of these biases, heuristics and logical fallacies, team leaders can guide their teams to improve the quality of the decision-making processes. Naturally it is impossible to highlight all biases and heuristics and they can also serve a particular purpose in teams. However, team leaders should guide their teams to be aware of the impact thereof and should put mitigating practices in place. For example, scrutiny of facts, allowing and promoting challenges to current thinking, revisiting of assumptions, critical review of decisions and giving opportunity to opposing views and different opinions held by members in the team can all be employed to good effect.

Representation

Cognitive decision biases and heuristics	Logical fallacies
Affect heuristic	Ad hominem attack
Affect insight bias	Appeal to age or tradition
Anchoring	Appeal to emotion or fear
Availability heuristic	Appeal to novelty
Bandwagon effect	Appeal to questionable authority
Base rate fallacy	Appeal to ridicule
Clustering bias	Begging the question
Confirmation bias	Biased sample
Existence bias	Confusion of cause and effect
Framing effect	Explaining by naming
Hindsight bias	False dichotomy
Illusions of control	Faulty analogy
Longevity bias	Glittering generality
Loss aversion	Hasty generalisation
Negativity bias	Loaded question
Normalcy effect	Middle ground
Ostrich effect	Neglect of a common cause
Overconfidence	Oversimplification
Status quo bias	Post hoc, ergo propter hoc
Sunk cost fallacy	Slippery slope
Temporal discounting	Straw man
	Wishful thinking

Figure 11.4: Cognitive biases and heuristics

References

Hoffman, B.G. (2017). *Red teaming: Transform your business by thinking like the enemy*. London: Piatkus.

Jones, P.E. & Roelofsma, M.P. (2000). The Potential for Social Contextual and Group Biases in Team Decision-Making: Biases, Conditions and Psychological Mechanisms, *Ergonomics,* 43(8), 1129–1152.

Kahneman, D. (2011). *Thinking, fast and slow*. London: Penguin Books Ltd.

| **Common decision-making pitfalls**

Introduction

Thompson pointed to four common decision-making pitfalls that manifest in teams. In the first instance the phenomenon of groupthink is addressed. This occurs when teams fail to be sufficiently critical among themselves about options available to them because they are more concerned with maintaining a consensus than ensuring optimum decisions. The second problem relates to the so-called Abilene paradox, which happens when all members of the team decide to do something because they believe someone else in the team or the team expects that. However, in the end the individual does what he or she does not want to do and it turns out the team did not expect that from the individual in the first place. The phenomenon of aggravation in groups is discussed next. This refers to the fact that teams tend to take more extreme positions than when individuals are polled individually. Lastly, escalation of commitment is where teams persist with behaviour and decisions to the detriment of the team because they are overly committed to the current action.

In a nutshell

Four common decision-making pitfalls, namely groupthink, Abilene paradox, aggravation in groups and escalation of commitment.

Purpose

To highlight common decision-making problems in teams.

To assist teams to minimise the impact of common pitfalls.

To increase quality of decision-making.

Description

Four common decision-making pitfalls that teams often fall victim to are described below:

Groupthink

Groupthink happens when teams prioritise consensus above all other priorities because there is pressure on the team to conform. It is facilitated by deteriorating mental efficiency, a lack of reality testing and poor moral judgements. When there is over-emphasis on the desirability of consensus, and there is someone present with expertise and a compelling argument, the risk for groupthink increases. Where members lack confidence in their own contributions and perceive their contributions as being limited, unimportant or meaningless, there is more chance of groupthink occurring. A number of preceding factors or antecedents of groupthink can be identified, including:

- compliance: a high level of compliance as caused by organisational or national culture, enforced by authoritarian leadership or personal disposition;

- closed-mindedness: where the team is not prepared to entertain alternative views;

- high cohesion: a high level of commitment to each other and the team;

- group insulation: when teams are isolated and insulated from other stakeholders and where the mental models of the team are not tested;

- group homogeneity in terms of background and ideology;

- crisis (time pressure): where external threats and/or views of a common enemy prevail;

- perceived difficult decision: the difficulty level of a decision the team has to make;

- recent group failure: where pressure is mounting on a team because of a recent failure; and

- leadership and equality of group members: a large interpersonal distance between the leader and team members sometimes leads members to agree in order to appease the leader, which can lead to groupthink.

Groupthink also occurs because it provides members with certain psychological and structural benefits. For example, an increased sense of belonging, cohesion and camaraderie feed into groupthink and give psychological benefits to sustain its occurrence. Pride (individual ego or team ego) is increased by groupthink and confirmation bias is a futher perceived benefit. Structural forces include organisational cultural pressures ("the way we do things here"), political pressure from people in power or those who want to maintain certain advantages, and competition between various teams in terms of resources, goals and performance. Groupthink manifests as:

- illusions of invulnerability: belief the group cannot fail;

- morality: where motives are good and correct, it is perceived that the actions and behaviours of the team should not be questioned;

- rationalising: explaining away contradictory data or information because of closed-mindedness or an incomplete survey of alternatives and options;

- stereotyping: tendency to portray opponents as evil or stupid;

- self-censorship: members keeping doubts to themselves feeds into insufficient levels of information;

- illusions of unanimity: caused by a belief that silence is the same as agreement and a failure to reappraise rejected alternatives or to examine risks;

- mind guards: self-appointed thought-police that shield the team from information that might challenge assumptions;

- conformity: where dissent is viewed as disloyalty; and

- consensus: over-emphasis on the desirability of consensus.

Abilene paradox

The notion of the Abilene paradox originated in a story that was popularised through the work of Harvey. It documents the narrative of four people resident in Coleman, Texas, who in the middle of soaring heat in July decided to take a trip to Abilene, 106 miles away. Afterwards, when each one was questioned they all stated that none of them was actually in the mood to go to Abilene, but each one decided to go because they thought the others wanted to go. Thus, the paradox that none wanted to go, but in the end they all agreed to go to avoid conflict. The Abilene paradox refers to decisions that individuals would not have made individually. It stems from a desire to limit or avoid conflict and therefore members are prepared do things that they would not do individually for the sake of the team. Members imagine that other members in the team desire certain outcomes or decisions and they adopt a position because they think others in the team hold that position. Teams are at risk of this happening when they do not express their views and beliefs openly and therefore end up in "Abilene".

It is believed that there are six situations that can facilitate the Abilene paradox, namely:

- the presence of someone with authority and/or expertise;

- someone raising a compelling argument;

- pressure from others to conform to the team's decision;

- an unimportant or meaningless decision leading to less vigorous involvement of members;

- lack of confidence in a member's contribution; and

- dysfunctional decision-making climate and atmosphere.

Group aggravation

This refers to the notion that being in a team "aggravates" the risks a team takes compared to what an individual would have done. Conversely, teams also sometimes make more cautious decisions than individuals. These two aspects of group polarisation are called risky shift and cautious shift. The idea states that being in a group has the tendency to intensify group opinion and more extreme judgements are obtained than when individuals' views are sought separately. This does not mean that the decision-making processes are less rigorous or inherently more inclined towards risk or caution, but simply that team decisions tend to be more extreme.

Three psychological reasons for this phenomenon can be found, namely:

- the need to be right: the belief that the team must know better because more information is available;

- the need to be liked: this normative influence states that members are more focused on being liked and are therefore more likely to make decisions that they think the team as a whole would make; and

- the need to conform: the need not to be the "odd one out" or "compatibility influence" drives this behaviour.

Escalation of commitment

This phenomenon occurs when teams continue with the wrong course of action even in the face of clear evidence to the contrary and where it will be obvious from a more objective evaluation that the action should be terminated. While many instances occur where people continue with mistakes or errors, escalation commitment occurs where a team continues with the same decision they made earlier. Since members contributed to that decision they feel obliged to continue, yet would not have done so had they made individual decisions on the same issue. Teams often fall into this dilemma when they decide to commit resources e.g. time, energy or money to "turn the situation around". The difficulty of this is that it seems to be iterative, with multiple attempts to take corrective action leading to an escalation of the inappropriate commitment. The bigger the investment and the more severe the possible loss, the more likely it is that a team will be motivated to stick with the original decision in the hope it will turn the situation around. The process of escalation of commitment is as follows:

- Questionable or negative outcomes: this is the first stage where the team becomes aware of possible outcomes through available data. This could include loss of sales, revenue, or market, share or an increase in mistakes, complaints or accidents.

- Re-examination of current course of action: the team is confronted with the situation and a decision is required. The team evaluates two options: (1) the perceived utility of the current course of action, or (2) the perceived utility of withdrawal and/or a change of behaviour or tactics. These alternatives are considered and it can even lead to thorough discussion and debate.

- Commitment to current action. The team decides to continue with the current course of action, even amidst clear indications that it may not be the correct way forward. The level of commitment affects this decision; if commitment is low, then the team may terminate. However, escalation of commitment occurs when commitment to the current course of action is high and the team therefore commits to the same course of action again. This may be because of any of the following:

  - Psychological determinants, including personal rewards of team members in the project (this will increase willingness to continue when high rewards are expected); the team's reputation could be on the line; confirmation bias where the team believes what they want to believe or think they already know; when individual ego is at stake; and where there is a natural sense of optimism that the situation will be turned around.

○ Structural determinants, such as the project being institutionalised and therefore not questioned, or because it is politically safer to continue.

○ Social determinants, including members' needs to belong, to affiliate and to be accepted, and therefore it may be difficult to "pull the plug" in the face of others' views that the project or course of action must be continued.

Tips for team leaders

The impact of escalation of commitment can be minimised by the setting of clear deadlines, limits and lines in the sand that are not to be crossed and can act as "external" guidelines. Leaders can help to avoid tunnel vision and allow for external review and/or for deliberate alternative views to be considered. The team should recognise sunk costs as just that and try to limit their emotional attachment to the fact that they have already occurred. Furthermore, differences of opinion should be encouraged and leaders should avoid the bystander effect where a member does not want to rock the boat.

Monitor team size as larger teams are more susceptible to groupthink, and allow for face-saving mechanisms to help the team deal with evaluation from others. It is also helpful to encourage discussion on the risks of particular decisions, to invite different perspectives and to find ways to protect alternative views. It sometimes helps to appoint a Devil's advocate or to deliberately devise a second solution. By appointing a Devil's advocate and questioning each decision and decision-maker carefully, the likelihood of the Abilene paradox manifesting itself can be minimised. Thus, leaders should allow dissent and a formal structure for controversial views. It is also helpful to minimise status difference and to frame the task as a decision and not a personal quest. Lastly, a formal forum for controversial/contradictory views could be set up.

Representation

The process a team follows where escalation of commitment occurs is indicated in the following flowchart:

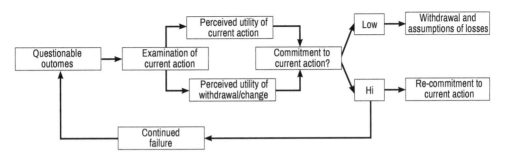

Figure 11.5: Escalation of commitment process

References

Thompson, L. (2007). *Making the team: A guide for managers* (3rd ed.). Upper Saddle River, NJ: Pearson Prentice Hall.

12

CONFLICT MANAGEMENT

Conflict is an inevitable part of life and as a consequence it also manifests in teams. This section starts with an overview of types of conflict that occur in teams: task conflict, relationship conflict, process conflict and status conflict. The next part deals with one potential source of conflict, namely "difficult" people. As many as ten different types of difficult people have been identified.

Two conflict management theories, namely the Thomas-Kilman and the Sequential-contingency theory, are then explained. The first uses a matrix upon which are plotted the level of assertiveness and the level of cooperation needed to solve any particular conflict, which leads to an analysis of different conflict management positions. The Sequential-contingency model of conflict management suggests that the number of conflict episodes experienced, the levels of intensity thereof and the duration of the conflict episode impact on how people react to conflict. Proponents of this model view the previous model as limiting as it restricts a team or its members to one style of conflict management instead of acknowledging that during a conflict episode a member may have to use more than one approach.

The last part of this section deals with handling conflict through an analysis of "crucial conversations". The recommended stages of a crucial conversation are described. This process helps leaders and members in teams to understand the stages of dealing with conflict and how to undertake crucial conversations.

Introduction

Conflict is a part of life and therefore also inevitably part of teams and teamwork. Conflict manifests in different forms and in teams four different types of conflict have been identified: task, relationship, process and status conflict. It must be remembered that the discussion here relates to intra-team conflict.

In a nutshell

Types of team conflict, namely task, relationship, process and status conflict.

Purpose

To help teams understand different types of conflict in teams.

To help teams deal with conflict.

Description

The four common types of intra-team conflict are described below:

Task conflict

This type of conflict stems from disagreements about task content and can include differences of opinion on what to do, how to do it or who is responsible for a particular task. This type of conflict happens naturally in a team and while there is still uncertainty about the benefits of such conflict, it would seem that it can sometimes help a team to find better and improved ways to deal with various tasks.

Antecedents of task conflict include informational or functional diversity, team members' need for achievement and the context wherein the team operates (including its atmosphere). Research indicates that interpersonal conflict that stems from task conflict negates the benefits that may arise from task conflict and that true optimisation of task conflict only manifests in the absence of relationship conflict. Thus, teams will only benefit from task conflict in contexts where they focus on tasks only. In order to facilitate such a context, teams can, for example, focus on the composition of the team in terms of personality, conflict-handling strategies, team atmosphere and communication. In this regard, where members are less likely to personalise task issues and where they are open and emotionally stable, it assists teams to focus on task conflict only. In terms of behaviours displayed to manage conflict it seems that teams should find a balance between actively managing conflict and allowing the conflict to manifest, and therefore provide the team an opportunity to find confidence in the manner they can deal with conflict. This curvilinear nature of managing conflict is critical if a team is to optimise the benefits of task conflict. In an atmosphere that is trusting and where intra-team trust is high, as well as in a context where the importance of the task to the team is deemed to be high, the focus of the team is more likely to remain on task and therefore for the conflict to be less contaminated with interpersonal conflict. In addition, it seems that task conflict is more positive for non-routine and more creative decision-making tasks than for routine tasks where task conflict has a more negative impact and also offers greater risk that it will escalate into interpersonal conflict. Finally, open communication, psychological safety and positive social interactions also allow task conflict to be resolved more easily, to the benefit of the team.

Relationship conflict

Relationship conflict is emotional in nature and impacts on interpersonal relationships. It influences relationships in that it decreases trust, cohesion and willingness to cooperate and may even induce somatic consequences. As a result team performance is compromised. The impact of relationship conflict is particularly high in teams where there is a high level of emotionality and where management strategies of avoiding or ignoring the conflict are employed. Thus, it would seem that the composition of the team could lead to relationship conflict in cases where members are more prone to identify emotions and recognise them appropriately, as well as where members have a low need for affiliation. In the latter instance it seems that since there is a lower need for belonging, members are more likely to forfeit relationships and more willing to engage in conflict. It would also seem that demographic diversity increases the likelihood of relationship conflict and requires deliberate action from the team and its leadership. Team atmosphere also influences the extent of relationship conflict in a context where a lack of feedback and low levels of trust and cohesion increase the likelihood of conflict. Time urgency, experience of respect and a history of effective interaction limit conflict. In addition, shared identity, shared context, shared experience and spontaneous and open communication minimise the occurrence of relationship conflict. Task conflict can lead to relationship conflict and occurs especially where the team has low levels of trust, where performance overrides a need for learning, where there are high levels of competition and where visible emotions are displayed in face-to-face interactions. The nature of the task also influences the likelihood of relationship conflict, being more likely when the task is of lower importance to the team, highly emotional, and with a low chance of resolution.

Process conflict

The third type of conflict identified (originally by Jehn) is process conflict. This is regarded as the most negative type and also has potentially the most direct impact on outcome. This type of conflict also has a more long-lasting and more emotionally impactful effect on teams because process conflict relates to perceptions of justice and equity. Furthermore, process conflict is related to power and resource control, e.g. the delegation of valued resources or allocation of time and tasks. The potential circularity between power holders and allocation of resources on the one hand, and how these actions are perceived in terms of justice and equity on the other, is evident. The severity of this type of conflict is also pronounced because it is often not verbalised or brought out into the open, but rather remains less transparent than other forms of conflict. It is therefore not surprising that this type of conflict is harmful to the team and could lead to a negative climate, lower decision-making quality and creativity, and lower productivity. Process conflict can be reduced in a team when role sub-groups are minimised, negative emotional triggers are limited and the team atmosphere allows for open conversation and honest discussion. Teams with high levels of value- and cultural diversity tend to have higher levels of process conflict, as do teams composed of persons with higher power levels. Process conflict is also higher in teams where there are lower levels of trust, respect and cohesion, but high levels of competition among members.

Status conflict

Bendersky and Hayes added a fourth type of conflict to the original three, namely status conflict. This refers to disputes over the status that various members occupy in the social hierarchy of the team. A member's status in a team is dependent on consensus among members and is socially conferred on individuals in the team. Status is established as a complex negotiated social order and manifests in every social system (teams included); it offers multiple benefits including access to influence, resources and information. It seems that status obtained in a meritocratic context incentivises and spurs teams on to perform optimally. However, where status is obtained through political manoeuvring it leads to increased levels of conflict and subsequent lower output. Increased levels of status conflict occur in situations where high power individuals are present (and therefore others feel a need to guard their power), as well as in situations where there are limited opportunities to advance one's status. It is particularly destructive where someone with a low status level is in in a powerful position, as this can lead to damaged team contexts and lowered output. Status conflict seems to be highly personal as it relates to the opportunities in a team for achievement, esteem, standing and belonging, and is therefore connected to the motivational drivers of individuals. It thus comes as no surprise that when these influences spill over into the team domain, the effects could be damaging to the team.

Tips for team leaders

It is helpful to remember that different individuals experience antecedents and effects of conflict differently. It would seem that discussions on team performance and norms and tasks associated with each may minimise conflict.

Representation

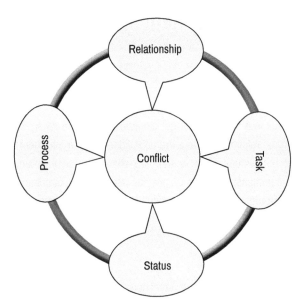

Figure 12.1: Types of team conflict

References

Berdensky, C. & Hayes, N.A. (2012). Status Conflict in Groups. *Organisation Science*, 23(2), 323–340.

Jehn, K.A. (1995). A Multimethod Examination of the Benefits and Detriments of Intragroup Conflict. *Administrative Science Quarterly*, 40(2), 256–282.

Greer, L.L. & Dannals, J.E. (2017). Conflict in teams. In E. Salas, Rico, R. & Passmore, J. (eds.), *The Wiley Blackwell handbook of the psychology of team working and collaborative processes*. Chichester, UK: John Wiley & Sons.

Introduction

It is inevitable that members in a team will not get along with everyone all the time. There are bound to be difficulties in interpersonal relationships and the behaviour of some members will give rise to conflict. Scholars have identified behavioural patterns that are shared by such potential "difficult people" by studying various problem communication styles. Thus, the use of particular communication and associated behaviour styles may alert leaders to potentially difficult members in the team, and help them to find ways to deal with them.

In a nutshell

Ten difficult team communication styles are identified: tanks, snipers, grenades, whiners, nothing ("whatever") persons, yes-people, no-people, know-it-alls, balloons and maybe-people.

Purpose

To help recognise difficult communication styles.

To highlight behavioural characteristics of each style.

To help leaders identify potential problem areas in the team.

To help members understand the behaviour of colleagues.

Description

Ten different types of "difficult people" are identified by pointing out the behavioural and communication styles of each. They are discussed below.

Tanks

These members display confrontational, pushy and aggressive behaviour and are often experienced as hostile, bullying, and intimidating. They use directive and controlling behaviour and may intimidate other employees by yelling, maintaining strong eye contact, or using abusive behaviour. They use nonverbal behaviour to convey status, control space and influence situations. They rarely believe other persons' opinions are correct or of any value to themselves and they also do not believe that others are skilful enough to contribute to their levels of expectation. They believe they are always right and rarely allow anyone else to confront them. The effect of their behaviour is that team members avoid them and the presence of such people severely limits the potential of the team.

Snipers

These team members are also hostile or aggressive, but the style presents in a different manner. Where tanks are open and directly aggressive, snipers manifest through sarcasm, rudeness or biting comments. Although they do not scream and shout, their aggressive and potentially hurtful behaviour is equally damaging to the team. They may maintain nonverbal behaviour that emphasises difference in status, authority and control. Through their "one-up" attitude and rudeness they make others feel inferior and foolish. They maintain friendly facial expressions and seem to convey pleasant relationships, but through innuendo and sniping comments they leave uncertainty about their intent. The overall effect is that members stop giving feedback or sharing ideas in teams because of the risk of being made to look foolish, feeling belittled or being treated without respect. They therefore reduce others to inaction and stifle participation.

Grenades

Grenades throw temper tantrums in situations where they perceive their ideas are being challenged or when they feel under threat. Although they do not shout in every situation, outbursts may happen suddenly and unexpectedly and they may yell and make a scene. Outbursts often happen when they perceive input by others as criticism and feel threatened or not valued. They may express feelings of guilt after an explosion and may fall into the trap of over-compensating afterwards. This may lead to a lack of trust as members may not know how to respond to the "real" grenade and may be wary of them. In addition, it may lead to limited participation as members may want to avoid explosions.

Whiners

These people are difficult because they blame others for personal or professional issues and they do not believe they have the ability to make a difference. They pretend to care and show concern for a person who is the target of gossip in the mode of "I really feel for her, but…". In reality they can be backstabbers or gossipers and they are not trusted by other team members. They rarely complain directly to a person, but prefer to let their views be known by nearly everyone except the one that the problem is about. As whiners they express dislike or concern about most situations, but while they complain and offer views, they do not offer solutions. It is in their interest to maintain the status quo as it allows opportunity to whine and complain. They seldom apologise or admit they are wrong, but remain focused on the problem. They have a negative influence on the mood of others and their bad mood often has a demoralising effect on the team. They feel powerless about their work and they do not feel confident that they can change their personal or professional situations. Thus, their complaining could be a cry for help about how they feel about themselves and for assistance in helping them cope. Some sensitivity by both the leader and the team is therefore called for.

Nothing ("whatever") persons

These people are generally apathetic and non-communicators. They convey a message that they do not care and "whatever" is generally what they regard as good for them. Their usual response to questions or request for feedback is a shrug and they rarely give concrete feedback or input. They respond with statements like "I do not care", "Whatever," or "It does not matter to me". It comes across to the team that they are not interested in anything and that they do not have an opinion about anything. This leaves the team at sea as they do not know what these people are thinking or if they approve of a particular idea. This can cause discomfort and create negativity, especially since their nonverbal behaviours and unresponsiveness are interpreted as judgmental. However, it is more likely that the source of this behaviour lies in fear of conflict, fear of rejection or a desire to be liked. Such people therefore risk being perceived negatively by not committing themselves or offering any response and feel safer by not risking conflict at all.

"Yes"-people

This type of person is difficult in spite of the fact that they are positive and supportive. They are friendly, responsible and eager to volunteer or help. They are prepared to do extra work as they believe it is the right thing to do and what is required to move forward and progress towards their goals. They show their support in assisting and agreeing with what the team and the leader wants. They dislike conflict and confrontation and generally want to please (leaders and members). They often feel conflicted in their efforts to help and feel caught in the middle. They find it difficult to say no and therefore over-commit, which may result in them finding it difficult to keep commitments and deliver. They are often over-involved in the team's collective business as they offer to make peace and to keep relationships healthy. Due to their taking on extra work or helping other members, their own performance could be compromised. They deflect negative messages and potential conflict through humour and kindness. They show support in non-verbal ways such as head nodding, or lifting an eyebrow to indicate agreement or support, communicate liking, or merely convey that they are listening and are involved.

"No"-people

These people are on the other end of the spectrum from "yes"-people, as they hardly say yes to anything and find it nearly impossible to be positive about anything. They find fault with any suggestion. They are pessimistic and negative and their attitudes have a demoralising and negative impact on the morale of the team. They are often mild-mannered and relatively quiet and tend to go about things in their own way. However, they do not believe in the need to change and it is very difficult to move them beyond current positions. They do not believe in anything new and do not believe any idea (old or new) will work. They have an attitude of "been there, done that and since it did not work then, it will not work now". Their negativity and pessimism rubs off on others quickly and stifles creative and innovative efforts.

Know-it-Alls

People that display this style are usually well-informed and knowledgeable and know a great deal about many things. They may be specialists or experts in a particular field and they do not miss an opportunity to make people aware of such expertise or experience. In making sure other people appreciate this area of speciality and the range of their knowledge they use story-telling about themselves. Often, a scenario will unfold where the "Know-it-All" will start with "I remember a similar situation which I handled this way..." Although their levels of skill and knowledge are often legitimate, they have the need to let everyone know about their knowledge and speciality. However, unfortunately often their very intelligence and expertise trip them up because they come to believe that they really have all the answers. This is the difficult and unhelpful part for teams, as it leads the "Know it all" to blame others if their suggestions turn out to be wrong or on occasions where they do not have the answers. They generally display disdain for authority, and since people in positions of authority are perceived to be inferior to their own levels of intelligence, knowledge and expertise, they show their disdain non-verbally. They are unlikely to ask for help or feedback from other team members and therefore tend to be isolated over time.

Balloons

Balloons are similar to the previous difficult style, but whereas the Know-it-All is informed, intelligent and knowledgeable to a very high degree, balloons have an inflated idea of their knowledge levels. Usually they know a lot less than they claim and can be caught speaking with great authority about subjects they actually know little about. They like to brag about their accomplishments, what they have done or know, and may embellish stories: sometimes to the point of being untruthful. They offer solutions and answers even before someone explains the problem, which may be an effort to divert the discussion into areas where they feel more comfortable. They are often agreeable and pleasant people and may bring energy to the team. However, the impact of their contribution may slow down the efforts of the team.

"Maybe"-people

The last style of difficult team members discussed here is maybe-persons. They find it difficult to make decisions and this indecision leads to procrastination. The greater the likelihood of conflict, the more they procrastinate, and if and when they finally decide, it is generally too late. They are positive and encouraging and supportive of others' decisions. They tend to be cautious and often will revert to "Maybe", "I'm not sure...", "Does it make sense...?" or "This may not be the right decision, but . . ."

Tips for team leaders

As relationship conflict is one of the main areas of conflict in teams, it is helpful for leaders to know the behavioural patterns and styles of difficult team members. Being able to identify these archetypical communication styles equips leaders to devise mechanisms to deal with members who display destructive behaviour. For example, it is better to deal with whiners by not listening to them or trying to point out alternatives. Balloons are best managed by giving little attention to them. One can focus on statistics and external verification and give them opportunity to save face. By devising techniques to deal with the types of communication style that manifest in a team, the leader can channel the contribution of these members to be more useful. It must be remembered that different individuals may present with some of these behaviours and yet not be regarded as difficult. The levels of disruption and discomfort they bring about depend on the extent to which they manifest these patterns, as well as on the other individuals in the team, their reaction to the behaviour and the group dynamics at play.

Representation

Communication style	Description of style
Tank	Confrontational and aggressive and always wants to be right
Sniper	Maintain one-up status through non-verbal behaviour
Grenade	Sudden and unexpected outbursts to get their way
Whiner	Continuous complaining and believe they can not make a difference
Nothing (whatever) person	Generally apathetic and disinterested
Yes-person	Agrees on everything and overly supportive and positive
No-person	Negative and find fault with anything
Know-it-all	Specialists who knows a lot and show this knowledge
Balloons	Inflated idea of their own knowledge and expertise
Maybe-person	Indecisive and may often procrastinate because they can not decide

Figure 12.2: Ten difficult team communication styles

Reference

Raynes, B. L. (2001). Predicting Difficult Employees: The Relationship between Vocational Interests, Self-esteem, and Problem Communication Styles, *Applied H.R.M. Research,* 6(1), 33–66.

Thomas-Kilman dimensional model

Introduction

Conflict can manifest on an intergroup, intragroup, interpersonal and intrapersonal level; the management of conflict can be defined as the actions a person takes in response to such conflict in order to achieve a desired goal. Conflict manifests through task, relationship and process differences, and people react behaviourally, emotionally and cognitively to such conflicts. Modern day teams have to acknowledge that conflict is a normal part of life and the potential benefits of conflict should be explored. The traditional Thomas-Kilman two-dimensional approach is presented here for its enduring value.

In a nutshell

Managing conflict through avoidance, accommodation, confrontation, compromise or collaboration.

Purpose

To highlight different approaches to conflict.

To help team members reflect on their fixed or default conflict management styles.

To help teams decide on appropriate conflict management styles.

Description

Conflict is a normal part of everyday life and therefore also part of organisational life. It is the manner in which conflict is dealt with that is critical. Healthy conflict can propel the team to be more effective. However, conflict can also be destructive to a team. Conflict in teams is a natural phenomenon and when dealt with correctly can be energising and move the team forward. It can arise from various sources, including:

- operational issues where tasks and roles overlap or there is lack of clarity in terms of responsibilities related to tasks and roles;

- relational issues: differences in communication behaviour and interaction;

- political issues: where there are hidden agendas to advance certain goals, which manifest in different beliefs about the motives and behaviour of team members;

- value differences: which are the most fundamental thing upon which human beings base their decisions and actions;

- resources: or more correctly the lack of resources;

- structural conflicts that stem from organisational structure, authority or hierarchy;

263

- personality differences of style and behaviour; and

- motivational differences, with people attaching different values to the various requirements in the team.

However, since the variety of sources listed here only serves to highlight how broad the spectrum (of where conflict stems from) is, it is more important to focus on the effect of conflict and how leaders can manage conflict in teams.

Thomas and Kilman offered a helpful matrix to analyse the dimensions and various types of conflict management styles. They contended that in a conflict situation one can either be cooperative or not, which is shown on the horizontal axis. On the vertical axis they depict the level of assertiveness one can adopt, from high to low. Combining these allows for five different conflict management styles to emerge.

Avoidance

This style is characterised by low assertiveness and a lack of cooperation. The conflict situations and issues are avoided and the team denies that there are problems. The team hopes that the conflict will go away by itself.

Accommodation

While also low on assertiveness, this style is high on cooperation; when this style is displayed it is often done with a concerted effort to accommodate the other points of view. Members are prepared to give up their position or point of view in an effort to accommodate those of other. They are cooperative, but it may not be the optimal solution.

Confrontation

With this high level of assertiveness the member is trying to win at all costs, where winning is more important than an optimal solution. It is helpful when quick decisions are needed and clear positions regarding the issues at hand need to be stated.

Compromise

This provides for a good balance where there is give and take from both sides. Compromise is often regarded as inadequate by both parties and teams tend to use this when they regard the issues to be of only moderate importance. However, when the parties present with equal power and there are time constraints, it tends to be a valuable style to adopt. Often solutions found through this approach are regarded as temporary and a substitute for failed competing or collaborating approaches.

Collaboration

This is an approach where win-win solutions are sought and where the cooperation and respect of both parties are required to arrive at a solution that suits both. It is helpful to get both parties involved in finding integrated solutions, to merge perspectives and to gain commitment, particularly where the long-term success of the relationship is critical.

Tips for team leaders

A team can use all these approaches and at different times they could get different results. However, just as there are benefits to each of these approaches, so they can also be destructive. For example, avoidance, accommodation and confrontation may sound intuitively appealing, but they create winners and losers and the impact thereof could reverberate throughout the team. Often this method of dealing with issues is repeated and it could be that the team may find it difficult to implement these decisions and compromises. Compromise also seems a good idea as it could maintain positions and relationships, but it can lead to less than optimal decisions because the most beneficial alternative could be forsaken due to the compromise. Teams should strive to use collaboration as an approach to solve conflict, as it encourages creativity, builds trust, maintains and enhances relationships, energises a team's sense of potency and leads to greater support and commitment to decisions.

The Thomas-Kilman Conflict Model Instrument (TKI) can be used to assess team members' preferred styles.

Representation

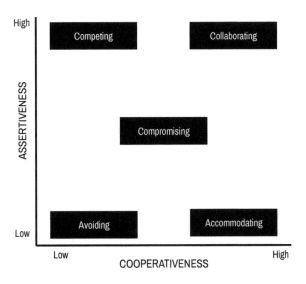

Figure 12.3: Thomas-Kilman dimensional model

References

Kilman, R.H. & Thomas, K.W. (1975). Interpersonal Conflict-Handling Behaviour as Reflections of Jungian Personality Dimensions. *Psychological Reports*, 37(3), 971–980.

Thomas, K.W. (1974). *Thomas-Kilmann conflict mode instrument*. New York: Xicom Tuxedo.

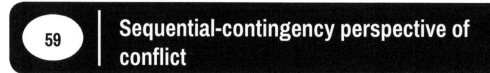

59 | Sequential-contingency perspective of conflict

Introduction

The Thomas-Kilman model implies that there is "one correct way", or alternatively that the team has to make a decision to apply *one* particular approach according to situational demands. In addition, modern-day team operations may be too complex to be dealt with in one way. In real life it is often necessary for the team to apply a mixture of these approaches throughout the same conflict period. Furthermore, during that period the team may move sequentially through a variety of different affective, cognitive and process modes.

In a nutshell

To view elements of conflict, including conflict characteristics, conflict management strategy, individual characteristics, relationship characteristics and outcome.

Purpose

To highlight different elements of conflict.

To find the key characteristics to concentrate on during conflict.

To allow flexibility to use different styles.

To understand the complexity of conflict.

Description

Speakman and Ryals promoted a model that acknowledges the complexity of conflict episodes, elicits antecedents of conflict, expands the conflict types, determines the components of conflict episodes, and relates conflict to cognitions, emotions and processes. Their sequential-contingency perspective looks at influencing factors in the micro-environment, the number of conflict episodes, the composition thereof and changes in the behaviours of the actors involved. In this way it offers a more positive, functional approach to conflict. They regarded conflict as ubiquitous, ever-present and ever-changing in terms of its nature or composition, and distinguished between the following types of conflict:

- Emotional conflict, which includes what team members think and feel about their relationships during the episode, and how they feel about others in relation to trust, status and interdependence.

- Cognitive conflicts, about what members know and understand about their task and the tasks of others.

- Process conflicts, related to the situation and the organisational setting.

Each instance of conflict is regarded as unique and the team deals with it on multiple levels, moving through various sequential contingencies. In each case of conflict, affective, cognitive and process components play a part in the number of episodes experienced, the levels of intensity and the duration of episodes. Thus, instead of the participant in a conflict situation adopting "one best solution", a variety of complex, mutually influencing factors will impact the behavioural options and strategies employed. It also makes the process more dynamic. For example, it includes the micro-environment in which other conflict situations and relationships influence conflict management behaviours. Thus, in dealing with conflict, team members use different behaviours and may have to deal with multiple conflicts simultaneously. Moreover, people change affect, cognitions and behaviour during conflict, which may influence the resolution of the current and future conflicts, both in approach and expectation of outcome. This means teams need to view conflict with an eye on the future and maintain a degree of cooperation, as opposed to adopting behaviour(s) which resolve(s) discrete isolated incidents of conflict at a given time.

To assist teams in this broader view of conflict management, the authors offered the following dimensions of conflict:

Conflict characteristics

The characteristics of the conflict situation can be varied, and include differences regarding the composition, type and development of affective, cognitive and process elements. Thus, assessing the number of episodes, levels of intensity and duration thereof, as well as the impact this has on various levels, helps teams to determine appropriate responses.

Conflict management strategy

This includes the familiar five strategies described in the previous part (i.e. avoiding, accommodating, compromising, competing and collaborating), but two additional styles are proposed. The first is confronting, which means drawing attention to one's own discontent about an issue and the subsequent actions taken to initiate resolution; in other words launching the conflict issue and addressing it. The second is process controlling, which is aimed at dominating, asserting influence, and controlling the setting and rules of the game, the agenda and the flow of conflict resolution.

Individual characteristics

This relates to personality characteristics such as adaptability, influencing skills, control, knowledge, needs, beliefs, roles and goals, which can all influence a person's predisposition to conflict and their style and approach to conflict situations.

Relationship characteristics

The characteristics of the relationship between people involved in conflict, such as levels of trust, commitment, power, and satisfaction, and the degree of interdependence, can impact the resolution efforts used to address the conflict.

Outcome

The outcome of the conflict is viewed in terms of whether it will have a mitigating or agitating effect, and a functional or dysfunctional effect. Again, the perceived outcome influences the manner in which conflict is approached.

Tips for team leaders

The sequential-contingency perspective is comprehensive and provides leaders with key points of reference to understand conflict. It can be used to ascertain elements of conflict, to determine styles of intervention, and to determine the impact of a particular conflict situation.

Representation

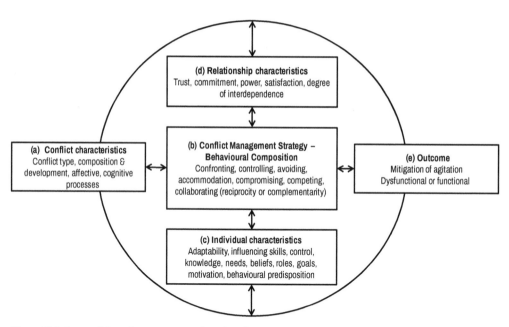

Figure 12.4: Sequential-contingency perspective of conflict

References

Euwema, M.C., Van de Vliert, E. & Bakker, A.B. (2003). Substantive and Relational Effectiveness of Organizational Conflict Behavior. *International Journal of Conflict Management*, 14(2), 119–39.

Speakman, J. & Ryals, L. (2010). A Re-evaluation of Conflict Theory for the Management of Multiple, Simultaneous Conflict Episodes. *International Journal of Conflict Management*, 21(2), 186–201.

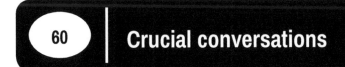

60 | Crucial conversations

Introduction

Often conflict arises in teams because of interpersonal difficulties or because of challenges with personalities. However, where these are the more obvious causes of conflict, it also sometimes comes to the fore because of other reasons that are more operational. In either case it requires communication to deal with such conflict. In their acclaimed book *Crucial Conversations: Tools for Talking when the Stakes are High*, Kerry Patterson, Joseph Grenny, Ron McMillan and Al Switzler provided a helpful tool for conducting crucial conversations. Their process allows for a planned structure and is helpful for individuals and teams in conflict situations in dyads, sub-groups or the whole team.

In a nutshell

Steps to facilitate crucial conversations.

Purpose

To help teams structure crucial conversations.

To provide a process of solving conflict.

To improve conflict management skills.

To empower the team to deal effectively with conflict.

Description

The authors offer a systematic process whereby a person can prepare for a crucial conversation and use the guidelines to conduct such a conversation. The process can be summarised in the following steps:

Start with heart

The process starts with a focus on the initiator or facilitator of the crucial conversation. You first evaluate your own position, i.e. "start with me". This is done by determining what you want for yourself, for others and for the relationship. It is also useful to determine what you do not want and to find new ways of looking at the problem.

Learn to look

The second stage involves interpreting certain signs in a crucial conversation, in particular whether these signs indicate a lack of shared meaning and/or safety concerns. This becomes evident through:

- silence behaviour i.e. withdrawing, avoiding or masking; or

- violence behaviour i.e. controlling, labelling or attacking.

Once these are detected one has to determine whether they are caused by one's own perceptions of the issue, and in particular what assumptions or motives/intent are present and what can be done to expand understanding.

Make it safe

The next step (to make it safe) requires being real, building a safe environment and questioning your own commitment. In the effort to create safety the parties should commit to seeking mutual purpose and maintaining mutual respect. Thus, during this stage it is helpful to:

- commit to seeking mutual purpose (e.g. "It seems we're both forcing our views. I commit to staying in the discussion until we find a solution for both of us.");

- recognise the purpose behind the strategy you observe (e.g. "What do you really want? What will a solution be for you?");

- invent a mutual purpose (e.g. "Ok if we can not get that what about…?"); and

- brainstorm new strategies.

This may entail having to apologise when appropriate. Another helpful approach is to clarify what is not your intent and what could be misconstrued, and contrast this with what the other person thinks you do mean.

Master my stories

This entails being sure about your own viewpoint or assumptions in preparation for the discussion. Be sure that you can "map" your own story. This includes reflection on your own evaluation of the state of affairs. Therefore it is helpful to retrace your path, understand your point of view and to be clear on "What is my story?"

State my path

At this stage you share your facts and tell your story. You should ask for other paths of thinking. It is helpful when you state your side to talk tentatively and to encourage testing.

Explore others' paths

Listening to the other story is the next stage. Here your opponent is given an opportunity to retrace their story and state their case. Ask yourself if you are actively exploring other views. Be sure to keep safety conditions in place and to listen for "stockpile templates", such as victim, villain or helpless. Try to defuse these as follows, "You are a villain" - can I make it human? Victim - can I help the other to become an actor rather than a victim? Helpless - can I enable? During this stage it helps to mirror the behaviours and emotions of the other, to paraphrase and to acknowledge understanding.

Move to action

In the last stage you determine the next steps, in particular how you will document what has been discussed and agreed upon: who will do what, by when and whether follow-up is required. It is helpful to build on what you are in agreement on and where opportunity exists to build further. Finally you can compare where you differ and identify the differences clearly.

Tips for team leaders

This is a helpful process as it gives an opportunity to reflect on your own position and to consider the views of others. It is specifically helpful to teams as it directs attention to the value of shared meaning, and addresses individuals' needs to go beyond silence or violence. The method is practical and effective and can be of great benefit to teams to structure crucial conversations to deal with any kind of conflict, such as disagreement, interpersonal strife, or mistakes or failures, and any conversations regarding performance.

Representation

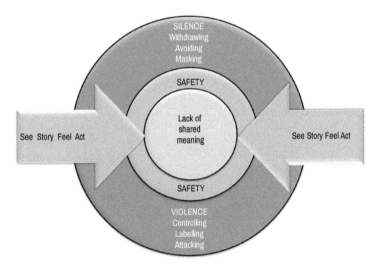

Figure 12.5: Crucial Conversations

Reference

Patterson, K., Grenny, J., McMillan, R. & Switzler, A. (2002). *Crucial conversations: Tools for talking when the stakes are high.* New York: McGraw-Hill.

13

COMMUNICATION

Communication is critical for coordination, collaboration and cooperation efforts in the team. Communication is a complex process and includes the manner in which different individuals communicate in a team, as well as how the team interacts collectively. The first part of this section presents the notion of communication patterns in teams and the drivers of such patterning. The second part is dedicated to a discussion on the types of interaction that occur during team meetings. Kauffeld and Lehmann-Willenbrock ascertained that communication in a team manifests through four different types of statements: problem-focused, procedural, socio-emotional and action-oriented. In the third part, the structural dynamics communication model of Kantor is presented. Next, focus is put on the communication of agile teams to see if other teams can benefit from following their example. Agile teams developed in the world of software development as that industry increasingly optimised the human interactional side of programming (including communication). Another type of team whose communication warrants scrutiny is virtual teams, i.e. a team is a team whose members are not in the same location and cannot communicate face-to-face. As modern business increasingly uses technology and teams are increasingly global, the use of virtual teams increases as well. In this situation good communication becomes even more vital.

61 | # Communication patterns

Introduction

The pattern or network of a team is the configuration of relationships among the various members. As soon as the operation of the team starts, different members interact with one another. These interactions lead to relationships forming between the members. The pattern of communication in a particular team is detectable by focusing on how, where and when different members of the team interact with one another. In other words, a communication pattern describes the way in which the communication network between members of the team is configured.

In a nutshell

The team determines the patterns of communication in terms of density, centrality, level, content, sequence, duration, direction and mode.

Purpose

To help identify communication patterns operative in a team.

To understand the determinants of a pattern.

To assist in evaluating whether a particular pattern is useful to the team.

To help determine default or fixed patterns and evaluate their utility.

To allow experimentation with different patterns.

Description

Communication is at the heart of teamwork and plays a critical role in team performance and ensuring that effective teams are built. Pentland identified that in successful teams:

- every member talks and listens in equal measure;

- contributions are short and to the point;

- face-to-face interaction facilitates energetic conversation;

- members connect directly with one another and not only with or "through" the leader;

- communication and conversation outside the team's formal meetings happen and are useful; and

- members periodically explore outside the team and bring back information into the team.

As a team communicates through various means (verbally and non-verbally), a pattern develops. This pattern in the team as a whole (i.e. as a system) can be analysed by looking at the contributions that various members make. Ties refer to relationships or connections between individuals (e.g. when one person speaks to another in a group they form a tie), while a node represents a particular individual or point of contact. Thus, ties exist between nodes. These contributions can be analysed in terms of the following dimensions. In understanding communication patterns it is helpful to distinguish between nodes and ties.

Density

Density refers to the number of ties in relation to all possible ties, i.e. the number of connections between two nodes and in relation to all other ties that are possible between members. It indicates how well-connected different team members are to each other. It can indicate a measure of socio-emotional relationships, but can also be influenced by task-related connections. It is an overall group assessment and shows the number of contributions in relation to all the available relations and connections. In essence, the higher the level of density, the easier the flow of information is. However, the flip side is that it could lead to less specialisation and higher redundancy. If there are a large number of connections there is less reason for a particular individual's contribution to be valued.

Centrality

This gives a notion of how focal (i.e. regarded as important for the communication in the team) a given node is in a social network. Wolfson and Mathieu distinguished between the various types of centrality as follows: degree, betweenness, closeness and Eigenvector centrality.

Degree centrality

This describes the node with the most connections and the individual through whom most of the work goes. It is determined by establishing which member has the most connections with other members. This can be called the hub or crossroads of the team, depending on the different attributes applied to the network. For example one member could be the knowledge node while another could be the social glue.

Betweenness centrality

This is a communication node that indicates the person in the team who acts as broker or gatekeeper and is in a position to link or connect different parts of the team or connect with other teams.

Closeness centrality

The node that is the closest to all other nodes gives an indication of the time it takes to disseminate information. It can be seen as an indication of how close a member is to the team or to other individuals.

Eigenvector centrality

This refers to the node that is best connected overall and also best connected to the most important other elements in the team's stakeholder network. This centrality does not require the member to be connected to all other members, but the uniqueness of the node lies in that it is connected to other key nodes or hubs. Members with a high Eigenvector centrality have the ability to mobilise others because they connect to key enablers in the team. They are also good at disseminating information or coordinating action.

Content

The type of content that is assessed to determine a network pattern can also vary, for example a network can be determined in relation to the levels of authority, interdependence, familiarity or knowledge, skills or abilities. Naturally each of these could be assessed separately, but various attributes can also be superimposed to show integrated networks. Although they could become complex, such more comprehensive networks allow the team to experience a richness of connection and interdependence that allows for development of the team to happen.

Sequence

Various ways of sequencing contributions can be analysed and questioned in terms of their possible contribution to the process level of the team. Examples of sequence are who talks after whom, or who talks first or last in a session or outside the team operations (it can happen that unofficial circumstances are used to communicate about the team). This pattern can reveal a number of issues, such as trust (it could be perceived as dangerous to raise the point formally), or lobbying for position (information could be sought, disclosed or distorted to benefit the member's own position).

Duration

This refers to the length of time that a particular member occupies the attention of the team, i.e. the length of each contribution in relation to others. For instance some members hold the floor for extended periods of time. The focus will of necessity be on that person the whole time they are speaking. This may be related to personality. Other people hardly ever speak and when they do it is for short periods of time.

Direction

This looks at to whom a comment or contribution is directed. The addressee of a contribution, statement or sentence may not be the one the speaker is really addressing. For instance, a member could make a contribution apparently for the benefit of everyone, but in fact with the specific aim of sending a message to a specific member of the team. In helping the team to detect a pattern, it is helpful to determine to whom contributions are in fact addressed, as this may give an indication of power structures, authority or leadership issues.

Mode

The mode of a team's pattern refers to the non-verbal content of a team's communication. Non-verbal content can be expressed through:

- body language: examples include facial expressions (e.g. frowning, laughing or looking depressed or not interested); leaving the room; making noises (e.g. finger- or foot tapping); signs or gestures (e.g. a specific manner of greeting); making or preventing eye-contact; hand gestures (e.g. finger pointing, talking behind one's hand); or mirroring of behaviour (e.g. replicating behaviour of another person e.g. the team leader);

- tone of voice: examples include loud and abrasive responses or a team member who is soft-spoken whispering in a team session;

- physiological responses: examples include perspiration, fiddling or ticking, gasping for air while talking; stuttering;

- style of response: the style of response is a combination of factors that tend to cluster in a pattern of presentation. Thus, body language and posture could be used along with a specific tone of voice to portray a certain style. For example, a submissive style would manifest as a soft, unsure tone of voice together with a lack of eye-contact, fiddling and perspiration; and

- operational: in an operational context non-verbal content can be expressed through go-slows, decreased (or increased) levels of production, or absenteeism.

Tips for team leaders

It should be kept in mind that the pattern of a team is not necessarily fixed. It evolves and distinct changes can occur as the team develops. For instance, in case of a crisis a different pattern can be used than the one used for the daily operation of the team. It could be that the role of the leader receives more prominence during a crisis and that the team displays its cohesion by rallying behind the leader. Leaders should keep in mind that they can use the various elements of the team's communication pattern to change or adjust any pattern in the team. For example, they can ask members to respond more or less often or change the sequence or direction of contributions of various members. Furthermore, leaders can follow the advice of Pentland, who identified the following key elements of communication in teams, and ensure that the communication in the pattern serves one of the following purposes:

- Generate energy: the level of energy in the team is not static, but fluid and is dependent on the type of information shared. It is determined by the number and nature of exchanges of members.

- Facilitate engagement: the distribution of energy among members reflects the level of involvement of members in the team's deliberations. One-to-group conversations, where the contributions of various members are shared in equal measure, should be about half the time of interaction. The other half of conversation time includes one-on-one conversations, including those that go beyond work-related topics and include side-exchanges.

- Allow exploration: the levels of energy that exist between the team and other teams it interacts with. Teams that seek more external interactions perform better.

Representation

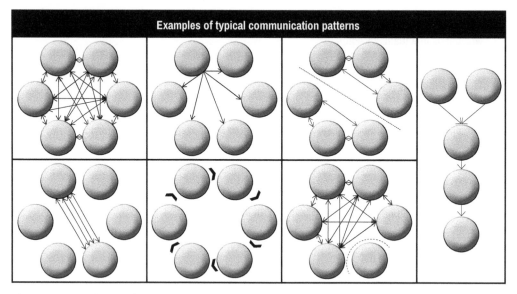

Examples of typical communication patterns

Figure 13.1: Examples of typical communication patterns

References

Pentland, A. (2012). The New Science of Building Great Teams. *Harvard Business Review*, 90(4), 60–69.

Wolfson, M.A. & Mathieu, J.E. (2017). Team composition. In E. Salas, R. Rico & J. Passmore (eds.). *The Wiley Blackwell handbook of the psychology of team working and collaborative processes*. Chichester, UK: John Wiley & Sons.

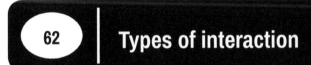

Introduction

It is common knowledge that the demands on teams to perform are becoming ever more challenging in the current age. One way that teams are required to excel is in the way they hold meetings and communicate with one another. Kauffeld and Lehmann-Willenbrock identified four types of communication statements and five communication roles that team members tend to adopt.

In a nutshell

Communication statements can be problem-focused, procedural, socio-emotional or action-oriented, while team members can adopt the role of complainer, solution-seeker, problem-analyst, indifferent or procedural facilitator.

Purpose

To improve the quality of team meetings.

To help teams understand different types of interactions.

Description

Types of communication statements

Problem-focused statements

The first type of statement is problem-focused and relates to understanding the issue at hand, making connections with a problem and proposing a solution. These types of statements include:

- focusing on the problem by identifying a (partial) problem and describing it;
- cross-linking a problem by making connections such as naming causes and effects;
- differentiating by finding an alternative solution;
- cross-linking a solution by providing new solutions and connections of the problem to the solution;
- statements about the organisation (e.g. organisational knowledge) that include knowledge about processes and systems; and
- statements about knowledge management, such as who knows what, and questioning opinions, content and experience.

Procedural statements

Procedural statements can be positive or negative:

- Positive procedural communication includes statements that are aimed at goal orientation where statements lead the team back to the topic; clarifying statements that are to the point; and procedural suggestions or questions. Comments that help the team to prioritise, manage its time and distribute its tasks are regarded as positive procedural statements, as are visualising, weighing costs/benefits; and summarising.

- Negative procedural statements are those where members lose their train of thought, go into too much detail or too many examples that are irrelevant to the goal, or deliver monologues unrelated to the current tasks.

Socio-emotional statements

These types of statements are also divided into positive and negative.

- Positive statements are those kinds of contributions that encourage participation, e.g. addressing quiet participants, providing support, actively listening, e.g. signalling interest ("hmm," "yes"), giving feedback and lightening the atmosphere, e.g. with jokes and funny remarks. When they state disagreement it is reasoned and contradictions are based on fact. Comments where members help the team to separate opinions from facts, express feelings or offer praise are further examples of positive socio-emotional statements.

- Negative socio-emotional statements include criticising or running someone down, constant interrupting, side conversations and self-promotion.

Action-orientated statements

Action-oriented statements manifest as either positive and proactive, or negative and counteractive:

- Positive, proactive statements include statements that express an interest in change; statements about personal responsibility; and action planning (i.e. agreeing upon tasks to be carried out).

- Negative, counteractive statements include no interest in change, complaints, empty talk, denying responsibility, seeking someone to blame, and terminating a discussion prematurely.

Communication roles

The authors also identified five different communication roles that members of a team prefer to enact. Understanding these roles helps team leaders to identify the contributions of different members to align them with the different modes of communication:

- Complainers use negative procedural statements and counteractive statements, and complain and criticise more.

- Solution-seekers contribute toward the differentiation of solutions, tend to cross-link and contribute proactive statements.

- Problem analysts raise and describe problems and connect them to other problems.

- Indifferents tend to make negative socio-emotional contributions in side conversation, get involved in discussions outside of the team and provide no relevant contribution to the conversation.

- Procedural facilitators make contributions regarding knowledge management, make positive structuring remarks, ask procedural questions and make suggestions, do not hesitate to question the topic, and finally clarify and summarise on the team's behalf.

Tips for team leaders

Team leaders can understand how the team is communicating in terms of the various types of interactions and the communication roles members play in the team. They can use this understanding to facilitate communication and to allow members to contribute according to their strengths.

Representation

Problem-focused statements	Procedural statements	Socio-emotional statements	Action-oriented statements
Differentiate a problem *Identify and describe problem* **Cross-linking a problem** *Connections with a problem* **Differentiate a solution** *Define the objective* *Offer a solution* *Describe a solution* **Cross-linking a solution** *Voice a problem with the solution* *Connections with a solution* **Statements about the organisation** *Organisational knowledge* **Knowledge management** *Knowing who* *Questioning opinions*	**Positive procedural statements** *Goal orientation* *Clarifying* *Procedural suggestions* *Procedural questions* *Prioritising* *Time management* *Task distribution* *Visualising* *Weighing costs/benefits* *Summarising* **Negative procedural statements** *Losing train of thought* *Lack of interest* *Sabotaging*	**Positive socio-emotional statements** *Encouraging participation* *Providing support* *Active listening* *Reasoned disagreement* *Giving feedback* *Lightening the atmosphere* *Separating opinion from facts* *Expressing feelings* *Offering praise* **Negative socio-emotional statements** *Criticising or running someone down* *Interrupting* *Side conversations* *Self-promotion*	**Positive, proactive statements** *Interest in change* *Personal responsibility* *Action planning* **Negative, counteractive statements** *No interest in change* *Complaining* *Empty talk* *Seeking someone to blame* *Denying responsibility* *Terminating the discussion*

Figure 13.2: Types of interaction

References

Kauffeld, S. & Lehmann-Willenbrock, N. (2012). Meetings Matter: Effects of Work Group Communication on Organizational Success. *Small Group Research*, 43(2), 130–158.

Lehmann-Willenbrock, N., Beck, S.J. & Kauffeld, S. (2016). Emergent Team Roles in Organizational Meetings: Identifying Communication Patterns via Cluster Analysis. *Communication Studies*, 67(1), 37–57.

Introduction

Structural dynamics is based on systems theory and sees any speech as an "act". Devised by Kantor over a life-time of studying couples, families, teams and organisations, it can be applied meaningfully to communication patterns at play in a team. Kantor described three levels of communication that influence group dynamics: the structure of communication, the content (topics, opinions, facts) and style (forms of etiquette, rules of order). In his view, structure is a fundamental, powerful and invisible behavioural profile operative in a team. It starts with speech as an act, i.e. the use of speech to accomplish something. This manifests on four levels, described by Kantor as action stances, communication domains, operating systems and childhood stories. While the latter is critical and determines behavioural profiles and preferences of individuals, it remains invisible and therefore less obvious in determining communication sequences and patterns.

In a nutshell

The action stances (moving, following, contrasting and bystanding), domains (affect, power and meaning) and systems (open, closed and random) that impact on group dynamics.

Purpose

To allow leaders to understand the "dynamics" in a team.

To facilitate improved communcation.

To help understand motives of communication.

To expand the communication repertoires of teams.

Description

Kantor's first three stages, namely action stances, domains and systems, are presented here, as the basic tenet is that any piece of communication that enters the team affects the team in one way or the other.

Action stances

Action stances can be identified as having a moving, following, contrasting or bystanding effect. Individuals' contributions tend over time to cluster in one of these types, in other words, people tend to have a dominant communication style. However, as this is played out in teams some members may display more than one stance. According to Kantor, the manifestation of action stances can be pure, compound or mixed, with mixed being the more difficult to discern and requiring more explanation.

Moving

A person who takes this kind of stance is a "mover" who initiates communication. Such a person proposes ideas, takes charge, initiates action, and focuses on attaining perfection and clarity. This helps the team to find direction. Without this action, a team could lack direction and focus. However, persons acting as movers in a team can be viewed as omnipotent, dictatorial and impatient, and be seen as too bossy.

Following

This is the type of communication offered by a "supporter", and includes appreciating, adding, expanding, agreeing, going along with, and helping the team to complete its tasks. This person is empathetic and compassionate, appreciates what is happening in the team and through loyalty ensures service and continuity. On the down side, such people are sometimes perceived to be pliant and a yes-person; someone who is indecisive and over-accommodating. Too much of this behaviour could lead to wishy-washy solutions.

Opposing

In a team this communication stance manifests by members acting as Devil's advocate, disagreeing, proposing contrasting views and challenging what is being proposed. This provides balance and gives the team the opportunity to correct its actions and consider opposing views. Without this perspective, a team could settle for half-baked solutions, while on the other hand too much of this type of intervention can cause the team to be overly negative or critical. A "challenger" can be seen as acting with integrity and courage, wanting to ensure the survival of the team. However, the "challenger" can be viewed as blaming, defensive, and overly-critical.

Bystanding

The "observer" is quietly attentive, observes, reflects and gives feedback. The team gains perspective by allowing this type of communication. The intention of an "observer" is to provide perspective and preservation. They have the ability to be self-reflective and can be perceived as patient, however they can be seen as disengaged and aloof. This perceived distance could be seen as judgmental and the lack of contribution could be disconcerting.

Kantor went on to show that action stances occur as action structures (i.e. two of them used repeatedly e.g. move-oppose), action sequences (i.e. longer combinations of action structures that form discernible patterns) or structural patterns (i.e. the repetition of patterns during the team's communication processes that become fixed and preferred). He described archetypal patterns such as point-counterpoint (move-oppose patterns that often leave teams stuck in the face of impending change); courteous compliance (where cultural norms or unwillingness to "rock the boat" leads to a "following" stance); and covert opposition (patterns that resemble compliance, but mask unhappiness, oppositional thoughts and potential sabotage).

Communication domains

In addition, Kantor identified three domains in which action stances are communicated and which relate to the aim or purpose of that stance:

Affect

This domain relates to how people connect with the world and includes nurture, intimacy and relationships. It is the language of emotion, caring and connection. Thus, it is oriented towards feeling and relationships and the territory it operates in includes focus on how people in the team are feeling and being cared for. The domain is characterised through words like empathy, sensitivity, well-being, care and feeling. He warned that psychobabble could be a potential dysfunction in this domain.

Power

This domain results from the fact that individuals are free to express what they want and to strive to achieve their aims. It refers to getting things done and focuses on action and productivity. Goals associated with this domain include competence, efficacy and completion. It is associated with clear sets of opposites: on the one hand power manifests in control, coercion and/or authority, while on the other hand power could cause immobilisation, inertia and lack of freedom to act.

Meaning

This domain is about thinking, logic and ideas, while the territory is defined as thought and searching for answers. Communication of this nature relates to identity and integration and strives for purpose and higher ideals. It is often used to test our sense of understanding and identity, and leads to scrutiny, finding more information, and a search for truth through analytical or philosophical means. Note that meaning is often context-bound as teams can define what they regard as meaningful in relation to the specifics of the environment.

Operating systems

Operating systems are the implicit set of rules of how boundaries, behaviour and relationships are governed and regulated in a system. The operating system a team employs helps to control speech through the way it enables, monitors and discourages the use of different speech acts. Building on the principles of systems theory, Kantor regarded the following as key to understanding structural dynamics:

*   Circular causal reasoning: here the focus is on how human behaviour (and communication) is circular ("I do things, that lead you to do things, that lead me to do things, etc.").

- Feedback loops: here it is acknowledged that feedback from a system has the power to increase or constrain output. Positive feedback can be used in teams to amplify positive behaviour while the opposite is true of negative feedback, which can increase instability and imbalance, as a result of which change is thwarted.

- Control devices: how controls are put in place to regulate feedback and progress in systems, such as by people with a personal agenda. This constrains and guides the flow and acceleration of change in a team and helps to fix a pattern.

The operating systems of communication in a team are also characterised by their orientation (whose needs get prioritised), values (the things people in the system care about), boundaries (i.e. who is within the system and how entry into the system is controlled) and limits on speech (who can speak, about what, for how long, and so on). The type of operating system also affects feedback mechanisms. These mechanisms allow for changes to be implemented and, indicate how such changes can be implemented, or how deviations from agreed processes are dealt with.

Communication

Kantor described three systems of communication, namely open, closed and random.

Open

This system is directed at the collective and helps the team by facilitating adaptive and participative behaviour and communication. It is characterised by teamwork and prefers to be ruled by processes rather than formal leadership. Its aim is to manage and balance the good of the whole and of the individual. It values the opinions of members and offers everyone the opportunity to be heard. It operates with permeable boundaries and allows for insights and views from external sources to enrich its own views. Information is shared and minimal limits on participation and speech are set. In such a system there is a balance between positive and closed feedback loops.

Closed

Closed systems are oriented towards the leader and the organisation and less towards individual members. Its territory is hierarchy, order, security and stability. It has clearly set values with a strong propensity to stay within the rules and to follow processes. In such a system there are formal leaders who favour strong planning and control systems. The leader manages the good of the whole, which can lead to the "tyranny of monarchy" where authority rests completely in leadership. Members have clearly defined goals and roles, and the system regulates the behaviour of its members, e.g. by tracking time and activities during the day. Loyalty, history and belonging to the team are prioritised over individual needs. There are clear boundaries and membership is controlled by regulating access. There are clear limits in terms of who is allowed to voice their opinion and what is allowed to be discussed. The system displays negative feedback loops, which leads to inertia and balance.

Random

These systems are characterised by a focus on the individual and allow exploration, experimentation and improvisation. They thrive on creativity and innovation, and lack formal structures, processes and leadership. These systems can sometimes resemble anarchy, where each individual's needs get preference, autonomy and freedom are valued, and there is unfiltered access. High levels of innovation, start-ups and fast-moving settings are clear examples of random systems.

Tips for team leaders

Kantor contended that in each communication system the three levels of action stance, communication domain, and operating system interact to form a structured pattern. This can be analysed and used to help the team in its performance. The diagram shows how the subdivisions of each level relate to each other. As these interact, standardised patterns tend to evolve that can be beneficial or limiting to a team. Leaders can use this analysis to determine the dynamics operative in the team and can employ this knowledge to facilitate more helpful communication. For example, leaders should help members avoid being locked into a single action.

Representation

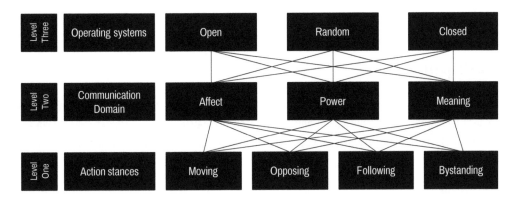

Figure 13.3: Structural dynamics

References

Kantor, D. (2012). *Reading the room: Group dynamics for coaches and leaders.* San Francisco, CA: Jossey-Bass.

64 | **Agile teams**

Introduction

The term "agile teams" strictly speaking refers to a particular type of team and originated in the world of software development. Yet they infused (as a key departure to traditional software development) the practice of software development with a new set of skills and techniques based on behavioural and social concerns and added a "people" focus into development practice. This included a set of communication techniques, which are discussed here to illustrate the influence of this growing field of interest.

In a nutshell

Principles and techniques of agile teams.

Purpose

To understand principles of agile teams.

To illustrate agile team techniques.

Description

Moe, Dingsøyr and Røyrvik identified five principles that influence agile teams, but this has been augmented by a sixth factor, namely communication and coordination (Karhatsu, Ikonen, Kettunen, Fagerholm and Abrahamsson). These principles are described first, after which some agile communication techniques are introduced.

Principles

Shared leadership

This principle refers to shared decision-making, where leadership is distributed according to knowledge, skills and abilities, and where shared mental models determine how leadership is utilised. This is successful if the direction of the team is well-defined and the team is designed to be fit for purpose.

Team orientation

Through a shared orientation, agile teams build cohesion by aligning individuals' tasks and responsibilities clearly to team goals, and creating contexts where such goals are given priority over individual goals. This requires a communication regime that allows for voicing of and acceptance of alternative suggestions from any member of the team.

Redundancy

Cross-functionality is akin to multi-skilling and allows members of the team to substitute for each other or to offer back-up behaviour. The principle states that any particular member in a team should in a sense be "redundant" because other members (being multi-skilled) of the team can step in and do another's work. This limits dependence on a particular member, which can lead to bottle-necks and delays. Agile teams understand the risks involved in relying on the specialisation of only some members and actively promote cross-functionality.

Learning

Learning in agile teams refers to the acquisition of interdisciplinary knowledge where team members acquire broad knowledge outside their direct scope of expertise to promote self-optimisation in a wider environment. This is characterised by job rotation, evaluation of development and communication processes, and integration of knowledge from different domains to improve the team's knowledge, operations and development. Agile teams therefore take responsibility for their own evaluation and improvement.

Autonomy

Agile teams require autonomy as one of its basic premises since it builds a sense of total responsibility over the outcomes of the team. External influences (e.g. demands on resources and management or organisational requests) limit the freedom to act in the best interests of the team and stifle the principle of self-management. In the agile approach, tasks in the team are directed, coordinated and decided upon by the team itself and not driven from a plan or through a "command and control" management perspective. Utilising this principle of autonomy, agile teams are set up to be self-managing. This entails the authority to set their own assignments, priorities and monitoring of measures and standards.

Communication and coordination

Karhatsu added communication and coordination to the original five factors. They regarded communication as the sending and receiving of information while they thought of coordination as "actively working together to deliver a work product or make a decision". They highlighted the importance of communication and coordination for many reasons, including that it facilitates active participation in decision-making and helps with shared skills and specialisations.

Techniques

These are some of the communication techniques that can be used to create agile teams:

Scrum

This is an adaptive process that replaces the traditional command-and-control type of communication with collaborative self-managing teams. The original context is software development projects and one of its main tenets is that it brings decision-making authority to the level of operational problems, challenges and uncertainties. Thus, scrum is a technique where a small cross-functional team is assigned to address an opportunity, challenge or problem. While one person (i.e. initiative or product owner) is ultimately responsible to deliver the required outputs of the team, responsibilities are shared and that person does not direct or "lead" the team by instructing them what to do, planning their tasks or assigning timelines. Rather, the team maps a journey with plans for activities that will not change before execution. The team divides the tasks into modules, decides on how to execute them according to clear measurements (i.e. what does "done" mean?) and starts working in a series of short development phases or iterations ("sprints"), where working versions of the product are typically completed in two to four weeks. During such sprints the team selects from what has been developed and chooses first those of highest value to the customer. Prototypes of part or all of the offering are regularly tested with customers and if positive reactions are obtained they may be released immediately.

Kanban

Kanban is an approach based on the Japanese production management practice where minimum stock is held and supply is done "just-in-time". Applied to software development teams and beyond, it leverages the same principles to match the amount of work in progress (WIP) to the team's capacity. This allows for more flexible planning and faster output, transparency and speed through the development cycle. It must be remembered that while Kanban shares some features with "scrum", it differs in that it focuses on more continuous planning (and not sprints), does not use specific team roles, and allows for change to come throughout a cycle.

Daily stand-up

A clear communication contribution of agile team methodology is the practice of "stand-up" meetings. In these meetings no-one sits, they are very short in duration and happen every day. The purpose of the meeting is feedback on progress, commitment to action and communication on potential problems or challenges related to the specific sprint. Only three questions are answered: What did I do yesterday? What will I do today? What impediments are in my way? This builds on the value agile methods put on face-to-face interactions (i.e. team-to-customer and intra-team) where knowledge sharing takes place and where experimentation, testing and progress can be reported. In agile teams knowledge-as-relationship is fundamental because it underscores the socially-constructed nature of communication. It also allows for stories, narratives, and metaphors to be used as means of transferring and sharing knowledge.

Retrospective

This refers to the evaluation of a completed stage or project by reflecting on the experience. It offers a review of the iteration by collating the collective wisdom of the team, identifying what to appreciate or improve, and learning from failings and failures. This can be done visually (e.g. through the use of metaphors indicating helping and restricting factors) or verbally (e.g. what the team learnt, liked, lacked and longed for). Often it is helpful to ask four questions at the end of a session or project:

- What did we learn?

- What are still unclear or puzzling?

- What will we do differently next time?

- Who should know about the lessons we learnt?

Non-verbal, visual display

A non-verbal display of progress is a very helpful part of the agile team toolkit. For this, storyboards, story cards and visual representations of "radiators" or scrum/Kanban boards are used. Storyboards provide a visual overview of the project and helps the team to decide on the key priorities members need to focus on. Cards are used to indicate key tasks, while radiators, like burnout boards, indicate progress in easily understandable graphs. Kanban boards offer a workflow visualisation by requiring each task to be labelled as backlog, to do, doing, testing or done.

Backlog	To do	In progress	Testing	Done
Activity	Activity	Activity	Activity	Activity
Activity	Activity	Activity	Activity	Activity
Activity	Activity	Activity		
	Activity	Activity		
		Activity		

Figure 13.4: Communication as agile teams

Tips for team leaders

One of the challenges faced by leaders of agile teams is managing the potential conflicts associated with self-organising teams. In this regard, individual versus team-level autonomy and goal pursuit could be contrasting. Leaders can adopt specific practices such as collective decision-making processes, shared and visible tracking, and rotating tasks to address these paradoxes.

Representation

Principles	Techniques
Shared Leadership	Scrum
Team orientation	Kanban
Redundancy	Daily Stand-up
Learning	Retrospectives
Autonomy	Non-verbal, visual display
Communication and coordination	

Figure 13.5: Principles and techniques of agile teams

References

Karhatsu, H., Ikonen, M., Kettunen, P., Fagerholm, F. & Abrahamsson, P. (2010). *Building Blocks for Self-Organizing Software Development Teams: A Framework Model and Empirical Pilot Study.* Paper presented at the 2nd International Conference on Software Technology and Engineering (ICSTE), San Juan, PR, USA.

Moe, N.B., Dingsøyr, T. & Dybå, T. (2009). A Teamwork Model for Understanding an Agile Team: A Case Study Of A Scrum Project. *Information and Software Technology, 52*(5), 480–491.

Moe, N.B., Dingsøyr, T. & Røyrvik, E.A. (2009). Putting agile teamwork to the test — A preliminary instrument for empirically assessing and improving agile software development. In P. Abrahamsson, M. Marchesi, & F. Maurer (eds.). *Agile processes in software engineering and extreme programming. Lecture Notes in Business Information Processing.* Berlin: Springer.

65 | **Virtual team communication**

Introduction

One of the most daunting challenges of modern-day business is to keep up with the increasingly demanding nature of technology that has entered every sphere of organisational life. The same holds true for teams and the manner in which communication occurs when it happens primarily through virtual tools. Marlow, Lacerenza and Salas provided a conceptual model to consider when addressing communication in virtual teams. In particular they highlighted the difference made by the frequency, quality, and content of communication as part of an Input-Moderated-Output-Input approach.

In a nutshell

Communication challenges in virtual teams.

Purpose

To highlight challenges in communication of virtual teams.

To improve communication in virtual teams.

Description

In their conceptual model on what influences communication in virtual teams, the authors discussed such teams in the framework of input, communication, emergent states, task and team characteristics, and output.

Input

Levels of diversity in the composition of the team influence the quality of communication. High levels of diversity (as manifested through differences in culture, language, knowledge, and backgrounds) can lead to a lack of common understanding and less accurate and overlapping mental models. In virtual teams this can be even more pronounced as there is less opportunity to speak and interact and subsequently fewer opportunities to clarify any misunderstandings. Highly diverse virtual teams therefore need to take care to supply more and accurate information to ensure the formation of accurate mental models on task and relational processes. As with face-to-face teams, high levels of diversity bring different perspectives to the team and an opportunity to be more creative. However, in virtual teams there should be a particular effort to exchange accurate information to integrate and understand unique member perspectives.

Communication

Three aspects of communication pertinent to virtual teams, frequency, quality and content, are listed.

Frequency

The volume of information that people receive today is mind-boggling and for the greater part electronic means of communication have facilitated this explosion. In virtual teams, it is even more the case that team members are bombarded with information related to the team and beyond. However, cognitive load theory suggests that human beings have limited capacity to process information. In terms of virtual teams this means that extra effort should be put in place to limit excess and irrelevant information. It would seem that in virtual teams the negative effect on performance of higher volumes and more frequent irrelevant information is more pronounced. However, this is related to the development level of a team, as at the forming stage of a virtual team the members will depend on information. The challenge is to keep the balance and ensure the right amount of relevant information is conveyed for the development stage the team is in.

Quality

In virtual teams, quality of communication must be prioritised over frequency. Marlow and her colleagues described communication quality as "the extent to which communication among team members is clear, effective, complete, fluent, and on time". Thus, quality refers to the degree of accuracy of the communication as well as how well it is understood, all of which influence the manner in which team members understand how to contribute to interdependent tasks and relationships. A further aspect influencing quality of communication is the timeliness of communication, which can be compromised since it may be asynchronous (e.g. different time zones). In virtual teams closed-loop communication is particularly valuable in this situation. This means that a member sends a message, another receives, interprets and acknowledges the message, and the originator of the message then checks that it is received and understood. It is said that in virtual teams closed-loop communication is more critical than in traditional teams.

Content

The third element of communication identified relates to task-oriented interaction (communication focused on task completion) and relational interaction (communication of an interpersonal nature). While it may seem counter-intuitive, evidence suggests that virtual teams are capable of conveying requisite communication content to develop affective states through sharing relational information virtually. However, deliberate action is required to ensure this occurs.

Emergent states

Through the team's operations (and in this case its use of communication in particular), cognitive and affective "states" emerge. Two such "emergent states" (see the next section) are described by the authors to indicate their impact on virtual team communication. In relation to the discussion above on content, these authors noted that it is possible for virtual teams to establish requisite levels of trust through high quality communication that is frequent, timely and of an interpersonal nature. Once this occurs, trust levels can be established and maintained. However, it is postulated that levels of trust are established more quickly if an initial face-to-face meeting takes place. Another emergent state that is influenced by communication is cognition. In this regard it seems that while virtual teams need high levels of cognition to perform, they may be challenged to achieve that because the communication pattern limits interpersonal contact, it is more difficult to share and coordinate knowledge because members are dispersed, and finally the opportunities to communicate are more limited in virtual teams than in traditional teams. Furthermore, virtual teams are often of shorter duration and team cognition may develop at a slower rate or there may not be sufficient opportunity to learn from one another or to allow back-up behaviour through which cognition takes place to occur. Thus, the relationship between cognition and performance may be weaker in highly virtual teams and performance could be compromised.

Team and task characteristics

Three characteristics of teams influence the communication that virtual teams employ. Firstly, where interdependence is high, higher levels of communication in terms of quality and content are required. Secondly, the level of virtuality moderates performance and teams that augment their communication through multiple mediums of virtual communication are more likely to have increased performance than those that rely on a single or minimum means of communication. Lastly, where team tasks are more complex the impact of virtuality is more pronounced, as relationships need to be stronger when task complexity is high and need not be as strong when task complexity is low.

Outcomes

The authors saw viability, performance and satisfaction as the outcomes of virtual teams.

Tips for team leaders

Leaders can consider structural support systems such as joint information or group communication systems (web-based chat groups and the like) to support their virtual teams.

Representation

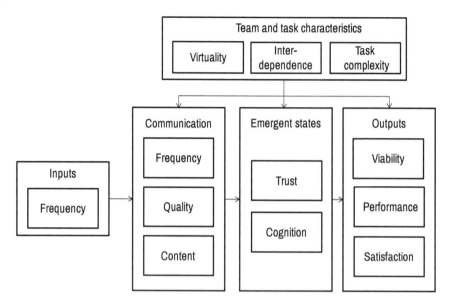

Figure 13.6: Role of communication in virtual teams

References

Marlow, S.L., Lacerenza, C.N. & Salas, E. (2017). Communication in Virtual Teams: A Conceptual Framework and Research Agenda. *Human Resource Management Review,* 27(4), 575–589.

Thompson, L. (2007). *Making the team: A guide for managers* (3rd ed.). Upper Saddle River, NJ: Pearson Prentice Hall.

14 EMERGENT STATES

Emergent states are established as a team functions and interaction between members and the environment takes place. These emergent states, which can be cognitive, emotional, behavioural or motivational, guide and influence the operations and performance of a team. Teams are social systems and therefore interpersonal and psychological dynamics are at play when people get together to complete tasks. Understanding and mobilising the emergent states could help to enhance performance, e.g. to alleviate tension, to improve cohesion, to manage power struggles or to unlock creativity. In addition there are always other, deeper-seated (i.e. "unconscious") forces at play in a team, which facilitate the development of emergent states.

Here five different emergent states are discussed, namely cognition, learning, affective, flow and (A)CIBART. The first part is devoted to cognition as an emergent state and three elements thereof are discussed, namely shared mental models, transactive memory systems and situational awareness. Learning is discussed next; this refers to the ability teams require to reflect on their work, evaluate their actions and performance, and adjust their behaviour accordingly. Affect as an emergent state refers to the affective reactions within a group, including how it deals with emotions and moods as a team completes its tasks and develop in time. The fourth emergent state that receives attention here is the particularly well-studied affective state of "flow". This indicates a state where members in a team feel challenged, yet confident in their ability to deal with these challenges as they feel they have influence over their jobs. Thus, it is an emotional state a team experiences collectively when they become completely absorbed in their attention to the task at hand. This shared experience emerges from collective commitment and team dynamic and depends on the levels of interaction and interdependence between members. The last emergent state described is the so-called "unconscious" forces that influence a team without members necessarily being aware of them. Building on the acronym (A)CIBART the following are described: anxiety, conflict, identity, boundary, authority, roles and tasks.

It is important to realise that the value of including emergent states in understanding and leading teams lies in the fact that they are both outcomes of interaction (i.e. they evolve through the functioning of the team) and also inputs into the team as they influence ongoing team performance.

66 Cognition

Introduction

As teams operate in the environment they have to react to information and cues from various contexts and make sense out of the data they receive. The manner in which such information is processed, stored, retrieved, dispersed among members and used in creating shared mental models of what is required of the team constitutes cognition in a team. Cognition is thus the shared knowledge and awareness that emerge when a team interacts and executes activities towards pursuing its goals and vision. Three elements of cognition are dealt with here, namely shared mental models, transactive memory systems (TMS) and situation awareness. The first is the collective mental maps a team employs while TMS relates to the collective distribution of information and knowledge; in other words, the first relates to information held in common while the second refers to information that is held by individuals and then dispersed throughout the team. Situational awareness is the manner in which a team perceives, comprehends and predicts changes in its environment.

In a nutshell

Cognitive states operative in a team, namely shared mental models, transactive memory systems and situational awareness.

Purpose

To help the team analyse cognitions.

To understand how shared mental models, transactive memory systems and situational awareness can help to optimise operations.

Description

Team cognition refers to how knowledge is represented, distributed and utilised in a team and enables the team to organise and acquire information it needs to operate and to perform. If each member of a team interprets information in a similar way to the other members, the team will be able to coordinate its actions.

Shared mental models

Shared mental models (SMM) have been identified as particularly helpful to teams and can be seen as the mental models or mental maps influencing the team's behaviours. While these are individually generated, a "shared, collective" mental map emerges as members work in teams. Examples are SMMs around the strategy, goals, environment, challenges, team membership, required behaviours, coordination requirements or time. When the mental models are shared it allows the team to sing from the proverbial same hymn sheet and provides for accurate and corresponding views on what should be done. They capture the shared understanding and mental representations of information, values and beliefs that the team regards as important. An SMM consists of words, images and stories that occupy the thinking processes in a team. For example, it could refer to the collective sense of what is required to "get the deal" or to "visualise" the successful completion of a project or product. The cognitive elements employed by a team are based on individual members' perceptions, thoughts, beliefs, and expectations, but extended beyond individual cognitions to become a team element. This means the representations are either identical (e.g. shared views on tasks, behaviours and outcomes) or distinct, but sufficiently overlapping. They help teams to understand, describe and explain phenomena they have to deal with collectively and assist them to predict and determine what to expect in future. They can be seen as the implicit coordination between members that facilitate their decision-making in difficult and complex environments.

Domains

For a team to operate, create understanding among each other and facilitate operations, there need to be shared mental models in each of the following four domains:

- Equipment (tools and material required to do the tasks of the team).

- Task (agreement on what the team has to deliver including performance levels, goals and potential challenges).

- Composition (a shared view on who is on the team and what the roles and expectations of various members are).

- Teamwork (what is required from the team in terms of cooperation and coordination to be effective).

Dimensions

Critical dimensions of shared mental models of teams are:

- sharedness: the extent to which a particular mental model is held in common across the team;

- accuracy: the extent to which the team's model corresponds with reality; and

- correspondence: this refers to the level of overlap between different members or alternatively whether each member perceives a particular phenomenon in a similar way.

When there is a high level of these three dimensions, the team is assured that critical information is shared, goals and tasks are aligned and according to assigned and (tacitly) agreed roles, and that knowledge interdependencies are acknowledged, shared and utilised. It is important to realise that the SMMs employed in a team relate to both the task and interpersonal realms of teamwork, and that both of these are dependent on the manner in which they are shared.

Transactive memory system

This refers to the encoding, storing, and retrieving of information by particular team members and resultant collective team "memory" when all of these individually held sets of information are collated. The second key part of a TMS is the fact that members remember who knows what and there is a shared awareness of who knows what. Thus, it is helpful to view this as a network with various nodes where each individual knows specialised information, but where there is understanding where information is located in the network. For example, in a management team, the team will hold the financial manager responsible for remembering certain accounting information and the team will expect him or her to be knowledgeable about this particular part of the team's collective memory. For the system to work optimally, each member takes responsibility for a particular set of information and team members channel information to the particular individual. The team therefore knows who the expert on a particular piece of collective memory is, and how to access information from this particular resource.

The key implications of shared cognition in a team relates to how the information in a team is either:

*   specialised: this refers to the notion that some information requires expertise to acquire and interpret; or

*   distributed: the alternative to specialised information in a team is that it is not seated in a particular individual, but more readily available or obtainable; and

*   credible: indicating the level to which it is accurate and believable to the members.

Teams develop their TMS through sharing knowledge about what the various members know and do and facilitating the distribution of information by tracking information, directing information to the responsible and applicable node in the network, and allowing members access to the information distributed across the network.

Situational awareness

Situational awareness refers to the cognitive abilities and skills needed to be aware of and responsive to the environment in which the team operates. It is a multi-faceted concept, but teams need to be aware how it impacts on their ability to make sense of the environment and how such cognitive efforts influence their actions and decision-making. Three levels or components of situation awareness are identified. They can be seen as the degree or extent to which each member holds sufficient information and awareness to be able to perform.

Perception

This is members' awareness of which elements in the environment are of importance to the team. In this regard the team needs to display insight about the environment and key factors that impact on the team. Perception relates to what is observed, what stimuli from the environment are reacted to, and in what manner aspects from the environment (maybe erroneously) are not taken into account.

Comprehension

The next level of situational awareness refers to the ability teams have to make sense of changes in the environment. Thus, where the first level requires the ability to be aware of and to sense changes, this level goes a step further by requiring the team to be aware of what value and meaning they place on the aspects that they perceive. Thus, "What does what we view mean for us?" and "How do we attach significance to it?" The sense-making abilities of a team are related to the manner in which teams construct meaning and assign significance to particular environmental changes and conditions.

Projection or anticipation

This element refers to the ability of a team to project how a context will change in future and then to act on such anticipation. Once the team has noticed environmental stimuli and made sense of them, the team projects these onto the anticipated future and its behaviour is influenced by such projections and anticipations.

Situational awareness develops sequentially, with the prior level required as input to the next. Furthermore, it would seem that the development thereof is both compositional (overlapping mental models on the content of the levels required) and compilational (where the shared mental model is built through the joint efforts of members in the team). In addition, it would seem that communication, training, and cultural and personal differences, as well as the interplay the team has with technology, are key antecedents to the development of situational awareness.

Tips for team leaders

The implication of these concepts for teams is that they help to determine the "value" of a contribution to a team. If some information is highly specialised it will be vested in a particular individual and not form part of the shared mental model. The value of this member increases relative to the importance of the information. On the other hand, if the information is readily available it is less dependent on the expertise of a particular member and leaders may use reflexivity to guide the team to reflect upon their operations and to facilitate the development of shared mental models. This includes reflection on the taskwork, teamwork, communication and levels of interaction of team members, as well as the extent to which the team reflects and communicates about goals, actions, strategies and processes. Since the context of the team is dynamic, ever-changing and "choardic" (a combination of chaotic and organised), it is key for any team to constantly reflect on its operations. This includes the team's constant monitoring of its environment and refers to how the team makes sense of happenings in its context. It requires a critical stance, with the ability to observe while the team is operating.

Representation

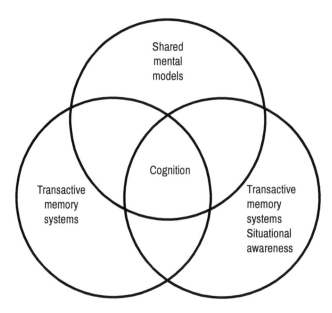

Figure 14.1: Cognitive states operative in a team

References

Bell, B.S., Kozlowski, S.W.J. & Blawath, S. (2012). Team learning: A review and integration. In S.W.J. Kozlowski (ed.). *The Oxford handbook of organizational psychology*, 2. Oxford, UK: Oxford University Press.

Kozlowski, S.W.J. & Ilgen, D.R. (2006). Enhancing the Effectiveness of Work Groups and Teams. *Psychological Science in the Public Interest*, 7(3), 77–124.

Lewis, K., Belliveau, M., Herndon, B. & Keller, J. (2007). Group Cognition, Membership Change, and Performance: Investigating the Benefits and Detriments of Collective Knowledge. *Organizational Behaviour and Human Decision Processes*, 103(2), 159–178.

Mohammed, S., Hamilton, K., Sánshez-Manzannares, M. & Rico, R. (2017). Team cognition: Team mental models and situation awareness. In E. Salas, R. Rico, J. Passmore (eds.), *The Wiley Blackwell handbook of the psychology of team working a collaborative processes*. Chichester, UK: John Wiley & Sons.

Mohammed, S., Ferzandi, L. & Hamilton, K. (2010). Metaphor No More: A 15-Year Review of the Team Mental Model Construct. *Journal of Management*, 36(4), 876–910.

67 | # Learning

Introduction

Kozlowski and Ilgen defined team learning as "the acquisition of knowledge, skills, and performance capabilities of an interdependent set of individuals through interaction and experience. Team learning is fundamentally based on individual learning, but when viewed as more than a mere pooling of individual knowledge it can be distinguished as a team-level property that captures the collective knowledge pool, potential synergies among team members, and unique individual contributions". By using team learning, members combine their individual knowledge, skills and experiences to reach a common goal, and the manner in which members combine these resources reflects the level of team learning operative in the team.

In a nutshell

Activities and products of team learning.

Purpose

To help a team understand the activities needed to facilitate team learning.

To know the products of team learning.

Description

Team learning as an emergent state points to the efforts a team makes to acquire knowledge, skills and performance capabilities to ensure it can deliver on its mandate. This acquisition takes place through the process of interaction and experience and refers to both individual learning and the broader collective effort and synergies of a team pooling their skills and knowledge. As a learning process this cognitive state is particular to a context and bounded in a social space. In combination with other emergent states this leads to a context wherein teams are accepting of behaviour including feedback, sharing information, experimenting, asking for help and discussing errors. One particular element of team learning is the ability to be reflexive. This entails the team's reflection upon its objectives, strategies and processes, and how the team learns from such reflection to adjust these elements of team performance. For team learning to happen, some activities, i.e. processes whereby learning can take place, are performed to deliver outcomes or products of such learning. These are dependent on some antecedents being in place, and therefore the three dimensions of team learning can be stated as activities, products and antecedents.

Activities

Activities that teams perform as part of team learning include knowledge sharing, team reflection and storage and retrieval. These activities are processes whereby the team collaboratively processes information to allow access to knowledge, to facilitate increased shared and accurate mental models, and to adapt behaviours accordingly.

Knowledge sharing

This activity reflects the manner in which members pass new information among each other and is the sine qua non for knowledge acquisition to occur. While knowledge acquisition happens on an individual level, the sharing of knowledge is a team function and learning is facilitated through the manner in which such sharing takes place among members.

Team reflection

This activity refers to the manner in which the team collectively questions, plans, explores and makes use of new information and reviews past and current actions. It involves overt and specific verbal efforts to discuss the team's tasks, objectives, strategies, processes, relationships and operations. It is not only focused on current tasks and environments, but is also reflective about how new actions should be introduced. Team reflection can be directed at current and future actions, but is often also focused on deeper-level questioning of the team's assumptions, values, strategies and methods, interaction processes and commitment to its purpose, which require more critical reflection. The former is focused on immediate challenges and issues faced by the team and is mainly related to its tasks, while the latter questions basic assumptions and mechanisms. Furthermore, the processes the team employs also require reflection as the team evaluates how the levels of coordination, interdependence and collaboration influence its performance levels.

Storage and retrieval

The last activity related to team learning refers to the processes the team employs to store and retrieve shared and relevant material and knowledge. Storage and retrieval refers to the overlap between mental models of individuals and those of the team as a whole. Thus, both the individual and collective memories are stored and retrieved and the team employs repositories for each. Such knowledge can also be stored and retrieved through structural processes and systems that teams employ when they follow standardised rules and procedures. Naturally teams also employ formal repositories (e.g. documents, protocols or databases) to store and retrieve relevant material.

Products

Shared mental models

As was explained elsewhere in this book, shared mental models are developed through activities of sense-making and communication among team members. These common cognitive frameworks enable teams to tap into shared experiences, knowledge and perceptions on the team's goals, tasks and relationships.

Behavioural products

Behavioural products involve the knowledge teams need to be able to complete their tasks and reach their goals. However, this goes beyond task related behaviour to include interactional processes that the team needs to employ to perform optimally.

Process of team learning

While offered as a more general view of how organisations learn, Crossan, Lane and White's "four I's" are helpful in understanding the developmental process of team learning. In the first stage (Intuiting) teams are aware of preconscious recognition of patterns and/or possibilities that manifest to an individual and only affect others once the individual interacts with others. The second stage is Interpreting, during which ideas or views are explained through words or actions and through which language develops to communicate the interpreted views. Teams then start to Integrate this knowledge through shared understanding, coordinated action and formal or ad hoc events. The last stage (Institutionalising) refers to processes that ensure that routinised action occurs, tasks are defined, actions specified and organisational mechanisms are put in place to embed the learning through structures, procedures and strategy.

Tips for team leaders

Leaders can facilitate learning by focusing on the processes required to develop team learning and by highlighting the mechanisms through which learning activities are performed.

Representation

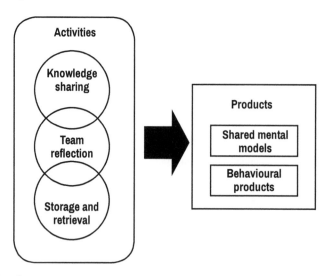

Figure 14.2: Team learning

References

Crossan, M.M., Lane, H.W. & White, R.E. (1999). An Organizational Learning Framework: From Intuition to Institution. *Academy of Management Review, 24*(3), 522–537.

Kozlowski, S.W.J. & Ilgen, D.R. (2006). Enhancing the Effectiveness of Work Groups and Teams. *Psychological Science in the Public Interest, 7*(3), 77–124.

| 68 | Affect |

Introduction

The affective emergent states operative in a team are related to the feelings and moods operative as a team completes its tasks and develops. Feelings refer to specific affective characteristics that occur for a finite period of time and are directed toward specific identifiable objects or events. Moods, on the other hand, last longer. Teams also share emotional states that develop and emerge collectively. The emotional state of a team allows for an affective climate to develop and the emergence thereof as a "state" impacts on the operations of a team as well.

In a nutshell

The difference between mood and emotion; the spectrum of emotions as seen on a circumplex.

Purpose

To focus on the spectrum of emotions.

To help the team to identify various emotions.

Description

As affect comprises mood and emotions it is required to differentiate between the two components of this emergent state first. Thereafter an emotional circumplex will be provided to help the team identify manifestations of emotions.

Mood

Moods can be seen as the affective backdrop experienced over time, independent from events. Thus, they are longer lasting than emotions, but tend to be more nebulous and lingering and often seem to have no cause. Moods are more durable and stable and are often not as easily identifiable as emotions. Moods are experienced less intensely, but can be the background wherein emotions are embedded.

Emotions

Emotions are dynamic, brief and distinctive reactions to events and can last from seconds to hours. They are influenced by context. Emotions manifest with more clarity than moods (i.e. they are more visible and easier to detect) and they are brief, reactive and shorter in duration than moods. It has been shown how the influence of a member in a team can limit or deflate emotions operative in a team, while emotions can also provide energy to a team and enthuse the members. Sometimes a team can be excited and happy because of a success or a positive development in the team. Alternatively, the team can feel depressed, despondent or negative because of perceived frustrations with leadership, interpersonal relations or multiple other influences. Feelings are sensations in the body, always changing, but always there. Some people are more comfortable with feelings, others not. Some feelings (and reactions to them) are unpredictable or unexpected. The research focus on affective states has been dominated by an interest in emotions, and therefore the spectrum of emotions that can manifest in a team and its members are discussed here.

Emotional circumplex

Building on the original work of James Russel, Colibazzi and his colleagues used a circumplex to show the spectrum of emotions. They started with a basic matrix with arousal on one axis and valence on the other. On the vertical axis emotions can thus be activated or not activated. On the horizontal axis emotions are shown as either pleasant or unpleasant. Utilising the idea of emotions as binary, pairs of emotions can be obtained that fit onto a circumplex. Teams can use this classification to determine the current emotions operant in a team.

These pairs of opposite emotions are:

Tense – calm	Being nervous, anxious versus still, tranquil, quiet or serene
Nervous – relaxed	Anxious, edgy or excitable versus comfortable and without care or worry
Stressed – serene	Pressure or tension versus calm, peaceful, and tranquil
Upset – contented	Troubled, perturbed and unsettled versus still, quiet and at peace
Sad – happy	Sorrowful, miserable and unhappy versus cheerful, delighted or in good spirits
Depressed – elated	Miserable, sorrowful, dejected and heavy-hearted versus delighted, excited or exultant
Bored – excited	Feeling weary and impatient because one is unoccupied or lacks interest versus thrilled, exhilarated or stirred
Fatigued – alert	Tired, drained or weary versus aware, watchful, attentive or heedful

Keeping these differences in mind can help the team to understand different emotions as they manifest in the team.

Tips for team leaders

By using the cirmcumplex leaders (and members) can expand their repertoire of emotions; it can help to detect emotions more correctly and can help leaders to manage emotions and the subsequent development of mood.

Representation

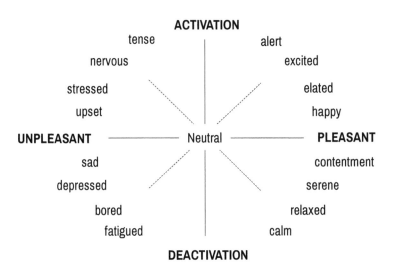

Figure 14.3: Spectrum of emotions

References

Colibazzi, T., Posner, J., Wang, Z., Gorman, D., Gerber, A., Yu, S., Zhu, H., Kangarlu, A., Duan, Y., Russell, J.A. & Peterson, B.S. (2010). Neural Systems Subserving Valence and Arousal During the Experience of Induced Emotions. *Emotion*, 10(3), 377–389.

Introduction

One manifestation of an emergent state of an affective nature is the concept of flow. Flow is the emotional state someone is in when the level of challenge of their job is matched by their ability, so they are neither overwhelmed or bored, but absorbed and functioning optimally. Flow also plays a role in team development and functioning. When individuals experience such flow collectively a collective emergent state develops. Team flow is therefore a shared experience that emerges from collective commitment and team dynamics, as well as the interaction and interdependence between members when they execute their tasks.

In a nutshell

Flow and team flow are affective states arising from being absorbed in something with the right balance of challenge and ability.

Purpose

To understand the concept of flow.

To put conditions in place to elicit flow.

Description

While flow manifests on an individual level its occurrence influences team behaviour as well. Furthermore, a team can collectively be in a state of team flow. This is independent of whether all the members are in individual flow or not. Here, a description of individual flow is provided, after which team flow is discussed.

Flow

Flow is the psychological state a person enters into when they are fully immersed in an activity that requires balancing ability and challenge. However, when one of these two determinants dominates the other it results in sub-optimal conditions for actively engaging with the task. The full range of possible emotional experiences and responses, depending on the level of challenge versus the level of perceived ability, are described and are shown on the diagram below. Flow (as indicated on the graph below) is part of a range of emotions unlocked given the extent of challenge or perception of ability members feel, including:

- anxiety: this emotion is experienced when a task is perceived to be too challenging and the person's perception of his or her own competence is low;

- worry: when there is low confidence in one's own ability, but there is a moderate sense of challenge, this may lead to feelings of worry. This emotional state is dominated by stress, sadness or despondency;

- apathy: this occurs when the task is experienced as void of challenge and the abilities required to perform the task are perceived as low. Sadness, depression and unhappiness result;

- arousal: when a high level of challenge is experienced with moderate confidence in one's own ability, the result is a sense of arousal. The member could be focused and alert, but not yet in an optimum state for performing;

- boredom: this will manifest when a person feels moderately confident in the abilities required for a task, but a low level of challenge is perceived;

- relaxation: when the perceived ability is high, but the task is seen as presenting no challenge, this can lead to relaxation, confidence and contentment; and

- control: this state occurs when the person is happy and confident because they experience a moderate challenge, but are fully confident of their ability.

Characteristics of flow

We have seen that flow is experienced when a person perceives that their abilities match the challenge presented. It is a state of happiness, focus and being actively engaged. When flow is experienced the following are present or emerge:

- clarity of goals;

- immediate feedback on progress;

- a balance between skills and challenge;

- intense, focused and total concentration on the activity at hand where the participant is oblivious to distraction;

- a sense of control with no fear of failure;

- effortlessness as actions and behaviours happen spontaneously, harmoniously and with ease and motivation for the action is driven by autotelic forces (i.e. intrinsic motivation for the sake of the action itself);

- a merger of action, awareness and consciousness where required behaviour becomes automatic;

- a sense of unity with the activity develops (e.g. an instrument is perceived as an extension of the self); and

- distorted perception of time until finally the activity is done for its own sake and for its intrinsic reward.

311

Of these the first three are prerequisites for flow. The next three can influence flow (like prerequisites), but are also indicative of flow (like characteristics). The final three are true experiences of flow.

Team flow

Van den Hout contends that when flow occurs simultaneously and with all members, team flow is experienced. He defined team flow as "a shared experience of flow during the execution of interdependent personal tasks in the interest of the team, originating from an optimised team dynamic". Thus, as with individuals, team members can also collectively experience challenges on a spectrum from low to high in relation to their perceived levels of skills or ability (again from low to high). The impact of this combination leaves an emotional effect. This full array of emotional responses emerges as affective states. Van den Hout et al. suggested that teams can put conditions in place to help individuals in teams to reach flow, and identified seven prerequisites and four characteristics that need to be in place for team flow to occur.

Prerequisites for team flow

Collective ambition

This entails a shared sense of intrinsic motivation to operate at optimal levels and is consistent with the team's shared values, recognition of complementary skills, participation for its own sake as well as willingness and effort to engage with the team to tackle additional challenges. It is based on a team's sense of potency and shaped by a sense of shared values and intrinsic motivation to engage.

Common goal

A team's common goal should be compelling, meaningful and clear. It must align with, complement and be compatible with individual members' goals and should energise the team. It should be internalised by team members and help to facilitate intrinsic motivation as it mobilises the team.

Aligned personal goals

This prerequisite is based on the same principles that apply to individual goal-setting theory, which states that if proximal goals are clear and the required resources are in place, they will act to inspire and motivate people. Applied to the context of team flow it means that team goals must be sufficiently well-stated and accommodating to individual goals to facilitate motivational aspects. It also requires the involvement of members in setting individual and team goals to provide the requisite sense of involvement.

Skill integration

Teams are by definition used to do tasks that individuals cannot complete on their own. This means that a sense of interdependence is needed to accomplish tasks, and a level of integration of skills is assumed. Team flow occurs when a high level of skill integration is needed and experienced when solving challenging tasks. As a balance between skills and challenge is required for flow to be experienced, it is necessary that

312

members know each other's skills and the team tries to optimise individual skill levels with challenging team tasks. In addition, the team tasks should rely on complementary skills and coordinated action.

Open communication

As is the case with individual flow, clear and unambiguous feedback is a key prerequisite for a state of flow to develop in a team. This feedback should be timely, open and related to the performance of tasks. It must be consistent and based on the agreed principle of mutual accountability, and it must assist to align and connect individuals' contributions through coordinated and cooperative means. To facilitate flow, communication in the team must be about achievement of goals, must include active and close listening, and should be constructive and appropriate.

Sense of psychological safety

A sense of safety is built on the notion that failure is an important element of growth and development in a team and that such failure needs to be tolerated and accepted to ensure that members feel they are free to take risks to fail. Thus, psychological safety as a prerequisite for flow encourages and rewards effort rather than success and allows risks to be taken. It does not punish failure, but rather fosters a sense of being in control and experiencing learning and growth. It encourages commitment to optimal effort.

Mutual commitment

This prerequisite is the team equivalent of total concentration and oblivion to distraction. This is facilitated by full attention to tasks on an individual level, awareness of and commitment to the common goal, acknowledgement and appreciation of all members' contributions towards the common goal, and alignment with the team's purpose and reason for being. This commitment to the goals of the team allows for full concentration and undivided attention to the team's common task and helps members to keep one another on task, given the interdependence required, the team dynamics at play and the need for collective action to reach the team's goals.

Characteristics of team flow

Once these pre-conditions are in place they enable team members to experience the characteristics of team flow, namely a sense of unity, a sense of joint progress, mutual trust and holistic focus.

Sense of unity

This characteristic refers to the sense of belonging and cohesion that a team experiences. This requires a loss of self-consciousness (i.e. driving individual needs) in favour of contributing to the team's goals and purpose. Accepting the shared goals of the team and participating in joint effort helps to merge action and awareness, as required by individual flow. A sense of unity is furthermore fostered by a blending of egos, which facilitates a sense of identity, relatedness and belonging.

313

Sense of joint progress

As a team's sense of unity and the understanding of commitment and dependence on one another develop, the actions of the team become integrated and the team's collective awareness merges with how it operates. This inevitably relies on an increased sense of coordinated effort and synergistic actions and a narrowing of action to be focused on that of the team. As team members' actions are increasingly directed at pursuing the collective goal of the team, members increasingly build on each other's work and create a sense of progress, achievement and accomplishment.

Mutual trust

As a consequence of safety an environment of mutual trust develops that entails a willingness to be vulnerable, mutual respect, and confidence in the working environment, in particular leaders, team members and organisation. This mutual trust directs action towards the goals of the team and fosters potency (as a team) and self-efficacy (as individuals).

Holistic focus

When a team is characterised by holistic focus, it means all members are fully concentrating on the tasks at hand, exhibit complete alignment of each of those tasks to the common goal and direct their attention to the team as a whole and the common and shared goal. This can entail team members becoming completely immersed in the team to the extent that they can lose track of time and experience distortion of time.

Tips for team leaders

The list of prerequisites can be used as a checklist to assist the team find the emotional state that can be characterised as flow. As both individual and team flow are discussed, leaders can elect to use this concept with individuals or with the team as a whole.

Representation

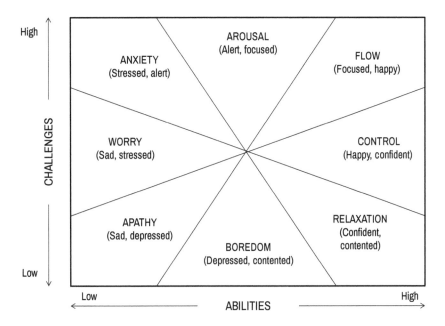

Figure 14.4: Flow

References

Csikszentmihalyi, M. (1990). *Flow: The psychology of optimal experience*. New York: Harper & Row, Publishers.

Van den Hout, J.J.J. (2016). *Team flow: From concept to application*. Unpublished Doctoral Dissertation. Eindhoven: Technische Universiteit.

Van den Hout, J.J.J., Davis, O.C. & Walraven, B. (2016). The application of team flow theory. In L. Harmat, F. Ørsted, F. Andersen, J. Ullén, J. Wright & G. Sadlo. *Flow experience: Empirical research and applications*. Berlin: Springer International.

70 | **(A)CIBART**

Introduction

The term "systems psychodynamics" refers to the whole repertoire of psychological behaviours within and between groups and organisations, where teams are seen as emotional places influenced by motivating forces emanating from the interconnectedness of various sub-systems. These motivating forces are embedded in the consciousness of individuals, teams and organisations. By focusing in particular on the role of the unconscious, the systems psychodynamic approach shifts attention to unknown, unwanted and threatening instincts and feelings, i.e. unconscious drives, needs and behaviour affecting team performance. A helpful tool in this regard is BART, an acronym for boundaries, authority, roles and task, proposed by Cytrynbaum and Noumair. However, in their development of a consulting model, Cilliers and Koortzen added conflict and identity, which resulted in CIBART. In turn, Van Niekerk added anxiety to complete the elements of the approach when used as a tool of analysis in a team.

In a nutshell

A team analysed through the dimensions of anxiety, conflict, identity, boundary, authority, roles and tasks.

Purpose

To highlight the role that unconscious drives and needs play in team behaviour and performance.

To help understand the impact of anxiety, conflict, identity, boundary, authority, roles and tasks in teams.

Description

Each of the elements of (A)CIBART are described below:

Anxiety

According to systems psychodynamic theory, anxiety is a ubiquitous force that drives individuals (and therefore also teams) to deal with their universal fear of the future. In order to deal with this anxiety team members employ three types of defence mechanisms, namely individual defences, social defences and system domain defences. Social defences manifest in the basic assumption of group sameness to the detriment of individual identity and needs, while system domain defences relate to previous experiences in organisations that are transferred into current situations. Individual defences were identified by Bion, and to his original three basic assumptions Turquet and Lawrence each added another, resulting in five basic assumptions regarding individual defences.

Dependency

The first assumption asserts that as during childhood where the child is dependent on the parent (or parental figure), team members project needs for dependency on the team and its leadership. If the focus of teamwork is not on fulfilling these needs, members are left frustrated, helpless, powerless and disempowered. It often manifests in a need for structure and direction, where the leader is perceived as omnipotent and responsible for rescuing the team and providing for their needs. Team members are prepared to follow the leader, but "they require him or her to take all the initiative, do all the thinking, be the major catalyst".

Fight/flight

The fight/flight assumption contends that team members either use fight (e.g. aggression, jealousy, competition, inter-team rivalry and in-fighting) or flight (e.g. avoidance, absenteeism, desperation, or giving up) behaviour to manage the assumed anxiety-producing environment.

Pairing

The last assumption identified by Bion, pairing, focuses on mechanisms that members put in place to avoid anxiety and alienation. Members are seen to pair with perceived powerful other team members or sub-groups to create a sense of security and safety. Members can also try to split up the team to form smaller subsystems in which they can feel safe and to which they belong. Often this goes along with conflict, as "ganging up" or aggression against a "mythical" other is needed to create the sense of belonging.

One-ness

Turquet added this assumption, namely one-ness, to describe a situation where everyone is assumed to be similar and differences are denied. This over-emphasis on cohesion and synergy leads to the team losing its capacity to think independently, as it is supposed that strength found in the one-ness will allow them to deal with the challenges they face.

Me-ness

The counter-effect to one-ness is me-ness where the team operates as an undifferentiated group with an emphasis on individual needs and drives. This is based on the fear of being engulfed or lost in the team, so that team members retreat into their own inner worlds as a defence against perceived challenges from a hostile external environment.

Other individual defences often employed in the workplace include introjection (internalisation of people and objects that are induced as mental images and representations); projection (when impulses and unconscious wishes such as ambition, envy or taboos are "projected" or dumped onto the leader or team); and/or splitting (when a mental structure loses its integrity and "splits" into separate parts such as in-groups and out-groups).

317

Conflict

Conflict is perceived as a normal part of team operation and behaviour and can manifest on various levels:

- Intrapersonal conflict: conflict between personal values and what the team requires of the individual.

- Interpersonal conflict: this may arise from competition amongst team members or with the leader.

- Intra-team conflict: conflict between sub-groups in the team.

- Inter-group conflict: conflict between the team and other parts or sub-systems of the organisation or even groups external to the organisation.

Identity

Cilliers and Koortzen saw identity as the fingerprint of the system, whether an individual or group, for example what one stands for, who one is and how one relates to the rest of the system. Identity refers to the characteristics that make the group unique and different from other groups, namely its members, their task, the climate and the culture. The identity of a team is often more obvious with successful or effective teams where a clear espirit de corps can be identified. It is clear that the team exhibits something unique and that the relationships between them are special. Thus, the boundary of a team is dependent on the levels of social identification that the team establish in differentiating themselves from the rest of the environment, which determines the sense of belonging. This is often seen in contrast to a "them" attitude on an "us-them" continuum and implies a shared set of assumptions and beliefs regarding the identity of the team.

Boundary

The team is in constant interaction with its environment (the context of the team), however, the team needs to create a boundary for itself to define itself. It needs to determine its limits and identify what makes it unique in its environment. This allows the team to determine how it wants to relate to the context and enables it to facilitate its interaction with the environment. For the team to create this boundary, members have to have some level of dependency on each other. The very fact that they are a team means that there is a certain shared commitment of members towards a goal or aim. This generates dependency and establishes a level of commonality. The level of communality allows team members an opportunity to align expectations about mutual needs and assists in establishing levels of communication. Thus, a team creates a boundary through its interactions between members and between members and the environment. The team determines its boundary by defining the level/intensity at which it will allow non-members to cross the boundary. Thus, "visitors" are often allowed as part of a social context, but might not be allowed to share in the "work" of the team. This is an indication of how the team determines the permeability of its boundary.

The boundary of a team can be seen as falling on a continuum where teams can be either under-bounded or over-bounded. In the first case the team runs the risk of having too many external ties and being less well-defined from the rest of the environment. However, it could struggle to motivate members to pull together and to band together. Over-bounded teams, on the other hand, have high loyalty amongst members and act in a highly cohesive manner. However, they have an inability to integrate with others and are less likely to engage in necessary external activity. To facilitate the boundary and identity, the team needs to feel bonded, a sense of rapport and a desire to stay together. Examples of psychological boundaries are role, task, intellectual, property, emotional, space, physical and time boundaries.

Authority/power

Cilliers and Koortzen identified three levels of authority, namely representative, delegated and plenipotentiary authority:

- Representative authority: permission to observe on behalf of the team (i.e. in a team work session), but not allowed or trusted to make inputs towards the task.

- Negotiating or delegated authority: the member has permission to interact, but within specific confines of the task or within specified boundaries.

- Plenipotentiary authority: here the member or representative has full authority and responsibility to act on behalf of the team without consultation.

Role

Cilliers and Koortzen aptly described role as "the boundary around work" and showed that it is the intersection between the individual and organisation (as manifested through tasks, structures, history, culture and norms). Three different roles are distinguished by the systems psychodynamic approach:

- Normative roles: the objective description of the content of a job within a particular context.

- Existential roles: how the team believes they are performing.

- Phenomenal roles: inferences e.g. projections by other members of the team that are mostly unconscious and attributed to particular members.

Task

This is the basic component of work and what the individual is supposed to perform. Clarity in terms of what is expected from the team member facilitates performance and limits confusion and conflict between members.

Tips for team leaders

Unconscious forces and drivers can be found in any team and their influence can be surprisingly powerful. However, it is best to enlist the assistance of a specialist in this field to avoid running the risk of "psychologising" the team. Leaders should also take their own unconscious forces, drivers and needs into consideration when analysing their own reactions to teams and team members.

Representation

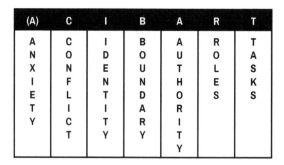

(A)	C	I	B	A	R	T
A N X I E T Y	C O N F L I C T	I D E N T I T Y	B O U N D A R Y	A U T H O R I T Y	R O L E S	T A S K S

Figure 14.5: Elements of (A)CIBART

References

Bion, W.R. (1975). Selections from experiences in groups. In A. D. Colman & W. H. Bexton (eds.). *Group relations reader 1*. Washington DC: A. K. Rice Institute.

Cilliers, F. & Koortzen, P. (2012). Special Edition on Systems Psychodynamics in South African Organisations. *South African Journal of Industrial Psychology*, 38(2), 3.

Cilliers, F. & Koortzen, P. (2005). Working with Conflict in Teams: The CIBART Model. *HR Future*, October, 51–52.

Cytrynbaum, S. & Noumair, D.A. (2004). Group Dynamics, Organisational Irrationality, and Social Complexity. *Group Relations Reader 3*. Jupiter, FL: A.K. Rice Institute.

Czander, W.M. (1993). *The psychodynamics of work and organisations: Theory and application*. New York, NY: Guilford Press.

Kets de Vries, M.F.R. (2001). *The leadership mystique*. London: Prentice Hall.

Van Niekerk, E. (2011). *The systems psychodynamic world of the fund manager*. Unpublished doctoral dissertation. Pretoria: University of South Africa.

15

MOTIVATIONAL STATES

The previous section described emergent states that evolve in all teams. Some emergent states, however, have a particular impact on the levels of motivation that members experience. Motivation therefore merits specific attention. Five motivational states are described here, namely confidence, trust, safety, cohesion and interdependence.

Confidence refers to the sense a team has that they can succeed collectively; trust refers to an individual's willingness to take risks or to be vulnerable, for which a context of safety is required; safety is a team construct that includes a climate consisting of trust, respect and caring about each other; cohesion is defined as the combined forces acting on member to stay in the team.

Behavioural emergent states are related to how a team operates and interacts and are therefore difficult to distinguish from processes described earlier. However, one particular defining element of behavioural states is described here in more detail, namely interdependence.

These five motivational states are therefore specific emergent states that motivate and inspire members to commit to the team.

71 | Confidence

Introduction

A team's sense of confidence refers to the collective belief that they can be successful and points to the collective capability of a team to organise and succeed. Confidence that the team can be successful in what it is supposed to deliver can be a powerful motivational driver to a team. It is therefore helpful for teams to know what constitutes confidence to assist them to optimise the potential benefits of increasing confidence in the team. Three related elements form part of the broader notion of confidence, namely self-efficacy, potency and team-efficacy.

In a nutshell

Confidence as self-efficacy, potency and team-efficacy.

Purpose

To understand confidence as a motivational emergent state.

To assist a team to benefit from confidence.

To help teams utilise motivational emergent states to improve performance.

Description

The three elements of confidence, namely self-efficacy, potency and team-efficacy, differ in scope and target. While the first refers to individual confidence, the other two are team concepts that evolve independently from individual perceptions of personal efficacy. Thus, a team may feel confident that it has the capability to deliver, yet there could be a member in the team with doubts about his or her own efficacy levels. The confidence levels of a team influence what goals the team prefers to pursue, the extent of effort they invest, and the levels of persistence and endurance they offer in the face of adversity.

Self-efficacy

This concept refers to the individual's belief in their ability to effectively deliver the task at hand, and to achieve a particular level of performance when aiming to reach a goal. This relation to goal-setting is key to the development of self-efficacy in individuals for two reasons: on the one hand reaching lower level goals builds efficacy and leads to higher goal standards, while on the other hand assessments of current levels of performance give feedback to members about their progress towards the goal. If these are accurate they can lead to the building of a sense of self-efficacy.

Potency

Potency is a more general belief in the team's ability to be successful beyond the demands of current tasks. Both beliefs influence the performance of a team, however the two concepts differ in that self-efficacy is a private experience while potency develops collectively. Both provide the team with a common understanding of what is expected, who is responsible for what task and what members can anticipate from one another. Potency also guides members' understanding of each other's needs and thereby facilitates collective action and helps teams to work in a coordinated manner. A critical element of potency is the fact that it operates on a group level and should be shared. The sense that the group can be successful is independent from individual beliefs in their own ability. Teams with higher levels of potency tend to have higher expectations of their ability to reach goals and therefore tend to set higher goals. These teams are more prepared to attempt difficult tasks and in general are more satisfied by being part of the team. Higher levels of potency and collective efficacy lead teams to believe that they are better able to deliver on their mandate and improve team performance. Teams with a higher sense of potency will work harder and remain more persistently focused on attaining goals. The level of potency also influences the manner teams adapt, change and challenge their actions to meet increased task complexity.

Team-efficacy

Whereas potency has a broader, more general focus, team efficacy refers to a team's confidence that it can carry out a specific task. Kozlowski and Ilgen defined it as shared and consensual views held across members: "a shared belief in a group's collective capability to organize and execute courses of action required to produce given levels of goal attainment". Thus, it is narrower in scope than potency and relates to specific tasks and contexts. Collins and Parker distinguished two subdomains, namely team process efficacy and team outcome efficacy.

Team process efficacy

The first element of team efficacy relates to how confidence is influenced through the views members hold around the processes they need to employ to be successful. It specifically pertains to the confidence members have that they can work together collectively and effectively. Team process efficacy refers to members' belief about the processes they employ when working together, how their interactions evolve and how they coordinate and combine resources throughout the lifespan of the team. It refers to their confidence in their ability to work collectively, their shared beliefs about within-team agreements and their sense of interdependence.

Team outcome efficacy

This refers to the belief a team holds that it has the capabilities needed to deliver on its expected and desired outcomes. The former can relate to the quantity (e.g. numerical sales targets) or quality (e.g. levels of satisfaction). Thus, a team may believe it has adequate processes in place, yet if it does not believe it will reach its goals (even with effective processes in place) it will be less confident.

Tips for team leaders

Shared leadership and high levels of interdependence increase levels of confidence in teams and it is also helpful to ensure that the confidence levels are widely shared. Leaders can use all three elements of confidence when they build the conditions to motivate the team members, as all three act as motivators to assist individuals and teams to improve their performance. Leaders play a key role in eliciting the levels of confidence members possess to the benefit of the team. Team leaders need to remember that these concepts are not fixed, but are dynamic and develop over time, so there can be fluctuations in the team's levels of confidence at different times.

Representation

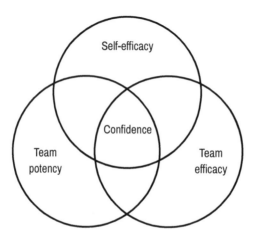

Figure 15.1: Three elements of confidence

References

Collins, C.G. & Parker, S.K. (2010). Team Capability Beliefs Over Time: Distinguishing between Team Potency, Team Outcome Efficacy, and Team Process Efficacy. *Journal of Occupational and Organizational Psychology*, 83(4), 1003–1023.

Gully, S.M., Incalcaterra, K.A., Joshi, A. & Beaubien, J.M. (2002). A Meta-Analysis of Team-Efficacy, Potency, and Performance: Interdependence and Level of Analysis as Moderators of Observed Relationships. *Journal of Applied Psychology*, 87(5), 819–832.

Guzzo, R.A., Yost, P.R. & Shea, G.P. (1993). Potency in Groups: Articulating a Construct. *British Journal of Psychology*, 32(1), 87–106.

Kozlowski, S.W.J. & Ilgen, D.R. (2006). Enhancing the Effectiveness of Work Groups and Teams. *Psychological Science in the Public Interest*, 7(3), 77–124.

Introduction

Mayer, Davis and Schoorman provided a widely used definition of trust, i.e. "the willingness of a party to be vulnerable to the actions of another party based on the expectation that the other will perform a particular action important to the trustor, irrespective of the ability to monitor or control that other party". Trust is a very commonly discussed concept in relation to teams, and its development or emergence in a team is a key contributor to success, especially if one regards personal growth and team satisfaction as outcomes.

In a nutshell

Trust and the antecedents of team trust.

Purpose

To help teams understand the drivers or antecedents of trust.

To highlight the multidimensional nature of trust.

Description

Trust is an individual construct that is essentially the willingness to risk being vulnerable and to direct one's attention towards future outcomes knowing that you can be yourself. Trust is a precondition for safety to manifest on a team level, and is the confidence that a member has in another individual or the team that commitments made to the individual will be honoured. It is the ability to depend on one another, and relates to a team member's evaluation and attribution about others' intentions and motives about the potential of such behaviour to be harmful or not. Trust is based on perceptions regarding the other party's interests, motives and ideas, and rests on the notion that commitments will be kept. It is dependent on the willingness of the one member to believe as well as on the believability of the intentions and trustworthiness of the other, and a context of sufficient trust leads to cooperation and commitment. It is the expectation that others' future actions will be favourable to one's interests and therefore one is willing to be vulnerable to those actions. Trust is important to create an atmosphere that the team can function in. For example, if the team is required to generate new ideas and be creative, there are certain risks involved such as the risk of exposure, ridicule or scepticism. An atmosphere of trust creates the opportunity to venture new ideas and to treat other team members' contributions with respect. The latter will be used to illustrate the impact of values on team behaviour. The following behaviours are expected from people who are trusted: openness (willingness to share information, thoughts and feelings as well as provide reactions consistent with the values of the team); community (behaviour that allows the team to reach its objectives by providing materials and resources to facilitate reaching team goals); and empowerment (allowing team members to achieve the task in their own way). At the same time, trustworthy behaviours include: respect (recognition of the contribution of team members and the belief in each other's ability to cope with the situation at hand); cooperation (cooperative behaviour and empathy); and dependability (keeping diligently to what is promised).

Antecedents of team trust

Costa and Anderson acknowledged the multidimensional nature of trust and highlighted how individual and organisational level antecedents of trust impact on a team.

Organisation-level antecedents

Organisation climate

Climate refers to the shared perceptions employees have about what events, practices and procedures are rewarded, supported and expected. Climate impacts on teams and a team has its own climate within that of the larger system. However, the boundaries between them, i.e. which impacts at what level on the team, are difficult to determine. One can rather say that given the systemic principle that the whole is in the part and the part is in the whole, both have an equally important influence on the development of trust. Climates that focus on collaboration, cooperative action, fairness, justice, equality and transparency, as well as a consistent application of procedures and systems, are more likely to facilitate the establishment of trust in a team.

Organisational structure

This refers to whether decision-making in the organisation is centralised or decentralised. This has an impact on the degree to which members feel able to influence organisational decision-making. Loose and decentralised structures allow for more freedom and a sense of autonomy and control that is diverted to individuals or teams. Subsequently such structures foster trusting teams more readily than highly authoritarian and bureaucratic regimes.

Human resource management practices

How employees view the human resource management in an organisation impacts on the formation and development of trust in a team. Human resource management practices that are seen to be enhancing growth and development opportunities impact positively on team trust.

Team-level antecedents

Interpersonal ties

Strong interpersonal ties and commitment to each other build team trust. Members of teams where there are strong ties and bonds are more emotionally attached to the team and each other, more cohesive and more likely to commit to team goals and a shared vision. They are prepared to take more risks and are more willing to trust one another, which reduces the need for monitoring and controlling.

Interaction processes

Trust as a dynamic process develops over time, and as it develops the circularity between trust and cooperative behaviour start to manifest. Trust leads to cooperation, but the extent and experience of such cooperation in turn builds trust. A further interactional process that influences the development of trust is the need to monitor and control. Where this is linked to empowering behaviour, trust develops more dynamically. It would also seem that conflict and a history of success in dealing with conflict helps teams to develop trust.

Team climate

A team climate that is built on participative safety and shared norms allows for the emergence of trust. Team climate is also part of a circularity where trust is needed to build a climate characterised by safety, which in turns influences the levels of trust in the team.

Team leadership

Team leadership helps to develop trust in a team in the manner in which it creates conditions that allow members to experiment and take risks and where reciprocation manifests in the ability members have to show vulnerability. Where leaders are driven by relationships, are open and allow emotional accessibility, the levels of trust increase.

Team structure

The levels of diversity and difference in a team can also impact on the formation of trust. It would appear that where there are higher levels of diversity a team's cognitive-based or competence-based trust develops earlier, while affective-based or similarity-based trust levels develop more slowly.

Communication medium

It has been found that face-to-face teams develop trust more readily than computer- or electronically facilitated communication. Where virtual teams do exist, deliberate actions like the delivery of timeous and meaningful responses as well as providing relevant information can mitigate the potentially detrimental impact of such contextual factors on team trust.

Individual-level antecedents

Trustor characteristics

The propensity to trust moderates trust in a relationship and in a team. This is based on past experience and the willingness to take risks in general. It is also influenced by personal differences, identity, and the culture and development context.

Trustee characteristics

The evaluation and assessment of the trustee is based on three key factors, namely ability, benevolence and integrity. Ability can be identified as the group of skills, competencies, and characteristics that enable someone to have influence within some specific domain in a particular context. This ability is context-specific and trust is afforded to someone within such a domain. It should be acknowledged that this perception of trust allows it to manifest through the behaviour within such competence or expertise, i.e. making the expertise salient builds trust. Benevolence is the extent to which a trustee is believed to want to do good to the trustor. It also refers to the extent to which the trustee's actions are perceived as working to the benefit of the trustor. However, since the experience of trust is particular to a specific relationship, attachment between the two parties influences the extent of trust between these parties and the act of trusting. This presupposes a personal component to the relationship that can impact the dyad, but the trustee's intentions can also be perceived to extend to the team and more broadly to a commitment to the greater good. Integrity is a basic belief that the trustee holds a set of principles or values that are acceptable to the trustor. Here again it is the person who is evaluated and this assessment can be based on past actions, the credibility of communication from such an individual, and the honesty and authenticity the person displays. It is also based on the evaluation of how congruent the trustee's actions are to what is espoused, and the sense of justice, fairness and equity that is conveyed and manifested.

Trustor-trustee relationship

As noted above, the relationship between the trustor and trustee also influences the development of trust. It is postulated that past experience, i.e. the process of the development of trust, is a key determining factor. In this regard the history of the relationship, such as where trust was put in the trustee and how it was handled, influences the trusting relationship. It has also been found that similarity in what is important for each party allows for a trusting relationship to develop faster and more deeply.

Outcomes of trust

The authors further described the outcomes of trust that manifest on an organisational level (better communication and knowledge exchange between individuals and groups), team level (team satisfaction, risk-taking, cooperation, information-sharing, knowledge creation, psychological safety, citizenship behaviours, conflict resolution and team performance), and individual level (positive job attitudes, risk-taking behaviours, information-sharing and knowledge transfer).

Tips for team leaders

Leaders can facilitate development of trust in the team by being willing to share information, thoughts and feelings as well as providing reactions consistent with the values of the team. They also help trust to develop through building a sense of community, i.e. behaviour that allows the team to reach its objectives by providing materials and resources to facilitate reaching team goals and empowerment. It is in particular helpful if the leader allows team members to achieve the task in their own way and to experience a sense of potency. On the other hand, trustworthy behaviours should be encouraged like respect (recognition of the contribution of team members and the belief in each other's ability to cope with the situation at hand); co-operation (lead in co-operative behaviour and empathy); and dependability (keep to what is promised diligently).

Representation

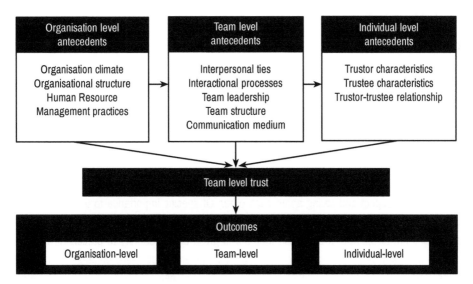

Figure 15.2: Trust and the antecedents of team trust

References

Costa, A.C. & Anderson, N. (2017). Team trust. In E. Salas, Rico, R. & J. Passmore (eds.). *The Wiley Blackwell handbook of the psychology of team working a collaborative processes.* Chichester, UK: John Wiley & Sons.

Mayer, R.C., Davis, J.H. & Schoorman, F.D. (1995). An Integrative Model of Organizational Trust. *Academy of Management Review*, 20(3), 709–734.

Schoorman, F.D., Mayer, R.C. & Davis, J.H. (2007). An Integrative Model of Organizational Trust: Past, Present, and Future. *Academy of Management Review*, 32(2), 344–354.

Introduction

Safety introduces a team construct that influences motivation and contains the conditions wherein trust can be experienced. The relationship between trust and psychological safety, both key team emergent states, needs careful consideration, as the latter goes "beyond" interpersonal trust and describes a team climate where trust and respect is such that members of the team can be themselves and feel safe.

In a nutshell

Psychological safety as an emergent state.

Purpose

To help teams build a context of safety.

To create the psychological space wherein team members can trust.

Description

Safety is a team construct that goes beyond the more individual concept of trust to include a climate consisting of trust, respect and caring about each other. Of specific importance to teams is the state of security and trust that develops as teams grow cohesive. As trust increases between members, this creates a safe environment to operate in and each member is given an opportunity to participate in the team. Furthermore it influences attitude positively and helps members to be more engaged and committed. Safety therefore refers to a shared belief that it is safe to take personal risk. In such an environment members feel that they can engage with the team as authentic selves, without risking being rejected as persons for their ideas, views or opinions. Where this safety exists, members are interested in one another for the people they are, they have positive intentions towards one another and they are able to deal with conflict in the team constructively. Because of the felt safety there is open communication and feedback on behaviour and members are prepared to voice their concerns about leadership, other team members, and so on. Here the results of two meta-analyses are combined to provide an overview of antecedents and outcomes of psychological safety in a team.

Antecedents

A number of antecedents have been identified as playing a part in facilitating the establishment of safety in a team, which can be divided into leader, team, task and organisational factors.

Leader

Research has found that positive leader relations as displayed through transformational leadership build the requisite trust in leadership to facilitate safety. Behaviour that supports this type of leadership includes support, resilience, consistency, competence and positive social exchanges between leaders and members.

Team

Certain team characteristics also facilitate safety, in particular the manner in which members of the team support one another through the social interaction that is brought about by building interpersonal relationships. Where a team succeeds in its problem-solving efforts and mechanisms, and where members in the team experience commitment and effort from one another, the team context supports safety.

Task

A further influence on safety is the characteristics of team tasks, in that the level of interdependence assists in the development of safety. This seems intuitively correct, as the requirement that my efforts are needed and valued, and that at the same time I depend on the efforts of others, fosters interdependence, which drives safety. Furthermore, where the team can act autonomously to influence its performance and where there is clarity on the various roles that individuals in the team have to fulfil, the team context serves as an antecedent to psychological safety.

Organisation

The last antecedent is the level of organisational support the team experiences. In this regard, human resource practices and team members' perceptions of how supportive human resource practices are, build commitment to the team and the organisation, as well as the level of social capital the organisation requires. This contributes to the development and sustenance of psychological safety.

Member characteristics

It is proposed that individual member factors moderate the impact of these antecedents on psychological safety, in particular aspects of personality that relate to proactive behaviour, emotional stability and openness to experience. Where these factors are involved along with levels of trust (willingness to be vulnerable) and where a learning orientation is present in the members, the development of psychological safety is positively influenced.

Outcomes

When there is sufficient safety in a team this drives performance, contributions, creativity and learning. A particular outcome of such safety is a higher level of engagement to the tasks, the team and the organisation. Task performance increases and there is more information- and knowledge-sharing, creativity and support in the team. Members are more willing to learn and experience higher levels of satisfaction with the team. A further outcome is that members are more willing to voice their opinions, positive or negative.

Tips for team leaders

The levels of security established by the team can be depicted as a spiral with discernible nodal points where the specific level of security is tested. This testing ensures that the security fabric of the team is intact and allows for the team to continue. Belief in security in the team is tacit and implies a sense that the environment is safe for interpersonal risk-taking – in other words, confidence that the team will accept members' actions and behaviour and allow for feelings congruent with their emotional states. It is therefore a shared belief in the consequences of individual and team actions.

Representation

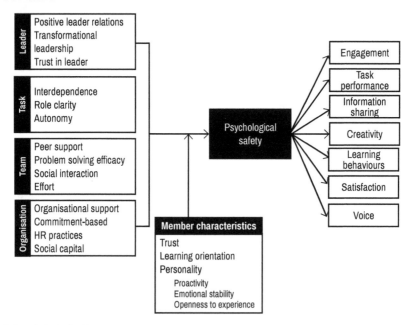

Figure 15.3: Psychological safety

References

Edmondson, A.C. & Lei, Z. (2014). Psychological Safety: The History, Renaissance, and Future of an Interpersonal Construct. *Annual Review of Organizational Psychology and Organizational Behaviour*, 1(1), 23–43.

Frazier, M.L., Fainshmidt, S., Klinger, R.L., Pezeshkan, A. & Vracheva, V. (2017). Psychological Safety: A Meta-Analytic Review and Extension. *Personnel Psychology*, 70(1), 113–165.

Cohesion

Introduction

Although the most often used definition of cohesion – "the resultant of all the forces acting on the members to remain in the group" – is old and dated, it still rings true and is widely used. Festinger's views of what comprise cohesion are still regarded as the three key elements thereof, namely member attraction, group activities (i.e. task commitment), and prestige or group pride.

In a nutshell

Key elements of cohesion, namely member attraction, task commitment and group pride.

Purpose

To help teams understand drivers of cohesion.

To build cohesive teams.

To help maximise benefits of cohesive teams.

Description

Cohesion can be seen as the processes a team employs to get members to stick together and to remain focused and committed to a common goal. It refers to a sense of rapport, camaraderie or "we-ness". It is the invisible binding ingredient that contributes to the team's solidarity, sense of community and fellow-feeling. Cohesion impacts on the tangible behaviour of the team. For example, a shared vision and agreed consent on how the team should proceed enable members to experience a bond between each other and a rhythm or flow starts to develop. This enables them to be in harmony with each other, which creates a sense of cohesion. The perception of strength in numbers and mutual dependence in light of adversity also strengthens the commitment of members to each other. Cohesion in a team becomes evident when members sit closer together, focus more attention on one another and show signs of mutual affection. Cohesion is created through members that appreciate each other's contributions and enjoy being in each other's company. The shared commitment to the team goal binds the team together and allows members to communicate and coordinate their task efforts more effectively. This instils a sense of pride that helps the team to grow its identity and sense of belonging. Cohesion is a multidimensional concept consisting of five dimensions, which are now discussed.

Member attraction

This refers to the degree of closeness, similarity and unity within the group, as well as the desire to develop and maintain social relationships in the team. It includes individuals' feelings about their personal involvement in the tasks of the team as well as involvement in the social interactions with one another. The social exchanges within a team establish group norms that in turn impact on how members feel, with positive exchanges increasing cohesion while the opposite is the case for punishing exchanges.

Task commitment

This element of cohesion refers to the attraction or bonding based on a shared commitment to the completion of the team tasks. This commitment to achieve the common goal of the team influences cooperation, coordination and interdependence, and thus facilitates performance. Behaviours that enhance commitment to the tasks and goals of the team may influence cohesion as critically as people's liking for one another.

Belonging

Whereas the first dimension refers to the attraction members have to each other and to the team, this dimension refers to the extent to which a member wants to be part of a team and be accepted by fellow members, and the degree to which the individual wants to remain in the team because of the other members. This desire to be part of the group also extends to a group as a whole.

Group pride

Members find pride in belonging to a particular team because they are attracted to the status of belonging to the team. It could also be that they want to belong because they agree with or wish to promote the ideologies, goals and aspirations of the team. The sense of purpose they find in being part of what the team represents leads to a sense of increased cohesion. A further aspect that influences a sense of pride in the team is the sense of shared importance it has to the members of the team to be part thereof.

Morale

A high degree of loyalty to team members characterises cohesive groups. Members are willing to back each other up and to assist and support one another. A sense of devotion and allegiance to one another that builds on a sense of dependability and trustworthiness commits members to the team and builds team morale. This commitment and loyalty to one another and to the team leads them to endure frustration on behalf of the team and to persist and to persevere on behalf of the team. Identification with a team that is valued has an impact on an individual's experience of the team and on their own self-esteem, and leads to a sense of efficacy and achievement.

Temporal issues

While time is not a dimension of cohesion, it is important to reflect on the role of time in the development of the cohesion of a team. The mere fact that teams develop and grow as proposed by many scholars (and as confirmed in this book) points to the fact that cohesion in a team is a dynamic process. Thus, while cohesion may not be strong at the outset, a team may develop into a cohesive unit over time. Initial levels of cohesion can be affected by first impressions, which can be influenced by surface-level group identities based on immediate features (such as race or gender). These initial reactions set the tone for the development of cohesion. As early interactions set the scene and provide the building blocks on which cohesion is built, it is helpful to make salient features available to teams to allow them to understand each other's values and beliefs better and to allow them to commit to the tasks of the team. It also goes without saying that events over the life-time of a team could impact on a team's cohesion, either positively or negatively. In this regard it could be that disappointments or moments where trust is broken diminish cohesion, while on the other hand times of success or the manner in which the team deals with collective torment, challenge or difficulties could improve cohesion levels.

Tips for team leaders

Research indicates that cohesion levels increase when the interdependence of tasks is greater and where members need to rely on one another more to perform.

Representation

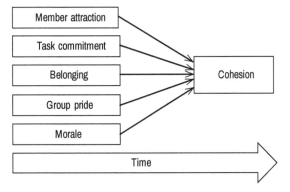

Figure 15.4: Key elements of cohesion

References

Festinger, L. (1950). Informal Social Communication. *Psychological Review*, 57(5), 271–282.

Kozlowski, S.W.J. & Chao, G.T. (2012). The Dynamics of Emergence: Cognition and Cohesion in Work Teams. *Managerial and Decision Economics*, 33 (5–6): 335–354.

Salas, E., Grossman, R., Hughes, A.M. & Coultas, C.W. (2015). Measuring Team Cohesion: Observations from the Science. *Human Factors*, 57(3), 365–374.

Introduction

Interdependence is a key prerequisite for a group of people to be a team, and for members in a team the sense of interdependence guides their behaviours. Interdependence fosters a sense that the individual's contribution is valued and needed by the team. On the other hand, the individual is assured that he or she needs the team and the contribution of the team enables the individual member to perform at levels that would not be possible alone. Thus, it is helpful to understand the different types of interdependence as well as the configuration of interdependent tasks.

In a nutshell

Configuration of interdependent tasks as pooled, sequential, reciprocal, conjunctive, disjunctive, discretionary, complementary and representative.

Purpose

To understand various ways to configure team tasks.

To design tasks to meet demands to reach team outcomes.

To optimise team interdependence.

To use interdependence to build motivational conditions for the team.

Description

Types of interdependence

In order to produce the required outcomes each member of a team has to complete a set of actions to finish the tasks allocated to him or her. However, to prevent these actions from being independent and non-aligned, team tasks need to be configured to create sufficient interdependence to ensure the team meets its outcomes. Different types of interdependence can be distinguished:

Psychological interdependence

This refers to the interpersonal contact that is required for working in a team. This type of interdependence acknowledges that team members depend on one another on a personal level in order to complete tasks, grow in the team and be content. Therefore, interdependence is the degree to which interpersonal relations affect performance, and manifests in supportive behaviour, willingness to help and the understanding that "we are there for each other".

Structural interdependence

The extent to which team members rely on one another because of the nature of the team's tasks is called structural interdependence. It refers to the technical, administrative or task requirements that teams need to fulfil and the degree to which members must share materials, information or expertise to complete tasks. As the complexity, difficulty and importance of tasks increase, the degree of interdependence typically increases as well because more interaction, coordination and assistance from each other is required. Structural interdependence manifests on a number of levels:

Horizontal interdependence

This refers to the degree to which each member's tasks and responsibilities influence other team members' tasks. An example is a classical production line where one member's input depends on the output or production of another "further down" the value chain. The greater this type of interdependence, the greater the impact that will be felt on social processes, interactions and outcomes.

Vertical interdependence

The next form of structural interdependence is the level of hierarchy present in the team. Sometimes teams are made up of members that hold different ranks or occupy different levels in the organisation, but who operate in the same team. Think, for instance, of an executive team that includes the Chief Operating Officer as well as the IT and HR managers, who report to her, but also have seats on the executive. Obviously the levels of interaction are complicated because of the vertical interdependence. The COO expects outcomes (e.g. deliverables) while those reporting to her may depend on her political influence or support to get the outcomes they need.

Goal interdependence

The degree to which the team is collectively responsible for reaching certain goals is what is meant by goal interdependence. It can be described as the qualitative and/or quantitative assessment of joint output in as far as the team reaches its overall objectives or meets its mission. Thus, if the team is responsible for a particular target, each member's individual contribution is perceived to have an impact on the achievement of these collective goals. The interdependence between individual goals and team goals may promote or inhibit such contributions because individual goals may encourage task strategies that maximise individual performance, whereas more cooperation and support may arise from instances where collective goals are clearly articulated.

Reward interdependence

This is the final structural type and refers to the degree to which members depend on one another to receive a reward for collective effort. As in any employment situation, individuals are required to perform certain tasks for which some reward eventuates. In a team, some or all of this reward (i.e. the consequences and outcomes of effort) may be shared by team members. Therefore, where members depend on one another to receive a reward, the reward for this collective effort and the level to which it is interdependent inform the degree of this type of structural interdependence.

Interactional interdependence

Various options on how to configure team tasks to ensure the interdependence of members have been put forward. Thompson offered one of the earliest views of how team tasks could be classified by identifying pooled, sequential and reciprocal tasks. In his classification system, Steiner used the term "additive" to denote pooled interdependence and denoted sequential tasks as conjunctive tasks. However, conjunctive tasks exhibit different characteristics (see below). Steiner thus retained sequential interdependence (calling it conjunctive) and adds compensatory and disjunctive interdependence to the classification system of Thompson.

Pooled interdependence

The configuration where team tasks are summed or collated to produce the outcome of the team is called pooled interdependence. In work environments this type of "pooled" interdependence requires each member's contribution to be completed independently and measured individually. However, the individual efforts are then combined to allow for a team output. Some call centres make use of a pooled interdependence design and measurement and reward are tied to the combined efforts of individuals although there could be minimal interaction between members.

Sequential interdependence

In this type of interdependence, the workflow is regularised and once a particular task is completed it is passed on to another member to continue with the task. Classical examples are assembly lines where each member plays a particular role that must be completed before his or her colleague takes over the product to perform the next step. In this case the task of each member of the team is used as input into the following member's task. Sometimes this type of design also applies on the team level where the output of the complete team is required as input into that of the next team.

Reciprocal interdependence

This type of configuration pertains where resources can be combined in any way to ensure success and where each member can do the tasks of one or more of the team mates, e.g. a team of real estate agents or a basketball team. In work teams this means that every member can complete any part of the tasks of the team at any given time. Reciprocal interdependence means that task allocation and completion do not take place in a linear fashion. Management actions during, for example open discussions or workshops take the shape of reciprocal interdependence. This is a helpful design as it gives the opportunity to maximise the input of each member and optimise their individual contributions.

Compensatory interdependence

This type of task is usually unitary and cannot be divided easily into sub-tasks, but rather focuses on optimisation and seeking a quality solution rather than prioritising quantity. It averages the input of members to provide a combined, single result, e.g. the average of a team. An example is where a management team has to create a set of scenarios of the future for strategy decisions, or making a sale, or forecast of a new product. It is a collective effort and members compensate for each other and are interdependent in a collective sense.

Conjunctive interdependence

This configuration is where members are required to perform at a minimally acceptable level and the team depends on the level of output of the worst performer.

Disjunctive interdependence

Disjunctive interdependence relates to the type of configuration where one team member's performance is required for the whole team to succeed and the output of the team depends heavily on the best individual performance.

Representative interdependence

Here the team depends on the efforts of a member "representing" them or doing tasks on their behalf, e.g. the leader representing the team at a meeting. These tasks are done on behalf of the team and team members are not present while they occur. Thus, the team allows the member to represent them and they entrust the task to the particular member to act on their behalf.

Tips for team leaders

Configuring the tasks of the team optimally is a challenging part of leading teams, as the level of interdependence determines in many cases the level of contribution members are prepared to offer. In particular this relates to how members view their contribution and subsequent reward, and whether they perceive that input-reward ratio to be fair in relation to the input-reward ratio of others in the team. It also requires team leaders to find ways to make individual contributions visible and link them to the overall goals of a team.

Representation

Psychological interdependence	Structural interdependence	Interactional interdependence
Psychological	Horizontal Vertical Goal Reward	Pooled Sequential Reciprocal Compensatory Conjunctive Disjunctive Representative

Figure 15.5: Configuration of interdependent tasks

References

Levi, D. (2007). *Group dynamics for teams*. Thousand Oaks, CA: Sage Publications, Inc.

Steiner, I.D. (1972). *Group process and productivity*. New York: Academic Press.

Tesluk, P.E., Mathieu, J.E., Zaccaro, S.J. & Marks, M.A. (1997). Task and aggregation issues in the analysis and assessment of team performance. In M.T. Brannick, E. Salas, & C. Prince (eds.). *Team performance and measurement: Theory, methods, and applications*. Mahwah, NJ: Erlbaum.

Thompson, J.D. (1967). *Organizations in action*. New York: McGraw-Hill.

Wageman, R. (1995). Interdependence and Group Effectiveness. *Administrative Science Quarterly*, 40, 145–180.

Wageman, R. (2001). The meaning of interdependence. In M.E. Turner (ed.). *Groups at work: Theory and research*. Mahwah, NJ: Erlbaum.

16

MOTIVATION THEORY

How to motivate employees to perform optimally remains one of the most demanding challenges faced by all leaders. Here a number of classic motivation theories that can be used to influence behaviour in teams are offered. Three classical needs-based theories are presented first, namely Maslow's Hierarchy of Needs, Alderfer's ERG, and Hertzberg's Two Factor theory.

The next theory of motivation included here is expectancy theory. The basic tenet of this theory is that motivation is a process and is not based on needs only. This is followed by a description of Self Determination Theory, which distinguishes between intrinsic and extrinsic motivation and describes how psychological needs are attained. Equity theory expands the boundaries of the team and includes equity as a key principle in setting up motivated workers and work systems. This theory contends that individuals evaluate their own performance in relation to the outcomes thereof, and that they also evaluate the distribution of justice in other parts of the organisation where team members evaluate other input in relation to what reward they get.

The last theory that can help with the motivation efforts of teams is called "nudging". This concept (coined by Thaler and Sundstein) is built on the notion that human behaviour is determined by the environment and not always by logical and conscious processes.

Introduction

The first cluster of motivation theories are all based on the notion that individuals have needs and that we are motivated by the drive to have these needs satisfied. Three different theories are included here to give an idea of how needs can be operative in motivating members in teams as well. These are the well-known theory of needs by Maslow, the so-called Existence-Relatedness-Growth (ERG) model of Alderfer, and Hertzberg's Hygiene-Motivation distinction.

In a nutshell

Three needs-based theories show how needs drive motivation.

Purpose

To understand the role of needs in motivation.

To get an idea of different types of needs and their impact on motivation in teams.

Description

Maslow's Hierarchy of Needs

The well-known hierarchy of needs as devised by Maslow has both intuitive and practical appeal and is a useful guide to leaders of teams to understand needs in teams. He hypothesised that individuals progress "upwards along" a hierarchy of needs, however the needs on the lower level must be satisfied before the individual moves to the next level. His five levels of needs are as follows:

- Physiological: basic survival needs, including food, water, warmth, sex and rest. These are the most basic needs essential to sustain life. When you are employed, your job gives you a salary to sustain your basic necessities.

- Safety: the need to be free from fear and to operate with certainty, stability and order. After the physiological needs are met, security or safety needs arise. In the work environment, this is comparable to having a job free of natural stress, calamity, continuous unpredictable change or anything related to fear.

- Affiliation: the need for a sense of belonging and relationships. This is driven by a need for affection and love and is what allows a person to belong to a group, or in this case a team. A sense of belonging and affiliation to a team gives a person the feeling that he or she is wanted and loved. Humans are naturally social beings, therefore friends, family and relationships are essential for living.

- Esteem: the need for self-belief and satisfaction with one's reputation, status and respect. This is divided into the need for esteem from others and the need for self-esteem. The need for esteem from others is met externally and includes the desire for status and dominance, while the need for self-esteem, which includes independence and mastery, is met internally. Maslow believed the healthiest way to satisfy both types of esteem needs was for them to be met as a result of a person's authentic nature, so that any respect gained would be merited rather than derived from presenting a false self.

- Self-actualisation: the final level in Maslow's hierarchy is where the need for reaching one's full potential and fulfilment is satisfied. After all the previous needs have been met, an individual is capable of achieving self-actualisation or self-realisation. This is more focused on a spiritual plane, with the meaning and purpose of one's life being the fundamental driver.

Maslow's theory is intuitively appealing, but it is only conceptual and does not have substantial research backing. It should therefore be used with care as an individual's development is not only linear; multiple iterations could occur and different needs could take prominence at different stages in one's life. It is also not clear that all previous needs are prerequisites for the following needs, however it introduces the concept of needs well and can be used by teams to understand how different people are motivated by different needs.

Existence-Relatedness-Growth (ERG)

Alderfer provided an empirically tested theory of human needs that was similar to that of Maslow, but improved on it in a number of ways. Firstly, it states that although there is indication of some linear progress, individuals do not necessarily only move upward, but can regress with ease to lower levels. He also mentioned that multiple needs can play a part in motivating individuals simultaneously, and motivation does not stem from one source or level only. Also, when an individual's needs in a higher category are not met, they tend to focus on related needs in a lower category. He identified the following three needs:

- Existence: concerns with survival and physiological well-being, including the need to have food, shelter and water.

- Relatedness: the importance of interpersonal relationships and social relations.

- Growth: driven by an inner desire for personal development, which includes respect and self-actualisation.

Although the similarity with Maslow is obvious, this author combined the first two levels of Maslow into the Existence level. He also could not find empirical proof of Maslow's fourth level, suggesting that the two types of esteem needs be split between the two adjacent levels. Thus, status becomes part of relatedness while self-esteem forms part of growth.

Herzberg's two-factor theory

Herzberg identified motivating factors and "hygiene" factors that are at play to motivate people. The former create satisfaction and provide an inner source of motivation. Hygiene factors do not satisfy people per se, but if they are missing or drop below levels of acceptance, this can be a source of dissatisfaction to the team. Thus, they do not spur people on, but they assist in keeping people unhappy when they are not present at sufficient levels:

- Hygiene factors: pay, company policies, relationship with supervisors, working conditions, and feelings associated with status and security.

- Motivating factors: recognition, achievement, advancement, nature of the work, responsibility.

For example, if I am an accountant I can experience many hygiene factors (e.g. a good salary, good working conditions and good relationship with supervisors and colleagues), but that will not necessarily motivate me to the same degree as internally focused factors such as the nature of the work or the opportunity for development. If I do not like being an accountant, no matter how many hygiene factors are in place, they may not be sufficiently motivating.

Tips for team leaders

The important thing to remember when using these theories to motivate team members is that it is critical to focus on the different needs that individuals try to satisfy. Furthermore, there are a number of different needs and various needs can be at play simultaneously.

Representation

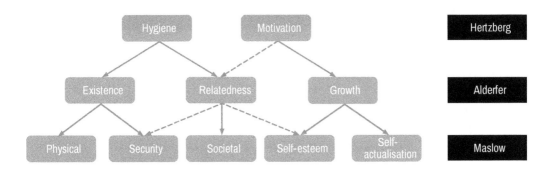

Figure 16.1: Three needs-based theories to show how needs drive motivation

References

Alderfer, C.P. (1969). An Empirical Test of a New Theory of Human Needs. *Organizational Behaviour and Human Performance, 4*(2), 142–175.

Herzberg, F., Mausner, B. & Snyderman, B. (1959). *The motivation to work* (2nd ed.). New York: Wiley.

Maslow, A.H. (1954). *Motivation and personality.* New York: Harper.

77 | **Expectancy theory**

Introduction

Vroom proposed a motivation theory that focuses on the "process" of motivation than on individuals being motivated by needs. This theory is based on the notion that individuals make decisions on what motivates them and how they will react to that. Expectancy theory tries to clarify why people behave in a certain way when they have options. It is based on the notion that behaviour results from conscious choices among alternatives to minimise pain and maximise pleasure, and crucially focuses on an individual's perceptions. However, the theory makes room for various individual factors that influence these perceptions, such as personality, knowledge, experience, skills, abilities and preferences.

In a nutshell

Motivation as a process between expectancy, instrumentality and valence.

Purpose

To guide leaders to structure tasks.

To design tasks to be motivating through expectancy, instrumentality and valence.

To help leaders understand motivation as a process.

To allow the three elements team members use when evaluating a task's motivating impact.

Description

Vroom's expectancy theory suggests that individuals behave in particular ways because they expect that a desired reward (valence) will accrue once a particular act (within their control) has been completed. An employee's beliefs about the expectancy, instrumentality and valence of a task interact psychologically to create a motivational force, such that the employee acts in ways that bring pleasure and avoid pain. Vroom expressed expectancy theory as a mathematical formula, i.e. $M = E.I.V$ where M is motivation, E is expectancy, I is instrumentality and V is valence. These three elements are explained below:

Expectancy

Expectancy is based on the belief that an outcome will happen, or the probability that it will happen. Thus, behind expectancy lies the question: If I try, will I succeed? If you think trying harder will not help, then you can let go. This relates to the subjective evaluation that one will get the expected results. However, since employees differ they have different expectations, which also applies to their own levels of confidence about what they are capable of doing. This influences their expectations about their possible success or failure. Their expectations are also affected by having the required resources, e.g. time, physical resources and materials, the required capabilities, and sufficient support. To assist team members, leaders must offer the resources, training or supervision the employees need.

Instrumentality

This part of Vroom's equation builds on the notion that individuals are prepared to put in effort in the knowledge that it will give results. It refers to the perception of employees as to whether they will actually get what they desire even if it has been promised. Thus, it is based on the belief that an increase in performance will lead to outcomes. An employee asks: If I succeed will I be rewarded? Or, alternatively, If I give this performance, is it likely to give me what I want? Management must ensure that promises of rewards are fulfilled and that employees are aware that this will happen. Instrumentality therefore refers to the extent to which a team member believes that the relevant authorities will deliver the promised rewards. By contrast, expectancy is dependent on the resources, requisite levels of skill and support the team member requires.

Valence

The third part of the equation refers to the extent to which the outcome is deemed desirable; it measures the value a person attaches to the reward associated with the task. This includes extrinsic reward (monetary rewards, tangible outcomes, promotions or benefits) and intrinsic rewards (inner satisfaction). If the reward is seen to be worthwhile extra effort will be offered, but if not, even capable people may not be motivated. It therefore refers to the emotional orientation people hold towards outcomes. A task or situation is motivating only when it is regarded as inspiring, challenging and coveted. Therefore, the value individuals put on the expected reward reflects their depth of want.

Tips for team leaders

Managers must take note of the effect of incentives and must structure assignments with all three of the elements of expectancy theory in mind, bearing in mind that this theory is based on individualised perceptions. As it is based on expectations and perception, what is real and actual is immaterial; while a leader may think everything is in place, it may not be perceived like that by all members of the team. This relates in particular to beliefs members may have about the support and resources they receive from leaders and to their beliefs about their own abilities. It is therefore helpful to understand these perceptions by looking at a person's personality, abilities, skills, knowledge and past experience.

Representation

$$M = (E)(I)(V)$$

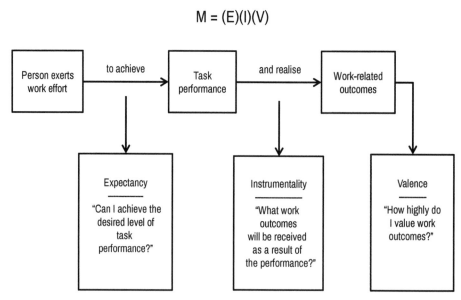

Figure 16.2: Expectancy theory

References

Vroom, V.H. (1964). *Work and motivation*. New York, NY: Wiley.

Introduction

Decy and Ryan proposed a motivation theory called Self-Determination Theory (SDT). They distinguished between intrinsic and extrinsic motivation, as described in the previous section under valence. Extrinsic motivation occurs when someone completes a task for an external goal or reward, while intrinsic motivation is an experience of volition or autonomy that emanates from the person him or herself, and is based on the individual's own interests, their belief in the activity or the meaning they find in the activity. The authors furthermore contended that intrinsic motivation is attained when three psychological needs are gained, namely autonomy, competence and relatedness.

In a nutshell

Intrinsic motivation as experienced once psychological needs are met.

Purpose

To help leaders understand the difference between intrinsic and extrinsic motivation.

To guide leader behaviour to create motivational conditions through competence, relatedness and autonomy.

Description

Decy and Ryan contended that humans want their internal drives, emotions and needs to be satisfied and are actively involved in wanting to master these forces. Furthermore, humans are proactive in wanting to grow and develop, yet this does not occur automatically and conditions need to be in place for optimal development to take place. They distinguished between motivation – what energises your behaviour and moves you through the day – and energy itself. According to them, it is necessary to consider where energy comes from, how it is utilised and how it is facilitated. They identified three types of motivation, namely amotivation, extrinsic motivation and intrinsic motivation, and distinguished between four forms of extrinsic motivation:

- Amotivation: this is non-self-determined and in terms of regulatory style there is non-regulation. It can be seen as the absence of motivation.

- Extrinsic motivation: the type of motivation where something is done to get a goal or reward external to the self or beyond the actual activity comes in four different types:

- ○ External regulation: motivation is obtained by attempts to satisfy external demands or possible rewards, like doing something only to make money.

- ○ Introjected regulation: this resembles internalised motivation and seems as if it is driven by value, but it is actually driven from outside, such as where actions are completed, but because of guilt, ego or status. For example, when someone aims to be on time in order not to feel bad, it is driven by introjected (and partial) internalisation as it is done because of pressure by internal contingencies, not true self-regulation.

- ○ Identification: this is more valued and autonomously driven as it involves conscious effort to value a goal and regulation is perceived to be personally important.

- ○ Integrated: this type of motivation drives behaviour that is actually for purposes external to the self, but it is so assimilated with the self that they are included in an individual's self-evaluations and personal needs. For example to go to gym may be internalised, but it could be for the external benefit and not because of the internalised pleasure of the activity itself.

- Intrinsic: this type of behaviour stems from intrinsic motivation and flow; engagement with the task where you lose track of time is experienced. This autonomous motivation is intrinsic (or identified/integrated) as the activity is perceived to be interesting and enjoyable for its own sake or in itself. For example playing golf, cello or whatever, because you really love the task. It is based on personal satisfaction and the intrinsic curiosity leads to a desire to master the task for the enjoyment and pleasure it gives in itself.

They posited that intrinsic motivation follows once three primary psychological needs essential for effective functioning have been met. These three psychological needs are competence, autonomy and relatedness. The SDT states that individuals need all three of these psychological needs to be satisfied to be truly motivated, and that if any one of them is not present, optimal levels of motivation and subsequent behaviour will not ensue. The theory is based on the general notion that people have the innate desire to grow, develop, and flourish and are generally ready to be challenged to pursue this desire.

Competence

This is a sense of efficacy and confidence that you can effect change and impact on the context or the inherent belief that you are good at something. It refers to the sense a person has of being effective or confident about their ability and their behaviour.

Autonomy

The second psychological need is the sense an individual gets of being fully and actively engaged in what they are doing, and experiencing the act with freedom as if it was their own choice, or at least because they endorse the action. In other words, the activity the person is engaged in is accomplished with a feeling of volition, willingness, concurrence and choice.

Relatedness

This refers to the universal need to be connected, to care and be cared for. This relatedness is essential to human wellness. This sense of belonging applies to team relationships as well.

Tips for team leaders

The leader needs to ensure that the correct conditions for motivation (i.e. relatedness, competence and autonomy) are available to foster and allow intrinsic motivation to come to the fore. Intrinsic motivation:

- is increased when the individual has choice over his or her action;

- fulfils innate needs of autonomy, competence and relatedness;

- enhances well being and growth (either personal, cognitive or social goals); and

- seeks new challenges and possibilities to help facilitate growth.

Representation

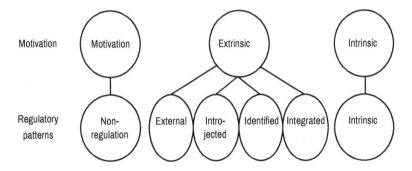

Figure 16.3: Self-determination theory

References

Deci, E.L. & Ryan, R.M. (2008). Self-determination Theory: A Macro Theory of Human Motivation, Development, and Health. *Canadian Psychology/Psychologie Canadienne*, 49(3), 182–185.

Deci, E.L. & Ryan, R.M. (2012). Motivation, personality, and development within embedded social contexts: An overview of self-determination theory. In R.M. Ryan (ed.). *Oxford handbook of human motivation*. Oxford, UK: Oxford University Press.

Ryan, R.M. & Deci, E.L. (2002). Self-determination Theory and the Facilitation of Intrinsic Motivation, Social Development, and Well-being. *American Psychologist*, 55(1), 68–78.

Ryan, R.M. & Deci, E.L. (2017). *Self-determination theory: Basic psychological needs in motivation, development, and wellness*. New York: Guilford Publishing.

Introduction

Equity theory was devised by Adams and contends that people are motivated when they perceive that they are being treated equitably and fairly. It is based on the idea that individuals are motivated by fairness and is helpful for assessing motivation to evaluate the perceived fairness of a situation.

In a nutshell

Motivation is related to members' perceptions about whether they are treated fairly and whether others are treated fairly.

Purpose

To help leaders create perceived equity in the workplace.

To allow members to provide optimum output.

To help create a climate for team motivation.

Description

Three different elements of perceived equity are assessed, namely evaluation of inputs, evaluation of ratio between input and reward, and finally evaluation of the levels and extent of justice in the system.

Evaluation of own input-reward ratio

The theory is based on the assumption that individuals evaluate the outputs they receive from an organisation in relation to inputs. Inputs are those things that we invest and are prepared to give to the organisation to ensure outcomes eventuate. For example we put time, effort, loyalty, willingness to sacrifice long hours, working extra for tight deadlines, knowledge and performance into our jobs. According to equity theory we compare these inputs with what we get from the organisation, such as pay, prestige and recognition. These outputs can be tangible (e.g. pay, flexible times for work, time off) or intangible (e.g. satisfaction, autonomy or internal purposes being met). Thus, we evaluate and see what we get in terms of what we invest. Optimally we want the input to match output and this balance is the preferred state. When this is not perceived as being equitable it leads to an imbalance. This perceived imbalance means that we either believe that we put more in than we receive or the other way around. In case of the former we will then try to create balance by getting more or doing less. Alternatively, if we think we get more than we put in we may improve our efforts.

Evaluation of others' input-reward ratio

The second part of the theory states that we not only look at our own input-output ratio, but we also evaluate that of others and compare ours to theirs. If individuals see what they regard as inequity between their own input-output ratio and that of others they may adjust their behaviour, in other words the motivation drops. A sense of fairness in the system therefore acts as a motivator and individuals either are motivated to do more, or conversely unfairness will be demotivating.

Thus, an individual evaluates:

*   own performance;
*   others' performance;
*   fairness of treatment re own performance; and
*   fairness of treatment re others' performance.

(N.B. The referent groups used in this regard are also important, as this theory does not mean that individuals think that everyone should be paid the same. Rather, workers make this evaluation from a broad perspective, accepting for example that senior executives' remuneration may be based on a different set of criteria, such as the degree of sacrifice in work-life balance, responsibility, and stress.)

If a worker perceives an imbalance, they could:

*   change their inputs;
*   change their expectation of outputs;
*   adjust their perception of self;
*   distort perception of others;
*   choose a different referent; and
*   leave the field.

Evaluation of extent of equity

The third element of equity theory is that these perceptions, which are based on individual preferences and judgments, lead to a view or perception of organisational justice. Organisational justice includes:

*   distributive justice: fairness of outcome and whether deliverables are evaluated fairly;
*   interpersonal justice: the degree to which members feel they are treated with dignity and respect; and
*   process justice: the perceived fairness of the methods used to determine outcomes and allocate rewards.

Tips for team leaders

The leader has to make sure there is fairness in compensation. No disparity should be tolerated in the evaluation and treatment of individuals in the team with regard to performance. Leaders should understand that perceptions of this fairness are shaped individually, and remain aware that treatment of one member in the team reverberates throughout the team and influences the perceptions of others. In terms of rewards, leaders should only use rewards that are available, should make sure all employees are eligible, and make rewards visible, contingent, timely and reversible.

Representation

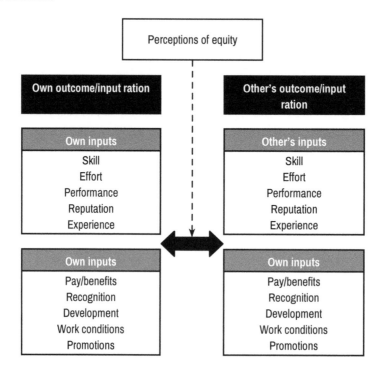

Figure 16.4: Equity theory

Reference

Adams, J. S. (1964). Inequity in social exchange. In Berkowitz, L. *Advances in Experimental Social Psychology*, 2, 26–299. New York: Academic Press.

Introduction

Developed from the fairly new field of Behavioural Economics, the term "nudging" got its popularity from the ground-breaking book Nudge by Nobel-prize winner Richard Thaler (written with Cass Sundstein). The fundamental idea is that people need to be nudged by the context to get them to do desirable behaviour, i.e. to motivate them to do what is required. For example, people find it easier to do things when they have clear instructions on how to do them. As a tool to be used in leading teams this concept can be applied to shape the context to help the team reach its goal. The mnemonic MINDSPACE (devised by Dolan), is presented to help teams in this effort.

In a nutshell

Create a MINDSPACE in the environment to nudge the team towards its goal.

Purpose

To use the environment as motivating tool.

To set principles of nudging in place to help members deliver the required output.

Description

Dolan provided a helpful acronym (MINDSPACE) to demonstrate the principles underlying nudging and described what can be used to design context that can motivate changes in behaviour. The following aspects of the environment of the team should be considered:

Messenger

People are influenced by who communicates information, which in teams can be seen as the manner in which organisational information is conveyed to the team. When instruction, clarification or goal direction is conveyed, team members will respond differently depending on who the communication is from, e.g. if it is from a respected supervisor as opposed to someone not well-regarded.

Incentives

This relates to the reward we expect for acting in a particular way. Elsewhere in the book it has been shown that rewards need to be meaningful to individuals to act as sufficient incentive to motivate preferred behaviour. Moreover, incentives are intrinsic or extrinsic and the impact of these different types of incentives is different for each individual. However, it is true that leaders can influence the context (i.e. "nudge" their followers) by co-creating a space where there is sufficient motivation for people to follow. In this regard, tangible and intangible rewards can be matched with individuals' needs for autonomy, relatedness, achievement and meaning. Once the incentives in the team are aligned with these motivational drives, action is possible.

Norms

We are strongly influenced by what others do and collectively teams put norms in place to shape their behaviour. Norms imply a shared understanding of what is correct behaviour. Teams regulate and direct behaviour through establishing norms that can be prescriptive (indicating what should be done) or proscriptive (highlighting what should be avoided). Thus, norms act as peer pressure and in a given context nudging can be facilitated by observing how members react to each other, determining what they regard as appropriate behaviour.

Default

This refers to the human preference to go to our "pre-set options", i.e. default behaviour. This is best explained by thinking about your computer set-up; we just go with the default site or setting and we use that. Thus, defaults are passive commitments we make, often without realising it, simply because they are the easiest option and that makes them comfortable. In contrast, a new habit is built by stating the specific behaviour in terms of when and where it is to occur and to articulate clearly what is required. Once a specific trigger (see below) is applied to such behaviour, it makes it easier for it to become default behaviour. However, these defaults must serve a clear purpose and must be easy to embrace.

Salience

People are drawn to things that are interesting to them, therefore the environment can be shaped to offer interesting and unexpected nudges. Determining of nudging requires these contextual influences to be noticeable and relevant. In other words, if a nudge is to impact on behaviours in a team, the context must provide sufficient cues for individuals to react to them.

Priming

In a team, as in general, our behaviour is influenced by unconscious cues. Thus, to nudge a team it is helpful to encourage desired habits and create behavioural "autopilot settings", norms and associations to guide behaviour. Even small changes can be effected if we are forced to notice the need for them. Helpful in this regard could be to build in action triggers as mental preparation. This is a kind of preloading, whereby people are reminded of things that they know they have to do. This allows control to be "passed" on to the environment and makes it easier for the individual because s/he is triggered to do something and thus a new default is created. Priming happens when we script critical moves and include triggers to spur us into action.

Affect

As teams interact they connect emotionally as well. It is clear that the emotional climate of the team impacts on members to move in a particular direction or way. Therefore, leaders can nudge people towards the desired behaviour by building in opportunities for positive emotions to be displayed and for people to build on the positive emotional experiences of colleagues.

Commitment

As we have already discussed, people take seriously what other people do and what other people set as norms. Therefore, we should also take seriously what we think people expect of us once we have made a commitment. In general we seek to be consistent with our public promises and when we make a promise we want to keep it. In this way people can be nudged by making public commitments to do something, and by being in the "spotlight" they are more likely to keep to such behaviour and promises. This is probably because we want to limit cognitive dissonance where we think something, but have to act differently. Therefore, if we are nudged by the environment, the mere exposure to new behaviour will make such behaviour easier and will lessen cognitive dissonance.

Ego

This nudging by the environment should allow people to feel better about themselves. This will occur if it allows them to act according to their needs of autonomy, belonging, achievement and meaning. In particular, if the context gives the opportunity for team members to balance purpose with pleasure, the context will nudge them towards required change.

Tips for team leaders

The benefit of nudging lies in the opportunity leaders have to shape the context wherein teams operate to facilitate change. Thus, the context is used to shape behaviour and in teams this approach helps leaders to motivate members.

Representation

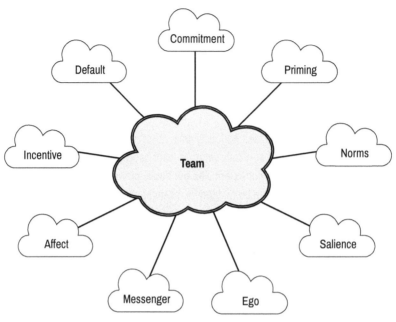

Figure 16.5: MINDSPACE – demonstrate the principles underlying nudging

References

Dolan, P. (2014). *Happiness by design: Finding pleasure and purpose in everyday life*. London: Hudson Street Press.

Thaler, R. H. & Sundstein, C. R. (2008). *Nudge: Improving decisions about health, wealth, and happiness*. Yale University Press, New Haven.

17

TEAM LEADERSHIP

While leadership theory has received ample scholarly attention and research on leadership has increased exponentially over the last few decades, the same cannot be said of team leadership. While it is safe to assume that much of what leadership theory can teach us can be applied to teams as well, especially as this is the system where leaders have a very direct impact, there is a disproportionately low level of research on team leadership per se. Here the leadership theory of Hill and the dynamic development theory of Kozlowski and his colleagues are presented, followed by a description of participative leadership as it can be applied to teams. This is augmented by a discussion of two "traditional" leadership theories (i.e. transformational and authentic leadership). The section is concluded with a general view of leadership from Barling, which he offered as a "summary" after his excellent review of the science of leadership and overview of some traditional leadership theories.

Introduction

Hill offered a leadership model that is specifically aimed at helping teams. It highlights the role leaders have to play in terms of taking action or monitoring team behaviour, and helps leaders decide on the type of intervention that is required. It was further designed to help provide leaders with an overall view of their team needs to assist with their monitoring requirements, and proposes suggestions on how leaders can take corrective action. It therefore assumes a direct, and proposes relationship between leadership actions and team effectiveness.

In a nutshell

A set of three decision nodes to help leaders shape their monitoring and action behaviour in leading teams.

Purpose

To help leaders diagnose team processes.

To help leaders decide on the type of intervention – act or monitor.

To help leaders determine where and how to intervene.

To make complex team leadership decisions easier.

To give a mental road map for team leadership.

Description

The model starts with the requirement that leaders are clear about the context, the situation at hand and what they regard as the problem, i.e. the mental model the leader applies is a critical point of departure. Once the leader has assessed the situation he or she has to make some key decisions. Three decision nodes are distinguished to guide the leader:

Decision node 1

The first decision node is to determine whether monitoring or action taking is the most appropriate intervention. According to the model, these are the two critical leadership behaviours that influence team effectiveness, thus leaders need to be comfortable and skilled with either of these. Monitoring requires leaders to scan the environment for information (and in particular to be clear on the mental model guiding this environment-scanning) and to interpret this information effectively. Thus, while the leader finds the information, it must also be analysed, organised and interpreted to enable the leader to guide his or her action.

Decision node 2

The next level of decision-making relates to whether the issue is an internal or external one. If monitoring is required, external monitoring entails scanning the environment for changes and potential impacts on the team. If the leader's assessment of the issue at hand requires action, the leader again has to decide whether it is an internal or external issue. If external, the leader takes action to prevent or reduce the impact of any environmental issue on the team. To do this, the leader:

* networks and forms alliances by gathering information and increasing influence;

* advocates and represents the team to various stakeholders;

* negotiates to secure required resources, support and recognition;

* buffers the team from distractions;

* assesses indicators of team effectiveness as required by the external environment including performance; and

* shares relevant information with the team.

However, if the required action is deemed to be internal, a further key decision (i.e. Decision 3) is required from the leader.

Decision node 3

The leader must determine whether the nature of the problem is task or relational in nature. Again, depending on the answer to this, the internal action of the leader is adjusted. When it is task-related the leader's actions are directed at:

* goal focusing by clarifying direction, using it to energise the team and ensure commitment to the goal;

* structuring for results through planning, visioning, organising, clarifying roles and delegating;

* facilitating decision-making including informing, controlling, coordinating, mediating, synthesising and focusing on issues;

* training team members in task skills by educating and developing them; and

* maintaining standards of excellence through assessing performance and dealing with deviation from the required standards.

However, if the issue at hand is of a relational nature, the leader's actions should be directed at:

* coaching in interpersonal skills;

* stressing the importance of collaboration and participation;

- managing conflict and power issues;

- building commitment and cohesion through being optimistic, innovative, envisioning, socialising, rewarding and recognising;

- satisfying needs by trusting, supporting and advocating; and

- modelling ethical and principled practices.

The effect or outcomes of these actions are that the team's effectiveness increases. It is necessary to note that Hill regarded effectiveness as both performance-related and having a development focus.

Tips for team leaders

This approach is accompanied by a valuable flow diagram to assist leaders with the process of deciding what interventions are required. The model is practical and guides the leader to make decisions systematically.

Representation

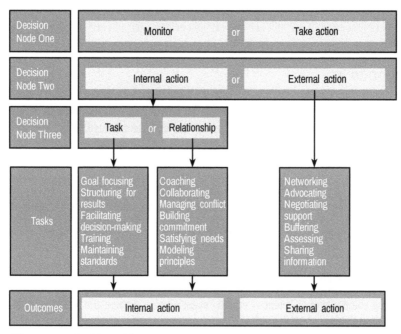

Figure 17.1: Hill's Team Leadership model

Reference

Kogler Hill, S.E. (2001). Team leadership. In P. G. Northouse (Ed.), *Leadership: Theory and practice* (2nd ed.). Thousand Oaks, CA: Sage.

Dynamic team leadership

Introduction

Kozlowski and his colleagues offered a development process named dynamic team leadership, which resembles the frameworks described earlier and which could easily have been discussed there. However, the specific contribution of this view is that it focuses on how team leaders' tasks change over the various stages of a team's life. It is this emphasis that is discussed here as it provides information on how leaders need to shape their tasks through the development of a team. The scholars pointed out the iterative nature of such tasks and showed that these tasks repeat within stages, but also provide a backdrop for leaders to gauge the development processes of a team and the transitions between development phases. The preparation, action and reflection tasks that leaders enact are discussed for each of the development phases, namely team formation, task and role development, team development and team improvement.

In a nutshell

Team leaders' tasks, which are described as preparation, action and reflection, occur at each stage of team development.

Purpose

To help leaders direct their tasks.

To understand the components of the various tasks.

To focus on how different tasks need to be applied to different stages.

Description

While Kozlowski et al. described the tasks sequentially, aligned with the proposed developmental phases, here the focus will be on the various tasks the leaders fulfil during each phase. However, before describing the tasks, the four phases are presented briefly to provide context for the description of the tasks. (In the representation below, the four phases are described on the rows of the table, and the tasks for each phase in the columns of the table.)

Development phases

Four phases are identified and described:

Team formation

During this phase, members identify with the team by associating themselves with the team's qualities, characteristics and views, and commit to the team by accepting and supporting the team's vision, mission, values and goals.

Task and role development

During this phase, members build their work capabilities through routines, priorities and strategies; negotiate social roles to improve coordination by clarifying their expectations of one another; and develop role acceptance and attachment.

Team development

Emphasis moves from the individual to the team during this phase, in order to improve team performance through the set of behaviours, cognitions, and attitudes that are required to facilitate improved output. The individual task mastery obtained during the previous phase allows for coordination to be improved, trust to be built, and for the team to understand how their tasks fit within those of the overall team.

Team improvement

The last phase is dominated by the need the team has to adapt to change and changing task demands, and to improve their adaptability.

Team leaders' tasks

The authors described how in each of these phases team leaders' tasks are comprised of preparation, action and reflection, with the cycle repeating iteratively. During preparation, developmental goals (task and social) are set and an action strategy is formulated, while action refers to how the leader monitors and develops attitudes, behaviours and cognitions. It also shows how leaders intervene (when necessary) to address task performance and team coordination, adjust the strategy and update the team on the situation it is facing. Reflection comprises diagnosing deficiencies and facilitating process feedback. As there are multiple iterations of this process in each phase, the leader has a series of opportunities to build the requisite team skills, and as members acquire the skills the team progresses to the next development phase. As development materialises the team members take on more responsibility and attain a higher degree of self-management, which enables them to meet the demands and adaptations set by the dynamic context. The team leaders' tasks take on different content in each phase, as is described in more detail below.

Preparation

During each of the four phases, leaders have to ensure that development goals are devised and an action strategy is formulated.

Developmental goals

Preparing developmental goals will take on different foci as the team develops. During the team formation phase the task-related goals are structured around orientating the team behind its mission and objectives, while the social goals include the establishment of norms and social integration. In the task development phase, the focus of preparation efforts is on taskwork; individual task mastery takes prominence and the leader helps individual members to experience a sense of self-efficacy in their respective tasks. The social aspect of preparation is dedicated to role socialisation, where members accept certain roles and grow attached to such roles. During the third phase the focus is on teamwork (task role interactions and task role revision), while cooperation (i.e. role interaction and mutual trust) characterises the social component of the leader's preparation task. The last phase is dedicated to the team's adaptive capability; through preparing development goals the team leader ensures adaptation so that the team's self-management and continuous improvement is strengthened. The social element in this phase is accomplished by strengthening social cohesion through synergistic interaction and effective conflict management.

Action strategy

The action strategy should be formed during phase one. During phase two, the leader provides the rationale for the action strategy. During phase three, the leader's task is to facilitate implementation of the strategy, while in the fourth phase, the leader should facilitate the forming of new strategies to align with the demands on the team to adapt and renew.

Action

This group of tasks refers to the action the leader must take in each phase after preparation is completed. Action comprises monitoring, developing (attitudes, behaviours and cognitions are distinguished) and intervening. Again, these take on a different focus in each of the phases and the main elements of action (i.e. monitor, development of attitudes, behaviours and cognitions; and intervention) each receive their own focus during each stage.

Monitor

During the team formation phase the leader monitors member interaction, while during the task and role development phase the focus is on individual performance. The leader then needs to monitor team performance, while during the final phase the team's adaptive performance is monitored.

Develop

Attitudes

Commitment to the team mission and to other members of the team must be developed during the team formation phase, and self-efficacy during the task and role development phase. During the subsequent two phases, the leader's focus with regard to attitudes should be directed at team efficacy (including the development of mutual respect and trust), while during the last phase (team improvement), team potency is developed through focusing on attitudes towards novel team tasks and new team contexts.

Behaviours

During the team formation phase, leaders develop behaviours to facilitate interaction to enable bonding and reciprocal commitment to evolve. Taskwork behaviour (such as self-regulation and individual help-seeking) is developed during the second phase. Teamwork is developed through coordination and back-up behaviour in the team development phase. In the last phase, the leader should develop behaviours to ensure adaptation through shared leadership, exploration and risk-taking.

Cognitions

During the team formation phase, the leader takes responsibility for developing cognitions that lead to team identity, characterised through the setting of boundaries and establishment of shared responsibilities. During the task and role development phase the leader should develop cognitions relating to individual mental modes, and team members should develop a conducive task mental model and an interpersonal mental model. This is followed during the team development phase by the development of a shared mental model as a collective endeavour. During the final (i.e. team improvement) phase, leaders develop a compatible mental model based on specialisation of knowledge in the team and utilising the team's transactive memory.

Intervene

The third component of leaders' "action" relates to how they intervene. During the first two phases intervention is directed at individual task assistance and team coordination, while during the team development phase the focus is on team coordination and the revision of tasks, strategies and goals. In the last phase intervention takes the form of updating the situation and context of the team and facilitating final decision-making.

Reflection

The third task in the iterative cycle is reflection. In the first phase the leader reflects by diagnosing deficiencies and determining where to offer individual-level developmental feedback. In the next phase the focus changes in that leaders facilitate team members' own reflections, while continuing to provide individual-level feedback. In the third phase reflection is directed at team-level reflection and team-level developmental feedback, while in the last phase the leader monitors team reflection and developmental feedback.

Tips for team leaders

The key focus of this approach is the notion that team leader tasks are iterative and are repeated intra-phase, while altering in focus as the team's work progresses and as adjustments are made.

Representation

	Leader tasks								
	Preparation			Action					Reflection
	Developmental goals		Action strategy	Monitor	Develop			Intervention	
	Task-related	Social			Affective	Behavioural	Cognitive		
Team Formation	Team orientation Mission objectives	Team socialisation Norms Social integration	Provide action strategy	Member interaction	Commitment Team mission Other members	Interaction Bonding Reciprocal commitment	Identity Boundaries Shared responsibility	Individual task assistance Team coordination	Diagnose deficiencies Provide individual-level developmental feedback
Task & Role Development	Taskwork Individual task mastery Self-efficacy	Role socialisation Acceptance Attachment	Provide rationale for Action strategy	Individual performance	Self efficacy Individual's task focus Social self-efficacy	Taskwork Self-regulation Individual help-seeking	Individual mental models Task mental model Interpersonal mental model	Individual task assistance Team coordination	Facilitate member reflection Provide individual-level developmental feedback
Team Development	Teamwork Task role interactions Task role revision	Cooperation Role interaction Mutual trust	Facilitate action Strategy Selection	Team performance	Team efficacy Team task focus Mutual trust & respect	Teamwork Coordination Back-up behaviour	Shared mental models Members' task interactions	Team coordination Task, strategy & goal revisions	Facilitate team reflection Provide team-level developmental feedback
Team Improvement	Adaptation Team self-management Continuous improvement	Social cohesion Synergistic interaction Conflict management	Facilitate development of new action strategies	Adaptive performance	Team potency Novel team task focus New team contexts	Adaptation Shared leadership Exploration & risk-taking	Compatible mental models Knowledge specialisation Transactive memory	Situation update Final decisions	Monitor team-level reflection & developmental feedback

Figure 17.2: Leader tasks

References

Kozlowski, S.W.J., Watola, D.J., Nowakowski, J.M., Kim, B.H. & Botero, I.C. (2009). Developing adaptive teams: A theory of dynamic team leadership. In E. Salas, G.F. Goodwin, & C.S Burke (eds.). *Team effectiveness in complex organisations: Cross-disciplinary perspectives and approaches*. Mahwah, NJ: LEA.

83 | **Traditional leadership theory**

Introduction

Traditional leadership theories are also helpful. While they are broader in scope, going beyond team leadership, they can be usefully applied to leading teams. Two of these (traditional) theories are offered here as they have endured through sustained research and been applied to many situations, and their focus could specifically transcend to the team as a system. The two theories chosen for this purpose are transformational leadership and authentic leadership.

In a nutshell

Traditional leadership theories with a team focus: transformational leadership and authentic leadership.

Purpose

To guide leaders on how to work with members.

To facilitate change through leadership behaviour.

Description

While there is clear overlap between some aspects of transformational and authentic leadership theories, these are not key to the current discussion and exponents of both will be mentioned here in as far as they could be helpful in leading teams. Transformational leadership is discussed through the use of full-range leadership, while the views of George and Luthans and Avolio illustrate authentic leadership.

Transformational leadership theory

Although the origins of this concept date back some decades to the work of Burns, it remains a powerful force in leadership theory through links, overlaps and alignment between it and various other leadership theories (notably authentic leadership, see below). For the purposes of using it as a tool to help in leading teams, we chose the "full range" conceptualisation as it introduces four major concepts that can be helpful in teams and also gives the opportunity to link with other team theories in a framework. Full range leadership makes use of a matrix to describe the development of leadership theory. The vertical axis represents effective to ineffective leadership, while the horizontal axis ranges from passive to active. Passive leaders do not take the required action while active leadership behaviour is displayed towards the other end of the spectrum. The theory holds that leadership develops diagonally across the matrix from the lower left quandrant of the matrix to the upper right quadrant. This allows the authors to link transformational leadership as the culmination of various other leadership actions and describe transformational leadership as the pinnacle of development. They identified two behaviours that they viewed as ineffective and passive. The first is Laissez-Faire leadership, which they regard as no leadership as it is non-transactional and has little effect. The second is Management by Exception (Passive), where leaders identify exceptions, but fail to take appropriate action. The third factor is somewhat neutral in both its effectiveness and the level of exertion displayed by the leader. This is Management by Exception (Active), where the leader takes action to address the management issue, being aware that it goes beyond normal and expected behaviour, but the focus remains on the operational and managerial. The fourth factor (Contingency Reward) relates to what can be called transactional leadership. The focus of the leader is on how reward is used to motivate, manage and move people. While there could be some success in using this type of leadership in conjunction with motivation theory the focus on this section is on transformational leadership, which is deemed to take place in the upper right quadrant. Four actions that leaders should take to facilitate transformational leadership are described:

Intellectual stimulation

This allows members of the team to be involved in the creative processes of the team to help to find solutions; it is basically vested in the idea that members' knowledge, skills and creativity can be an invaluable asset to propel the team forward. It allows members (here also called followers) to take initiative, to address issues on their own and to find ways to address issues the team struggles with. It encourages team members to think for themselves and to offer new and novel ways to address issues and challenges. Characteristic of this factor is the ability to allow members to challenge assumptions – both about themselves and about work-related issues. Leaders are also adept at soliciting ideas from followers about their work, the team and the future, and are prepared to risk more and to push the boundaries of conventional wisdom and norms.

Inspirational motivation

The role leaders play in motivating followers towards the goal of the team is the focus of this factor, which highlights how leaders can put high expectations to followers, support them to follow through with actions and communicate direction to the team. It emphasises the emotional component of the team as manifested through passion, drive and team spirit. Such leaders are prepared to raise the bar, expect more and drive to reach the goals of the team. They display the ability to energise, to build on the good of the team and foster a sense of optimism and hope. Through inspirational motivation, leaders drive expectations beyond currently held limits and motivate followers to dream and reach higher. They develop a sense of self-efficacy in their members and drive them to higher performance.

Individualised consideration

The notion here is that a leader who creates a supportive environment and listens to the team members will be effective in getting the team motivated to the goal. Transformational leaders use this factor by coaching, mentoring and helping members to reach their potential, to care for them and to develop them. They need to ensure that each member feels individually important and aware that his or her contribution is valued and expected by the rest of the team. The leader is therefore focused on the needs of their followers and is prepared to give full attention to their concerns, issues and needs. This demonstrates a developmental focus; the empathetic, caring and coaching focus of this factor fosters a sense that the follower is valued and respected.

Idealised influence

This links to the ethical and moral aspect of transformational leadership and has both a "do" and a "be" component. Transformational leaders do the right things, act morally, ethically and correctly, and ensure that the team adheres to strict codes of conduct. They are prepared to make a stand for what they believe in and display deep conviction in what they value. The inherent focus of these leaders is on what is good for the greater good and not only for individual and short-term gain. Beyond these behavioural traits there is also an attributional factor where members attribute certain behaviour to the leader and expect the leader to be the ideal. This relates to the emotional component of leadership and refers to how followers idealise leaders and attempt to follow them.

Authentic leadership theory

Authentic leadership theories are a cluster of theories that focus on the authenticity of the leader and his or her consistency with values. Although there is substantial overlap on many issues, some differences lead this set of theories to display a rather disparate character. Authentic leadership can be viewed from a (intra-) personal perspective where the focus on the leader's self-knowledge, self-regulation and self-concept, but it could also be seen as interpersonal with a focus on the relational quality between individuals. Thus, whether it is about the leader's internal needs and drives or whether it involves others, it is clear that these theories apply to teams in general. Two authentic leadership perspectives are described here to assist team leaders to reflect on their own authenticity; firstly the views of George and then those of Luthans and Avolio are presented.

George

George had a successful leadership career and after retiring interviewed more than a hundred leaders to try and understand leadership. He identified five characteristics of leaders and a behavioural competence for each that can be developed in order for the characteristic to manifest itself. A pair consisting of a value and a behaviour is identified in each of the five cases. The idea is that the value provides the driver that manifests in the behaviour and these are applicable to teams too.

Purpose – passion

Purpose relates to the sense leaders have regarding on where they are going, in other words their "true North", and what inherent drives, needs and values propel them forward. This manifests in a passion for what they do through intrinsic motivation. This spurs them on because they enjoy what they do, are interested in it and truly care about their work.

Values – behaviour

Authentic leaders have a clear sense of their values and are able to use them as guiding principles independent of the particular context. Even in the face of adversity and when times are tough, they rely on their sense of values to continue to lead during these periods of difficulty. Everything they do – personally and professionally – is guided by their values and manifests in their behaviour towards others.

Relationship – connection

By focusing on relationships leaders use communication (e.g. stories, narratives and focused listening) to build connections with their followers. Through this, transparency, trust and commitment are built and the relationship between the leader and the follower is strengthened.

Self-discipline – consistency

Leaders are dedicated to their goals and reach them through self-discipline, which drives focus and determination. This relates to how they pursue their own goals, but also manifests in the way they hold others accountable. This creates a sense of stability and security and enables communication with followers.

Heart – compassion

The last aspect indicates that leaders are driven by a real deep-seated concern and sensitivity for others (heart). This manifests in sincere compassion in that the stories, lives and journeys of others matter to authentic leaders, who open themselves up to the plight of others and are ready to help.

Luthans and Avolio

These authors scrutinised leadership literature and identified four key characteristics that constitute authentic leadership, namely:

Self-awareness

This refers to insights leaders have on their own strengths and weaknesses, passions and values, and the impact these have on the rest of the team. It includes a sense of identity, emotions, drives and needs, goals and an understanding of intrapersonal dynamics. It also focuses on emotional intelligence (the ability to recognise and regulate emotions of self and others).

Relational transparency

Authentic leaders are comfortable in their relationships to risk and expose their "real" selves without fear and without holding back. They are prepared to share their feelings, motives and inclinations with others in appropriate ways through open and direct communication. These interpersonal relationships are perceived as real and include positive and negative elements of the leader, e.g. strengths and weaknesses, being shared.

Balanced processing

Authentic leaders have the ability to balance their own views with those of others and process the value of the different points of view. They solicit and entertain alternative views because they believe that in considering different points of view their own views become clearer. Since this is a regulatory function, authentic leaders use this to evaluate the level of bias and favouritism they perceive in relationships, and the balanced nature of this prevents it from influencing the leader inappropriately.

Internalised moral perspective

This is the self-regulatory process that leaders employ to guide their behaviour when under pressure. Leaders often find themselves in situations where they have to deal with multiple stakeholders with various and often opposing demands on the leader. The manner in which they use their internal moral compass to guide behaviour and decisions should be based on this internally based moral perspective. When leaders' actions are consistent with their moral principles, they are perceived to be authentic by followers.

Critical life events

In addition, there are always events, positive or negative, that befall the leader on his or her life journey. It is inevitable that we all experience a variety of events in our lives, which may impact the way a leader reacts and behaves. These events require reflection, change and adjustment, and also shape the person's leadership journey. They are often the impetus for growth or even the decision to continue leading or not. The manner in which authentic leaders respond to critical life events and how this facilitates the development of the authentic leadership characteristics described above are influenced by two sets of factors, namely, moral reasoning and positive psychological influences.

Moral reasoning

This refers to the ability leaders have to make moral decisions amidst difficult situations and to apply decisions according to his or her value system. Thus, in the face of adversity, leaders need to find the moral courage and authority to rise above individual differences and to mobilise team members behind what is right and good. The ability to make these decisions on behalf of the team, sometimes also in the face of difficult and conflicting situations, influences the level of authenticity a leader can display.

Positive psychological influences

Although it goes without saying that each individual is influenced and shaped by life history and events, the manner in which such experiences and in particular critical events can facilitate positive psychological influences in the leadership of a person facilitate the authenticity of such leadership. These influences include:

- optimism: through this cognitive process they view situations in a positive light and believe in favourable expectations for the future;

- hope: they inspire others because of their belief that they will succeed through will power and driving to reach their goals;

- confidence: the belief leaders have that they are able to deliver and meet the challenges of leadership; and

- resilience: authentic leaders have the ability to recover from hardship, difficult times and suffering, and to feel strengthened and more resourceful as the result of such events.

Tips for team leaders

It is necessary for leaders to be flexible and to employ more than one style, as well as to discern when to use a particular style. However, as we tend to prefer a particular style it is necessary that leaders are aware not to over-use this preferred style as a go-to behaviour and run the risk of using it inappropriately. Finding ways to implement the four "I"s in their daily leadership actions will assist them in motivating their teams towards the goals. This also allows for leadership to be "in the moment" and not necessarily dependent on grand actions, to allow leadership to unfold during the mundane and daily interactions, and to connect with members of the team.

Representation

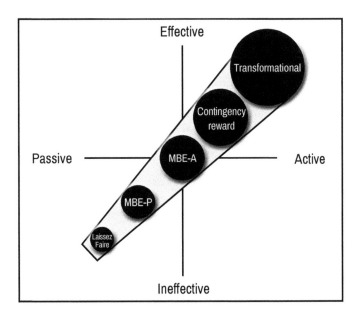

Figure 17.3: Full-range leadership

Reference

Bass, B.M. & Avolio, B. J. (1997). *Full range leadership development: Manual for the multifactor leadership questionnaire*. Redwood City, CA. Mind Garden.

George, B. (2010). *True north: Finding your authentic leadership*. San Francisco, CA: Jossey-Bass.

Goleman, D., Boyatzis, R.E. & McKee, A. (2002). *Primal leadership: Realizing the power of emotional intelligence*. Boston: Harvard Business School Press.

Luthans, F., & Avolio, B.J. (2003). Authentic leadership development. In K. S. Cameron, J. E. Dutton, & R. E. Quinn (eds.). *Positive organizational scholarship* (pp. 241–258). San Francisco: Berrett-Koehler.

84 | Participative leadership

Introduction

More recently, leadership research interest has moved away from the leader being "special" or having unique traits, skills or behaviours and, with attention increasingly falling on how leadership is a co-constructing process between leaders and their followers. A team where this relationship is direct and immediate makes for an ideal setting where such participative actions can take place and for leadership to emerge. Although theories specifically designed for teams from this perspective are still maturing, an illustration of how participative and co-constructed leadership can be viewed is presented through describing shared leadership, empowering leadership and complexity leadership theories.

In a nutshell

Participative leadership theories applied to teams, namely shared leadership, empowering leadership and complexity leadership theories.

Purpose

To illustrate how teams are involved in the leadership process.

To find benefits in mobilising team participation.

To direct attention to co-constructing leadership roles in teams.

Description

Leadership theories that focus on teams highlight the unique settings of teams and try to take account of this context, in contrast to general leadership theories that include the individual and non-team or even organisational settings. In particular, team theories emphasise the unique leadership required to lead in complex and creative contexts where decision-making and problem-solving are needed. This requires teams to make use of the particular benefits that teams offer organisations, i.e. the synergies that can arise from combining resources (skills, expertise and information) to excel beyond individual performance. Shared leadership, empowering leadership and complexity leadership are briefly described.

Shared leadership

D'Innocenzo, Mathieu, and Kukenberger defined shared leadership as "an emergent and dynamic team phenomenon whereby leadership roles and influence are distributed among team members". This type of leadership allows each member of the team to at least share the leadership of the team to a certain extent. In fact, the main objective of shared leadership is for members to lead one another to ensure the team achieves its aims. It relies on the proactive engagement of members in the team's tasks to unleash the synergistic benefits of working together. The principle behind this form of leadership is that the team needs to be empowered by being given responsibility and encouragement to use such responsibility, as well as being trusted. Shared leadership moves away from traditional approaches (i.e. "vertical leadership") and views leadership in a team as being distributed across multiple team members whose interactions influence each other to improve performance. These two opposites are in fact perceived to be on a continuum, from focused leadership vested in a single member to broadly distributed and shared leadership where everyone in the team is allowed the opportunity to lead. Where the latter is present leadership may shift, be shared or be rotated according to context, including the levels of skills required according to where the team is in terms of challenges faced, the phase of its life cycle and development cycle, or the tasks that need to be delivered. This demands members of the team to be ready to lead or to accept leadership from other members at various stages of the team's operations. Naturally this points to the fact that such leadership is relational and creates and maintains patterns of influence and communication across the team. It furthermore assumes that in shared leadership teams there is a willingness by all to act as leaders and for members to accept the leadership and influence of others. To facilitate this, members must be committed to a shared purpose. Furthermore, the team context must facilitate social support where members are willing to act on each other's behalf, recognise and acknowledge efforts by various members, and provide operational and psychological help to one another. Team contexts that support shared leadership also encourage and support members to voice their opinions and be open to alternative views.

Pearce and colleagues identified four ways in which shared leadership can manifest in organisations, and how it can be used in teams as well:

- Rotated shared leadership consists of conscious strategies the team adapts to rotate leadership. This can be as basic as an agreement that different people will chair the meetings of a team, while understanding that a rotational system is in place and that the role will become the responsibility of someone else at a different stage.

- Integrated shared leadership is similar to the above, but does not require formal agreement or a formal system of rotation, but leadership rotates more seamlessly.

- Distributed shared leadership manifests where leadership roles and accountability are dispersed more broadly in an organisation. Here members of teams are required to take shared responsibility for leadership as part of the larger organisational culture.

- Comprehensive shared leadership is present where leadership is inculcated throughout many or all of the organisation's or team's operations. Modern day phenomena like agile teams build on this view of shared leadership.

Empowering leadership

Empowering leadership in a team can be seen as a set of behaviours by leaders that enhance team members' experience of potency, meaningfulness, autonomy and impact. It consists of the act(s) whereby leaders delegate authority and responsibility to the team so that leadership is shared and the team experiences a greater sense of self-determination and perceived impact. This form of leadership encourages subordinates to take initiative, to start tasks and deliver on what is expected of them. Team members are empowered to make their own decisions and engage in self-leadership. When leaders share information and provide motivational support it enhances the opportunity for team members to be inventive and resourceful. Empowering leaders encourage initiative, further the team's drive towards its goals and engage in efficacy support. Such leaders are inspirational to the team through supporting development of followers, modelling excellence and offering guidance. Behaviours associated with empowering leadership, as defined by Arnold and his colleagues, are:

- leading by example: the leader displays commitment to his or her own work and performs it with excellence- meeting or exceeding expectations;

- coaching: helping, educating and developing team members to become self-reliant;

- participative decision-making: team members share information and take part in discussions and making decisions;

- showing concern: indication of a general regard for team members' well-being; and

- informing: the manner in which the leader disseminates information.

At a team level this type of leadership leads to the members believing in the potency of the team, the meaningfulness of their work, and its impact on the organisation as a whole. They experience autonomy in the independence they are allowed to express.

Thus, at its core, empowering leadership is a set of behaviours and processes whereby team members are empowered to take initiative, perform, and feel inspired because they have enhanced autonomy and motivation.

Complexity Leadership Theory

This theory is concerned with the need that systems (organisations and teams) have to be adaptive to change. Applied to teams, one aspect of the theory is particularly pertinent, namely the concept of adaptive spaces. An adaptive space is one in which leaders enable the team to provide solutions and adaptations to operate in a complex and changing environment. The authors describe the pressures, practices and principles associated with adaptive spaces.

Adaptive pressures

Within any adaptive space there is bound to be tension and according to complexity leadership theory, the pressures that come with these tensions allow for new solutions to emerge. Thus, in the face of change these pressures allow the team to move out of balance, stability and equilibrium in a safe and secure place. The role of the team is to articulate challenges, enable the adaptive space and leverage pressures. In particular, team leaders are required to utilise or handle the following components of adaptive pressures:

- novelty: the pressure to find a new alternative or solution as the status quo cannot endure;

- relationships: finding or fostering new partnerships by bridging new perspectives, linking different stakeholders and building new relationships;

- conflicting perspectives: finding value in conflict instead of suppressing areas of disagreement; and

- interdependence: building on the fact that members in the team need each other to be successful.

Adaptive practices

Adaptive practices are practices used consistently over a period of time to allow benefits from the adaptive space to evolve. Examples include liberating structures, design thinking and collaborations.

Adaptive principles

Adaptive principles are the guidelines that act as the driving force to sustain the adaptive space and other parts of the complex (organisational) system. The authors recommended the following:

- Find a Friend. Build and leverage current relationships i.e. local allies.

- Follow the Energy. Link up with existing ideas, strategies and views.

- Set Boundaries. Limit engagement to a group or sub-system of the team to existing and intersecting natural networks.

- Embrace the Conflict. Utilise opportunities of conflict to bring to shape an idea that could be meaningful for the team or the larger system.

- Create Network Closure. Allow for connection back into larger systems through acceptance by other stakeholders.

Tips for team leaders

Leaders can use these leadership perspectives to shape their own leadership and allow team leadership to a participative process.

Representation

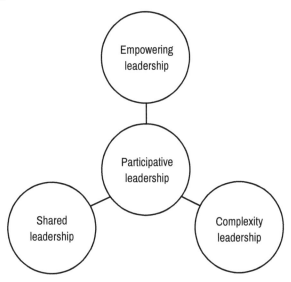

Figure 17.4: Participative leadership

References

Arnold, J.A., Arad, S., Rhoades, J.A. & Drasgow, F. (2000). The Empowering Leadership Questionnaire: The Construction and Validation of a New Scale for Measuring Leader Behaviours. *Journal of Organizational Behaviour*, 21(3), 249–269.

D'Innocenzo, L., Mathieu, J.E. & Kukenberger, M.R. (2016). A Meta-Analysis of Different Forms of Shared Leadership–Team Performance Relations. *Journal of Management*, 42(7), 1964–1991.

Kirkman, B.L. & Rosen, B. (1999). Beyond Self-Management: Antecedents and Consequences of Team Empowerment. *The Academy of Management Journal*, 42(1), 58–74.

Pearce, C. L., & Conger, J. A. 2003. *Shared leadership: Reframing the hows and whys of leadership*. Thousand Oaks, CA: Sage.

Uhl-Bien, M. & Arena, M. (2017). Complexity Leadership: Enabling People and Organizations for Adaptability. *Organizational Dynamics*, 46(1), 9–20.

85 | # Barling: "The Science of Leadership"

Introduction

In his excellent review of the science of leadership, Julian Barling gives a summary of what research has established about leadership. While the review goes beyond team leadership it can be applied to teams as well, and his category of follower work experiences (including team cohesion) is helpful for leaders of teams.

In a nutshell

Leader influence on a team through follower self-perception, follower work experiences and leader-member relationships.

Purpose

To direct a leader's attention to elements of a team that can be impacted.

To highlight follower self-perception.

To guide leaders on how to influence follower work experience.

To build leader-follower relationships.

Description

Barling highlighted that individual, team and organisational outputs are influenced by quality leadership. He contended that leaders can influence follower self-perception, follower work experience and the relationship between the leader and the follower to improve these outputs. He also pointed to three moderators that can affect leadership, namely leader characteristics, organisational characteristics and the external environment.

Follower self-perception

Aspects of follower self-perception that are influenced by the leader-member relationship include self-efficacy belief and mood.

Self-efficacy belief

This refers to an individual's belief that he or she is able to do what is required; this belief influences the initiation, maintenance and persistence of the behaviour of individuals, while belief in team efficacy works in the same way on the behaviour of the team as a collective. Three factors influence belief in oneself, namely personal mastery experiences, vicarious experiences and verbal persuasion. A leader plays a vitally important role in confirming their belief in the efficacy of members and the team.

Mood

While self-efficacy belief relates to how followers feel about their competence, how they feel about themselves is also important. Leaders can influence this aspect of followers' self-perception.

Follower work experience

Six factors are highlighted that impact on work experience:

Meaningfulness at work

Meaningful work is experienced beyond extrinsic motivational factors such as remuneration. Examples are latent or psychological factors such as social contacts, purposefulness, identity and our relations with others. Leaders can influence people's perception of meaningfulness at work by focusing on purpose and higher goals, highlighting a sense of autonomy or mastery, and using individualised consideration to connect with the relationship needs that individuals find in a team. The sense of meaningfulness can also be enhanced by bringing team members in contact with the beneficiaries of their efforts. Believing that what one does is meaningful increases intrinsic motivation.

Team cohesion and potency

A sense of belonging to the team, commitment to its goals and belief that the team is able to deliver on what is required (i.e. potency) can be enhanced by leaders.

Commitment to the organisation

Quality leadership influences followers' commitment to the organisation by increasing a sense of pride and attachment to the organisation. While followers are influenced by the behaviour of leaders more distal to the team (i.e. leaders higher up in the organisational hierarchy), commitment to the team and to the team's performance is directly influenced by the relationship the leader has with his or her team members.

Empowerment and engagement

Within a team a leader can influence the empowerment the team experiences. Empowerment is seen as a form of intrinsic motivation that depends on the belief members have that they are competent to do what is required, their belief about the impact of their tasks on what the team needs to deliver, the autonomy they have in making decisions, and the subjective importance they ascribe to specific tasks. Engagement, on the other hand, relates to how leaders influence followers to such a degree that individuals move beyond mere job satisfaction and engage more intensely with the task, team and organisation.

High-performance work systems

Leaders can influence follower work experience by the way they impact on the performance systems at play in the team. Whether such systems are more controlled or hierarchical on the one hand, or more emerging and encouraging of commitment and involvement on the other, the manner in which leaders focus on high performance and the norms associated with high performance affects the experience members have in a team.

Safety climate

The safety climate associated with follower work experience has a psychological component, where emotional risk taking is allowed, and a behavioural component, which relates to the behaviours that are needed for the team to be physically safe and secure in what it does. This is enhanced through shared views on what safety is, whether leaders act according to safety requirements, and the importance leaders attach to safety measures.

Leader-follower relationship

The final aspects by which the relationship between leaders and followers is influenced are trust in the leader, identification with the leader, value congruence and leader-member exchange.

Trust in one's leader

Trust is seen as the willingness to be vulnerable, as well as the leader will react when such vulnerability is shown according to what the team member personally values. This will happen more readily if leaders believe in members, and allow and encourage them to think for themselves. Such leaders also promote and act for the greater good of the team and display other-centered values. Trust is furthermore built through caring, listening and mentoring behaviour that enhances the social bond between a member and leader.

Identification with the leader

Identification occurs when members of the team experience that the leader's values can be respected and trusted, and that his or her intentions and behaviours can be trusted. This leads to an increased bond between them which is strengthened even more if a sense that the leader cares for them is experienced. If members experience such care and this is reciprocated, the identification with the leader intensifies. It is key for leaders to know that the identification of the members could be with the leader or with the team. It is often better that members identify with the team and that success is perceived to be based on collective effort, which enhances commitment to the team. On the other hand, if identification is only with the leader, then the incentive to operate as a team is diminished and dependence on the leader can ensue.

Value congruence

Leaders need to articulate values associated with a better future and other-centered values based on the collective good. This leads to shared values, which will spur members on to work with and for the team.

Leader-member exchange

In the sense Barling used the term "leader-member exchange", it relates to the manner in which a high quality of leadership stimulates the relationship between leader and follower and how this impacts on follower behaviour. He stated that such relationships have a positive impact on individual, team and organisational performance.

Moderators

Barling also held that the manner in which quality leadership behaviour influences followers, as well as the way in which follower self-perception, follower work experience and leader-follower relationships impact on outcome and performance, are moderated by three factors:

Leader characteristics

The characteristics of the leader that moderate the effect of leadership on followers are manifold and include at least personality, style, gender, values and communication. The leader as a person interacts with followers, therefore the nature of that relationship is determined by the characteristics the leader brings to the interaction.

Organisational context

The relationship between leader and follower is also moderated by the organisation, and here culture, physical distance and size play a role. In terms of how teams are affected by these factors one has only to think of how a team will be influenced by differences in culture or to think how factors driven by organisational demands such as virtual teams, proximity or demographic make-up could impact on a team.

External environmental factors

External factors were discussed earlier, but one particular aspect mentioned by Barling relates to how the leader-member relationship is influenced by changes and uncertainty in the external environment. Demands on leaders to facilitate safety and security are increased in such contexts.

Tips for team leaders

This overview of research is valuable in the way it shows leaders what they should focus on in building relationships with their followers.

Representation

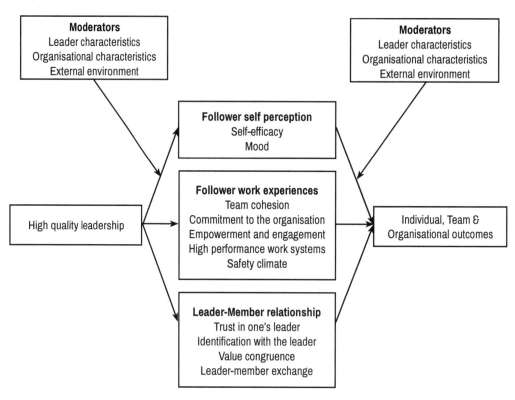

Figure 17.5: Barling: "The Science of Leadership"

Reference

Barling, J. (2014). *The science of leadership: Lessons from research for organizational leaders.* Oxford: Oxford University Press.

.

18 TASKS OF TEAM LEADERS

The tasks that leaders of teams perform have also received research and practitioner attention and offer some valuable information to increase team performance. In this section the functional tasks that need to be performed are presented first as a general overview of the tasks of team leaders. Focus then moves to the tasks of leaders during times of change, both organisational and personal. The last two parts of this section describe implementation techniques. Disciplines of execution is a technique with four strategies or essential dimensions that help teams to focus their attention appropriately. Finally, various other implementation techniques are described, including tools such as Gantt charts and flowcharts.

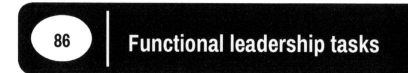

Introduction

The processes a team performs during its life time are structured in a series of episodes that are organised as transition and action phases. During the transition phase the team's focus is on activities related to structuring the team, planning its work and evaluating whether it is performing to the extent that will ensure it achieves its goals. For example, it ensures its composition is such that it has the correct people on board and that it is clear on what it has to accomplish as a team. During the action phase the team focuses its attention on how it delivers its work and how it performs. The leader performs functional tasks during each of these phases.

In a nutshell

The functional tasks of team leaders during transition phases and action phases.

Purpose

To provide an understanding of action and transition phase tasks.

To help leaders monitor and evaluate their own task performances.

To act as a gauge for the actions leaders fulfil in a team.

To act as a tool to facilitate development.

Description

Each task in each of the two phases is discussed.

Transition phase leadership functions

Compose team

The leader has to ensure that between them, the members who comprise the team have the requisite characteristics and attributes, and that these are distributed appropriately to ensure the team functions optimally over time as it develops and meets environmental challenges. These requirements include knowledge, skills, abilities, prior experience, interpersonal skills and levels of motivation. For a new team, this involves selecting appropriate members, while in an existing team it involves evaluating the current levels of characteristics and attributes, adjusting the composition by redeploying or replacing members, and adjusting the team to the demands of the environment. Finally, the leader has to ensure that the team's interpersonal relationships are conducive to optimal functioning.

Define mission

The leader has to help the team devise a clear, compelling and challenging mission, and ensure that all members have a common understanding thereof. This helps the team to fulfil members' expectations, makes them feel part of the team and the processes, and directs them towards goal accomplishment. It also helps the team to build a common identity, form cohesive relationships and devise tactical plans to accomplish the team's goal and purpose.

Establish expectations and goals

Establishing performance expectations and setting team goals is the next task of leaders. The leader helps members to set challenging, but realistic goals and in collaboration with the other members of the team, sets out clear performance expectations. This is particularly helpful to teams as it directs individual action to achieve those targets, builds identity and shared commitment to performance, and helps them to act as a cohesive unit.

Train and develop

When leaders identify that members in the team lack certain knowledge, skills or capabilities, they have to address that through training and development. These skills could be operational or interpersonal in nature, and could be addressed by direct training, coaching, encouraging the use of educational resources offered by the organisation and/or facilitating developmental opportunities. The leader can also help with cross-training and reflection about performance.

Structure and plan

Once the team has its goals determined, the next step is to structure and plan its work by determining how work needs to be completed (i.e. method), who will do which aspects of the work (i.e. role clarification), and when the work will done (i.e. timing, scheduling, work flow). To ensure this happens a plan is devised to direct and coordinate team effort, to develop appropriate performance strategies, and to develop and standardise team processes.

Sense-making

As the team performs its tasks and develops in time it is natural that it will encounter events, challenges and changes that will disrupt its operations and plans. The sense-making task a leader has to fulfil requires him or her to scan the environment, identify significant signs in the context, interpret them for potential impact on the team and communicate that with the team. It involves identifying key events and influences on the team from its environment and helping the team to interpret and get a sense of meaning from such events. External sources, open discussion and clarification are used to help the team explore the potential implications of such events.

Provide feedback

As part of the leader's responsibility to manage the regulatory mechanisms that ensure the functioning, maintenance, and development of the system over time, the leader has to provide feedback to the team. Through feedback, members can evaluate past performance and make adjustments to ensure future success. Thus, feedback is the mechanism through which the leader helps the team to evaluate its performance against established milestones, metrics, and expectations, and through which the leader assists the team to adjust and adapt where they do not meet expectations or standards.

Action phase leadership functions

During the action phase the leaders' tasks are activities that contribute directly to the team accomplishing its goals.

Monitor team

The monitoring function is accomplished by evaluating whether the team is performing optimally and is aware of external contextual factors that may impact on its performance. In particular, the leader should evaluate the team's progress toward task completion, examine the team processes, determine whether it has sufficient resources, and monitor the context for potential changes and challenges that could impact on the team's performance.

Manage team boundaries

This function entails managing the relationships between the team and the organisational context and ensuring appropriate levels of cooperation and coordination between the team and other parts of the organisation. It requires the leader to manage the tension between a tight (over-bounded) or a loose (under-bounded) relationship with the rest of the organisation. In other words, it requires walking the tightrope between buffering from external sources, events and influences, and integration with other parts of the organisation.

Challenge team

Challenging the team's performance, confronting its assumptions, methods and processes, and creating new approaches and being innovative fall within this functional task. It is required of the team leader to stretch the team and to unleash energy from the drive that comes from the team being committed to new challenges. Challenges could be of a personal or task nature where the leader challenges individuals, but could also be broader where the team is required to collectively consider new challenges.

Perform team tasks

Team leaders usually have their own operational functions in a team as well as leading the other members, and are required to deliver on specific areas of competence. Leaders are also required to participate, intervene and perform some of the work of the team. Thus, the leader often takes responsibility for executing tasks within the team or for finishing team tasks.

Solve problems

A further critical function of leaders is to help the team solve problems. Indeed, the ubiquitous nature of problems in teams make this one of the most enduring tasks of leaders. Solving problems has functional or operational and interpersonal components. The responsibility of the leader is to assist the team to find solutions. In some cases leaders are well suited to provide the solution and should offer it. In other cases, leaders can facilitate appropriate processes to allow the team to find solutions themselves.

Provide resources

This task requires leaders to obtain and provide the resources the team requires to perform optimally. These resources could be of an informational nature, to ensure members know what they have to do. Other resources are financial and material, to ensure the team is equipped with the means to complete its task, and even personnel resources where members in the team need certain skills, knowledge and abilities to perform optimally.

Encourage team self-management

This more supportive and indirect task encourages the team to manage itself. Part of the development task leaders fulfil is to allow teams to grow to the level where they take responsibility for themselves and where concern for one another and for the team drives behaviour. Thus, the leader helps the team to perform some of its own leadership functions. Leaders encourage the team to resolve task- and teamwork-related problems themselves without intervention or interference from outside influences, or external stakeholders or experts. This allows a sense of empowerment that leads the team to be more adaptable and resilient.

Support social climate

Leaders perform this function when they support the social climate of the team by attending to its social environment and by intervening where interpersonal issues may interfere with team performance. The team as a social system requires interaction throughout its life cycle and the leader plays a part during all stages of the team's development. Leaders assist in supporting the social climate through solving conflicts, building cohesion, setting the team climate, demonstrating consideration and empowering team members.

Tips for team leaders

The tasks that leaders have to complete are extensive and require constant evaluation and monitoring of their own and the team's actions. This list provides a helpful "checklist" for leaders to evaluate their own actions.

Representation

Transition phase tasks	Action phase tasks
Compose team	Monitor team
Define mission	Manage team boundaries
Establish expectations and goals	Challenge team
Structure and plan	Perform team task
Train and develop	Solve problems
Sensemaking	Provide resources
Provide feedback	Support social climate

Figure 18.1: List of functional tasks for leaders

References

Morgeson, F.P., Scott DeRue, D. & Karam, E.P. (2010). Leadership in Teams: A Functional Approach to Understanding Leadership Structures and Processes. *Journal of Management*, 36(1), 5–39.

87 | # Leading change

Introduction

It is helpful for team leaders to understand key models about change and how they can assist them in leading teams. Here the classification system of change "images" offered by Palmer, Dunford and Akin is explained as an introduction to different change approaches. While these refer to instances of larger organisational change, the same perspectives are useful for leading change efforts in teams as well, and leaders can adapt these to fit the needs of their teams.

In a nutshell

Six metaphors a change leader can adopt, namely director, coach, navigator, interpreter, caretaker and nurturer.

Purpose

To indicate different stances that are available for leaders to facilitate change.

To assist in a flexible approach to change.

To direct leaders to meet the demands of their teams with appropriate change approaches.

Description

Palmer and his colleagues created a six-block matrix that provides "images" of managing change. This relates to how metaphors and symbols guide humans' views of the world. For example, to view an organisation as a machine we are likely to look for "breakdowns", while a different metaphor such as a "political arena" may conjure up different images.

On the horizontal axis of the matrix the authors differentiated between controlling activities and shaping capabilities. Management as control is seen as the historically most enduring view and is associated with a top-down approach; management regards the organisation as a "machine" where employees are assigned particular roles and management "drives" the organisation to its desired end. Management as shaping is a more recent phenomenon and refers to a participative style of management where people are involved in improving the organisation and management's role is more to shape particular outcomes. The emphasis is less on control and more on co-directing organisational effort, and therefore this anthropomorphised view of organisations brings images of a living organism to the fore rather than those of an inanimate machine.

On the vertical axis the authors differentiated between change outcomes as either intended, partially intended or unintended. Intended change is based on the idea that the consequences of change can be pre-determined and organisational change efforts can be shaped and directed to reach such outcomes. Partially intended change refers to the view that leaders' actions do not always lead to what was intended. Unintended change refers to the view that leaders cannot control the effects of change efforts and rather have to acknowledge the internal and external forces at play in shaping organisational destiny.

Once these two views of management and three views of change are combined, six different possible approaches are arrived at. Each is associated with an image or metaphor that describes the approach to change. Furthermore, the authors stated that the approach associated with each of the images makes use of particular tools, methods and techniques to drive the change from this particular vantage point. The six approaches to change are as follows:

Director (control and intended outcome)

The leader directs change as a strategic choice and guides the team to pre-determined outcomes. The classic so-called "n-step" models of change, where the team follows steps towards the end result, are examples of this metaphor of change. The most well-known of these is the Kotter change model that offers eight change steps, namely create a sense of urgency, find a guiding coalition, develop a vision, communicate the vision, empower staff, ensure there are small wins, consolidate gains, and embed in the larger organisational culture. The guiding idea here is that the control that the change agent exerts is such that it will achieve what was intended.

Navigator (control and partially intended outcome)

By espousing this approach managers keep control, but know that the outcomes may not be as intended. They direct their approach towards a goal, but through multiple adjustments the change process in the team follows its own course within the broad strategic direction proposed by the leader. The image assumes that while management keeps a high level of control and plays a key role in achieving outcomes, only partially intended change will occur. A major part of a manager's responsibility is to navigate the resources in the team in such a way that external influences are minimised to ensure that a greater part of the intended change is achieved.

Caretaker (control and unintended outcome)

While the dominant image is still one of control, this view acknowledges the role of internal and external factors that propel change independently from managers' intent. In this regard the control is "passed on" to systems and processes beyond the intervention of the leader. A classic example is the life-cycle theory of team development, which determines the level of change that can be reached at a particular stage. Thus, the leader is a caretaker of the development of the team, as this development is outside his or her control, but is rather determined by the development cycle of the team. The role of the change agent is therefore to guide the team along well-established routes.

Coach (shaping and intended outcome)

The change leader as a coach refers to the ability leaders have to influence and shape change processes. The classical Organisational Development approach can be used to illustrate this. Here the leader as coach (very much like a sports coach) applies their own view of what skills, techniques, processes or modes of operation are needed, and hones these to benefit what they think the team needs. In this way the team is shaped towards an intended outcome through the following steps: identify a problem, gather data and diagnose the problem, determine future intended outcome, plan joint action, implement change actions, and gather further data.

Interpreter (shaping and partially intended outcome)

By leading change from this perspective the leader takes on the position of interpreting what is happening in the team and in its external environment on behalf of and with the team. This sense-making effort is the task of making meaning for the team of what is happening and guiding how reaction to that should be shaped. The interpretive role of leaders is seen in how they determine which are dominant influences and how what is happening influences team behaviour. In particular, sense-making efforts of team leaders could be directed at identity construction (who are we as a team?), social sense-making (what are the social influences from other actors on the team?), extracted cues (what are the cues, ideas or actions that the team regard as important and act on in the change process?), ongoing sense-making (which cues are enduring and which are new, and to which does the team react as it progresses through its development?), retrospection (how does the team make sense of events that have passed?), plausibility (what does the leader have to do to "sell" the change in the face of various political, personal, social and other forces in the team?), enactment (how does the team react to its sense-making efforts by changing them into action?) and projective sense-making (how is sense interjected on a situation or event so that the team is influenced and helped in its meaning-making activities?).

Nurturer (shaping and unintended outcome)

Set within chaos theory, this view of change is built on the notion that systems are unpredictable and chart their own routes and processes. The leader merely nurtures the self-organisational ability of the team and has little impact or influence on where it is going, believing instead in its own empowered ability to find its best course. This change agent facilitates organisational qualities and capabilities to ensure that self-organising is enabled, but realises that they have little control over the outcomes of change and as a consequence the outcomes are described as unintended.

Tips for team leaders

The various metaphors allow leaders to adjust the change approach they need to apply to a given change situation. This allows for more direct and specific action and gives leaders an opportunity to use more focused approaches to connect their teams' internal and external change processes. By starting at the outcome expected of the change, the leader can adjust his or her approach and ensure the most optimal approach is used to facilitate change.

Representation

		Images of managing	
		Controlling...	Shaping...
Images of change outcomes	Intended	DIRECTOR	COACH
	Partially intended	NAVIGATOR	INTERPRETER
	Unintended	CARETAKER	NURTURER

Figure 18.2: Leading change

References

Kotter, J.P. (1996). *Leading change*. Boston, MA: Harvard Business School Press.

Palmer, I., Dunford, R. & Akin, G. (2009). *Managing organizational change: A multiple perspectives approach*. New York: McGraw–Hill Education.

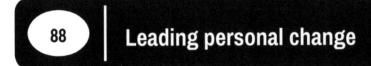

Introduction

Key to any leader's tasks in managing and leading a team is to facilitate change. After all, to move from a current position to a desired state in the future implies progress from one to another state. However, apart from such incremental change from one state to another, teams sometimes experience turbulence and disruptive events that require different skills and coping mechanisms from the leader and the members. To understand the principles and processes behind change is therefore critical, and beyond knowing the different approaches to change described above, it is also helpful for leaders to understand the process team members go through when they undergo disruptive change. A number of theories have been proposed to help with exactly this challenge of team leadership, and two will be discussed briefly here, namely those of Lewin and Kubler-Ross. In addition, a more recent approach (i.e. Fisher's view) on how change is perceived from a personal perspective is also presented to help leaders direct attention to individual members.

In a nutshell

The process team members go through in dealing with change.

Purpose

To understand the stages of the change process.

To help members cope with the challenges associated with change.

To guide members through the emotional components of change.

Description

The discussion starts with foundation theories of change, after which focus is put on the personal transition curve of Fisher to help leaders understand change processes.

Lewin

How people deal with change was highlighted through the work of Kurt Lewin of the National Training Laboratories and his work in the middle of the last century. He directed attention to three phases of change, which are described here from a team perspective:

- Freezing: the original state the team finds itself in and from where change needs to happen. This could be a state that is perceived to be undesirable or untenable because of demands from the context that are changing and forcing change.

- Unfreezing: the intervention by the leader to facilitate and generate change whereby a process is enacted to move the team from a period of inertia to the next stage. This is perceived to be a turbulent period that is unsettling and brings with it emotions of discomfort, resistance and reluctance to accept the need for movement.

- Refreezing: once the process of addressing the change has been completed the team settles into a new rhythm and a more stable period ensues.

Kubler-Ross

Arguably the most influential theory on personal change and a true classic is the study that Kubler-Ross carried out on terminally ill patients' reactions to the fact of their imminent death, but it has since been adopted and adapted in many other contexts, including situations of organisational change. The familiar five stages a person goes through when confronted with change are perceived to be universal to human experience.

Denial

The first reaction to change (especially change perceived to be unpleasant) is denial; the impact of the change is ignored and the team clings to a false sense of security that the change will not happen or impact on the team.

Anger

This is characterised by emotional responses in which the change is perceived as loss and the leader, organisation or team members are blamed for the view that the change will negatively impact on the individual. This leads to feelings of frustration, anger and blame.

Bargaining

This ensues once the inevitability of the change is recognised; the team tries to negotiate a position where the current state will be preserved, but with a compromise, that is with some changes in attitude and or behaviour.

Depression

When the inevitability of the change and its impact on the individual and the team is acknowledged, and since there is no way out of the change and the potential impact thereof, and attempts to bargain or negotiate have been unsuccessful, a stage of depression and desperation is experienced.

Acceptance

A final stage where the new future is accepted and embraced and where the new opportunities can be viewed as potentially energising and positive.

Fisher

Fisher provided a comprehensive and extended linear model of how personal change is experienced. Its major contribution lies in the fact that it also identifies some inflection points where the linear process can be exited and where the individual can opt out of the change.

Anxiety

According to this theory, the first emotional response to a change event relates to the understanding that the event is out of one's control. This leads to anxiety and to questioning whether one will be able to cope. This feeling stems from the fact that the individual does not have an adequate picture of the future or is not able to anticipate a new context in future.

Happiness

Once the initial anxiety subsides, happiness ensues in the knowledge that other members share the experience. Regardless of whether the current state is perceived as positive or negative, the excitement of change and a new beginning provide energy during this stage. The happiness is often based on a sense of redemption as it is perceived as confirmation that the feelings that the current state is inadequate or bound to change are vindicated. However, there is a risk that these feelings may be over-stated and the change perceived to be too positive, with the effect that it may not live up to expectations. To leaders of teams this offers a very helpful opportunity to intervene as the team's readiness for change and a sense that at least something is going to be done about the current situation provides fertile ground for intervention.

Inflection Point One: Denial

Once the individual considers the impact the change will have, the sense of happiness may subside and be replaced with denial. The realisation that the change is going to be bigger than initially thought leads to denial where the impact of the change is ignored and the false idea that everything will continue as before is believed.

Fear

Even if not denied, the impact of the change on the individual is evaluated and this leads to fear. Here the focus is on whether you will be able to cope and whether the new situation will provide the expected better future. As a consequence of their assessment of the future impact, this sense of fear makes members believe they will not have to change and will be able to continue in the previous operating mode.

Threat

In the face of this fear, the change is suddenly experienced as a threat. Members realise that their old choices, behaviours and actions will not be sufficient in face of the new reality. They therefore question whether they will be able to cope, act or react to the demands of the new situation where "old rules" no longer apply and "new" ones are not established as yet.

Guilt

According to Fisher, this stage entails exploration of one's self-perception and evaluation of actions in the past. This leads to identifying core beliefs and assessing how they play out in the team in terms of their appropriateness. This in turn leads to feelings of guilt.

Inflection Point Two: Disillusionment

At this second potential exit point, the individual assesses his or her position in relation to the change and the expected new future. If it is assessed as "not for me", the person may decide to leave the team.

Depression

From guilt follows a sense of depression. This is characterised by inertia, lack of motivation and confusion. Individuals are uncertain as to what the future holds and how they can fit into the future "world".

Inflection Point Three: Hostility

If no future is seen, but the member decides to stay in the team, reactions to the change process resemble hostility and (passive aggressive) anger.

Gradual acceptance

However, once the potential benefit and value of the change process starts to be understood, a general sense of acceptance may evolve. This links in with an increasing level of self-confidence, when we feel good that we are doing the right things in the right way.

Moving forward

A sense of positivity and renewed energy ensues and the member and team are reinvigorated with acceptance of the change and commitment to future action.

Complacency

As a final stage, emphasising the circularity of the process, the team settles into a new, stable state and complacency sets in.

Tips for team leaders

Apart from being more comprehensive and focused on individual behaviour, this approach also allows for exits from the more linear approach of Kubler-Ross. Leaders can use this process to guide members through accepting the changes faced by their teams.

Representation

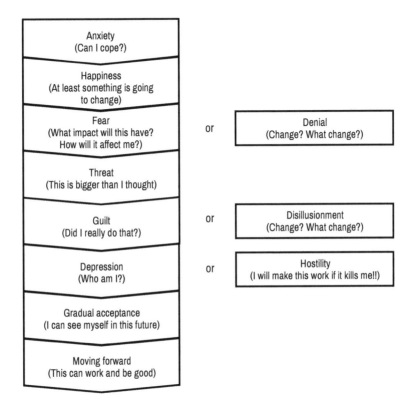

Figure 18.3: Leading personal change

References

Fisher J.M. (2000). Creating the future? In J.W. Scheer (ed.). *The person in society: Challenges to a constructivist theory.* Giessen: Psychosozial-Verlag.

Fisher J.M. (2012a). *The Process of Transition: Fisher's Personal Transition Curve.* Available from: https://www.csu.edu.au/__data/assets/pdf_file/0006/949533/fisher-transition-curve-2012.pdf

Fisher, J.M. (2012b). *Personal Change Stages.* Available from: https://www.businessballs.com/change-management/personal-change-stages-john-fisher-162/.

Kubler-Ross, E. (1969). *On death and dying.* New York: Touchstone.

Lewin, K. (1952). Group decision and social change. In G. E. Swanson, T. M. Newcomb, & E. L. Hartley (eds.). *Readings in social psychology.* New York: Henry Holt.

Introduction

In their book focusing on execution, McChesney, Covey and Huling outlined how to ensure more effective implementation, which can easily be applied to teams as well. These "disciplines" can be adopted by teams and can be of value in guiding task implementation. The tool helps teams to determine which activity is the most critical and the one that should attract the immediate attention of the team, and subsequently what the team needs to do to ensure its implementation.

In a nutshell

Four implementation disciplines, namely define your wildly important goals (WIG), determine how to achieve these goals, design a scorecard and establish a cadence of accountability.

Purpose

To identify the team's most critical goal.

To focus attention on one key objective.

To highlight lead goals.

To track progress.

To create a rhythm of accountability.

Description

The authors described normal business activity as a "whirlwind" that often keeps the team away from what it is supposed to do. Work can be interrupted by any unexpected problem or distraction. They pointed out that in this daily "whirlpool" of activity, teams get so caught up in what they are doing that everything seems important, but they are often prevented from making progress. They therefore suggested a process to ensure the effective implementation of the most critical goals at the same time as the team carries out its daily operations.

Discipline 1: Focus on your WIG

All goals of teams are important, but some are obviously more critical than others. The concept of a WIG (a wildly important goal) emphasises that energy and movement in a team should be focused on this goal. While all urgent goals remain on the radar, a team's WIG is the most critical at any given stage and the focus should be on that one. The team does not abandon the rest, but they do not take WIG-like focus.

Thus, the team must determine what its WIG is and how it can be maintained. In order to do this it must determine whether, if all goals remain, what single goal i.e. WIG (when attained) will move all the others forward simultaneously. If everything remains as is, the WIG is that one achievement that will make the rest secondary. This WIG should be expressed as "from x to y by z".

Discipline 2: Determine measures that will ensure you reach this

The authors distinguished between "lag" goals and "lead" goals. The former are goals that you only know you have reached at the end of a particular period, e.g. whether a quarterly sales target has been achieved can only be assessed at the end of a particular quarter. Lead goals, on the other hand, can be assessed along the way; inputs that will ensure that a particular output or goal will be reached by the designated point in time can be measured. In other words, the journey is measured. The team determines what behaviours need to be measured to influence the lead goal, in other words, what behaviours are necessary to achieve the lead goal because if the lead goal is reached the lag goal will automatically be reached. However, since behaviours are within the control of the team and generally closer to the action, the effect of measuring them (and the effect on the lead goal) is that they can be influenced on a day-to-day basis as they are something that you can improve and measure every day. These behaviours should therefore be:

- predictable i.e. the results will determine measures that will ensure you reach the lead goal (if you do this you can predict that the lead goal will be attained); and

- influenceable (you must be able to change action to influence the behaviours that will lead to achieving the goal), as this gives leverage to the team and is the measure that influences the WIG most critically.

Thus, while the lag goal tells if you have reached your goal, lead goals provide a measure of the behaviours you have to complete to influence the lag goal, and since they are predictable you know that when you adopt these behaviours the lag goal will be reached as a consequence of your actions. The focus thus moves from measuring end states to measuring behaviour that is immediate, influenceable and will ensure successful execution.

Discipline 3: Design a scorecard

A scorecard helps members to play differently if they see the score and therefore the team has to see if it is winning or losing during efforts to reach the WIG. The behavioural measures indicated by movement on the lead goals will have no meaning unless members know there is movement. If behaviours can influence lead, they can influence lag. The scoreboard must be designed so that members can see the state of play and to prevent disengagement because members of the team do not know the current score. It should also include input from the team and preferably be designed by the team. A simple and easily understandable format is preferred to ensure that data necessary to win are clearly visible and indicate movement on both lead and lag goals. It is also critical that the scorecard gives immediate indication of winning or losing.

Discipline 4: Cadence of accountability

The team creates a cadence of accountability by scheduling specific times to work on its goal attainment through deliberate practice. This entails defining a specific stretch goal (it can be a weakness or strength) and the team gives full attention and effort to this action by setting aside deliberate time. It installs a cadence of accountability through a specific routine where commitments are made to change and where each member commits to each other to do this in a particular timespan. The authors proposed that this accountability meeting happens weekly, for no longer than twenty minutes, on the same day and at the same time every week. This gives a particular rhythm and helps team members to commit to each other. During this meeting focus is exclusively on the WIG and no other "whirlpool" discussion is tolerated. At this meeting members each report on what they have done to influence the measurement, review the scoreboard, and commit to new actions for the next week. This becomes a personal promise and once the impact on the lead goal is seen, this positive impact influences behaviour.

Tips for team leaders

Leaders must evaluate whether the planned action impacts the lead goal – if it does not, it must go back to the drawing board and when it is reached then it goes back into the whirlpool and a new WIG becomes the focus of the team's actions. Once they have received informative feedback they reflect on the experience, refine their response and repeat the deliberate practice. It is furthermore necessary to realise that the power of these disciplines lies in the fact that they introduce a set of principles that guide behaviour and they are not merely activities or practices. Thus, they are more enduring and ubiquitous and apply to all behaviours of the team. The authors also warned that implementation of these disciplines may require resistance as they seem counter-intuitive and deceptively basic. However, according to the authors, these disciplines are powerful and facilitate effective implementation of a team's plans, but require commitment, focus and the set-up of a complete management system to ensure effectiveness. Leaders should also remember that the ideal of the disciplines is to focus on the one goal that will ensure that all the others move as well.

Representation

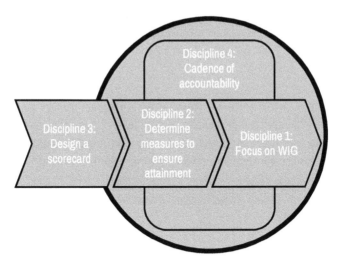

Figure 18.4: Disciplines of action

Reference

McChesney, C., Covey, S. & Huling, J. (2012). *The 4 Disciplines of execution*. New York: Free Press.

Introduction

As is clear from the above, leaders have the responsibility to plan and monitor, but also to take action. Thus, they need to help their teams in their implementation tasks. A number of implementation tools and techniques available to help teams implement their plans from Project Management, including Work Breakdown Structure, Gantt charts, Critical Path Network, Flowcharts, RACI matrix, Task matrix, and Impact matrix and are included here to guide teams in their implementation efforts. In addition, a description of a Task matrix and an Impact matrix are offered to help the team with its implementation.

In a nutshell

Implementation techinques including Work Breakdown Structure, Gantt charts, Critical Path Network, Flowcharts, RACI matrix, Task matrix and Impact matrix.

Purpose

To facilitate implementation.

To assist teams assign tasks and activities to execute.

To communicate the state of progress in respect of the implementation plan.

To provide an aid for visualising the progress of the plan.

To understand the flow of goods and services.

Description

Work Breakdown Structure

Work Breakdown Structure is used to "break down" the different activities of the team and structure them according to their relationships. The team lists all the activities it has to complete. The different levels or sub-divisions of the tasks are determined and the team constructs a hierarchical framework of activities. This "cascading" of deliverables is normally done according to the level of detail required to complete the task. However, the team can also use levels of risk and control, or estimations of resources required, to complete a particular work package. The division and categorisation of activities should be according to the scope of the work and can include levels of tasks, products or geographical distribution. The activities must be structured so as to allow for "roll-up". This means that a higher level will include everything that is subdivided below that level.

Gantt charts

Gantt charts provide an effective and accurate presentation of the state of an implementation plan. The team lists all the activities required by the implementation plan in the left-hand column of a spreadsheet, indicating the duration of each activity, the person accountable for each activity, and the starting and finishing dates for each activity in the corresponding columns. They then decide on a time scale, which is normally given in days or weeks, but, depending on the plan, it could also be hours, months or years. Indicate the points on the chosen time scale in subsequent columns. For example, if the time scale is in months, they put January, February, ect. as the headings of the respective columns (e.g. obviously these should correspond with the starting date of the project). They then indicate the appropriate information (i.e. duration of the activity) on the Gantt chart and show the progress of the implementation plan. This technique is helpful for communicating information about the implementation plans. They are useful aids for smaller projects and can be helpful in visualising the basic structure of a complex project.

Critical Path Network

Critical Path Network (CPM) gives an indication of how the various tasks of the team interrelate and gives a general overview of the proposed implementation plan. The team lists all the actions or activities that are necessary to implement the plan. If a Work Breakdown Structure has been completed, the outcome of that process can be used. The logical relationships between the activities or actions are identified and noted. Keep in mind that activities can be in series (carried out one after the other) or in parallel (performed at the same time). The team must determine the sequence(s) in which actions or activities must occur and indicate the logical relationship and/or sequence on the network diagram. This rudimentary network can be improved through two subsequent processes, namely by adding duration and/or the critical path:

• Duration: define the activities or actions by indicating the start time or date and/or end time or date of each. Thus, the duration or lapsed time it takes to complete each activity or action must be available. Construct a network diagram by taking into account the duration of each activity as well as the required start and finish times. Work out the earliest and latest possible start times of each action or activity. This stage helps in sequencing the implementation plan and assists with the allocation of resources according to where the need will arise.

• Critical Path: the critical path indicates the minimum time required to complete the project. Although a network diagram is helpful to assist in sequencing, one of its major benefits is that it gives an indication of where any change would impact on the delivery time of the project. For example if a change (e.g. a delay or increase in speed of production) occurs on the critical path, the overall time of the project will be influenced. This is the critical path of the project. Thus, the logical sequence, duration of activities and the critical path helps to determine a network diagram of the implementation plan.

Flowcharts

Flowcharts are helpful to help the team understand the flow of goods or services through various stages in the implementation process. Four different, but related flowcharts are presented here, namely a flow diagram, a process chart, time function mapping and an example of a swim-lane chart.

Flow diagram

The flow that is mapped by the team is presented as stages in a process and each activity (task, job or operation that must be performed) is listed. The team can use its own symbols and determine its own rules of schematic representation.

Process chart

Process charts present flow by using symbols to indicate the flow of material through standardised "types" of activities.

Time–Function mapping

This type of flowchart adds the dimension of time to demonstrate how the activities flow and the duration of each activity.

Swim lanes

In a swim lane presentation each member or resource in the team is represented as a row or "swim lane". This means that the member of the team has his or her own set of responsibilities and the interconnection of the team in producing an outcome can be depicted. The movement of goods or service is depicted at any point where a member of the team (i.e. within a lane) is in contact with the product or has to make a decision regarding the flow thereof.

RACI chart

A RACI chart is used to record the actions required from various stakeholders in relation to various tasks. A basic matrix can be drawn up showing the members in the team and who is responsible for each task. The activities or tasks are entered on the vertical axis and the names of each stakeholder (team member) on the horizontal axis. Each name must be in a separate column. Thus, a matrix is formed with the activities in the rows and the stakeholders in the columns. At the intersection of any activity and any person involved with that activity, a code is entered that indicates the relationship between the activity and the person. The original four markers were Responsible, Accountable, Consulted and Informed, however the method can be used with any relevant markers. For example, the following extension could be used:

- C   Consulted: stakeholder(s) must be consulted

- G   General supervision of the project

- P   Primary responsibility

- S   Secondary responsibility

- N   Notified: stakeholder(s) must be notified

- A   Approval: stakeholder(s) must give approval

Task matrix

Byttebier offered this technique to help teams prioritise actions and to assist in compiling their action plans. It also helps the team decide which tasks to discontinue or postpone. A matrix is designed with actions currently being done or not being done on one axis, and actions the team want to do or do not want to do on the other axis. The four quadrants then reveal the following:

- Do not want to do, but do: this states current actions, but also indicates what members prefer to let go or not want to do in future anymore. This helps the team to determine what it (or particular members) need to do to limit, decrease or delegate actions.

- Want to do and do: these actions help the team to design action plans around preferences of members and assist in optimising its action plan.

- Want to do, but do not do: this indicates to the team what actions members are currently not doing or involved in, but would like to contribute to once the plan is in place.

- Do not want to do and do not do: this also assists the team to determine what they will not have to do in future and what the members are not currently doing. By stating these dislikes clearly and through critical evaluation of the validity of such actions, the team can use the information included here to exclude certain unnecessary actions.

Impact matrix

A final implementation tool that helps the team decides on future action is known as an impact matrix. This requires the team to reflect on future reactions and risks and their potential impact on future plans. First, possible difficulties are listed and sorted by degree of problem they would present. This is followed (as a second step) by an assessment of the probability that these difficulties will arise. Although the latter may be difficult to determine and require understanding of the assumptions behind them, it is a critical step. Each risk is categorised as low probability (unlikely to happen), medium (the team is undecided on the likelihood) and high (very likely to happen). Thirdly, the potential impact of each of these risks is indicated, again by allocating one of the three categories (low, medium and high). Each risk is entered in a matrix indicating likelihood of occurrence on one axis and degree of impact on the other (this provides nine blocks or clusters). Each risk is entered in the appropriate block according to the assessments. The team uses the resulting diagram to evaluate its plan of action.

Tips for team leaders

To facilitate work breakdown structuring, there should be no more than four to five different levels or subdivisions. One of the main benefits of the method is the numbering of activities. This allows for estimation and/or the allocation of people, money and time to each activity. Thus, the structure allows for control and management and is specifically helpful in allocating budgets and accounts. Gantt charts can be made more informative and expanded by colour-coding to indicate responsible members and help to balance the team in terms of responsibilities. CPM shows activities that need to occur simultaneously and which activities are blocked, and tracks the state of activities, in other words whether activities are behind schedule, ahead of schedule, or precisely as planned. The key benefit of flowcharts is that they can represent processes that are dynamic and assist in decision-making. They can also help to indicate feedback loops and to show where certain actions need to be completed before another action can commence. The rest of the techniques are valuable in that they give a clear indication of who is responsible for specific tasks and what the impact of the efforts of the team is on stakeholders.

Representation

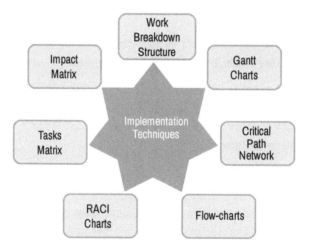

Figure 18.5: Implementation techniques

References

Kriek, H.S. (2007). *Creative problem solving: Techniques for South African teams*. Pretoria: Mindmuzik.

Project Management Institute. (2013). *A guide to the project management body of knowledge* (5th ed.). Newtown Square, PA: Project Management Institute.

19

COACHING

Coaching has undoubtedly taken the organisational world by storm and its perceived value can be seen in the popularity and extent of its use throughout many business and organisational contexts. While many coaching models and frameworks exist, the use of coaching in teams is less extensive than for individuals. Therefore, individual coaching models are first explained, illustrated by the RACSR-model used by the Centre for Creative Leadership. While these models were developed predominantly with individuals in mind, some models have been adjusted for use in teams. For example the well-known GROW-model of John Whitmore has been extended to be called GROUP, while the individual-focused CLEAR model of Hawkins had been enhanced for group settings, with the stages called CID-CLEAR. The next part of this section describes a later, more expanded description of leadership team coaching from Hawkins, followed by the team coaching model of Hackman and Wageman. The last coaching approach is based on the broader, philosophical work of Ken Wilber, which has found traction in organisational work (e.g. culture) and in what is known as integral coaching.

Introduction

The leader as coach acts in this role in the workplace and performs specific behaviours to enable the employee to perform, grow and develop. Some of these behaviours include listening, questioning, challenging, feedback, reflection, and goal setting. As a team leadership function, one important element of such interventions is the fact that they provide the space wherein employees find solutions and alternatives for themselves and thus provide a co-creating space. In the world of executive coaching many "models" of coaching now exist and have found their way into the skills set of the "manager as coach" as well. For some reason nearly all utilise an acronym, such as Palmer points out: ACHIEVE, OSKAR, ABCDE and PRACTICE. The RACSR model of the Centre for Creative Leadership has been chosen as an illustration because of its research-based focus and widespread use.

In a nutshell

A coaching conversation is structured through relations; assessment, challenge and support; and results.

Purpose

To use in coaching conversations.

To provide a guide to leaders on what to use.

To highlight key elements in the coaching process.

To act as a practical coaching tool.

Description

The coaching model developed by the Centre for Creative Leadership is presented here as an illustration of models that leaders can use in coaching individuals. The model was developed from principles used in adult learning, coaching and professional experience. It is a coaching tool used by executive and professional coaches, but the guiding principles of the model can be used for leaders coaching team members. The RACSR-model has three guiding principles, namely relationship; understanding of coachee through assessment, challenge and support; and finally results or outcomes.

Relationship

The RACSR approach uses the relationship between a coach and coachee, or in this case between a leader and team member, as the fundamental point of departure. The model regards the coaching relationship as a special kind of connection built on rapport, commitment and trust. Once this relationship is in place it allows the leader (as coach) to establish required boundaries for the intervention and helps the member to clarify his or her expectations. Through building trust and credibility the leader puts the foundations in place to use the coaching space as a safe, yet open space where the member can be challenged. As the relationship is seen as a collaborative effort it is kept intact through unconditional positive regard and security, based on clarified roles and rules and on respect.

Assessment, challenge, and support

The next three elements of RACSR are related as they inform the content of the coaching discussions.

Assessment

The purpose of assessment is to get a holistic understanding of the team member in terms of idiosyncrasies, context and challenges in the work setting, as well as areas for development. The assessment can take place through a variety of means and the leader can use interviews, instruments or observations to establish a thorough understanding of the individual, the leader-member relationship, and the experience of the individual with the team and other systems. Assessment allows the member to reflect, to increase self-awareness and to understand their strengths and weaknesses. The manner in which the leader gives feedback to the member about the results of assessment instruments and observations, about their experience of the member in the team, and about performance becomes a valuable input in the coaching relationship.

Challenge

Based on adult learning principles, which state that adults learn by being challenged, the coaching relationship also allows for such challenges or "stretching" by exposing the coachee to new or different behaviours and situations and by challenging the coachee's assumptions or beliefs. It also provides an opportunity to analyse what the coachee perceives as obstacles to their development and challenges them to find ways to overcome such obstacles. This part of the coaching process also encourages new ways of thinking and pushes boundaries through the relationship.

Support

Support is the third element of the content of the coaching relationship. The coach (or leader) must make sure they listen carefully, are empathetic, show curiosity, respect values and beliefs, and observe what is driving the conversation. The leader must also summarise key elements of the discussion.

Results

The purpose of a coaching relationship is to deliver results through improving performance and utilising development opportunities, thus, the coaching conversations should be aligned to the goals of the individual, the team and the organisation. The leader helps to set goals and clarify to the member what performance and developmental success would look like.

Tips for team leaders

Although this tool is designed primarily for an individual coaching relationship, leaders can use it in their "leader-as-coach" tasks as well and it can be applied with the benefit of the team in mind. The model focuses on the importance of the relationship between the two (and this factor is consistent with other leadership theories) and gives clear direction to the leader on where emphasis should be put in the coaching relationship. The other main benefit of RACSR is its focus on results.

Representation

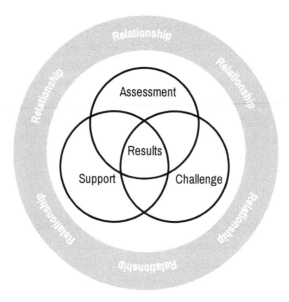

Figure 19.1: RACSR coaching model

References

Naudé J. (2016). Coaching and mentoring. In A. Viera & R. Kramer R. (eds.). *Management and leadership skills for medical faculty*. Cham, Switzerland: Springer.

Palmer, S. (2008). The PRACTICE Model of Coaching: Towards a Solution-Focused Approach. *Coaching Psychology International*, 1(1), 4–6.

Adjusted individual coaching models

Introduction

One of the earliest and most enduring coaching models is the so-called GROW-model proposed by Whitmore, which is used widely to structure and guide the coaching conversation. The CLEAR model by Hawkins is also popular and has received acclaim in academic and practitioner circles. Both of these primarily individual models have been adjusted to be used for teams and these adjustments are presented here. The GROW-model has been adjusted to be used as the GROUP model, while CID-CLEAR is the adjustment for the model proposed by Hawkins.

In a nutshell

A coaching conversation is structured by using the GROUP and CID-CLEAR coaching models.

Purpose

To coach teams through a structured process.

To guide the coaching conversation.

Description

GROW to GROUP

The GROW-model of Whitmore was adjusted to be used in teams through Brown and Grant's proposal, namely GROUP. The original model is briefly described here to provide background to the adjustment. The model derives its name from the acronym GROW, where each letter represents a stage in the coaching conversation.

- **G – Goals.** In the first stage the goals of the conversation are determined, where the aim is to agree on a specific objective and topic for the session. Where appropriate, long-term goals can be included during the initial stages of the conversation. The process starts with the coachee stating what they want to achieve in the session and this determines the focus of the session.

- **R – Reality.** The current reality of the coachee's situation is explored during the second stage. The main focus is on how the current situation is impacting on the coachee's goals. During the conversation the coach tries to obtain clarity and to make clear at the same time to the coachee what is happening regarding the situation. The coach invites self-assessment, tests the assumptions of self and coachee, and helps to raise awareness of present realities. The conversation provides the context and history of the topic related to the coaching and the coach checks what has been tried already.

- **O – Options.** During this stage options and alternatives are explored. The coach helps the coachee to evaluate possible options and explores what has already been tried and offers potential alternatives. This is a more creative stage, where focus is on guiding the resources of the individual, finding solutions and looking beyond the problem and its impact. Focus is on what the coachee might do and from the range of options possible options are selected.

- **W – Way Forward.** This refers to the follow-up steps and actions that are needed to implement the changes. Appropriate actions commensurate with the aim of the session and aligned with the proposed solution are devised. During this stage potential obstacles, as well as support systems are identified, and the impact thereof on preferred actions are investigated. Specific milestones to help the coachee track progress are also determined. As this is a motivational stage, emotions are also explored in terms of current thinking and the potential emotional impact of implementing alternatives.

As an extension of the GROW-model, Brown and Grant proposed an approach that can be applied for group coaching. Although they indicated that this approach is directed at groups, they included teams as a sub-set of groups. They used the acronym GROUP for the following five stages:

- **G – Goals.** The team clarifies what they want out of each session and thereby determine the focus of the coaching.

- **R – Reality.** The team evaluates what is happening in the team and efforts they have already tried; in this way awareness is raised of current realities and how these impact on the team's goals.

- **O – Options.** Available options are identified and alternatives are generated through solution-focused brainstorming.

- **U – Understanding.** This phase is designed to increase the team's awareness of its current reality, what systemic level challenges they are facing and the degree of openness to one another. It uses dialogue where the team thinks together; there is flow of meaning and a willingness to consider new possibilities about the team and members alike. It leads to increased understanding of one's own behaviour and the impact it might have on others. Understanding is further facilitated through dialogue, as it fosters synergies, opens creativity, generates insight and enhances connections between members. The coach helps the team in its quest to be more understanding by encouraging members to be open, to listen to each other, and to be comfortable with uncertainty, and by inviting reflection.

- **P – Performance.** In this conception of performance both action plans for the coaching sessions themselves and action plans that relate to external demands on the team are regarded as relevant. The authors saw performance as an iterative process where the team explores and enacts, but then comes back into coaching sessions to reflect and evaluate. This double-loop learning experience facilitates performance. They rely on principles related to design-thinking where they devise performance plans for the "future", and this anticipatory process provides motivation for the team to drive implementation plans. Thus, the concept of prototype is introduced, as it allows for design, testing and change and ensures a continuous evolutionary process where adaption, failure, "letting-go" and rethinking become part of the learning process.

Finally, the authors proposed two further steps to ensure continuity and continuous evaluation, namely:

- **review**: an overview and review of the actions taken between sessions; and

- **evaluate**: an assessment of the successes, failures, learning, barriers to and support of the implementation actions taken between sessions. These two steps guide the goal-setting of subsequent steps.

CID-CLEAR

In the team coaching process developed by Hawkins he expanded his CLEAR model to make it appropriate for team coaching. The resulting CID-CLEAR approach uses the following steps:

- **Contracting 1:** initial exploratory discussions. This refers to the initial discussions by the team leader with a coach and is not the same as contracting with the total team.

- **Inquiry:** this allows the coach an opportunity to get information regarding performance, initial impressions, group dynamics and relationships between various stakeholders. This stage can be completed through semi-structured interviews, a questionnaire, 360 degree assessments or stakeholder conversations, and a review of performance data.

- **Discovery, diagnosis and design:** the information acquired through the previous stage is used to determine where the team functions on each of the disciplines and to decide on an appropriate point of entry. For example a team in trouble and emotionally burdened will require a starting point from the co-creating stance.

The coaching process is then completed through using the CLEAR stages of contracting, listening, explore and experiment, action and review:

- **Contracting**: contracting with the team on the goals and expectations of the coaching session.

- **Listening**: this stage allows for active participation of the coach in trying to understand what is happening in the team through listening to data or facts; observing patterns of behaviour; and experiencing the emotional climate (i.e. the emotional expressions and relating through metaphors and non-verbal communication).

- **Explore and experiment**: the information revealed by previous stages is reviewed and explored and the team experiments with alternative ways to operate. This needs to be aligned with the discipline that is most at risk or with the manner in which the interaction between disciplines is facilitated.

- **Action**: during this stage focus is on how the team can act differently and perform better. The team plans for how new actions will be implemented and starts living these new intentions and plans immediately.

- **Review**: the process of implementing the new changes is monitored and feedback given to the team.

Tips for team leaders

These coaching models are helpful because they relate specifically to teams, and as expansions of individual models can be used to link some of the benefits from individual coaching into team coaching environments.

Representation

GROUP	CID-CLEAR
G-Goals R-Reality O-Options U-Understanding P-Performance	C-Contracting 1 I-Inquiry D-Discovery, diagnosis and design C-Contracting 2 L-Listening E-Explore and experiment A-Action R-Review

Figure 19.2: GROUP and CID-CLEAR coaching models

References

Brown, S.W. & Grant, A.M. (2010). From GROW to GROUP: Theoretical Issues and a Practical Model for Group Coaching in Organisations. *Coaching: An International Journal of Theory, Research and Practice*, 3(1), 30–45.

Hawkins, P. (2017). *Leadership team coaching: Developing collective transformational leadership*. London: Kogan Page.

Team coaching: Peter Hawkins

Introduction

Although presented as a coaching model for team leaders, the framework offered by Peter Hawkins provides a very helpful and practical perspective on coaching teams as it shows that development occurs in a spiral fashion.

In a nutshell

Teams use commission, clarification, co-creation, connection and core-learning to develop.

Purpose

To guide the team's development processes.

To allow for multiple iterations of development to unfold.

Description

Hawkins believed that most teams spend too much time and effort on internal dynamics and do not allow sufficiently for the role of external stakeholders. He also argued that too much time is spent on historical influences on the team, which leads to an over-emphasis on the past. Thus, he proposed that teams should adopt an approach directed by:

- future back: the team thinks "backwards" from where it wants to be in the future in order to determine what they have to do now; this provides the team with the required energy and drive to push towards this future-oriented goal; and

- external in: the team's very existence is dependent on the external environment since it is this dynamic that helps the team to always follow a moving target. Thus, what the team needs to do is always determined by external influences and external stakeholders provide the team with its scope and focus. Teams should therefore give greater emphasis to the external environment, and let this guide them with regards to what they are supposed to do.

Hawkins put forward a matrix with task and process on the vertical axis and internal and external on the horizontal axis. This allows for five "disciplines" that drive team behaviour.

Commission

Believing that external stakeholders' views should be reflected and considered when coaching teams, Hawkins contended that the views held by such stakeholders present the point of departure of a team. He suggested that the "commission" they give to the team (i.e. a clear vision and requisite performance measures and targets) provides the team with the required context to start working. Once this is in place, the external context (i.e. the vision) enables the selection of a leader who in turn selects the team and the key role of the commissioners becomes supportive. Thus, a clear commission includes targets, resources, information, learning and development, feedback, and technical and process support.

Clarify

Once the team's commission is in place the team clarifies how the challenge is energising and compelling and fosters interdependence. By articulating a mission that will enable the team to reach this goal, the team mobilises its collective energy and builds a sense of mutual accomplishment that meeting the goal will bring. Hawkins defined 'mission' as consisting of purpose, strategic narrative, goals and objectives, core values, vision for success, protocols and agreed ways of working, roles and expectations, and key performance objectives and indicators.

Co-create

This entails the manner in which the team cooperates to attain its mission. It requires the team to be self-reflective of when they perform below or above expectations. They must devise effective processes and agree on appropriate behaviour in meetings, informal gatherings and beyond the team's boundaries, including the way they handle conflict.

Connect

This stage refers to the manner in which the team connects with their stakeholders to improve their own performance and to involve stakeholders in their operations. Hawkins distinguished three types of connections a team makes within its environment, namely:

- ambassadorial: communicating what the team does and raising its profile;
- scouting and inquiry: determining what is influencing other stakeholders and its impact on team performance; and
- partnering: partnering with other stakeholders outside the team to enhance the output of the team beyond what they can do by themselves;

Core learning

Spanning all disciplines (and spatially in the middle of the graph), this offers a place where the team reflects objectively on its performance and processes. It consolidates learning already present and is focused on how performance can be enhanced by using the lessons learnt from current operations. The team also considers from such learning how long-term viability is effected by putting in place social support, team conflict resolution, support for members' learning and development, and finally team climate. Hawkins also stated that teams need to take deliberate action to move between these different "spaces" and suggested the following actions to connect the disciplines:

- Commission to mission dialogue: this should provide clarity of stakeholders' expectations of at least financial performance, output, reputation, innovation, people and transforming the organisation. When completed successfully it allows the leader to select a team to deliver and for the team to internalise and concretise their interpretation thereof in the mission (purpose, strategy, core values and vision). It also allows opportunity for feedback to the commissioners around what is attainable, to close the aspiration–realism gap, and to provide an agreeable and achievable roadmap of success.

- Policy-into-practice dialogue: this aligns aspiration and daily practice by involving the team through co-creating actions based on the core values of the team and focused on its strategy. It also allows for continuous adjustment of the team's strategy and actions to align with changing contextual demands.

- Co-creating with stakeholders: the team co-creates its own actions in alignment with its stakeholders. This is done through double-loops of engagement, including listening to stakeholders and stakeholders' stakeholders. This is shared with the team who adjust their actions co-constructively to offer these stakeholders win-win solutions.

- Stakeholder-commissioners' dialogue: this allows for the external context and its stakeholders to use the opportunity to feed it back to the commissioners of the team and to enable adjustment of their expectations.

- Core learning connecting to all disciplines: this higher order function gives the team the opportunity to reflect on the disciplines and the interactions between the members of the team, as well as between the team and its stakeholders. The team learns from how it interacts internally as well as with all stakeholders. It also gives the opportunity to reflect on behaviour, performance and success factors.

Thus, this offers a comprehensive coaching process that allows for many iterations and development to take place.

Tips for team leaders

Leaders can also use this approach by focusing on what the impact will be if one or all of these elements are not in place:

- Commission: lack of commission will lead to progress on something not needed by external stakeholders.

- Clarification: without clarification there will be no collectively devised vision and targets, and members will be chasing externally determined targets.

- Co-create: if this does not happen there will be no sense of collaboration, enjoyment and commitment; you may know what needs doing, but not who does it or could do it.

- Connect: if there is not connection the team may be unaware of changes in the external context and stakeholder expectations.

- Core learning: lack of core learning will lead to a long-term focus on improvement, with attention directed at the immediate only.

Representation

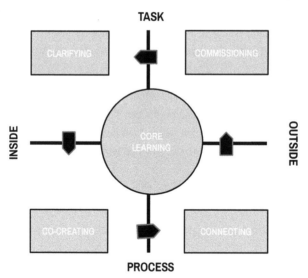

Figure 19.3: Leadership team coaching

References

Hawkins, P. (2017). *Leadership team coaching: Developing collective transformational leadership.* London: Kogan Page.

94 | Team coaching: Hackman and Wageman

Introduction

Hackman and Wageman defined team coaching as "direct interaction with a team intended to help members make coordinated and task-appropriate use of their collective resources in accomplishing the team's work". When appropriately applied it limits process loss and even facilitates process gain. This means that with appropriate coaching a team can perform at better levels than without. They stressed the functions that coaching serves for a team, the times at which interventions are more effective, and the conditions that need to be in place for coaching to succeed.

In a nutshell

The focus is on coaching functions, time of application and conditions for effectiveness.

Purpose

To help leaders and coaches determine the focus of specific coaching interventions.

To align coaching efforts with the appropriate time to intervene.

To ensure conditions for effective coaching are in place.

Description

This coaching approach differs from others in that it does not focus on interpersonal relationships between members, but rather on a team's task performance processes. This they defined as the:

- level of effort members collectively put into their task work;

- appropriateness to the task of the performance strategies the team uses; and

- knowledge and skills required.

They furthermore contended that each of these performance processes requires a particular type of coaching, namely:

- effort requires motivational coaching, which serves to limit free riding and build shared commitment;

- performance strategy requires strategic coaching functions to help teams minimise task performance routines that are not well-considered or are unnecessary; and

- knowledge and skills processes require coaching that is educational and ensures members' knowledge and skills are used optimally, and processes are developed appropriately.

A further key contribution of this team coaching model is the manner in which they link the team readiness to coaching to the Punctuated Equilibrium (or Midpoint Transition) model of team development (see Section 9). The model states that when teams have a clear deadline to complete a particular task or project, there are three main stages. These are (1) the start where a relative stable period exists, (2) the midpoint (approximately the calendar midpoint) where turbulence and change occur, and finally (3) the last half of the team's operations that are again fairly stable. This allows for three natural points of entry where the team is most ready and susceptible to intervention such as coaching. In particular they regarded readiness as the degree to which the issues to be addressed are those concerning the team in any event. Thus, team coaches need to optimise these opportunities. In particular the model states that teams are ready at:

- the beginning for motivational coaching, where focus is on the boundary of the team, roles of members, limiting anxieties and engaging them with the task at hand;

- the midpoint for strategic coaching, where the function is to assess past performance and adjust behaviour towards the accomplishment of the task; and

- the endpoint for educational coaching, with a focus on what lessons can be learnt from the process.

In addition, while teams are most susceptible for intervention at these stages ,"in-between" interventions are helpful when:

- task complexity is high and the team is inexperienced; at such times focus on the team's coordination efforts can be helpful;

- constructive behaviour is present, but not frequently used; here coaches can use techniques to emphasise good behaviour;

- teams have multiple tasks and multiple task cycles, as this gives more opportunity for a coach to use any of the three periods described above where teams display heightened readiness; and

- teams are continuous, with a perpetual task horizon, as this allows a coach to introduce rhythm and establish intervention periods commensurate with the midpoint transition model.

They also stated that these modes and periods of intervention are dependent on certain conditions and the degree to which these conditions are in place. In this regard they highlighted the degree to which key performance processes are externally constrained, i.e. the manner in which the processes (effort, performance strategy, and knowledge and skills) depend on external constraints. For example, the level of freedom members have in how they perform a task and the team's composition can both influence performance.

The authors further stated that each of the performance processes is influenced by the structural and contextual support that members experience. In this regard they contended that:

- effort is dependent on the design of the task (structural) and the reward system of the organisation (contextual);

- performance strategies are dependent on the norms of conduct in, and the information system of, the organisation (contextual); and

- knowledge and skills depend on the composition of the team as well as the education support system.

Lastly, they stated that four conditions need to be present for team coaching to be effective. These are:

- performance processes relatively unconstrained by task or organisational requirements. The team must have sufficient resources for the tasks at hand, and not be hampered or constrained by contextual variants;

- a well designed team and a supportive organisational context. A well-designed team is one with sufficient levels of skill, of optimal size and that manifests sufficient diversity;

- coaching directed at salient task performance processes and not at interpersonal relationships. This is a key difference of this model; and

- interventions aligned with when teams are most ready for such interventions.

Tips for team leaders

This is a helpful tool that guides interventions and prescribes to leaders and coaches what to focus on during coaching processes. The alignment of coaches' actions to what the team needs is highlighted, and when used appropriately contributes to the effectiveness of coaching interventions.

Representation

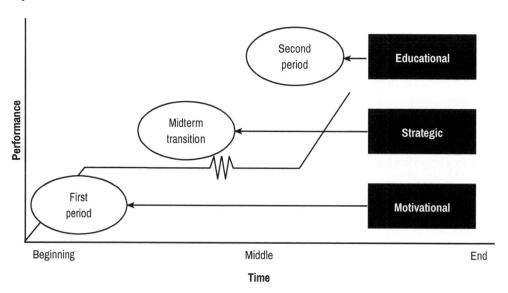

Figure 19.4: Hackman and Wageman team coaching model

References

Hackman, J.R. & Wageman, R. (2005). A Theory of Team Coaching. *Academy of Management Review*, 30(2), 269–287.

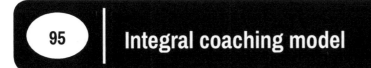

Introduction

Wilber is arguably one of the most well-known modern day philosophers and his Integral Theory is influential in many fields. In particular, his aim of integrating various disciplines adds to the influence of his thinking, and it comes as no surprise that it has also found its way into the world of organisations (notably the work of Laloux on culture (see Section 14)) and also into the growing field of coaching. His views can be used to guide coaching perspectives and discussions which leaders can use. Although the model is complex and exhaustive, an application of the theory in the coaching realm is presented here with the aim of assisting team leaders in their coaching endeavours.

In a nutshell

Using four quadrants – "I" (inner states), "IT" (behavioural), "ITS" (systems/structure) and "WE" (culture) – and a spiral of development, coaches can use integral theory as part of a coaching process.

Purpose

To guide the coaching process.

To understand individuals' coaching needs.

To use development processes in coaching.

Description

A brief overview of two elements (i.e. quadrants and levels) of Integral Theory that are particularly helpful to team coaching processes is provided here. Quadrants refers to the integrated nature of all systems while levels focuses on human consciousness development and its impact on behaviour.

Quadrants

Wilber aimed to provide a theory that encompasses "all" phenomena that humans encounter and integrates various elements of life on two axes, namely interior–exterior and individual–collective. Combining these allows for four quadrants, each focusing on a different element of human interaction.

- "I": the Inner States quadrant is the overlay between interior and individual. This refers to the individual's inner world and includes cognitions, emotions, and memories from past experiences, states of mind, perceptions, and immediate sensations. It relates to the subjective aspects of the consciousness or individual perception, as well as spiritual experience and self-identity dynamics. It includes the subjective views individuals hold about the world and their values, purpose and calling.

- "IT": the "Behaviour" quadrant is the overlay between exterior and individual. This refers to the individual's outside world, i.e. physical aspects including brain, body and behaviour. Actions, language, skills, competencies and body language are focused on during this part of the coaching process, as this gives an objective perspective of the world.

- "ITS": the Systems/Structure quadrant is the overlay between exterior and collective. This refers to the systems and structures shaping our lives (and therefore is inter-objective in perspective), including the social dimension wherein the individual lives. This quadrant enquires about how people are organised, and the policies and procedures, codes of conduct, economic and social context, geopolitical structures and ecosystems surrounding the individual.

- "WE": the Collective Interior Quadrant is the overlay between interior and collective. The "WE" quadrant represents the group or collective consciousness and indicates the values, feelings, beliefs and worldviews shared by individuals, in other words, the cultural space in which the individual operates. It is the intersubjective domain where political and community values, morality and culture give expression to meaning through music and art.

Levels

Integral theory builds on the work of Beck and Cowan by asking about the levels of human development. This theory contends that humans developed survival mechanisms to cope with the ever more complex demands from the environment. It states that human consciousness developed in a spiral fashion from the most basic to the more complex. However, each of the larger order states incorporates all of the states that preceded it in a holarchy i.e. like a Matryoshka (Russian) doll that can be opened up to reveal another doll inside that can be opened to reveal yet another, and so on. The following development stages of human consciousness are identified:

- Beige: Archaic-Instinctual. The level of basic survival where you are only concerned with what you must do to stay alive. Focus on their own survival through means to obtain food, water, warmth, sex, shelter and safety. The core value is survival.

- Purple: Magical-Animistic. This world is dominated by spirits and magic and the challenge is to keep them happy. This development stage is characterised by allegiance to chiefs and elders, and clans and ethnic tribes form that contain ancestral spirits and provide a place of bonding and kinship. Core values are the desire to serve the clan and magical spirits.

- Red: Power Gods. The first indication of an individual self apart from and distinguished from the tribe emerges. The self becomes egocentric and heroic and as powerful people they have the ability to determine the fate of others, to attract the adoration of followers, and to give protection in face of a world seen to be in danger from magical-mythic spirits, dragons and beasts. Impulsive drives, service to raw self-interest and immediate rewards drive this level.

- Blue: Mythic Order. The dominance of the system and the order associated with fitting in and complying are key drivers of this stage. A powerful order enforces moral codes of conduct based on "right and wrong" and "good and evil". Absolute principles with absolute truths dominate and a sense of "this is how it is done here" prevails. Adhering to rules, avoiding punishment and doing one's duty are elements of the fundamental value of complying that underscores this level.

- Orange: Scientific Achievement. In the so-called "age of reason" societies prosper through science, technology and competitiveness. The fundamental point of departure is that man can control nature by understanding and mastering its laws. The individual emerges from the system-dominated mythic order to act in their own self-interest and to drive achievement.

- Green: Sensitive Self. The focus is on connection and relationships where the individual is at peace with their inner self. They explore (with others) the caring dimensions of community and search to elicit the potential of individuals, communities and the world at large through care and nurturing. Emphasis is on dialogue, interaction and relationship-building, and the value underscoring this domain is "relate". Relations and serving the greater good are key values of this level.

- Yellow: Integrative. The domain is dominated by the experience of the wholeness of existence through mind and spirit. The world is viewed as a single, dynamic organism with its own collective mind. The self is both distinct and blended into a large, compassionate whole. The fact that everything is connected to everything else is accepted and there is ecological alignment. Personal responsibility drives this level.

- Turquoise: Holistic. A final developmental area where life is a natural hierarchy of holarchies and magnificence of existence is valued. Chaos and change are natural. This meme is still developing and as yet does not feature strongly in teams. To serve the entire ecosystem and all living beings are key values associated with this level.

Tips for team leaders

As a coaching tool the quadrants help members to understand the impact of various systems on individual and team behaviour, while knowing the role of levels helps members to understand their driving values and how they may be similar to or different from those of others in the team. The levels can help leaders to understand key values of team members.

Representation

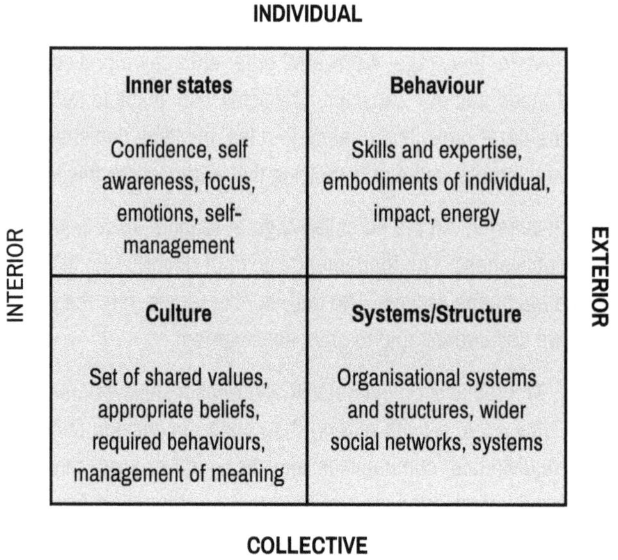

INDIVIDUAL

	Inner states	Behaviour
INTERIOR	Confidence, self awareness, focus, emotions, self-management	Skills and expertise, embodiments of individual, impact, energy
	Culture	Systems/Structure
	Set of shared values, appropriate beliefs, required behaviours, management of meaning	Organisational systems and structures, wider social networks, systems

COLLECTIVE

Figure 19.5: Integral coaching model

References

Beck, D.E. & Cowan, C. (2014). *Spiral dynamics: Mastering values, leadership and change*. Maiden: Blackwell Publishing.

Wilber, K. (2001). *A theory of everything: An integral vision for business, politics, science and spirituality*. Boston: Shambhala.

20 TEAMBUILDING

Teambuilding can be seen as a developmental process whereby teams are assisted to become more effective in executing their vision, completing their tasks and satisfying the needs of their members. Through teambuilding teams find new ways to provide the outcomes required of them, and build rapport, cohesion and a sense of belonging, which improves motivation and commitment. Teambuilding also offers an opportunity for members to get to know one another better, to improve their skill sets and to improve understanding of the operational and interpersonal tasks of the team and its members. It is a planned process that consists of a one-day or longer programme focused on the improvement of interpersonal relations, improved productivity or better alignment with organisational goals.

Teambuilding has become a specialised field with various approaches, as well as a variety of activities, techniques and instruments being employed. Here an integrated teambuilding perspective opens the discussion in order to provide a broad overview of some of the elements that influence teambuilding. Then the process of implementing teambuilding is introduced, before the focus of teambuilding is discussed. The latter comprises both the human-relations focus and task-related focus of teambuilding. The section is concluded with a description of two popular teambuilding approaches, namely activity-based teambuilding and positive approaches to teambuilding.

Introduction

In one of the rare attempts to provide an integrated theoretical model of teambuilding, Gilley, Lane Morris, Waite, Coates and Veliquette used a review of literature to determine the key elements that should inform building effective teams. They integrated teambuilding philosophy, selection theory and development theory, including the impact on team development, charge and charter theory, change curve theory, performance theory and synergistic relationship theory to provide the integration.

In a nutshell

An integrated teambuilding theory based on teambuilding philosophy, selection theory and development theory.

Purpose

To provide an integration of various theories impacting on teambuilding.

To guide teams on the key components influencing teambuilding efforts.

To offer a comprehensive model.

Description

The authors attempted to provide an integrated theory of teambuilding. They stated that four stages are required to facilitate effective teambuilding, namely develop an appropriate teambuilding philosophy, develop specific member selection criteria, identify the stages of team development and ascertain how they impact on the team's performance, and lastly, an examination of four theoretical constructs and their impact on team effectiveness.

Teambuilding philosophy

To develop an effective teambuilding philosophy leaders must consider all the following elements:

- An understanding of teambuilding: teambuilding is regarded as a process that helps the team to be more effective in accomplishing its tasks and to satisfy the needs of its members. However leaders and teams can have a variety of specific goals – improved performance of members, self-development, enhanced communication mechanisms, improved work environments, creating a sense of belonging, motivating members, discovering new ways to operate in the team, understanding different roles, generating shared goals and action plans, creating a sense of cohesiveness and commitment, and finally finding ways to deal with conflict and share resources. While all these could be addressed during an intervention, teams must be clear on what it is they want to accomplish.

- Type of team: this influences the type of intervention as characteristics particular to the team need to be addressed, e.g. virtual teams, self-management teams, production teams and creative teams may need different types of interventions.

- Purpose of the team: the use of a team to accomplish a particular outcome needs to be clear.

- Team effectiveness strategy: this relates to the levels of trust, commitment to goals and to each other, willingness of members to share risks and to assist one another, and is dependent on who is on the team i.e. its membership structure.

Selection criteria

The second phase of the integrated teambuilding model they proposed consists of selection criteria, namely the skills, knowledge and attitudes of team members; temperament type theory; and the theory of the characteristics of effective teams.

Skills, knowledge and attitudes of team members

As the membership influences the strategy that the team will adopt, the selection criteria used in finding the correct members is the next stage of an effective teambuilding process. It builds on members' strengths and weaknesses. Strengths are characterised by a passionate interest in something; high levels of personal satisfaction when performing a task or activity; rapid and continuous learning; and finally achieving exceptional results. They regarded the following as key competencies for effective teamwork:

- Ability to resolve conflict: as it is a natural phenomenon in teams, effectiveness will improve if members are adept at dealing with conflict.

- Problem solving: the ability to analyse a problem and find appropriate solutions.

- Communication: effective communication strategies including (but not limited to) active listening, questioning, encouraging, silence, dialogue, presentation, maintaining communication networks and consonance between verbal and non-verbal behaviour.

- Decision-making skills: Effective decision-making that includes judgement and ability to manage a process of deliberation.

- Goal setting and performance management skills: competency in setting goals and maintaining sufficient levels of performance to ensure attainment of such goals.

- Planning and task coordination: this skill is helpful to facilitate coordinated effort, synchronise activities and information, and manage interdependencies between various members in the team.

Temperament type theory

The authors acknowledged the role that different personalities, preferences and types play in influencing team behaviour. They identified four styles of personality:

- Analytical style: they tend to be task-oriented, precise, and thorough and are comfortable dealing with facts and concrete elements of work. They prefer to work methodically, according to standard operating procedures and within prescribed system bounds.

- Driver style: people who prefer this style are goal-oriented, and push for results, control and achievements.

- Amiable style: these are members who focus on people and are friendly, accepting and cooperative. They prefer to help others, and belonging and supporting each other are key drivers for this style.

- Expressive style: these people are idea oriented, vigorous, enthusiastic and spontaneous. They like to initiate relationships and motivate others toward goals.

The authors contend that knowing these preferences of members and finding the right balance, and aligning them with members' task- and relationship expectations are important drivers in effective teambuilding.

Characteristics of effective teams

The authors supported the five characteristics identified by Hackman (see Section 19) as the characteristics of effective teams. These are a team's direction, effective leadership, tasks that are suited for teamwork, appropriate resources provided by a supporting context, and whether it is a "real" team.

Team development theory

In their approach to team development, the authors relied on the familiar theory of Tuckman (see Section 1) which has described above. However, they stated that when used in teambuilding, an intervention must be designed to be commensurate with the particular stage the team is in. Furthermore, they contended that effective teambuilding can make use of four supporting theories:

Charge and charter theory

The first theoretical construct the authors regarded as influential to team development (i.e. progressing through the stages) is what they called charge and charter theory, which is based on the work of Whichard and Kees. This theory contends that teams that find clarity on what they need to deliver are more successful. They stated that the charter of the team needs to consist of:

- a purpose: a clear explanation of why a team exists, how it relates to the overall organisational strategy, to whom it is responsible, and how it will benefit the organisation;

- the goals of the team: details about what the team will do, how it will accomplish its responsibilities, who will assume responsibility for what, and when the activities will be accomplished;

- the roles of each team member: this delineates the responsibilities of each member, aligned with the member's characteristics; and

- the procedures a team will follow: how it expects to work together and the interactions (social), activities (technical) and procedures the team wants to adopt.

Change curve theory

The authors referred to four stages that teams use in adapting to change. The first is the denial phase, characterised as a period of uninformed enthusiasm where members either deny that the change will affect them or because of a lack of knowledge are prepared to join because they think it could benefit the organisation. The second stage, the resistance phase, is the period where members realise the complexity and understand how difficult the change will be to accomplish. The next stage is called the exploration phase, where members start to investigate whether the change will or will not bring positive results. They enter a period of hopeful adoption, where they accept values, display professional behaviour and start to operate according to shared and agreed norms. The final stage (commitment) refers to acceptance of the charge and charter and adoption of new ways of doing things in the team.

Performance theory

The change curve theory indicates that as teams develop effectively their performance levels increase. However, for this to happen teams have to complete the development tasks as described by Katzenbach and Smith (see Section 2) and move from a loosely formed group to an effective, high-performing team. In such teams members not only assist one another to meet team goals, but are also committed to each other's personal well-being, goals and development.

Synergistic relationship theory

This refers to the relationship skills members need and employ to create a positive, comfortable and non-threatening climate. These skills are characterised by effective communication where members discuss organisational issues, problems and other topics openly and honestly, without fear of reprisal. The synergistic element refers to the level of interdependence, which allows for collective effort towards a shared goal and wherein members experience sufficient opportunity for growth and development. In such a context members experience enhanced self-esteem, increased productivity, positive communication channels, enhanced organisational understanding and enhanced commitment to the team and the organisation. Through such an environment of care, respect and cooperation, rapport develops and this in turn facilitates increased performance and attained outcomes.

Tips for team leaders

This is a helpful and comprehensive model that leaders can use to guide their teambuilding efforts and help them to determine what appropriate interventions should be. The model provides a practical approach that gives a general overview of elements needed in building teams, but is also sufficiently detailed for leaders and practitioners to find valuable tools on how to constitute and lead teams.

Representation

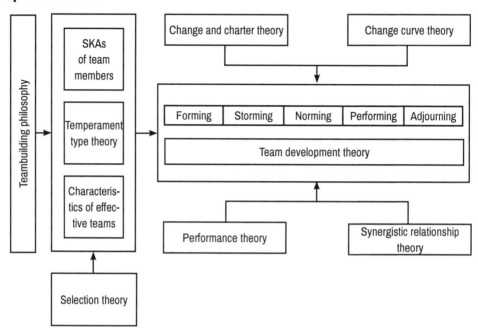

Figure 20.1: Integrated model of teambuilding

References

Gilley, J.W., Lane Morris, M., Waite, A.M., Coates, T. & Veliquette, A. (2010). Integrated Theoretical Model for Building Effective Teams. *Advances in Developing Human Resources*, 12(1), 7–28.

Whichard, J. & Kees, N.L. (2006). *Manager as facilitator*. Hartford, CT: Praeger.

Introduction

When team leaders want to improve performance through teambuilding they have to decide on a process. The process of designing an intervention and the process intervention "on the day". The process of designing an intervention is represented here by the traditional linear Organisational Development (OD) process, while a process with exit points (called sequential here) and an iterative view are also presented.

In a nutshell

The overall design of a teambuilding process can be completed as linear or iterative.

Purpose

To help in developing effective teambuilding interventions.

To guide the process of teambuilding.

Description

Firstly the processes required to design the overall intervention are introduced, followed by a description of the "on-the-day" process.

Overall design

OD process

As teambuilding originated from Organisation Development (OD), most teambuilding processes offered follow the "classic" original OD strategy of determining needs and designing potential interventions to meet those needs. The process refers to the contact with a team, the application of an intervention and the subsequent follow-up processes. The following stages are listed:

- Introduction: this refers to the initial contact between the team and the teambuilding expert. Most often this initial contact is a request from the leader of the team, but it can also be a request from other stakeholders and should end in a contractual agreement that takes into consideration both psychological and operational matters.

- Assessment: the assessment of the problems, e.g. interactional difficulties or operational challenges that necessitated the intervention, comes next. A variety of diagnostic techniques can be employed including psychometric assessment instruments, focus groups and individual interviews.

- Design: this stage comprises the design of the intervention and necessitates understanding the team members, as well as the context wherein the team operates, in order to align the proposed design with the needs of the team.

- Implementation: this stage comprises the actual intervention and the process of transferring what was gained from the intervention to the work situation. During this stage action plans are drawn up, feedback occasions are scheduled and the organisational context is prepared for the implementation plan.

- Follow-up: this comprises efforts to sustain the momentum of the intervention and includes measurements to evaluate progress.

- Feedback: although each of the stages requires feedback and evaluation, this stage is for the organisation to learn from the efforts of the team. The team reviews the efficiency of its efforts, evaluates the benefits, records lessons learnt, and communicates them to the organisation.

This view of the process can be seen as linear with little flexibility and no opportunity for the team to revisit previously completed stages. This is addressed in the process described next.

Sequential process

The sequential process was offered by Phillips and Elledge, who created a six-stage process that allows for a more iterative approach:

- Contracting: establishing a collaborative contract to determine when to proceed with the process of teambuilding.

- Data collection: different methods of gathering information on the team and its context.

- Data analysis: this stage includes coding, summarising, and interpreting data from the previous stage.

- Feedback: providing the information back to the team.

- Implementation: the actual intervention.

- Follow up: stressing the ongoing process of teambuilding.

As is clear from the diagram (see below) the team is allowed to "exit" the process after the Contracting (Phase I), Feedback (Phase IV) and Follow-up (Phase VI). In each case, if the answer to the corresponding question is negative the teambuilding process is terminated and alternatives are pursued. This approach highlights the role of the team in determining the process and charting the way forward. The first key feature is that the process allows for exit points based on the observations, evaluation and input from stakeholders. The second key feature is the feedback process, which includes feedback to the client (i.e.

the organisation) as well as to the team. These sets of evaluations and feedback allow for the process to be mapped out.

Iterative

Mealiea and Baltazar proposed a process that goes beyond viewing teambuilding interventions as linear processes. They highlighted the iterative nature of the intervention process, focusing on the possibility of revisiting earlier stages. They believed that successful teams display certain key "characteristics" and built the model to ensure that teams address those elements of success. They proposed seven steps:

- Identify the key characteristics predictive of the particular team.

- Measure the existing team climate and characteristics

- Identify team deficiencies.

- Determine an appropriate sequence of interventions.

- Identify interventions for overcoming deficiencies,.

- Select a set of strategies to improve deficiencies.

- Implement the intervention(s) and assess the team for improvement.

They acknowledged the circularity of the process by indicating that an understanding of the team's situation should be enhanced through observation and interaction, ongoing data collection, follow-up interviews and analysis of assessment instruments. Comparing this proposal to other models, the benefits of the various iterations stand out. However, a serious shortcoming of the programme is the perceived limited focus on evaluation and follow-up.

Tips for team leaders

To ensure effective interventions it is helpful for team leaders to ensure all members are committed to the effort and willing to take responsibility to make it work. It is also necessary that the goals and aims of the intervention should be clear and that decisions and commitments made during the intervention are implemented.

Representation

The process offered by Phillips and Elledge is offered here to illustrate a process of teambuilding.

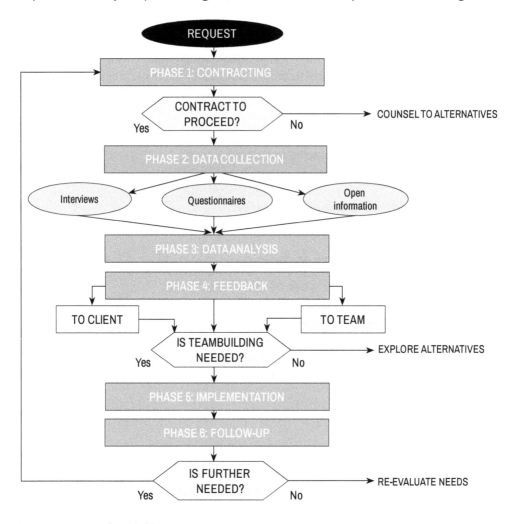

Figure 20.2: Process of teambuilding

Reference

Kriek, H.S. (2007). *Creative problem solving: Techniques for South African teams*. Pretoria: Mindmuzik.

Mealiea, L. & Baltazar, R. (2005). Strategic Guide for Building Effective Teams. *Public Personnel Management*. 34(2), 141–160.

Phillips, S.L. & Elledge, R.L. (1989). *The team-building source book*. San Diego: University Associates.

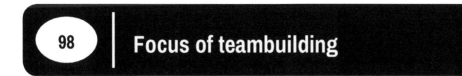

Introduction

Teambuilding is employed to improve the performance of teams, therefore the focus can be directed either at the relationships between team members or at its tasks. Both will be discussed here. The former, also called the human relations approach, assists the team to develop high levels of social and personal awareness among one another. The idea is that a better understanding of one another's personalities, as well as a better ability to communicate with one another, will help people to work together more easily. Task-based approaches emphasise the tasks of the team and the contribution members make to achieve such tasks, as well as how the team collectively coordinate their efforts to be effective.

In a nutshell

Focus of teambuilding interventions as either human relations or tasks.

Purpose

To improve interpersonal relationships.

To improve task performance.

To align coordination efforts to accomplish tasks.

Description

The two foci of teambuilding interventions are human relations and task, and although this makes for two distinct approaches, they are often used in conjunction with one another to ensure improved performance.

Human relations focus

This approach focuses on the interactions and interpersonal relationships between members. It is based on the assumption that when people know and understand each other better the experience in a team will be improved, communication flows will be better and the performance of members will increase. Thus, the human relations focus uses various approaches to assist teams in understanding one another better and to raise social and personal awareness among one another. The following variants of the interpersonal approach are presented:

Interpersonal relations

To improve interpersonal relationships, the human relations approach to teambuilding facilitates open and frank interrogation of relationships among team members, resolves conflicts and exposes hidden agendas. It is based on the assumption that teams with fewer interpersonal conflicts function more effectively and that when sufficient trust is built between team members, team outcomes are more easily attained. Thus, the approach focuses on mutual supportiveness, communication and sharing of feelings. A focus on interpersonal relations is often part of other types of teambuilding interventions as well. For example it is not uncommon for improvements in human relations to be facilitated through the use of experience, adventure or psychometric assessments. However, while it is common to use them in conjunction with other teambuilding approaches, they are also used on their own, most notably through the use of unstructured or semi-unstructured interventions. These types of interventions use minimum content (such as discussion on work issues or lecturing topics), but rather consist of facilitation of any issues the team "brings up". This free-for-all or "anything goes" approach is then used to facilitate the group dynamics. In semi-unstructured interventions some guided questions lead to open discussion, e.g. "Tell us your story" or "Describe the moment in the team's history that was most meaningful to you".

Interpersonal process skills

This is primarily viewed as a learning opportunity where team members learn skills like decision-making, problem-solving and negotiating. Members of the team learn to coordinate their efforts with other members of the team and to work together as a team. Typically "simulated activities or exercises" are used to practise these skills. Although closely related to the interpersonal relations approach, the manner in which Levi defines this stresses the process part of relationship. Thus, while the focus of the previous approach is only on the improvement of relationships, here this is extended as members acquire skills to improve the dynamics in future. It must be remembered that this type of intervention can be used without attention on the team's current issues, but rather with a broader focus of improving the process skills of the team.

Psychodynamic approach

Cilliers distinguished between traditional approaches and a psychodynamic approach, which advocates for the application of psychodynamic principles to the teambuilding intervention and illuminates unconscious behaviour to the team (i.e. "conventions that have developed collectively"). Psychodynamic drivers of behaviour manifest in a team context through various unconscious forces, such as anxiety, setting of boundaries, role uptake, handling of authority, relationship to leadership and issues related to the group as a whole. Through the team intervention members obtain understanding and insight of the impact of these behaviours on team performance and operation. This approach challenges the "rational" approach to teams and emphasises that a person is also subject to "many (often contradictory) wishes, fantasies, conflicts, defensive behavior, and anxieties – some conscious, other beyond consciousness" and that this should be considered where human beings operate in social settings such as teams. Different perspectives of this approach can be distinguished. It should be noted that the term psychodynamic is used here in a broad sense to refer to theories from the perspective of psychology and should not be confused with a narrower, psychoanalytical (Freudian) use of the term. It is used to include unconscious, intentional and interactional elements of group behaviour.

Tavistock Model

The so-called Tavistock model is applied as a teambuilding intervention as it focuses on unconscious needs and drives in team, including the possibility that members may enter a team with unfulfilled and unconscious family needs which may manifest without their necessarily being aware of it (see Section 70). Members bring unresolved conflict to the team and play out the need for power over siblings and parental figures in the team relationships. Three basic assumptions underlie this model, namely dependency, fight/ flight, and pairing:

- Dependency: the first assumption asserts that as during childhood where the child is dependent on the parent (or parental figure), team members project needs for dependency on the team and its leadership. As the focus of work teams is not on fulfilling these needs, members are left frustrated, helpless, powerless and disempowered. In team contexts this can manifest in needs for structure and direction where the leader is perceived as omnipotent, with the responsibility to rescue the team and provide for their needs.

- Fight/flight: this assumption contends that team members use either fight or flight behaviour to manage the assumed anxiety-producing environment. Fight manifests in constant conflict, aggression, jealousy, competition and jostling for position, while flight behaviour is characterised by avoidance, absenteeism and distancing issues from the self.

- Pairing: the last assumption focuses on a mechanism members put in place to avoid anxiety and alienation. Members pair with perceived powerful other team members or sub-groups to create a sense of security and safety. The members can also try to split up the team to form smaller subsystems in which they can feel safe and secure. Often this goes along with conflict, as "ganging up" or aggression against a mythical other is needed to create the sense of belonging.

Cohesion building/social identity approach

The aim of this approach is to "foster a sense of team spirit and build the interpersonal connections among team members" and to create "a sense of unity and belonging, a climate of mutual understanding, and a sense of pride in the team". Identification with the team and an increase of a sense of belonging are the main foci of this approach. It assumes that once members have their relationships firmly established, a greater commitment to the team goals will emerge. The main aims of the cohesion building approach are to:

- create a sense of unity and belonging;

- foster a climate of mutual understanding; and

- create a sense of pride in belonging to the particular team.

It is clear that a cohesion approach to teambuilding focuses on the interpersonal relationships between members. The thesis is that with more cohesion the interpersonal relations between members will improve, which in turn will impact on performance.

Task-based focus

The organisational tasks the team is expected to perform are the point of departure of this approach and team members are assisted in developing shared commitment to this task, for example by defining timetables, action plans and strategies to deal with obstacles that are preventing the team from performing optimally. Focus is placed on the skills of team members and on the interchange of information that ensures skills are utilised to the benefit of the whole team. It also analyses the team's tasks in terms of the resources, skills and practical steps it will use to carry out its tasks and roles. It assumes a team will be able to operate effectively and efficiently when each member has "a clear understanding of their place, role and responsibility" and of the tasks they have to fulfil. Although it will be clear that these aspects could be viewed as "interpersonal" in nature, the task-based approach is different in that it does not focus directly on people's individual feelings, beliefs and hidden conflicts, but on what people do and what they need from others. Two specific types of tasks are emphasised, namely goal-setting tasks and problem-solving tasks.

Goal-setting tasks

The goal-setting approach aims to clarify the purpose of the team and involves determining its goals and objectives. When this intervention is applied team members become involved in planning efforts on how to achieve these goals. Levi expanded this view, distinguishing between a "narrow" focus with emphasis on immediate performance criteria (e.g. goals, objectives and action plans) and a "broad" focus where the vision, values and purpose of the team are explored.

Problem-solving tasks

The problem-solving approach allows members to identify problems, generate relevant information, engage in problem-solving and action-planning, and implement and evaluate actions plans. The focus is to identify the problems of the team and to improve its operation through articulating its goals, aligning the goals, and mobilising the team behind accomplishing the goals. Thus, the problems the team face are addressed by focused action towards solving them. It uses planned experiences that are often facilitated by a third party, which are designed specifically to improve the team's operations through developing problem-solving procedures and skills. This approach focuses on problems and challenges in the team and includes both the development of problem-solving capacity and the solving of problems as part of this approach. The assumption underlying this type of intervention is that work teams become more effective through the experience of solving their major problems together. This approach works with real issues in the team and is not directed at learning problem solving skills or solving challenges that are not related to actual team operations.

Tips for team leaders

Members of the team learn to coordinate their efforts with other members of the team and to work together as a team. Typically, simulated activities or exercises, indoor or outdoor, are used to practise these skills.

Representation

Human-relations focus	Task-based focus
Interpersonal relations	Goal-setting approach
Interpersonal process skills	Problem-solving approach
Psychodynamic	
Tavistock	
Cohesion/Social identity	

Figure 20.3: Teambuilding focus

References

Aga, D.A., Noorderhaven, N. & Vallejo, B. (2016). Transformational Leadership and Project Success: The Mediating Role of Team-building. *International Journal of Project Management*, 34(5), 806–818.

Cilliers, F.v.N. (2000). Team Building from a Psychodynamic Perspective. *Journal of Industrial Psychology*, 26(1), 18–23.

Kets de Vries, M.F.R. (2011). *The hedgehog effect: The secrets of building high performance teams*. London: Wiley.

Levi, D. (2007). *Group dynamics for teams*. Thousand Oaks, CA: Sage Publications, Inc.

Introduction

It is inevitable that any intervention in a team will require activities that have a meaningful and sustainable impact. However, in some teambuilding activities the primary emphasis of the experience lies with the type of activity. Activity-based teambuilding is also called adventure-based or experiential learning, as it takes participants out of their regular work setting into unique and challenging environments and engages them in activities that are often fun and/or physical in nature. While this type of activity often makes use of problem-solving, this is not always the case.

In a nutshell

The use of activity-based teambuilding, including adventure, structured, social, and problem-solving activities.

Purpose

To change the context of the team to highlight group dynamics.

To facilitate interpersonal contact beyond normal business interaction.

To facilitate learning through experience.

To build teams through collective action.

Description

It is true that nearly all teambuilding interventions make use of activities to such a degree that almost the whole event consists of an activity and the activity becomes the driver to facilitate change, i.e. to enable the aims of other approaches. For example a river rafting intervention can be used to facilitate problem-solving, interpersonal relationships and role clarification. In other instances activities are used more sparingly or are specifically of a problem-solving nature. Often the value of these activities is unlocked by using the experiential learning model devised by David Kolb, which is therefore also included here.

Teambuilding activities

This type of intervention emphasises task accomplishment through group participation and requires participants to reflect upon their experiences. Four types of activity-based interventions are described, namely adventure activities, structured activities, social activities and problem-solving activities.

Adventure

The use of adventure or outdoor learning approaches to facilitate teambuilding has become increasingly popular, and adventure-based, outdoor-centred and wilderness programmes can be distinguished. The first uses specially designed (outdoor) activities to foster calculated risk-taking (perceived or real), problem-solving skills, trust and teamwork. In outdoor-centred programmes participants live and eat indoors, but most of the training consists of structured outdoor activities, while in wilderness programmes participants also live outdoors and engage in activities that are mainly outdoors. The variety of adventure activities is endless, but includes a.o. rope courses, river rafting, hiking, or wilderness experiences.

Structured activities

Many games, simulations and experiential activities that are not adventure-based are also employed in teambuilding of this nature. Whereas the adventure-based activities described above are often debriefed with a team focus and include reflection on group dynamics, structured activities can also be used to highlight one element the team needs to address. For example, a particular skill or learning need can be identified and an activity can be used to highlight just this aspect, such as a blindfold game to illustrate trust. In many cases these activities use the traditional Kolbian cycle, but in some instances they are used to drive and illustrate a particular learning point.

Social activities

While it is impossible to describe all the potential social activities that are used as teambuilding, it would seem that this category should be distinguished from more formal interventions where structured and adventure activities are used. In this regard, the established notion that familiarity breeds different levels of interaction and interpersonal relationships has led to the use of social events as teambuilding interventions. Events like karaoke, barbeques, filming or picnicking are all examples. While at least anecdotally these types of interventions have evoked diverse reactions ranging from positive to hesitant, they should nevertheless be included as teambuilding activities.

Problem-solving activities

Many of the activity-based interventions include problem-solving tasks, and such activities are used to build interpersonal relations, address group dynamics and help the team in its processes. However, this is distinct from task-based problem-solving as these activities are not operational tasks such as goal-setting or finding solutions to an operational issue, but are unrelated problems and challenges that the team has to solve. Through this approach of joint effort the team is built, but crucially the team's problem-solving capacity is increased at the same time. Thus, these problem-solving activities are used to allow the team to reflect on its own problem-solving processes and to acquire new ways to address challenges and problems.

Experiential learning

A further opportunity leaders can explore is the Kolb learning cycle, which is common to most activity-based teambuilding interventions, for potential experiential learning by using in other settings in the team as well. This theory focuses on four stages of learning:

- Concrete experience. The teambuilding activities are structured to facilitate this concrete experience. In most cases activities are used that are different from the work setting. Since these activities do not relate to specific work they allow for a different concrete experience in terms of intrapersonal and interpersonal relations.

- Reflective observation. Teams are assisted to reflect on the experience and to identify emotions, reactions and observations regarding the activity.

- Abstract conceptualisation. During this phase the team finds general principles on how they interact with one another, group dynamics, and how task-related challenges and principles that were applied in the concrete experience may be operative in the team's work activities.

- Active experimentation. Some principles and actions are identified and experimentation with new or revised behaviour is encouraged. This can take place during the activity or be focused on improving team behaviour at the workplace.

Tips for team leaders

It is helpful for leaders to identify clearly what the challenge is that they need to address and to select activities that are commensurate with the team's needs and that can facilitate and address specific issues. Members may not all be able to take part in activities that are physically demanding. Thorough debriefing of the emotional impact of the activity must be done by a skilled and trained professional. Transfer back to the workplace is critical, and sufficient time should be allocated to ensure effective transfer. While a problem-solving approach to teambuilding is certainly merited, it raises even more questions if it subsumes aspects from all the components of other teambuilding approaches and becomes very broad. However, it is helpful to guide teams to focus their teambuilding efforts to actual problems and in this way ensure that such efforts are beneficial to the team.

Representation

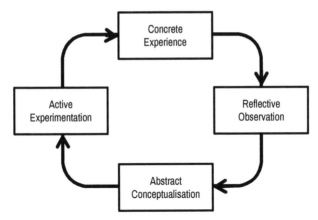

Figure 20.4: Kolb learning cycle

References

Hayes, N. (1997). *Successful team management*. London: International Thomson Business Press.

Kolb, D.A. (1984). *Experiential learning: Experience as the source of learning and development*. New Jersey: Pearson Education.

100 | Positive approaches to teambuilding

Introduction

Appreciative Inquiry (AI) is an approach to organisational development that focuses on the positives in the system (in this case the team) and "appreciates" the team's successes. It moves away from the focus on solving problems that characterises traditional approaches "because under that paradigm, groups and organizations are treated not only as if they have problems, but as if they are problems to be 'solved'". When used in teambuilding, this approach builds on the notion that teams should focus on the positive and indeed have a positive opinion about themselves, and it can therefore be defined as "the cooperative co-evolutionary search for the best in people, their organizations, and the world around them".

In a nutshell

Appreciating the positive in the team through Appreciative Inquiry (discover, dream, design, and destiny) or P-ICIA (illuminate, connect, inspire and achieve).

Purpose

To highlight what is good in the team.

To energise the team.

To foster a positive spirit.

To enable the team to find its own solutions.

Description

Two approaches based on positive psychology are presented, namely Appreciative Inquiry and P-ICIA.

Appreciative Inquiry

This approach is generative and is focused on success factors and what is currently working best in the system. This is in contrast to deficit approaches that focus on what is wrong and on fixing problems. Appreciative Inquiry uses a mind-set of finding the positives, strengths or parts in the team that are already functioning well or according to expectations, and uses those elements to develop the team. The principles underlying the AI approach were aptly described by Sharma:

- Constructionist Principle: participants in the system (i.e. team) co-create the reality therein and what is believed to be reality.

- Simultaneity Principle: inquiry and change are simultaneous events and therefore introducing a teambuilding event has some element of change to it already.

- Anticipatory Principle: stories forthcoming from AI interventions are future-orientated and assist to propel the system forward.

- Poetic Principle: this principle refers to the opportunity an AI intervention offers for interpretation and reinterpretation, or metaphorically a reading and rereading of the system. As the approach is principally focused on growth and development, i.e. the positive, this invokes new, innovative and generative energy.

- Heliotropic Principle: the metaphor of sunflowers turning to continually face the sun (positive phototaxis) illustrates this principle. Focusing on the positive this allows for hope, joy and energy to emerge.

Thus, by focusing on the positives in the team, the approach aims to "appreciate" the team's successes. The original Appreciative Inquiry process proposed the following four stages:

- Discover: AI allows for identification, recognition and discovery of what the team does best and what is positive in the team already. It aims to discover and build on successes and strengths in the team, and to elicit narratives that build on these positives.

- Dream: During this stage the future intent or ideal of the team is envisaged. The team is guided to utilise collective energy, find the inspiration to build on its strengths, and craft an inclusive vision of a future given an understanding of its current strengths and accomplishments.

- Design: This allows the team to make the dream realistic and reachable through practical actions supporting the envisioned future. This is a collaborative effort where everyone in the team is involved in constructing what the team should and could produce. The outcome of the process is a concrete action plan and/or strategy.

- Destiny: The process is completed by aligning the efforts of the previous stages and requires the team to focus on how to sustain its operations. This is a critical part of the process as it strengthens collective effort and through joint determination of the required actions helps the team to direct its actions. Focus is on what is needed to measure and sustain the efforts of the team to ensure it reaches its dream.

P-ICIA

Another variant that takes a positive outlook is the so-called P-ICIA approach proposed by Pavez, Alarcón and Salvatierra, which also stresses the strengths already present in the team. It builds on the notion that a team already has a particular image of itself that undergirds its operations, and if this image is positive the self-organising principles guiding the team can be mobilised. It distinguishes between the "expressive" and instrumental needs of the team and states that the former must be addressed first. Expressive needs refer to the relational needs among team members. These socio-emotional needs and interpersonal interactions need to be elicited and strengthened prior to operational or instrumental needs, which refer to aspects of productivity, efficiency and performance.

The process proposed has four stages:

- Illuminating: the focus is on highlighting operational and interpersonal strengths already present in the team. It builds on relationships among team members so that the team's expressive needs can come to the fore. This is then used as a basis to accomplish the instrumental needs of the team.

- Connectivity: the next step is to build relationships by reinforcing and increasing the levels of connectivity. Searching to nurture positive emotional states, this stage attempts to increase trust and collective efficacy by managing conflicts and the emotional impact thereof. It furthermore allows the team to build relationships and interaction given the image they have of themselves already.

- Inspiration: since this approach values the ability teams have to map their own way, find their own processes and creatively solve the challenges they deal with, the team's efforts in this regard are strengthened. In this stage focus therefore moves to how the team is inspired by working on its own transformational process. Again, the focus is on the positive. The collective, but autonomous action of the team to devise their own way is stressed. In this way positive emotional states energise the team in its transformational endeavour.

- Achieve: the team's efforts are directed to collectively implement developmental initiatives to achieve the desired future. Positive energy is unleashed to direct members to work towards becoming the team of their dreams.

Tips for team leaders

The focus on the positive is a big advantage of positive approaches and its interactive style helps to mobilise members in the team in a natural way. It facilitates ownership and team members feel empowered by being acknowledged, validated and included in actively seeking solutions.

Representation

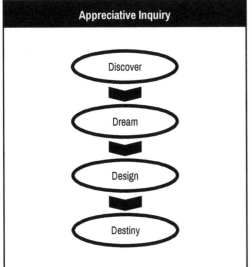
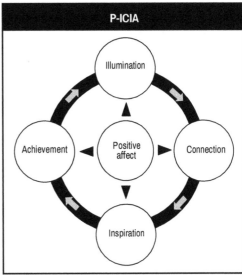

Figure 20.5: Positive approaches to teambuilding

References

Cooperrider, D.L., Whitney, D.K. & Stavros, J.M. (2008). *Appreciative inquiry handbook: For leaders of change*. San Francisco: Crown Custom Pub.

Pavez, I., Alarcón, L.F. & Salvatierra, J.L. (2015). Using Appreciative Inquiry as a Strategy to Accelerate Team Building on Site. *Proc. 23rd Ann. Conf. of the Int'l. Group for Lean Construction*. Perth, Australia, 29(31), 701–710.

LIST OF REFERENCES

Adams, J. S. (1964). Inequity in social exchange. In L. Berkowitz. *Advances in Experimental Social Psychology*, 2, 26–299. New York: Academic Press.

Aga, D.A., Noorderhaven, N. & Vallejo, B. (2016). Transformational Leadership and Project Success: The Mediating Role of Team-building. *International Journal of Project Management*, 34(5), 806–818.

Alderfer, C.P. (1969). An Empirical Test of a New Theory of Human Needs. *Organizational Behaviour and Human Performance*, 4(2), 142–175.

Anderson, N. & West, M.A. (1996). The Team Climate Inventory: Development of the TCI and its Applications in Teambuilding for Innovativeness. *European Journal of Work and Organizational Psychology*, 5(1), 53–66.

Arnold, J.A., Arad, S., Rhoades, J.A. & Drasgow, F. (2000). The Empowering Leadership Questionnaire: The Construction and Validation of a New Scale for Measuring Leader Behaviours. *Journal of Organizational Behaviour*, 21(3), 249–269.

Baghai, M. & Quigley, J. (2011). *As one*. New York, NY: Portfolio Hardcover.

Bang, H. (2017). *Technical manual on effect – an inventory for measuring management team effectiveness*. Oslo: University of Oslo.

Bang, H. & Midelfart, T.N. (2017). What Characterizes Effective Management Teams? A Research-Based Approach. *Consulting Psychology Journal: Practice and Research*, 69(4), 334–359.

Barling, J. (2014). *The science of leadership: Lessons from research for organizational leaders*. Oxford: Oxford University Press.

Bar-On, R. (1997). *Bar-On emotional quotient inventory: A measure of emotional intelligence*. Toronto: Multi-Health Systems Inc.

Bass, B.M. & Avolio, B. J. (1997). *Full range leadership development: Manual for the multifactor leadership questionnaire*. Redwood City, CA. Mind Garden.

Beck, D.E. & Cowan, C. (2014). *Spiral dynamics: Mastering values, leadership and change*. Maiden: Blackwell Publishing.

Belbin, R.M. (2004). *Management teams: Why they succeed or fail* (2nd ed.). Oxford, UK: Butterworth-Heinemann.

Bell, B.S., Kozlowski, S.W.J. & Blawath, S. (2012). Team learning: A review and integration. In S.W.J. Kozlowski (ed.). *The Oxford handbook of organizational psychology*, 2. Oxford, UK: Oxford University Press.

Berdensky, C. & Hayes, N.A. (2012). Status Conflict in Groups. *Organisation Science*, 23(2), 323–340.

Bion, W.R. (1975). Selections from experiences in groups. In A. D. Colman & W. H. Bexton (eds.). *Group relations reader 1*. Washington DC: A. K. Rice Institute.

Brown, S.W. & Grant, A.M. (2010). From GROW to GROUP: Theoretical Issues and a Practical Model for Group Coaching in Organisations. *Coaching: An International Journal of Theory, Research and Practice*, 3(1), 30–45.

Burke, W.W. & Litwin, G.H. (1992). A Causal Model of Organisational Performance and Change. *Journal of Management*, 8(3), 523–546.

Bushe, G.R. & Coetzer, G.H. (2007). Group Development and Team Effectiveness: Using Cognitive Representations to Measure Group Development and Predict Task Performance and Group Viability. *The Journal of Applied Behavioural Science*, June, 184–211.

Buzan, T. & Buzan, B. (1993). *The Mind Map book: How to use radiant thinking to maximize your brain's untapped potential*. New York: Plume.

Byttebier, I. (2002). *Creativiteit Hoe Zo?: Inzicht, inspiratie en toepassingen voor het optimal benutten van uw eigen creativiteit en die van uw organisatie*. Tielt: Lannoo.

Campion, M.A., Medsker, G.J. & Higgs, A.C. (1993). Relations Between Work Group Characteristics and Effectiveness: Implications for Designing Effective Work Groups. *Personnel Psychology*, 46(4), 823–850.

Cilliers, F. & Koortzen, P. (2012). Special Edition on Systems Psychodynamics in South African Organisations. *South African Journal of Industrial Psychology*, 38(2), 3.

Cilliers, F.v.N. (2000). Team Building from a Psychodynamic Perspective. *Journal of Industrial Psychology*, 26(1), 18–23.

Cilliers, F. & Koortzen, P. (2005). Working with Conflict in Teams: The CIBART Model. *HR Future*, October, 51–52.

Colibazzi, T., Posner, J., Wang, Z., Gorman, D., Gerber, A., Yu, S., Zhu, H., Kangarlu, A., Duan, Y., Russell, J.A. & Peterson, B.S. (2010). Neural Systems Subserving Valence and Arousal During the Experience of Induced Emotions. *Emotion*, 10(3), 377–389.

Collins, C.G. & Parker, S.K. (2010). Team Capability Beliefs Over Time: Distinguishing between Team Potency, Team Outcome Efficacy, and Team Process Efficacy. *Journal of Occupational and Organizational Psychology*, 83(4), 1003–1023.

Cooperrider, D.L., Whitney, D.K. & Stavros, J.M. (2008). *Appreciative inquiry handbook: For leaders of change.* San Francisco: Crown Custom Pub.

Costa, A.C. & Anderson, N. (2017). Team trust. In E. Salas, R. Rico. & J. Passmore (eds.). *The Wiley Blackwell handbook of the psychology of team working a collaborative processes.* Chichester, UK: John Wiley & Sons.

Crossan, M.M., Lane, H.W. & White, R.E. (1999). An Organizational Learning Framework: From Intuition to Institution. *Academy of Management Review*, 24(3), 522–537.

Csikszentmihalyi, M. (1990). *Flow: The psychology of optimal experience.* New York: Harper & Row, Publishers.

Cytrynbaum, S. & Noumair, D.A. (2004). Group Dynamics, Organisational Irrationality, and Social Complexity. *Group Relations Reader 3.* Jupiter, FL: A.K. Rice Institute.

Czander, W.M. (1993). *The psychodynamics of work and organisations: Theory and application.* New York, NY: Guilford Press.

D'Innocenzo, L., Mathieu, J.E. & Kukenberger, M.R. (2016). A Meta-Analysis of Different Forms of Shared Leadership–Team Performance Relations. *Journal of Management*, 42(7), 1964–1991.

Davis, G.A. & Scott, S.A. (1978). *Training creative thinking.* Huntington: Krieger.

De Meuse, K. (2009). *Driving Team Effectiveness. A Comparative Analysis of the Korn/Ferry T7 Model with Other Popular Team Models.* Available from: https://www.kornferry.com/media/lominger_pdf/teamswhitepaper080409.pdf.

Deci, E.L. & Ryan, R.M. (2008). Self-determination Theory: A Macro Theory of Human Motivation, Development, and Health. *Canadian Psychology/Psychologie Canadienne*, 49(3), 182–185.

Deci, E.L. & Ryan, R.M. (2012). Motivation, personality, and development within embedded social contexts: An overview of self-determination theory. In R.M. Ryan (ed.). *Oxford handbook of human motivation.* Oxford, UK: Oxford University Press.

Delbecq, A.L., Van de Ven, A.H. & Gustafson, D.H. (1975). *Group techniques for programme planning.* Glenview: Scott, Foresman.

Devine, D., Clayton, L., Philips, J., Dunford, B. & Melner, S. (1999). Teams in Organizations: Prevalence, Characteristics, and Effectiveness. *Small Group Research*, 30(6), 678.

DeYoung, C.G. (2010). Personality Neuroscience and the Biology of Traits. *Social and Personality Psychology Compass*, 4(12), 1165–1180.

DeYoung, C.G., Hirsh, J.B., Shane, M., Jones, C.S. & Hartley, N.T. (2013). Comparing Correlations between Four-Quadrant and Five-Factor Personality Assessments. *American Journal of Business Education*, 6(4), 459–470.

Dinh, J.V. & Salas, E. (2017). Factors that influence teamwork. In E. Salas, R. Rico, & J. Passmore. (eds.). *The Wiley Blackwell handbook of the psychology of team working and collaborative processes.* Chichester, UK: John Wiley & Sons.

Dolan, P. (2014). *Happiness by design: Finding pleasure and purpose in everyday life.* London: Hudson Street Press.

Doran, G.T. (1981). There's a S.M.A.R.T. Way to Write Management's Goals and Objectives. *Management Review* 70(11), 35–36.

Drexler, A.B., Sibbet, D. & Forrester, R.H. (1988). The team performance model. In W. B. Reddy & K. Jamison (eds.). *Team building: Blueprints for productivity and satisfaction.* Alexandria, VA: National Institute for Applied Behavioral Science & Pfeiffer.

Eberle, R. (1996). *Games for imagination development.* Buffalo: D.O.K. Press.

Edison, T. (2008). The Team Development Life Cycle: A New Look. *Defence AT& L*, 37(3), 14–17.

Edmondson, A.C. & Lei, Z. (2014). Psychological Safety: The History, Renaissance, and Future of an Interpersonal Construct. *Annual Review of Organizational Psychology and Organizational Behaviour*, 1(1), 23–43.

Euwema, M.C., Van de Vliert, E. & Bakker, A.B. (2003). Substantive and Relational Effectiveness of Organizational Conflict Behavior. *International Journal of Conflict Management*, 14(2), 119–39.

Festinger, L. (1950). Informal Social Communication. *Psychological Review*, 57(5), 271–282.

Fisher J.M. (2000). Creating the future? In J.W. Scheer (ed.). *The person in society: Challenges to a constructivist theory*. Giessen: Psychosozial-Verlag.

Fisher J.M. (2012a). *The Process of Transition: Fisher's Personal Transition Curve*. Available from: https://www.csu.edu.au/__data/assets/pdf_file/0006/949533/fisher-transition-curve-2012.pdf

Fisher, J.M. (2012b). *Personal Change Stages*. Available from: https://www.businessballs.com/change-management/personal-change-stages-john-fisher-162/.

Frazier, M.L., Fainshmidt, S., Klinger, R.L., Pezeshkan, A. & Vracheva, V. (2017). Psychological Safety: A Meta-Analytic Review and Extension. *Personnel Psychology*, 70(1), 113–165.

George, B. (2010). *True north: Finding your authentic leadership*. San Francisco, CA: Jossey-Bass.

Gersick, C.J. (1988). Time and Transition in Work Teams: Toward a New Model of Group Development. *Academy of Management Journal*, 31, 9–41.

Gersick, C.J. (1989). Marking Time: Predictable Transitions in Task Groups. *Academy of Management Journal*, 32, 274–309.

Geschka, H., Schaude, G.R. & Schlicksupp, H. (1973). Modern Techniques for Problem Solving. *Chemical Engineering*, Aug, 91–97.

Gilley, J.W., Lane Morris, M., Waite, A.M., Coates, T. & Veliquette, A. (2010). Integrated Theoretical Model for Building Effective Teams. *Advances in Developing Human Resources*, 12(1), 7–28.

Glaser, R.O. & Glaser, C. (1992). *Team Effectiveness Profile: How is your team working?* King of Prussia, PA: Organization Design and Development.

Goleman, D. (1995). *Emotional intelligence: Why it can matter more than IQ*. New York: Bantam.

Goleman, D., Boyatzis, R.E. & McKee, A. (2002). *Primal leadership: Realizing the power of emotional intelligence*. Boston: Harvard Business School Press.

Gordon, J. (2002). A Perspective on Team Building. *Journal of American Academy of Business*, 2(1), 185–188.

Greer, L.L. & Dannals, J.E. (2017). Conflict in teams. In E. Salas, R. Rico. & Passmore, J. (eds.), *The Wiley Blackwell handbook of the psychology of team working and collaborative processes*. Chichester, UK: John Wiley & Sons.

Gully, S.M., Incalcaterra, K.A., Joshi, A. & Beaubien, J.M. (2002). A Meta-Analysis of Team-Efficacy, Potency, and Performance: Interdependence and Level of Analysis as Moderators of Observed Relationships. *Journal of Applied Psychology*, 87(5), 819–832.

Guzzo, R.A., Yost, P.R. & Shea, G.P. (1993). Potency in Groups: Articulating a Construct. *British Journal of Psychology*, 32(1), 87–106.

Hackman, J.R. (2002). *Leading teams: Setting the stage for great performances*. Boston: Harvard Business School Press.

Hackman, J.R. & Oldham, G.R. (1975). Development of the Job Diagnostic Survey. *Journal of Applied Psychology*, 60, 159–170.

Hackman, J.R. & Oldham, G.R. (1976). Motivation Through the Design of Work: Test of a Theory. *Organizational Behaviour & Human Performance*, 16, 250–279.

Hackman, J.R. & Oldham, G.R. (1980). *Work redesign*. San Francisco, CA: Addison Wesley.

Hackman, J.R. & Wageman, R. (2005). A Theory of Team Coaching. *Academy of Management Review*, 30(2), 269–287.

Hansen, L.B. (2017). The dimensionality of management team effectiveness: A psychometric analysis of the team inventory "effect". Unpublished Master's Thesis, University of Oslo.

Harrison, D. A. & Klein, K. J. (2007). What's the Difference? Diversity Constructs as Separation, Variety, or Disparity in Organizations. *Academy of Management Review*, 32(4), 1199–1228.

Hawkins, P. (2017). *Leadership team coaching: Developing collective transformational leadership*. London: Kogan Page.

Hayes, N. (1997). *Successful team management*. London: International Thomson Business Press.

Heron, J. (1999). *The complete facilitator's handbook*. London: Kogan Page.

Herzberg, F., Mausner, B. & Snyderman, B. (1959). *The motivation to work* (2nd ed.). New York: Wiley.

Hoffman, B.G. (2017). *Red teaming: Transform your business by thinking like the enemy*. London: Piatkus.

Hogan, R. & Hogan, J. (1995). *Hogan personality inventory manual*. Tulsa, OK: Hogan Assessment Systems.

Hollenbeck, J.R., Beersma, B. & Schouten, M.E. (2012). Beyond Team Types and Taxonomies: A Dimensional Scaling Conceptualization for Team Description. *Academy of Management Review*, 37(1), 82–106. http://dx.doi.org/10.5465/amr.2010.0181.

Hughes, R.L., Ginnett, R.C. & Curphey, G.J. (2009). *Leadership: Enhancing the lessons of experience* (6th ed.). New York: McGraw-Hill.

Ilgen, D.R., Hollenbeck, J.R., Johnson, M. & Jundt, D. (2005). Teams in Organizations: From Input-Process-Output Models to IMOI Models. *Annual Review of Psychology*, 56(1), 517–543.

Ishikawa K. & Loftus, J.H. (1990). *Introduction to quality control*. Tokyo: 3A Corporation.

Jehn, K.A. (1995). A Multimethod Examination of the Benefits and Detriments of Intragroup Conflict. *Administrative Science Quarterly*, 40(2), 256–282.

Johnson, G. & Scholes, K. (1997). *Exploring corporate strategy*. Verlag: Prentice-Hall.

Jones, P.E. & Roelofsma, M.P. (2000). The Potential for Social Contextual and Group Biases in Team Decision-Making: Biases, Conditions and Psychological Mechanisms, *Ergonomics*, 43(8), 1129–1152.

Judge, T.A., Piccolo, R.F. & Kosalka, T. (2009). The Bright and Dark Sides of Leader Traits: A Review and Theoretical Extension of the Leader Trait Paradigm. *The Leadership Quarterly*, 20(6), 855–875.

Kahneman, D. (2011). *Thinking, fast and slow*. London: Penguin Books Ltd.

Kantor, D. (2012). *Reading the room: Group dynamics for coaches and leaders*. San Francisco, CA: Jossey-Bass.

Karhatsu, H., Ikonen, M., Kettunen, P., Fagerholm, F. & Abrahamsson, P. (2010). *Building Blocks for Self-Organizing Software Development Teams: A Framework Model and Empirical Pilot Study*. Paper presented at the 2nd International Conference on Software Technology and Engineering (ICSTE), San Juan, PR, USA.

Katzenbach, J., Smith, D. & Bookspan, M. (1993). *The wisdom of teams*: Boston: Harvard Business School Press.

Kauffeld, S. & Lehmann-Willenbrock, N. (2012). Meetings Matter: Effects of Work Group Communication on Organizational Success. *Small Group Research*, 43(2), 130–158.

Kets de Vries, M.F.R. (2001). *The leadership mystique*. London: Prentice Hall.

Kets de Vries, M.F.R. (2007). Decoding the Team Conundrum: The Eight Roles Executives Play. *Organizational Dynamics*, 36(1), 28–44.

Kets de Vries, M.F.R. (2011). *The hedgehog effect: The secrets of building high performance teams*. London: Wiley.

Kilman, R.H. & Thomas, K.W. (1975). Interpersonal Conflict-Handling Behaviour as Reflections of Jungian Personality Dimensions. *Psychological Reports*, 37(3), 971–980.

Kirkman, B.L. & Rosen, B. (1999). Beyond Self-Management: Antecedents and Consequences of Team Empowerment. *The Academy of Management Journal*, 42(1), 58–74.

Klein, R. (2008). *The Klein Group Instrument manual*. Gainesville, FL: The Centre for Applications of Psychological Type.

Kogler Hill, S.E. (2001). Team leadership. In P. G. Northouse (Ed.), *Leadership: Theory and practice* (2nd ed.). Thousand Oaks, CA: Sage.

Kolb, D.A. (1984). *Experiential learning: Experience as the source of learning and development*. New Jersey: Pearson Education.

Kotter, J.P. (1996). *Leading change*. Boston, MA: Harvard Business School Press.

Kozlowski, S.W.J. & Ilgen, D.R. (2006). Enhancing the Effectiveness of Work Groups and Teams. *Psychological Science in the Public Interest*, 7(3), 77–124.

Kozlowski, S.W.J. & Chao, G.T. (2012). The Dynamics of Emergence: Cognition and Cohesion in Work Teams. *Managerial and Decision Economics*, 33 (5–6): 335–354.

Kozlowski, S.W.J., Watola, D.J., Nowakowski, J.M., Kim, B.H. & Botero, I.C. (2009). Developing adaptive teams: A theory of dynamic team leadership. In E. Salas, G.F. Goodwin, & C.S Burke (eds.). *Team effectiveness in complex organisations: Cross-disciplinary perspectives and approaches*. Mahwah, NJ: LEA.

Kriek, H.S. (2007). *Creative problem solving: Techniques for South African teams*. Pretoria: Mindmuzik.

Kubler-Ross, E. (1969). *On death and dying*. New York: Touchstone.

LaFasto, F.M.J. & Larson, C.E. (2001). *When teams work best: 6,000 team members and leaders tell what it takes to succeed*. Newbury Park, CA: Sage.

Laloux, F. (2014). *Reinventing organizations: A guide to creating organizations inspired by the next stage in human consciousness*. Brussels, Belgium: Nelson Parker.

Larson, C.E. & LaFasto, F.M.J. (1989). *Teamwork: What must go right/ What can go wrong*. Newbury Park, CA: Brooks.

Lehmann-Willenbrock, N., Beck, S.J. & Kauffeld, S. (2016). Emergent Team Roles in Organizational Meetings: Identifying Communication Patterns via Cluster Analysis. *Communication Studies*, 67(1), 37–57.

Lencioni, P. (2002). *The five dysfunctions of a team*. San Francisco, CA: Jossey-Bass.

Lessem, R. (2016). *The integrators: The next evolution in leadership, knowledge and value creation*. London: Routledge.

Levi, D. (2007). *Group dynamics for teams*. Thousand Oaks, CA: Sage Publications, Inc.

Lewin, K. (1952). Group decision and social change. In G. E. Swanson, T. M. Newcomb, & E. L. Hartley (eds.). *Readings in social psychology*. New York: Henry Holt.

Lewis, K., Belliveau, M., Herndon, B. & Keller, J. (2007). Group Cognition, Membership Change, and Performance: Investigating the Benefits and Detriments of Collective Knowledge. *Organizational Behaviour and Human Decision Processes*, 103(2), 159–178.

Linkage Incorporated. (n.d.) *Team Effectiveness Assessment*. Available from: www.linkageinc.com.

Lipmanowicz, H. & McCandless, K. (2013). *The surprising power of liberating structures. Simple rules to unleash a culture of innovation*. Columbia, SC: Liberating Structures Press.

Locke, E.A. & Latham, G.P. (1990). *A theory of goal setting and task performance*. Englewood Cliffs, NJ: Prentice-Hall.

Lombardo, M.M. & Eichinger, R.W. (1995). *The team architect® user's manual*. Minneapolis, MN: Lominger Limited.

Luthans, F., & Avolio, B.J. (2003). Authentic leadership development. In K. S. Cameron, J. E. Dutton, & R. E. Quinn (eds.). *Positive organizational scholarship* (pp. 241–258). San Francisco: Berrett-Koehler.

Margerison, C. & McCann, D. (1984) Team Mapping: A New Approach to Managerial Leadership. *Journal of European Industrial Training*, 8(1), 12–16.

Margerison, C. & McCann, D. (1996). *Team management: Practical new approaches*. Chalford: Management Books.

Marks, M.A., Mathieu, J.E. & Zaccaro, S.I. (2001). A Temporally Based Framework and Taxonomy of Team Processes. *Academy of Management Review*, 26(3), 356–376.

Marlow, S.L., Lacerenza, C.N. & Salas, E. (2017). Communication in Virtual Teams: A Conceptual Framework and Research Agenda. *Human Resource Management Review*, 27(4), 575–589.

Maslow, A.H. (1954). *Motivation and personality*. New York: Harper.

Mathieu, J.E., Tannenbaum, S.I., Donsbach, J.S. & Alliger, G.M. (2014). A Review and Integration of Team Composition Models: Moving Toward a Dynamic and Temporal Framework. *Journal of Management*, 40(1), 130–160.

Mayer, J.D., Salovey, P. & Caruso, D.R. (2004). Emotional intelligence: Theory, Findings, and Implications. *Psychological Inquiry*, 15(3), 197–215.

Mayer, J.D., Salovey, P., Caruso, D.R. & Sitarenios, G. (2003). Measuring Emotional Intelligence with the MSCEIT V2.0. *Emotion*, 3(1), 97–105.

Mayer, R.C., Davis, J.H. & Schoorman, F.D. (1995). An Integrative Model of Organizational Trust. *Academy of Management Review*, 20(3), 709–734.

McChesney, C., Covey, S. & Huling, J. (2012). *The 4 Disciplines of execution.* New York: Free Press.

McGrath, J.E. (1984). *Groups: Interaction and performance.* Englewood Cliffs, NJ: Prentice Hall.

Mealiea, L. & Baltazar, R. (2005). Strategic Guide for Building Effective Teams. *Public Personnel Management.* 34(2), 141–160.

Moe, N.B., Dingsøyr, T. & Dybå, T. (2009). A Teamwork Model for Understanding an Agile Team: A Case Study Of A Scrum Project. *Information and Software Technology, 52*(5), 480–491.

Moe, N.B., Dingsøyr, T. & Røyrvik, E.A. (2009). Putting agile teamwork to the test — A preliminary instrument for empirically assessing and improving agile software development. In P. Abrahamsson, M. Marchesi, & F. Maurer (eds.). *Agile processes in software engineering and extreme programming. Lecture Notes in Business Information Processing.* Berlin: Springer.

Mohammed, S., Hamilton, K., Sánshez-Manzannares, M. & Rico, R. (2017). Team cognition: Team mental models and situation awareness. In E. Salas, R. Rico, J. Passmore (eds.), *The Wiley Blackwell handbook of the psychology of team working a collaborative processes.* Chichester, UK: John Wiley & Sons.

Mohammed, S., Ferzandi, L. & Hamilton, K. (2010). Metaphor No More: A 15-Year Review of the Team Mental Model Construct. *Journal of Management*, 36(4), 876–910.

Morgan, B. B., Salas, E. & Glickman, A. S. (1993). An Analysis of Team Evolution and Maturation. *Journal of General Psychology*, 120(3), 277–291.

Morgeson, F.P., Scott DeRue, D. & Karam, E.P. (2010). Leadership in Teams: A Functional Approach to Understanding Leadership Structures and Processes. *Journal of Management*, 36(1), 5–39.

Mumford, T.V., Campion, M.A. & Morgeson, F.P. (2006). Situational judgment in work teams: A team role typology. In J.A. Weekley & R.E. Ployhart (eds.). *Situational judgment tests: Theory, measurement, and application.* Mahwah, NJ: Erlbaum.

Mumford, T.V., Van Iddekinge, C.H., Morgeson, F.P. & Campion, M.A. (2008). The Team Role Test: Development and Validation of a Team Role Knowledge Situational Judgment Test, *Journal of Applied Psychology Association*, 93(2), 250 –267.

Myers, I.B. (2003). *MBTI manual: A guide to the development and use of the Myers-Briggs Type Indicator.* Mountain View, CA: CPP.

Naudé J. (2016). Coaching and mentoring. In A. Viera & R. Kramer R. (eds.). *Management and leadership skills for medical faculty.* Cham, Switzerland: Springer.

Osborne, A.F. (1963). *Applied imagination* (3rd ed.). New York: Scribner.

Osterwalder, A. & Pigneur, Y. (2010). *Business model generation: A handbook for visionaries, game changers, and challengers.* Hoboken, NJ: Wiley.

Palmer, I., Dunford, R. & Akin, G. (2009). *Managing organizational change: A multiple perspectives approach.* New York: McGraw–Hill Education.

Palmer, S. (2008). The PRACTICE Model of Coaching: Towards a Solution-Focused Approach. *Coaching Psychology International*, 1(1), 4–6.

Parker, S.K., Morgeson, F.P. & Johns, G. (2017). One Hundred Years of Work Design Research: Looking Back and Looking Forward. *Journal of Applied Psychology*, 102(3), 403–420.

Patterson, K., Grenny, J., McMillan, R. & Switzler, A. (2002). *Crucial conversations: Tools for talking when the stakes are high.* New York: McGraw-Hill.

Pavez, I., Alarcón, L.F. & Salvatierra, J.L. (2015). Using Appreciative Inquiry as a Strategy to Accelerate Team Building on Site. *Proc. 23rd Ann. Conf. of the Int'l. Group for Lean Construction.* Perth, Australia, 29(31), 701–710.

Pearce, C. L., & Conger, J. A. 2003. *Shared leadership: Reframing the hows and whys of leadership.* Thousand Oaks, CA: Sage.

Pentland, A. (2012). The New Science of Building Great Teams. *Harvard Business Review*, 90(4), 60–69.

Peters, T. & Waterman, R. (1982). *In search of excellence.* New York: Harper & Row.

Phillips, S.L. & Elledge, R.L. (1989). *The team-building source book.* San Diego: University Associates.

Porter, M. (1985). Competitive advantage: Creating and sustaining superior performance. New York, NY: The Free Press.

Project Management Institute. (2013). *A guide to the project management body of knowledge* (5th ed.). Newtown Square, PA: Project Management Institute.

Rath, T. (2008). *Strengths-based leadership: Great leaders, teams and why people follow.* New York: Gallup Press.

Ryan, R.M. & Deci, E.L. (2002). Self-determination Theory and the Facilitation of Intrinsic Motivation, Social Development, and Well-being. *American Psychologist*, 55(1), 68–78.

Ryan, R.M. & Deci, E.L. (2017). *Self-determination theory: Basic psychological needs in motivation, development, and wellness.* New York: Guilford Publishing.

Raynes, B. L. (2001). Predicting Difficult Employees: The Relationship between Vocational Interests, Self-esteem, and Problem Communication Styles, *Applied H.R.M. Research,* 6(1), 33–66.

Saaty, T.L. (1980). The *Analytic Hierarchy Process.* Available from: https://www.sciencedirect.com/science/article/pii/0270025587904738.

Saaty, T.L. & Vargas L.G. (2001). *Models, methods, concepts and applications of the analytic hierarchy process.* Dordrecht: Kluwer.

Salas, E., Grossman, R., Hughes, A.M. & Coultas, C.W. (2015). Measuring Team Cohesion: Observations from the Science. *Human Factors*, 57(3), 365–374.

Salas, E., Shuffler, M.L., Thayer, A.L., Bedwell, W.L. & Lazzara, E.H. (2015). Understanding and Improving Teamwork in Organizations: A Scientifically Based Practical Guide. *Human Resource Management,* 54(4), 599–622.

Schoorman, F.D., Mayer, R.C. & Davis, J.H. (2007). An Integrative Model of Organizational Trust: Past, Present, and Future. *Academy of Management Review*, 32(2), 344–354.

Sharma, R. (2008). Celebrating Change: The New Paradigm of Organizational Development. *ICFAI Journal of Soft Skills*, 2(3), 23-28.

Shore, S. (1972). *Creativity in action.* Sharon: Connecticut.

Speakman, J. & Ryals, L. (2010). A Re-evaluation of Conflict Theory for the Management of Multiple, Simultaneous Conflict Episodes. *International Journal of Conflict Management*, 21(2), 186–201.

Steiner, I.D. (1972). *Group process and productivity.* New York: Academic Press.

Strauss, S.G. (1999). Testing a Typology of Tasks: An Empirical Validation of McGrath's (1984) Group Task Circumplex. *Small Group Research*, 30(2), 166–187.

Sundstrom, E., McIntyre, M., Halfhill, T. & Richards, H. (2000). Work Groups: From the Hawthorne Studies to Work Teams of the 1990s and Beyond. *Group Dynamics: Theory, Research, and Practice*, 4(1), 44–67.

Tesluk, P.E., Mathieu, J.E., Zaccaro, S.J. & Marks, M.A. (1997). Task and aggregation issues in the analysis and assessment of team performance. In M.T. Brannick, E. Salas, & C. Prince (eds.). *Team performance and measurement: Theory, methods, and applications.* Mahwah, NJ: Erlbaum.

Thaler, R. H. & Sundstein, C. R. (2008). *Nudge: Improving decisions about health, wealth, and happiness.* Yale University Press, New Haven.

Thomas, K.W. (1974). *Thomas-Kilmann conflict mode instrument.* New York: Xicom Tuxedo.

Thompson, J.D. (1967). *Organizations in action.* New York: McGraw-Hill.

Thompson, L. (2007). *Making the team: A guide for managers* (3rd ed.). Upper Saddle River, NJ: Pearson Prentice Hall.

Tuckman, B. (1965). Developmental Sequence in Small Groups. *Psychological Bulletin*, 63(6), 384–399.

Tuckman, B. & Jensen, M. (1977). Stages of Small-group Development Revisited. *Group & Organization Management*, 2(4), 419–427.

Uhl-Bien, M. & Arena, M. (2017). Complexity Leadership: Enabling People and Organizations for Adaptability. *Organizational Dynamics*, 46(1), 9–20.

Van den Hout, J.J.J. (2016). *Team flow: From concept to application.* Unpublished Doctoral Dissertation. Eindhoven: Technische Universiteit.

Van den Hout, J.J.J., Davis, O.C. & Walraven, B. (2016). The application of team flow theory. In L. Harmat, F. Ørsted, F. Andersen, J. Ullén, J. Wright & G. Sadlo. *Flow experience: Empirical research and applications*. Berlin: Springer International.

Van Gundy, A.B. (1988). *Techniques of structured problem solving* (2nd ed.). New York: Van Nostrand Reinhold.

Van Knippenberg, D., De Dreu, C.K.W. & Homan, A.C. (2004). Work Group Diversity and Group Performance: An Integrative Model and Research Agenda. *Journal of Applied Psychology*, 89(6), 1008–1022.

Van Maurik, J. (1994). Facilitating Excellence: Styles and Processes of Facilitation. *Leadership & Organization Development Journal*, 15(8), 30–34.

Van Niekerk, E. (2011). *The systems psychodynamic world of the fund manager*. Unpublished doctoral dissertation. Pretoria: University of South Africa.

Vroom, V.H. (1964). *Work and motivation*. New York, NY: Wiley.

Vroom, V.H. (1974). Decision Making and the Leadership Process. *Journal of Contemporary Business*, 3(4), 47–64.

Vroom, V.H. (2000). Leadership and the Decision-making Process. *Organizational Dynamics*, 28(4), 82–94.

Vroom, V.H. & Jago, A.G. (1988). *The new leadership: Managing participation in organizations*. Englewood Cliffs, NJ: Prentice Hall.

Vroom, V.H. & Yetton, P.W. (1973). *Leadership and decision making*. Pittsburgh, PA: University of Pittsburgh Press.

Wageman, R. (1995). Interdependence and Group Effectiveness. *Administrative Science Quarterly*, 40, 145–180.

Wageman, R. (2001). The meaning of interdependence. In M.E. Turner (ed.). *Groups at work: Theory and research*. Mahwah, NJ: Erlbaum.

Waterman, R.H., Peters, T.J. & Phillips, J.R. (1980). *Structure is not organization*. Bridgeport, Conn.: M. Wiener.

Wheelan, S. (2016). *Creating effective teams: A guide for members and leaders* (5th ed.). Los Angeles: Sage.

Wheelan, S., Davidson, B. & Tilin, F. (2003). Group Development Across Time: Reality or illusion? *Small Group Research*, 34(2), 223–245.

Whichard, J. & Kees, N.L. (2006). *Manager as facilitator*. Hartford, CT: Praeger.

Whitmore, J. (1996). *Coaching for performance: Growing people, performance and purpose*. London: Nicholas Brealey.

Wilber, K. (2001). *A theory of everything: An integral vision for business, politics, science and spirituality*. Boston: Shambhala.

Wolfson, M.A. & Mathieu, J.E. (2017). Team composition. In E. Salas, R. Rico & J. Passmore (eds.). *The Wiley Blackwell handbook of the psychology of team working and collaborative processes*. Chichester, UK: John Wiley & Sons.

INDEX

Milton Keynes UK
Ingram Content Group UK Ltd.
UKHW050839271223
434976UK00008B/349